THEMES IN AFRICAN-GUYANESE HISTORY

EDITORS
Winston F. McGowan, James G. Rose
and David A. Granger

HANSIB

Published by Hansib Publications 2009
London & Hertfordshire
P.O. Box 226, Hertford, Hertfordshire, SG14 3WY, United Kingdom

Email: info@hansib-books.com
Website: www.hansib-books.com

First published by Free Press, Guyana, 1998

A catalogue record of this book is
available from the British Library

ISBN 978-1-906190-18-7

Production:
Keyboard input by Desma Granger and Merle Thompson; concept and design by David Granger; typesetting and layout by HMAK Systems.

Cover illustration:
Impression of the Demerara Revolt, 1823, by Barrington Braithwaite.

The publishers wish to acknowledge permission to use the maps from the University of Guyana on pages xxi and 226.

Printed and bound in the UK

Preface

The reprinting of this book coincides with the worldwide observance of the two-hundredth anniversary of the abolition of the trans-Atlantic trade in captive Africans. The United Nations General Assembly held a solemn ceremony on 26 March 2007 to commemorate the passing, on 25 March 1807, by Parliament, of the Slave Trade Act.

The Act prohibited British ships from transporting human cargo and participating in the trade. By that time, however, untold millions had perished in the trade, a crime against humanity which, for centuries, shaped the history of Africa, the Americas, the Caribbean and, to some extent, Western Europe.

Professor Rex Nettleford, Vice-Chancellor Emeritus of the University of the West Indies, addressed the ceremony drawing attention to the United Nations Educational, Scientific and Cultural Organisation (UNESCO) Slave Route Project which aimed to break the silence surrounding the trans-Atlantic slave trade.

The General Assembly was also addressed by Mr Denzil Douglas, Prime Minister of Saint Kitts and Nevis, who spoke on behalf of the Caribbean Community, the regional bloc that had helped push through the resolution that led to the United Nations recognition of the end of the trans-Atlantic trade.

It is fitting that this important book should be reprinted on such an occasion. *Themes in African-Guyanese History* has been one of the most important books of Guyanese history but, unfortunately, went out of print. Its reappearance is most welcome.

David A. Granger
June 2008

Contents

Part III : Pre-Independence Period

Part IV : Post-Independence Period

Illustrations

Maps

Figures

Tables

Acknowledgement

The editors wish to acknowledge with gratitude, the generous contribution of the United Nations Educational, Scientific and Cultural Organisation which made the publication of this volume possible.

Grateful acknowledgement is made to the following for permission to reprint previously published material:

Fitzroy Ambursley and Robin Cohen (eds.), Crisis in the Caribbean (London : Heinemam Educational Books Ltd. 1984).
Alan Gregor Cobley and Alvin Thompson (eds.), The African-Caribbean Connection : Historical and Cultural Perspectives (Bridgetown : Department of History, UWI and the National Cultural Foundation, Barbados, 1990).
Alvin O. Thompson, Colonialism and Underdevelopment in Guyana, 1580-1803 (Bridgetown : Carib Research & Publications Inc., 1987).
Winston Mc Gowan (ed.), Guyana Historical Journal, Vol. I (1989); Vol II (1990); Vol III (1991).
David Granger (ed.), History Gazette, No. 13 (1989); No. 22 (1990); No. 27 (1990).

We would like to thank also the numerous persons whose efforts helped in the production of this volume. In particular we recognise the work of Misses Desma Granger, Evadney Henriques and Merle Thompson, and Messrs. Barrington Braithwaite, Haseeb Khan and George N. Cave.

Contributors

Carl A. Braithwaite	*is a former Lecturer in the Department of Geography, University of Guyana.*
Winston F. McGowan	*is Senior Lecturer and Head of the Department of History, University of Guyana.*
Brian L. Moore	*is Senior Lecturer and Head of the Department of History, Mona Campus, University of the West Indies.*
Kimani S. Nehusi	*is Senior Lecturer and Director of African Studies, University of East London.*
James G. Rose	*is Senior Lecturer in the Department of History, University of Guyana.*
Clive Y. Thomas	*is Professor of Economics and Director of the Institute of Development Studies, University of Guyana.*
Alvin O. Thompson	*is Senior Lecturer in the Department of History, Cave Hill Campus, University of the West Indies.*
Hazel M. Woolford	*is a former Lecturer in the Department of History, University of Guyana.*

Abbreviations

ACDA	African Cultural and Development Association
BGBV	British Guiana Boundary Arbitration with the United States of Venezuela
BGEIA	British Guiana East Indian Association
BGLU	British Guiana Labour Union
CO	Colonial Office Records
CSSH	Comparative Studies in Society and History
EG	Egerton Papers
GHJ	Guyana Historical Journal
GHRA	Guyana Human Rights Association
GIWU	Guiana Industrial Workers' Union
GSO	Government Service Order
GUY REDEM	Guyana Regional Demographic Survey
HIES	Household Income and Expenditure Survey
HMSO	His/Her Majesty's Stationery Office
JAH	Journal of African History
JCH	Journal of Caribbean History
LCP	League of Coloured Peoples
LMS	London Missionary Society
LSMS	Living Standards Measurement Survey
MCC	Minutes of the Combined Court
MCP	Minutes of the Court of Policy
MEP	Malaria Eradication Programme
MPCA	Man Power Citizens Association
NAG	National Archives of Guyana
NPC	Negro Progress Convention
OAG	Officer Administering the Government
PAC	Political Affairs Committee
PNC	People's National Congress
PP	Parliamentary Papers
PPP	People's Progressive Party
PRO	Public Record Office
PWD	Public Works Department
SES	Social and Economic Studies
TUC	Trade Union Council
UGL	University of Guyana Library
USC	United States Commission on Boundary between Venezuela and British Guiana.
WIC	(Dutch) West India Company

Introduction

This book focuses on some of the major developments in the history of the African-Guyanese from the time of their arrival in what were then the Dutch colonies of Essequibo and Berbice in the first half of the seventeenth century to the present day. The term African-Guyanese is used to refer to residents of African descent of the area which constitutes the modern Republic of Guyana on the north coast of South America. It is generally employed in this text in preference to other synonymous terms such as Afro-Guyanese, Negroes, Blacks and Creoles. Similarly, the term 'plantation' is often used instead of 'estates' and 'Guyana' is utilised except in circumstances which clearly demand the use of 'British Guiana.'

Most African-Guyanese today are descendants of slaves who were victims of the trans-Atlantic slave trade, the forced migration of millions of Africans especially from West Africa to the Americas from the fifteenth to the nineteenth centuries. A tiny minority of them, however, are the descendants of a relatively small number of Africans (estimated at about 14,000) who came to Guyana in the post-Emancipation period, especially from Sierra Leone, between 1838 and 1865.

Understandably, this book begins with a focus on the African background of the slaves who were brought to Essequibo, Berbice and, after 1746, Demerara. These African slaves were not uncivilised barbarians, as some European writers assumed and asserted. Rather, they were members of societies which had been distinguished by significant achievements. They were therefore able to make a valuable contribution to the land to which they were taken against their will after a traumatic journey across the Atlantic.

This trans-Atlantic slave trade to Guyana which ended in 1807 is the focus of the second chapter which deals with an important but neglected aspect of the subject, namely, the volume of the traffic to Guyana. Unlike many other territories in the Caribbean, notably Jamaica and Cuba, the slave trade to Guyana was comparatively small, especially in view of the size of the territory and its insistent demand for slave labour. This explains the relatively small size of Guyana's population during the period of slavery. This paucity of population, though enhanced by the influx of a considerable number of other immigrants after the abolition of slavery in 1834, has remained one of the salient features of the country's demography, adversely affecting its development.

Slaves who survived the Atlantic crossing found themselves forced to live in societies where they were regarded primarily as property and units of production subject to the authoritarian control of masters who, for the most part, were a law unto themselves. Though conditions of life varied among different categories of slaves such as field labourers, artisans and domestics, the lot of all slaves was extremely difficult. Apart from hard work, slaves were victims of numerous other abuses, including restrictions in movement, cruel punishment, a diet which was deficient in quality and quantity, insufficient clothing and many other material and social burdens which characterised slave life. These issues are examined in detail in the third chapter, entitled "Slave Society during the Dutch Regime," in which some of the distinguishing conditions of slavery in Guyana, compared with the rest of the Caribbean, are highlighted.

The slave ancestors of the modern African-Guyanese responded in a variety of ways to their terrible plight. For example, they resisted slavery day by day by actions which were often not recognised by their masters as forms of resistance and are difficult to quantify. These actions, often described as "passive resistance" by scholars, included malingering, insolence, the damaging of tools and other plantation equipment, other forms of sabotage, the feigning of illness, theft, abortion and infanticide. They also resorted to more positive methods of resistance such as the poisoning of masters, arson, flight and armed rebellion.

Armed rebellion was the response most feared by the slaveowning class, for it posed the most formidable threat to their lives and property. Slave rebellions, however, were comparatively rare in Guyana and most other slave societies in the Americas. This lack of frequency was due to the fact that rebellions were difficult to organise without being discovered by masters, were virtually doomed to failure because of the superior military power and other advantages possessed by the slaveholding class, and resulted in the imposition of severe punishment on the rebels, especially the leaders.

Nevertheless, Guyana experienced two of the most massive slave uprisings witnessed in the Americas. These two rebellions are discussed in Chapters Four and Five, with special attention being directed to the causes, course and consequences of the revolts. The first uprising began in February 1763 in the colony of Berbice and lasted for a little more than a year. Apart from the successful revolt in Saint Domingue in the 1790s, this Berbice rebellion came nearer to overthrowing white rule and achieving the emancipation of the slaves and the establishment of a Black independent state than any other slave uprising in the history of the Americas. After experiencing significant success in the initial phase, however, the Berbice Revolt ultimately ended in failure.

Sixty years later, another massive revolt, involving about 11,000 to 12,000 slaves, occurred on the East Coast of Demerara. This revolt in 1823 was the second of three major rebellions staged by slaves in the British West Indies in the early decades of the nineteenth century. It followed in the wake of an uprising in Barbados in 1816 and preceded an even more massive insurrection in Jamaica in 1831. The rebellion by the African-Guyanese slaves in 1823 and the 1831 Jamaican revolt played an important role in helping to persuade the British Government to pass an act in 1833 abolishing slavery in British Guiana and the rest of the British Caribbean with effect from 1 August 1834.

Instead of becoming completely free immediately, however, the slaves were required to work for their masters for another four or six years under a system called "Apprenticeship", which was, in fact, a modified form of slavery. Eventually there was an early termination of Apprenticeship and all the African-Guyanese apprentices and their counterparts elsewhere in the British West Indies were granted full freedom on 1 August 1838. Emancipation on 1 August 1838 is perhaps the single most important event in the history of the African-Guyanese. It ushered in major changes in the lives not only of African-Guyanese but also of the entire society. One of the most obvious and significant changes was demographic.

The expectation and then the reality of an exodus of ex-apprentices from the plantations after Emancipation to seek some measure of independence resulted in the importation by planters from 1835 of thousands of indentured workers, especially Portuguese, East Indians and Chinese. The aim of the planters was to secure a cheap, immobile, easily controllable labour force as an alternative to the African-Guyanese. This immigration led to the emergence in Guyana of a multi-ethnic society comprised of six races instead of the three groups - Amerindians, Africans and Europeans - present in 1834. As a result, the African-Guyanese, who enjoyed a numerical preponderance in 1834, saw that dominance progressively undermined. By 1911, the racial balance of the Guyanese population had shifted to a numerical preponderance of East Indians over African-Guyanese culminating by 1988, 150 years after Emancipation, in an estimated 20 per cent difference in the proportion of the total accruing to these two principal ethnic groups.

These important demographic issues are discussed in Chapter Eight, which is entitled "The African-Guyanese Demographic Transition : An Analysis of Growth Trends, 1838-1988." The major phases in the social demography of the African-Guyanese population are traced and this population's dominant characteristics, especially its migratory behaviour and its low fecundity, are emphasised. Particularly striking is the fact that a preponderance of deaths over births contributed, until 1918, to a negative growth in the African-Guyanese population.

An appreciation of these demographic developments is crucial to an understanding of the social and economic history of the African-Guyanese after 1838. Emancipation was a great challenge to both the African-Guyanese ex-apprentices and the White ex-masters. It offered the ex-apprentices a welcome opportunity for economic and social advancement and for exercising greater control over their future, while it threatened to undermine the status, way of life and economic aspirations and prospects of the ex-masters. A struggle for supremacy ensued between these two ethnic groups or classes with competing, contradictory interests. This struggle took place especially in the economic and social spheres. Both groups fought for control of the economy, realising that the key to such control was the possession of land and good drainage. The Whites emerged victorious in the struggle and the African-Guyanese experienced economic and social subordination.

This important conflict for economic and social control or supremacy is analysed in Chapter Six on "The Social and Economic Subordination of the Guyanese Creoles after Emancipation." The White victors in this conflict profited from their possession of a virtual monopoly of local political power and support from the political and military power of the imperial state. In striking contrast, most African-Guyanese, in particular the ex-apprentices, had no political voice, for the qualifications for both the franchise and the membership of the political institutions were deliberately fixed beyond their reach.

White planters in particular used their privileged political position to restrict the access of African-Guyanese to land and credit and to impose on them burdensome discriminatory taxes and licences in order to hinder or limit their economic activity. They also utilised the support of the local government eventually to seize control of the administration of the African-Guyanese villages which were established after 1838 and over which initially they had little if any influence. The crucial importance of the possession of political power by the Whites in realising and maintaining the economic, social and political subjugation of the African-Guyanese after Emancipation is the central theme of Chapter Nine which is entitled "African-Guyanese Political Disempowerment during the Nineteenth Century."

The White plantocracy was able to preserve its control over the Colony's political system until 1891 when, largely in response to pressure from middle-class African-Guyanese, some modest changes were made in the Constitution of the Colony. As a result of these changes, the political power of the planters was eroded progressively and fell increasingly into the hands of African-Guyanese and coloured politicians. This shift of power into the hands of the African-Guyanese disturbed the planters, the local officials and the metropolitan authorities so much that eventually, in 1928, this trend was checked by the introduction of Crown Colony Government, the subject of Chapter Twelve.

In short, the lives of the African-Guyanese after Emancipation were distinguished by a relentless political, economic and social struggle. In the decade immediately after Emancipation they were engaged in a battle with the White planters for control of the labour market. This struggle was most evident in the occurrence in 1842 and 1848 of two general strikes which are discussed in Chapter Seven. The efforts of the strikers were successful in 1842, but were defeated in 1848, when the planters used East Indian immigrants as strike-breakers. This defeat in 1848 was a serious set-back to, and a major turning-point in, the affairs of the African-Guyanese labouring population. It illustrated that the planters' programme of immigration had begun to achieve its objective of lowering wages and breaking the African-Guyanese control of the labour market. Thereafter, immigrants were used increasingly to free the planters from their dependence on the African-Guyanese labour force.

Thus, by 1848, the planters had re-established their ascendancy over the African-Guyanese labouring population. They consolidated this dominance in the latter half of the century. African-Guyanese labourers became increasingly less important to the plantations. Yet, they had only a few options such as migration to the villages or towns, squatting in the interior or remaining on the plantations on disadvantageous terms dictated by the plantocracy. Many dissatisfied African-Guyanese drifted to the towns, especially as the peasant village economies began to fail. They, however, found life in Georgetown, in particular, unenviable with low wages, a high level of unemployment and underemployment, and a high cost of living. Their struggle against these conditions was punctuated by major protests such as the abortive one in 1905 which is the subject of Chapter Ten.

The African-Guyanese workers, especially those in Georgetown, gradually realised that their best hope of advancement was to become organised. This led eventually to the formation of the Colony's first trade union, the British Guiana Labour Union, in 1919. This Union was able to achieve some significant benefits for workers, but the formidable obstacles which it had to face ensured that its success was limited. Nevertheless, the birth and subsequent growth of the trade union movement, examined in Chapter Eleven, were important developments in the history of the Colony as a whole, and African-Guyanese in particular.

The limited success of the trade unions helped to make African-Guyanese and other workers become convinced that to improve their lot they also needed to gain access to political power and to secure an end to colonial rule. As Chapter Fourteen illustrates, African-Guyanese played an important role in the establishment and development of political organisations designed to secure constitutional changes to satisfy these aspirations. Eventually, their efforts were successful. African-Guyanese workers became eligible to vote in national elections and to sit in the legislature in 1953, when universal adult suffrage was granted and the discriminatory income and property qualifications for entry into the legislature were removed. They were also prominent in the nationalist struggle which culminated in the Colony's attainment of political independence from Britain in May 1966. African-Guyanese women were very active in these political struggles, as is emphasised and illustrated in Chapter Thirteen on "Women in Guyanese Politics, 1812-1964."

African-Guyanese hoped and expected that Independence would serve to enhance their lot. This optimism was understandable, for the ruling party, the People's National Congress, was led by African-Guyanese and was believed to be particularly committed to the welfare of the African-Guyanese. These hopes and aspirations, however, did not materialise. Many African-Guyanese eventually became disillusioned and dissatisfied with the Government whose policies impacted negatively on their welfare. These issues are discussed in Chapter Fifteen on "State Capitalism in Guyana : An Assessment of Burnham's Cooperative Socialist Republic."

After over three decades of Independence, there has not been any significant improvement in the economic conditions of many African-Guyanese. In fact, their plight is one of the disturbing features of modern Guyana. This contemporary problem is addressed in the final chapter which is entitled "The Situation of African-Guyanese in the Economy."

Many of the chapters in this book have appeared earlier elsewhere, mostly in publications which are little-known and are somewhat inaccessible. Several of them, however, have been written or revised expressly for inclusion in this work. The book seeks to deal in a more or less balanced way with the phases into which historians have often divided Guyanese history, namely, the pre-Emancipation period, which ended in 1838; the post-Emancipation period during the remainder of the nineteenth century; the pre-Independence period which ended in 1966; and the post-Independence period during the remainder of the twentieth century. The period of Dutch rule from about 1616 to 1796, a neglected era in many historical works, has been accorded better treatment than is normally the case. Similarly, more attention has been devoted to developments in the twentieth century than has been given in most accounts of Guyanese history.

Nevertheless, this book is not a history of the entire African-Guyanese experience. Its contents focus on the political, economic and social dimensions of that experience, largely to the neglect of cultural history. There is certainly scope for the publication of a supplementary volume dealing with social and cultural history. It is hoped that this book will inspire research that will result in many other publications, including an authoritative comprehensive account of the entire history of the African-Guyanese from the early seventeenth century to the present.

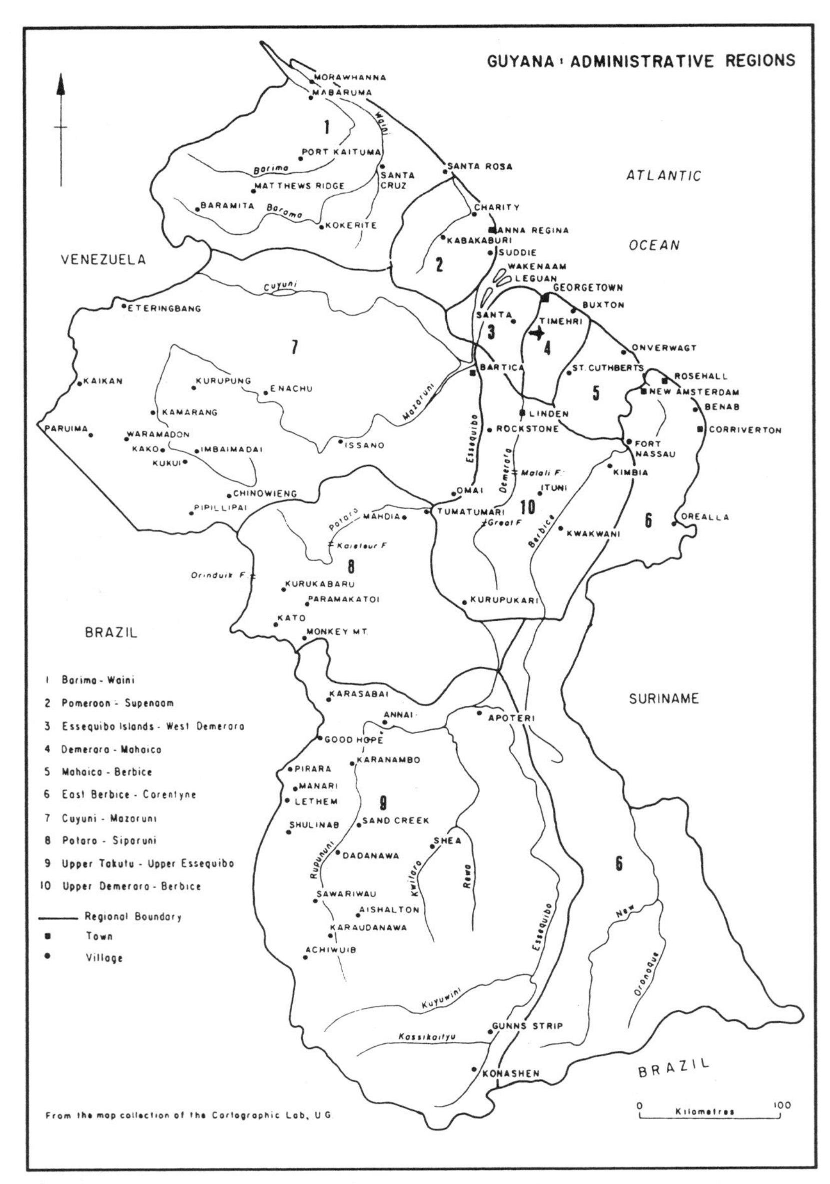

Map 1: General Map of Guyana in the late Twentieth Century

Map 2: Main States and Peoples of Western Africa in the Seventeenth Century

Part I

Pre-Emancipation Period

1: The Societies of Western Africa on the Eve of the Atlantic Slave Trade

by
Alvin O. Thompson

It is well known that the vast majority of slaves who reached the Americas came from western Africa and, more particularly, from the stretch of coastline and related hinterland between modern Senegal and modern Angola. At the time of the commencement of the Atlantic slave trade, little was known and much was assumed by Europeans about the nature of these societies. In general, Europeans assumed that Africans were 'primitive', 'savage' and the like.

About two centuries before Charles Darwin wrote his *Origin of the Species*, some Europeans were debating the genetic relationship between Africans and certain creatures living, or believed to be living, in Africa. Thus, Europeans wrote about 'satyrs' and 'gorgons' existing in western Africa. They wondered whether gorillas were 'ape-like men' or 'men-like apes'. One writer, speaking about albinos in Loango, suggested that they were the products of unions between African women and the Devil. Various other writers of the period declared that there were such marvels as snakes about a mile long, men whose heads were beneath their shoulders and women whose breasts were larger than the udders of goats.

Concerning the physical features of the West African environment, one view which gained much currency was that several parts of it were so hot that at times fire could be seen issuing upwards and that the rivers and seas sometimes appeared to be liquid fire. Before the Europeans passed Cape Bojador on the western Saharan coast in 1434, they believed that the region south of that landmark was the haunt of demons and that no European who went southwards would ever return. Although this myth was exploded by the Portuguese voyage of 1434, many of the other myths remained. Some indeed were reinforced by so-called first-hand accounts of travellers.

Concerning slavery and the slave trade, it was generally believed that these were quite prevalent and, in fact, large-scale, at the time of the European advent. Even as late as the mid-twentieth century few writers questioned these assumptions about slavery and the slave trade. Particularly during the period of the abolition of the British slave trade, pro-slavery interests expressed the view that the vast majority of Africans lived under the most abject conditions of slavery and poverty, and that their lords or masters could dispose of them with impunity.

The anti-slavery interests never attempted seriously to refute these charges. They focussed their attention upon the untold horrors of the slave trade in Africa and the equally horrifying effects of slavery in the Americas. Though more recent scholarship has attempted to address the issues relating to African slavery and the early African slave trade, the myths regarding these aspects of early western African history die hard.

To be fair, it must be pointed out that there were a few contemporary European writers who saw and wrote about positive aspects of the societies in western Africa. Indeed, it is to these writers that we sometimes have to turn to rebut many of the derogatory statements about these societies. But the fact is that the views of these early writers gained little currency in contemporary European discussions about Africa. Sometimes these writers themselves undermined the value of their works by placing major emphasis on what they regarded as negative aspects of western African societies. This essay therefore attempts to look at certain aspects of the societies in question, with a view to highlighting their achievements around the time of the advent of the Atlantic slave trade. It is not intended, however, to ignore (or overlook) the weaknesses in these societies.

Western Africa is a very large area, covering roughly 12,741,344 square kilometres of territory. It can be divided into two main vegetational zones. These are the savannah and grassland areas.

The grasslands are located mainly in the western and central Sudan, that is, the area directly south of the Sahara desert. There is also an area of savannah around the upper reaches of the Kasai and Lualaba rivers and most of the Kwango river, tributaries of the Congo (Zaire) river. The forest areas lie adjacent to the savannahs.

Grassland areas are usually more congenial to human habitation and the development of stratified societies. This was certainly the case in western Africa. The earliest states and empires were founded there. Between roughly A.D. 500 and A.D. 1600, three major empires existed in the western section of the savannah. They were the empires of Ghana, Mali and Songhai. The Mali empire succeeded that of Ghana, and the Songhai empire that of Mali. Each empire was larger than its predecessor, but lasted for a shorter period of time. At the time of the European advent into West Africa, the Songhai empire was at its height. (But the Europeans had also heard of the Mali empire, and of its famous ruler, Mansa Musa, who ruled between A.D. 1307 and A.D. 1337.). The Songhai empire was destroyed, while still a virile empire, through a daring expedition sent against it by the ruler of Morocco in 1591. The Moroccans introduced firearms for the first time into West Africa, at least as a combat weapon. This, plus tactical errors on the part of the Songhai rulers, led to the demise of the empire and the emergence of a number of small states contending for independence and supremacy.

A little further to the east of the empires mentioned above, lay the somewhat smaller but also significant empire of Kanem-Borno. This empire was founded around A.D. 800 and continued to exist until the 1890s when it was subjected to French imperialism. It was under the rule of a single dynasty from its foundation until 1846. It is therefore the empire with the longest dynastic rule in the history of mankind. This suggests that the empire, in spite of the many vicissitudes it experienced, possessed a remarkable degree of resilience and adaptability.

Apart from the empires noted above, there were a number of smaller states in existence in the savannah region before 1600.

Among these should be mentioned those in Hausaland (in the northern part of modern Nigeria), Gonja, Yatenga, Mossi and Dagomba (in present-day Mali and Upper Volta) and Oyo (in modern Yorubaland).

The forest regions experienced the beginnings of state- and empire-building at a later point in time than the savannah areas. It is thought that migrants with state-building ideas moving south and south-west from the main centres of power in the savannah areas, contributed in a significant way to the process of state-building in the forest areas. At any rate, by the thirteenth century, this process was clearly visible in a number of areas. By the sixteenth century, a congeries of states of varying sizes existed in various parts of the Guinea forest. Among these were the Mande kingdom of Sierra Leone, the Fante and Asante states of modern Ghana, and the states of Benin and Ife in southern Nigeria. Benin was the largest and most important of these at the time of the first European contacts with the Guinea coast.

Further south, in the area of modern Congo and Angola, the process of state development was also discernible in a number of instances. By the thirteenth century, and perhaps earlier, small Luba-Lunda states, as they were called, were in existence. By the sixteenth century, a few of them had become strong and stable but the largest and most stable of the kingdoms was that known as the Kongo kingdom. The Portuguese struck up a friendship with the kingdom, as they did also with Benin. In the process, the former disintegrated under the impact of the slave trade, while the latter atrophied, partly as a result of this trade. However, it was still in existence at the time of the British conquest of the area in the late nineteenth century.

It can be seen from the above that many areas of western Africa had arrived at fairly sophisticated levels of political stratification, as was true also of other parts of Africa. The large empires were divided into a number of states or provinces. Varying degrees of autonomy were allowed to these segments. It is true that from time to time the empires experienced a number of revolts, but it is equally true that they were usually able to put down these revolts and to hold their territories intact for long periods. For instance, the ancient empire of Ghana existed for at least 700 years; Mali for about 200 years; Songhai for about 150 years; and Borno for about 1,100 years. Some smaller states, such as those in Hausaland and Benin, existed for about 500 years or more. It is therefore obvious, contrary to the suggestion of some writers, that the rulers of these states and empires were able to devise mechanisms of control to maintain their territorial and political sovereignty for long periods.

All the states and empires mentioned above had councils of government (equivalent to modern cabinets), civil servants, laws governing the communities, and clearly defined sources of income. For instance, the Mali and Songhai empires had ministers of government who were in charge of the rivers, customs, production, etc. They had a large retinue of tax collectors. Government revenue was derived not only from tribute and customs, but from long-distance trade. This last aspect will receive further attention later on. It should be pointed out, however, that the known wealth of the western Sudan, particularly in gold, became a focus of envy and attention by the rulers of Morocco on the one hand and Portugal on the other. Several early Portuguese voyages were directed to capturing and controlling the gold-bearing areas. The Moroccan invasion of Songhai in 1591 was also directed mainly towards this end. At an earlier period, Arabs and Berbers from North Africa and the Middle East were attracted to the area, in search of trade.

The discussion so far has centred around the development of states and empires in western Africa. The capacity of peoples to build large states and empires is often viewed as an important yardstick in judging their advance from 'barbarism' to 'civilisation'. By this yardstick, several African communities of the period under discussion would have to be classified as 'civilised'. However, it is not the intention here to employ this dubious standard of measurement. A number of western African communities of the period never developed systems of political (and social) stratification as those mentioned earlier, but this did not make them less civilised than those which did.

Several communities along the seaboard did not develop highly stratified political systems up to 1600. They developed 'segmented' or 'stateless' societies. By this is meant that they developed communities which lacked hereditary and clearly defined hierarchical political and social structures. This was true of the Balantas of Upper Guinea, and the Ibo (Igbo) and Ibibio of Lower Guinea. In fact, the Ibo stoutly maintained their system of 'village democracies' (as they are sometimes called) up to the time of the British conquest of the area. They revolted during the colonial period when the British tried to unite their villages into larger political entities.

The point that is being made here is that western African societies displayed a wide spectrum of political and social organisation, ranging from empires on the one hand to stateless societies on the other. Though political fissioning and fragmentation were a part of the history of the region, the dominant tendency was towards political unification and enlargement, at the time of the European advent.

At the level of economic organisation, a similar variety was noticed. The larger states and empires derived their revenue from a variety of sources, including tribute from subordinate groups, customs duties, royal monopolies over certain items of production or trade, and agricultural settlements. These communities usually participated in long-distance trade which linked them ultimately with North Africa, the Mediterranean and the Indian Ocean. There were four main trade routes which linked the West African states of the Sudan with North Africa, though the importance of each route changed as time went by. The trans-Saharan trade which developed involved the transport of goods which were in demand by rich people and were highly priced. The main items exported from West Africa were gold, ivory, ostrich feathers, leather, kola nuts and slaves. Gold was by far the most important export. The region imported, in return, such items as horses, coats-of-mail, swords and glassware.

The lucrative nature of the trade can be gathered from the fact that North African and Middle Eastern merchants established trading centres in Western Africa, some of which later became fairly large cities. Among these should be mentioned Jenne and Timbuktu. The trade led to an accumulation of large amounts of wealth by certain individuals. For instance, Mansa Musa, emperor of Mali in the fourteenth century, took with him on a pilgrimage to Mecca 100 camel loads of gold and 500 pages, each bearing a gold staff weighing about four pounds. It is said that Askia Mohammed, the most famous of the Songhai emperors, was even more prodigal in his display of wealth on his pilgrimage to Mecca in the fifteenth century. There is also on record the case of a merchant involved in the trans-Saharan trade writing a cheque in Morocco in the tenth century for 42,000 dinars (the currency of the day), that is, about US$120,000.

Up to the time of the European contact with West Africa via the Atlantic, the exclusive orientation of the export trade was towards the Sahara and North Africa. This explains, to a great extent, why the largest kingdoms of that region emerged in the savannah rather than the forest areas. They were more strategically placed to engross the trade and to use the wealth accruing therefrom to strengthen further their kingdoms. Even in the heyday of the Atlantic slave trade, the northern trade remained an important factor in the export trade of the region. Apart from the export trade, there was a considerable amount of trade being carried on between the various states and empires of western Africa. In fact, in terms of volume, variety and importance of goods this trade was much more significant than the export trade to the communities as a whole. A large number of trade routes criss-crossed western Africa by 1600, linking the territories with one another both vertically and horizontally. Caravans or itinerant trading groups spent sometimes as long as one year away from their homelands, indulging in long-distance trade. They bought and sold commodities as they journeyed. The Hausa and Diula were the most well-known of these traders in West Africa.

Associated with these trade routes were the markets which developed in all parts of western Africa. The market centres were mainly of two kinds. There were the emporia, such as Jenne, Gao and Timbuktu, which became distribution centres for both local and exotic goods to other parts of western Africa. There were also smaller markets conducted weekly (or at short intervals) in the more rural areas. The market economy played a significant role in the overall economic life of western African societies.

What has been stated above is not intended to suggest that western African economies were more of an exchange nature than a subsistence one. Subsistence production remained the dominant feature of the economy for a long time after 1600. However, long before that date, the exchange economy had come into existence and formed a significant element in the economic life of the region.

In discussing the economic organisation of western African communities, specific and somewhat more detailed attention should be paid to food production. This is because one of the myths which had prevailed for long regarding these societies is that they had little if anything to eat. As a corollary to this, it is asserted that the introduction of certain exotic plants from the Americas by the Portuguese, particularly maize and cassava, created conditions for an agricultural revolution in Guinea during the era of the slave trade.

Sedentary agricultural practices began in West Africa at the latest by 2,000 B.C., and, according to some authorities, as early as 4,500 B.C. If the latter date is correct, it would mean that sedentary agriculture developed in West Africa at a time not much later than similar developments in Egypt and Abyssinia. There were two main agricultural zones in West Africa — savannah and forest. The crops cultivated in each area were basically different. The savannah peoples concentrated on the production of cereals, while those in the forest zones concentrated on tubers and root crops. In each case, environmental factors played a major role in determining the crops produced. As T. Lewicki has shown in his work, *West African Food in the Middle Ages*, the region as a whole produced a number of crops before the era of the Atlantic trade. These included sorghums, millets, rice, ground peas, yams, kidney beans, onions, watermelons, cucumbers, pumpkins, broad beans, palm oil and kola nuts. There were also a large number of fruit trees being cultivated or growing wild, from which food was acquired. Among these were the sycamore, tamarind, peach, lemon and wild orange. However, up to this point, the range of distribution of these trees has not been determined, especially in relation to the forest regions.

Animal husbandry was also practised in West Africa, mainly in the savannah area, for a long time before the beginning of the Christian era. The animals most commonly used for food, milk, butter and cheese were cattle, goats and sheep. Ecological factors played an important role in limiting the spread and number of these animals. Most of West Africa was affected by the dreaded tsetse fly which causes *trypanosomiasis* ('sleeping sickness') and which has a serious effect on animals in particular. Therefore, only selected areas mainly in the savannah region were able to keep fairly large herds of livestock. West Africa was known to have a variety of cattle, the *Ndama* breed, which were fairly resistant to sleeping sickness. However, they were not good producers of meat.

The forest communities had to depend much more than those in the savannah on hunting and fishing to provide their protein requirements. The animals hunted, both in the forest and the savannah regions, included giraffes, hippopotami, elephants, antelopes and crocodiles. A.J. Hopkins in his work, *An Economic History of West Africa*, states that during the dry season, when the demand for farm labour was not pressing, hunting became a highly organised activity in the forest zones. However, more substantial work has to be done on this subject to determine fully the range and importance of the chase in West African life.

Fishing was also an important means of acquiring protein. The many inland waterways were exploited from the earliest days for marine food. Many early settlements were built around the rivers. The large states and empires also sought to control them because of their potential as suppliers of food, and the facility which they offered sometimes as a means of communication. The peoples of the littoral were even more dependent than those inland upon marine food. In fact, the early settlements that grew up along the coast and many of those which existed around 1600 were basically fishing communities. They dried much of the fish caught and bartered it to the people of the immediate hinterland for various products. One gets the impression that, at the time of the European advent, a brisk trade in fish was going on, all along the coast.

The picture given above is that of a people attempting to come to grips with their environment and to utilise it to serve their needs, particularly in relation to food production. As time went by, they improved their techniques of production. Perhaps their most serious disadvantage up to 1500 was their lack of the wheel and the plough in cultivation. No satisfactory explanation has been advanced as to why the wheel in particular was not utilised. It was in use in Egypt, Abyssinia and the eastern Sudan for a long time. These were areas that influenced various aspects of western African life, for example, through the diffusion of iron technology. The use of iron tools had become widely diffused in western Africa by 1600, though it had not completely replaced stone tools up to that date. It is generally believed that the coming of the iron age to western Africa around the beginning of the Christian era, if not before, played a significant role in improving agricultural technology.

Other innovations of a technological nature in the field of agriculture included the cultivation of rice in the area of the modern republic of Guinea by a complex system of irrigation. The peoples of the Congo cultivated the hillsides by an equally sophisticated system of terracing. Dealing more generally with the subject of agriculture, Morgan and Pugh in their work, *West Africa*, point out that there were at least seven main methods of cultivation: rotational bush fallow, rotational planted fallow, mixed farming, permanent cultivation, tree cultivation, and flooded and irrigated farming. These methods were clearly developed by a society with a long tradition of agricultural production. On the whole, western Africa was only slightly, if at all, behind Europe in the field of agricultural technology. For instance, the methods of production employed on the plantations in the Americas up to the end of the eighteenth century were similar to those used in Africa at the time.

In the industrial field, western Africa also reached a high level of achievement in the production of certain articles. It should be pointed out here that industries were organised either at the level of the village or the cottage. No factories are known to have existed there at the period in question. In some societies, however, such as those in Hausaland, craftsmen would form themselves into guilds, relating to their specialities. But the non-existence of factories meant that the volume of production of a number of commodities would be limited, and this would cause the goods to be very expensive.

This was true of the production of cotton cloth and iron. Of course, production of these goods was also limited by the relative scarcity of raw materials. Cotton was produced in a few areas of the western and central Sudan, and much more rarely in the Guinea forest regions. Raffia, which was much more readily available, was used as the basic material for the manufacture of cloth. In regard to iron, only a few areas were known at the time to possess ore of a high quality. Moreover, it was only in those areas where wood was readily available for making charcoal that the iron industry could flourish. The main iron-bearing areas at the time in question were those of northern Yorubaland, the south-western part of modern Ghana, and the modern Republic of Guinea.

The production of cotton cloth and iron also required somewhat more advanced techniques than was the case with a number of other commodities produced at the time. On the other hand, the ceramic industry was widespread because of the greater availability of clay, a long tradition in pottery-making and a widely diffused technical competence in regard to that industry.

In regard to certain industries, West Africans had reached a high level of competence by 1600, in comparison with Europe and other non-African societies of the period. For instance, gold-mining (which was conducted mainly in areas of modern Mali, Guinea,

Burkina Faso and Ghana) was carried out both by working the alluvium and by shafting. Some mines in Burkina Faso went to a depth of 20 metres. As Davies states in his work, *West Africa before the Europeans*, " they must have been the work of skilled miners". The French scholar Raymond Mauny has suggested that, in the sixteenth century, West Africa was producing about nine tons of gold annually. This was a little less than half that produced during the colonial period. Basil Davidson reminds us that the development of mining in colonial Brazil owed much to the metallurgical techniques brought to that country by African slaves.

Leather was another commodity in regard to which Africans displayed a high level of technical competence. Leather, often originating in Kano and other Hausa states, frequently found its way to Morocco and was sold from there into Europe as Moroccan leather.

In relation to cloth-making, one Portuguese writer around the late sixteenth century declared that the Congolese were known to produce cloths similar to damask, velvet and taffeta. They also produced a cloth which was highly resistant to water and which the Portuguese used for making tents. The most well-known producers of cloth in West Africa were the peoples of Kano. Cloth produced by these people held its own against that produced by Europe and sold into Africa. It is also known that African weavers sometimes bought cotton cloths from Europeans, unravelled the threads and respun them according to African patterns, which were often far more intricate than those in Europe at the time. Similarly, it is said that African smiths often produced iron which was as good as that produced in Europe. The major differences between Europe and Africa at this point, in terms of production, were that the Europeans produced much larger quantities and a much wider range of goods than did the Africans. They sold these goods to the Africans at a relatively cheaper cost than the local products. This factor often caused the local industries to stagnate.

In regard to the plastic and graphic arts, West Africans also utilised a wide variety of materials and displayed a high level of sophistication. They are most widely known for their wood carvings and the manufacture of drums. Much less is known about their ivory carvings and their bronze or brass sculpting. Ivory carvings were carried out in several communities along the coast, and also inland. Portuguese records of the sixteenth century noted the high level of expertise reached by these people, especially those of Sierra Leone, in the carving of spoons, forks, salt-cellars, etc., made from ivory. Valentin Fernandes, a sixteenth-century Portuguese writer, was deeply impressed with his on-the-spot observation of their skill as carvers.

The greatest level of expertise in sculpting was attained by the 'bronze' sculptors of Ife and Benin, in modern Nigeria. Both of these territories had a long tradition in respect of this art form. Various writers have expressed the view that African art influenced the work of such European artists as Epstein and Picasso. Brian Fagg, one of the leading twentieth-century writers on African art, expressed the view that the 'bronzes' of Benin "dazzled Europe" when they were first seen in large quantities by European artists. Jean Claude, another modern writer, has commented that in 1920 Paul Guillaume thought that perhaps the impact of African sculpture on Western culture was as important as was "discovery of classical Hellenic antiquity for the Italian Renaissance". The bronzes and many of the most exquisite works produced from other materials were commissioned by members of the nobility. Several African rulers employed artists as functionaries of the court. In this sense, they often acted as patrons of the arts, as was the case in Italy during the Renaissance. Melville Herskovits, writing some years later about 'bronze' casting and cloth making in West Africa, declared that " the development of these two forms of art is to be regarded as a product of a populous society having a highly integrated culture ".

In relation to the literary arts, western Africa as a whole did not develop a strong tradition by 1500 or even by 1800. Most African societies remained at the pre-literate level up to the commencement of the colonial period in the late nineteenth century. However, some societies with which this essay is concerned did develop a long and strong literary tradition. These were mainly the states of the Sudan or grassland area. As a result of contact with Arab and Berber traders, Islam was introduced into various societies and Muslim schools were set up. Some centres became renowned for their scholarship and attracted Muslim scholars from North Africa and the Middle East. The most renowned of these centres was the Sankore mosque in Timbuktu in the fourteenth century, where the equivalent of a university education was offered. Its fame reached the main Islamic centres of learning at the time, including those in Fez (Morocco), Córdoba (Spain), Cairo (Egypt), Damascus (Syria) and Baghdad (Iraq). Other important Muslim centres in West Africa were Jenne and Gao. Many African scholars were studying Plato and Aristotle, works introduced to them by Arabs, at a time antecedent to the rediscovery of these authors by European scholars.

West African scholars also produced a variety of literary works in Arabic and in their own African language. A few of these works have survived up to today. The empires and states of Mali, Songhai, Borno and Hausaland made great use of literate men to assist in the running of the Government.

It must not be thought that those communities without a literate tradition had absolutely no organised or formal system of education. In fact, most communities had some formal, but rather limited, system of education. In a number of societies priests, diviners, herbalists and the like went through a long period of education, at the feet of more experienced men. Some of them underwent protracted periods of fasting and isolation from the rest of society in an effort to sharpen their spiritual insights. Secret societies were quite common in West Africa. The Poro in Sierra Leone, the Ogboni in Yorubaland, and the Ekpe (Egbo) in the Niger Delta were three of the most well-known secret societies in West Africa before 1800.

The discussion on western African societies would not be complete without at least a few brief observations on the antiquity and extent of the slave trade and slavery in western Africa before 1500. In relation to the slave trade, it is known that before the

Christian era African slaves were being sent to certain parts of the Mediterranean and the Middle East. It is also known that as time went by this trade covered a wider area and became more large-scale. However, the provenance of many of these slaves and the actual volume of this early trade remain serious points of contention among modern scholars. (This is equally so in the context of the Atlantic slave trade.)

Dealing specifically with West Africa, the relatively recent research of E.W. Boxhill, found in *The Golden Trade of the Moors* (originally published in 1958), has shown clearly that the Carthaginian and Roman trade with that region was mainly for carbuncle beads or stones, and that the slave trade played a minor role in the total trade of the region at that time. Moreover, throughout the period before 1600, the slave trade never assumed overriding importance in West Africa. The dominant export trade was in gold. Ivory was probably in second place, followed by a number of other commodities, including slaves. The main empires of the western Sudan clearly based their wealth upon the control and exploitation of the gold- and salt-bearing regions.

Even if one accepts the view that the slave trade from West Africa in the period before 1600 constituted a significant drain on the local population, one still has to draw a distinction, in this respect, between the savannah area on the one hand, and the forest and coastal areas on the other. It was from these two areas that the vast majority of slaves were drawn for export to the Americas. It is clear, however, that these areas had participated only indirectly in the trans-Saharan trade and that they had no important tradition of exporting slaves. The main commodities they sent northwards were gold, salt and kola nuts. For the coastal and forest regions, therefore, the European trans-Atlantic slave trade required a radical shift both in terms of the direction of their trade and the main commodity of export. The radical nature of this trade can also be gauged, to some extent, by the reluctance of various African societies to participate in the trade. For instance, the rulers of the Kongo kingdom in the late fifteenth and early sixteenth centuries made repeated efforts to put down the incipient slave trade organised by the Portuguese. As late as the early eighteenth century, Agaja, the ruler of Dahomey, sought unsuccessfully to arrest the growth of the trade there. Several small communities on the Upper Guinea coast, such as the Bulloms, Balantas and Banhuns, played only a minor part in the trade. These people recognised that the slave trade was a fire which was likely not only to burn them but to consume them.

The discussion immediately above also implies that slavery was not as widespread an institution in western Africa as it was generally made out to be by Europeans. This subject is an even more contentious one than that of the slave trade. This is so because, while it is recognised that several western African societies had institutions which denied people certain of their rights as human beings, not all of these institutions can rightly be called institutions of slavery, as many early writers have done. Several more recent writers have come around to the view that slavery was non-existent in many parts of western Africa and that, at other times, the institution in vogue was related more closely to European feudalism than to New World or Roman slavery. This view has been advanced notably by Walter Rodney and Basil Davidson. As these writers themselves have realised, there were a number of differences between European feudalism and the African institutions. Nevertheless, as a general framework of reference, the parallel holds good.

Western African societies were ordered more closely along the lines of lord and vassal, than along those of master and slave. It involved the notion of obligation on the part of the lord and duty on that of the vassal. Once this is appreciated, it throws a different light on the institution of slavery in western Africa.

Walter Rodney has argued that at least up to the seventeenth century in Upper Guinea there was no such institution as slavery. It is also known that in Calabar (Southern Nigeria) as late as the nineteenth century there were no special words for the European terms 'slave' and 'master'. The words used as equivalents were 'child' and 'father'. In Asante, the term used for a person in a servile condition was *odonko ba*, which carried with it no harsher connotation than 'slave child'. In several societies, such as those in Upper Guinea and the Niger Delta (and even farther afield, in places such as Zanzibar and Madagascar), the subjects of the rulers were often referred to as their slaves. This apparently caused some contemporary writers to declare that Africans were generally the slaves of imperious rulers. Even in certain parts of the Western Sudan where it is possible to discern more clearly an institution of slavery in vogue, the individuals involved often had a great number of rights and privileges within the societies.

It is difficult, if not impossible, to discern in western African societies in the period with which we are concerned any differences in the occupational roles or the life-styles of so-called slaves and the rest of the African population. At the lowest level, persons with varying degrees of unfreedom farmed the land, manufactured goods, traded, owned families, etc., just as the ordinary commoners did. Indeed, in some instances they could even inherit property, to the disadvantage of freeborn members of the family. At a higher social level, persons of servile origin occupied important positions within the Government, Civil Service and army. In Borno, the monarch usually placed several persons of servile origin over the province and the central administration. In Serer society (Senegal) the king's chamberlain was usually a man of servile origin. Among the Oyo (Yorubaland), the three most important court officials of the emperor were persons of servile origins. Though they had no seats on the Grand Council of State (which was reserved for freemen), they represented the emperor in his tripartite role as religious, judicial and executive head of state. Several other examples can be cited to show that men of servile origin often functioned in highly important capacities in African societies. In general, however, they were not allowed to become heads of state. But this was also true of commoners and of most of the nobility.

Unfree persons born in a given society often had certain imprescriptible rights within that society. They had certain rights to property and could not be sold except on the commission of certain crimes. There was therefore a sharp distinction between them and newly acquired prisoners-of-war. Moreover, no racial degradation was attached to their status as unfree persons.

This essay has attempted to highlight some of the prominent features of the societies of western Africa, roughly at the onset of the Atlantic slave trade. An attempt has been made to show that the peoples of the region encountered various economic, political and social problems. As is true everywhere in human societies, their environment imposed certain limitations upon them. The important point is that they sought to master this environment and to improve the quality of their lives. They made positive achievements in this respect. Over time, they increased considerably their range and quality of goods and services and in some areas they achieved levels of distinction comparable with those of the most advanced communities in Europe and elsewhere.

They made mistakes, too, but none that threatened their existence so gravely as the holocaust that was to come in the form of the Atlantic slave trade.

Further Reading

Ajayi, J. and M. Crowder (eds.). *History of West Africa*, vol. 1. London: Longman, 1971.
Boahen, A. *Topics in West African History*. London: Longman, 1966.
Boxill, E.W. *The Golden Trade of the Moors*, 2nd ed. London: Oxford University Press, 1970.
Curtin, P. *et al. African History*. London: Longman, 1978.
Davidson, B. *The Growth of African Civilisation. A History of West Africa 1000-1800, 2nd ed.* London: Longman, 1967.
Hopkins, A. *An Economic History of West Africa*. New York: Columbia University Press, 1973.
Rodney, W. *How Europe Underdevelopd Africa*. London: Bogle L'Ouverture, 1972.
Vansina, J. *Kingdoms of the Savanna*. Madison: University of Wisconsin Press, 1966.

2: The African Slave Trade to Guyana

by
Winston F. McGowan

The vast majority of African-Guyanese are descendants of victims of the trans-Atlantic slave trade, the forced migration of millions of Africans mostly from West and Central Africa to the Americas between the fifteenth and nineteenth centuries. Perhaps the most striking feature of the African slave trade to the area which today constitutes the Republic of Guyana was its relatively small volume, especially when compared with the size of the territory, its manpower needs and the scale of the traffic to other countries in the Caribbean. This characteristic was particularly pronounced during the period of Dutch occupation of the territory which virtually came to an end in 1796, when the British took possession of Berbice, Essequibo and Demerara. British occupation was followed by a considerable increase in the volume of the slave trade to these colonies from Africa until 1805, when the traffic was severely restricted by the British Government, before being completely prohibited in 1807.

This essay on the African slave trade to Guyana has two main objectives. Firstly, it seeks to examine the trade with a view to illustrating and explaining its small volume during the period of Dutch occupation and its marked growth in the initial phase of British rule. Secondly, it endeavours to assess the effects of the volume of the trade on the history of Guyana.

The attainment of these objectives has been rendered difficult by some of the problems inherent in the assessment of the volume of the Atlantic slave trade and the size of Caribbean slave populations. One major problem is posed by the extant Dutch historical records which, especially for certain years in the seventeenth century, are fragmentary or vague and often make it extremely difficult to determine precisely the volume of the slave traffic to the Guiana colonies. Furthermore, the use of official slave population statistics for the colonies is somewhat problematic for most of the figures were taken from tax returns and were widely believed to have been deliberately understated by slaveholders in an effort to evade taxes. But, even in cases where the returns may be accurate, they can be misleading for they often do not reflect exemptions given to slaveholders by virtue of the age of the slaves or the small number which they possessed. In these circumstances, it is always difficult to determine the exact size of the slave population at any given period.[1]

The precise origins of the African slave trade to Guyana are obscure. It is generally assumed that the trade began in the early decades of the seventeenth century to provide labour for the incipient Dutch settlements in Essequibo and Berbice. Initially, and for much of the remainder of the century, the trade was minimal. This was due partly to the fact that at first the main preoccupation of the Dutch settlers, especially those in Essequibo, was the promotion of trade with the indigenous Amerindian population rather than with plantation agriculture or any other activity requiring a substantial amount of African labour. The Dutch residents concentrated on exchanging European merchandise for timber, tobacco, resins, balsams, and, above all, anatto dye. While this preoccupation with trade lasted, there was only a limited demand for African slaves.[2]

The demand for African slaves probably did not increase significantly until after the 1650s when Dutch settlers in Essequibo embarked upon sugar cultivation, a labour-intensive activity which the sparsely distributed Amerindian population was unwilling or unsuited to undertake. In 1661, the first shipment of sugar was sent from Essequibo to the Netherlands. Sugar production, which was soon introduced into Berbice, began gradually to be given increasing importance though it is doubtful whether, at least in Essequibo, it superseded trade with the Amerindians in economic significance until the second or third decade of the eighteenth century.

Unlike the experience of several other European colonies in the Caribbean, notably Barbados,[3] the beginning of sugar cultivation in Essequibo and Berbice did not result immediately, or even for a long while, in any considerable growth in the African population to satisfy the demands of a labour-intensive industry. This may seem surprising for the Dutch in the latter half of the seventeenth century not only had the largest and most efficient merchant marine in Europe, but also a number of slave-trading stations in West Africa, especially on the Gold and Slave Coasts, as well as commercial contacts with the Congo-Angola region.[4] In fact, the development and extension of sugar cultivation in Essequibo and Berbice were severely retarded by a shortage of labour, resulting largely from an insufficient supply of slaves from Africa.

This situation stemmed mainly from the fact that the organisation of the African slave trade to Essequibo and Berbice was exclusively in the hands of the Dutch West India Company (WIC). This large state-chartered body, founded in 1621 essentially to challenge Portuguese dominance in West Africa and Spanish ascendancy in the Caribbean, enjoyed a monopoly of Dutch trade in West Africa and the Americas. Like the state-sponsored commercial companies elsewhere in Europe, the Dutch West India Company was severely hampered in its slave-trading operations by financial weakness, high overhead costs, dishonest employees and unfavourable circumstances in Africa and internationally.[5] Nevertheless, the Dutch Government did not follow the example of France (1672) and Britain (1698) in abandoning the system of monopoly control and in opening the trade legally to private individuals until 1730 — in fact, 1734 in the case of the slave traffic on the Gold Coast. By then, planters in Essequibo and Berbice were suffering from a serious shortage of slaves.[6]

The failure of the Dutch West India Company to supply the planters with the slaves they needed was related to three important features of its history and policy. Firstly, it was partly a result of the low volume of trade transacted by the Company, which, according to the most recent scholarly estimate, is said to have supplied the Americas annually with an average of 1,500 slaves between 1630 and 1674; 2,188 between 1675 and 1700; and 2,429 between 1701 and 1730.[7] This supply was not only inadequate to meet the needs of the Dutch West Indian colonies, but also was minute when compared with the British slave traffic. By the end of the seventeenth century, the British were landing more slaves annually in both Barbados and Jamaica than the total Dutch slave trade to the Americas. Between 1698 and 1707, for example, the Royal African Company and British private traders supplied an estimated 50,000 slaves to Barbados and 44,000 to Jamaica, an annual average of about 5,000 and 4,400 respectively, figures which were more than double the volume of the total Dutch trade to the Caribbean.[8]

A second and more important factor than the overall volume of the Dutch slave trade contributing to the inadequate supply of slaves to Essequibo and Demerara was the basic commercial policy of the Dutch West India Company. A preoccupation with the maximisation of profits and other considerations led the Company to supply many, if not most, of its slaves to the colonies of other European Powers, where prices were higher and the markets larger, rather than to Dutch possessions like Essequibo and Berbice.[9] The Company, for example, played a crucial role in the establishment of the sugar industry in Barbados. It was the principal supplier of slaves there, providing about 46,000 captives to the island between 1640 and 1663, when the introduction and enforcement of the Navigation Acts eliminated the Dutch role of suppliers to the British colonies and a monopoly of the British slave trade was granted to a new commercial body, the Company of the Royal Adventurers of England Trading into Africa.[10] Furthermore, the Dutch West India Company throughout the period of its monopoly sent a significant number of its slave cargoes to Curaçao and St. Eustatius for sale especially in the Spanish mainland territories, where it sought not only to fulfil the obligations of its *asiento* contracts between 1662 and 1713, but also to conduct contraband trade.[11]

The third feature which helped to minimise the supply of slaves to Essequibo and Berbice was the low esteem and priority accorded to them by the Directors of the Company compared to certain other Dutch possessions. Between 1630 and 1654, when the Dutch wrested the prosperous north-eastern part of Brazil from Portugal, the Company sought to satisfy the demand for slaves from Dutch settlers in Brazil in preference to that of any other Dutch American territory.[12] Similarly, after 1667, when the Dutch captured Suriname from the British, the Company regarded this new possession with its already flourishing and rapidly expanding plantation system as possessing far more value and potential than the incipient plantation colonies of Essequibo and Berbice, from which the Netherlands was deriving only minimal profit. It therefore pursued a deliberate policy of supplying slaves to Suriname in preference to Essequibo and Berbice.[13]

As a result of these three features of the history and policy of the Dutch West India Company, Essequibo and Berbice were greatly undersupplied with slaves in the latter half of the seventeenth and the early decades of the eighteenth centuries. It was not unusual then for two or more years to elapse without the arrival of a slave ship from Africa. For instance, only one slaver with 330 slaves arrived in Essequibo between August 1699 and May 1701.[14] Moreover, according to the Dutch historian, Goslinga, Essequibo and Berbice received only about 2,000 slaves out of an estimated 83,000 exported by the Company from Africa between 1675 and 1699, whereas Curaçao received about 61,500 during the same period and Suriname 9,462 between 1683 and 1699. This pattern of relative neglect of Essequibo and Berbice in the Company's slave exports is said to have continued in the final phase of the Company's legal monopoly of the Dutch traffic. Goslinga estimates that the Company landed only about 3,450 slaves in Essequibo and Berbice between 1700 and 1735, while Curaçao and Suriname respectively received 35,604 and 31,100 slaves during this same period.[15]

The lack of any significant growth in the slave trade to Berbice and Essequibo, in spite of the Dutch loss of the *asiento* contract to Britain in 1713, must have been a great disappointment to planters in the two colonies. In 1716, the Dutch West India Company gave a solemn promise to supply Essequibo with 200 to 250 slaves and Berbice with at least 50 each year, but these promises were not fulfilled. Similarly, in 1720 Berbice made an unsuccessful request for 400 slaves.[16] The Company continued to supply foreign powers with slaves at the expense of Dutch territories.[17] The need for a more abundant supply of African slaves to Berbice and Essequibo became more acute in the 1720s, when trade with the Amerindians dwindled and the economies of the two colonies began to be based almost completely on plantation agriculture.

Agriculture was diversified by the introduction of coffee cultivation in Berbice in 1721 and in Essequibo the following year, a development which increased the demand for slave labour. The two colonies in fact were undergoing changes which suggested that they could develop into important plantation settlements, if the urgent need for slaves was met.

The possibility of this need being satisfied was enhanced in 1730 by the end of the Dutch West India Company's monopoly of the Dutch slave trade and the advent of a new era where that commerce was dominated by private citizens. Dutch free traders, like their British and French counterparts, were able to supply a larger number of slaves than the state-chartered company, which eventually ceased sending slaves to the Americas in the 1750s. Estimates for the annual average supply of slaves by the Dutch to the Americas almost doubled between the 1720s and the 1760s, increasing from 3,264 in the 1720s, to 4,779 in the 1730s, to 5,524 in the 1740s, to 5,135 in the 1750s, and to 6,292 in the 1760s, before undergoing a decline in the 1770s.[18]

Several circumstances, however, prevented the increased supply of slaves provided by the Dutch free traders from alleviating the need for labour in Berbice and Essequibo after 1730. The individual traders, somewhat like the Company, showed a marked preference to supply slaves to Suriname where the continued expansion of cultivation resulted in a growing demand and attractive prices for slaves until 1770. In May 1743 alone five ships with a total of 1,014 slaves arrived in Suriname from the Congo while, in striking contrast, there were several years when not a single slave vessel came to the other Dutch Guiana colonies. In fact, the average annual importation of 2,000 -2,500 slaves into Suriname in the 1740s was probably equivalent to the total African slave population of Berbice or Essequibo.[19] The abundant supply of slaves from Africa enabled the slave population of Suriname to increase from an estimated 50,000 - 55,000 in 1738 to about 74,500 in 1762, while that of Berbice and Essequibo struggled to expand.[20] Thus, in 1762, Berbice is said to have had an African slave population of only 3,824, while that of Essequibo was even smaller, being estimated at 2,571.

The preoccupation with Suriname to the comparative neglect of the other Guiana colonies occurred at a time when there was an unprecedented demand for slaves there due to three major developments. The first development was the opening up of Essequibo in 1740 to foreign nationals, resulting in the influx especially of British planters, mostly from the older British West Indian islands such as Barbados and Antigua, where the soil was becoming increasingly exhausted and more difficult and expensive to cultivate. The second development was the establishment in 1746 of a new Dutch colony in Demerara where grants of land were made especially to British and Dutch planters who soon embarked on sugar and coffee cultivation. The third and final factor was the introduction of the cultivation of cotton in Essequibo in the mid-1740s and its spread later to Berbice and Demerara.

The increased demand for slaves stimulated by these developments was only partially met by the Dutch free traders. New British settlers were allowed to bring in slaves whom they owned in the islands. Some of them took advantage of this facility to import slaves illegally under the guise of being old property, when in fact they had just been purchased.[21] Some slaves were also smuggled into Essequibo and Demerara in particular by British and French traders. Nevertheless, by the 1750s, the colonies were critically short of slave labour. van's Gravesande, the Director-General of Essequibo and Demerara from 1750 to 1772, kept complaining to the metropolitan Government about the urgent need of slaves.[22] In July 1763, Gedney Clarke jr., the son of the most successful of the new British planters in Demerara, made a special visit to Holland to complain to the metropolitan Government about the inadequate slave supply and "to see what good he can get done for the Inhabitants of that Infant and African Starved Colony".[23] He presented to the authorities there a plan, centred on an adequate provision of slaves, which he contended would make Demerara become the most valuable Dutch territory in the Caribbean. In this plan he stated:

> About the year 1752 the first Settlements were begun In Demerary. The Inhabitants as was natural expected proper Encouragement from their Mother Country and were even promised it. Instead of which they have not to This Day received the least Supply of Negroes or any thing else towards the Advancement of their Estates, so that they have been obliged all along, with great Risque, to purchase Necessaries at St. Eustatius, the English Islands or wherever they could get them and at any Price. Without Negroes it is impossible for them to cultivate their Lands so that without a speedy supply of that Article In particular Demerary, fertile as it is, must dwindle and come to Nothing.[24]

The supply of African slaves to Essequibo, Berbice and Demerara did not improve significantly until the 1770s. This improvement was reflected in what must have been an unprecedented increase in the rate of growth of the slave population of these colonies. The number of slaves in Essequibo and Demerara, respectively, grew from an estimated 3,986 and 5,987 in 1769 to 8,700 and 12,559 in 1782, while that of Berbice is said to have increased from 3,370 in 1764 to 8,050 in 1782.[25] The growth in the slave supply to Demerara, Essequibo and Berbice in the 1770s occurred in spite of the fact that this decade witnessed the beginning of a marked decline in Dutch participation in the Atlantic slave trade. In short, a far greater proportion of the overall Dutch trade began to be conducted with these colonies than before.

This growth was due mainly to two developments. Firstly, it was partly a result of a decision made in 1770 to open the trade of Demerara and Essequibo to all the provinces in the Netherlands, instead of maintaining it as a preserve of Zeeland alone. Slavers from Holland therefore began to land slave cargoes in these colonies, thus supplementing the supplies provided by Zeeland traders.[26] The increase in the slave supply, however, was due, above all, to a serious economic crisis in Suriname which resulted in the withdrawal of credit, bankruptcy, the abandonment and sale of plantations and a marked fall in the demand for, and price of, slaves. The depression of the market prompted most Dutch slavers who arrived in Suriname after 1772 to refuse to sell their cargo there and to proceed instead to neighbouring Berbice, Demerara and Essequibo to dispose of it at higher prices. It is estimated that these colonies were supplied with about 7,000 - 8,000 slaves in this way in the 1770s.[27] Although this figure constituted a significant increase in slave supply, it was small compared to the imports of several other Caribbean territories, notably Jamaica, which, although it had a slave population of nearly 200,000, imported an estimated 18,448 slaves in 1774 alone.[28]

The 1780s witnessed a significant increase in the demand for slaves especially for cotton cultivation in the wake of the growing realisation that the saline coastal soils were the best lands for its growth.[29] Planters profited from the capture of the three colonies between 1781 and 1784 by the British and the French, the leading slave-trading nations. British and French traders seem to have supplied the colonies with a considerable number of slaves during these years. Barbados in particular provided the colonies with slaves and other necessaries during the period of British occupation from February 1781 to February 1782.[30]

This situation of improved slave supplies was affected after March 1784, when France restored Berbice, Demerara and Essequibo to the Netherlands for what proved to be virtually the last years (March 1784 - April 1796) of Dutch rule of these colonies. During this period, the Dutch slave trade to the Americas underwent a drastic decline to a level of about 1,000 slaves a year – a level never experienced since the initial phase of Dutch participation in the trade in the late sixteenth and early seventeenth centuries. Dutch traders provided only a few slave cargoes to Demerara, Essequibo and Berbice, and though the colonial authorities winked at contraband trade especially with the British West Indies, the supply of slaves reaching the three colonies seems to have fallen far short of the needs of the planters.

By 1795, a time of international war, Demerara, Essequibo and Berbice were in desperate straits owing to the imposition by Britain of a general embargo on Dutch ships and the growing insecurity facing Dutch vessels on the high seas where they were subject to attacks and seizure by British privateers. Hardly a Dutch ship dared cross the Atlantic and planters in Demerara, Essequibo and Berbice found it extremely difficult not only to import slaves, but also to export their produce to the Netherlands. It was this distressing situation which helped to make many of the planters willing to accept British rule, a status which would enable them to be supplied with slaves by British traders and to secure entry for their produce into the British market. These prospects became realities after April 1796, when Britain occupied the three colonies.[31]

British occupation marked the end of the Dutch slave trade to Demerara, Essequibo and Berbice. The most striking characteristic of this trade almost throughout its history was its low volume and its inadequacy to meet the demands of slaveholders. This trait was largely the result of the considerations of profit and priority that influenced the Dutch West India Company and, later, the individual Dutch traders.

It was due also to another significant factor, namely, the limited financial resources of many planters in the three colonies and the lack of credibility and creditworthiness with which the suppliers of slaves tended to view them. The suppliers were usually unwilling to extend to them the same favourable terms of credit granted to their counterparts in Suriname. For example, in the 1720s the Berbice Association, the new owner of the colony, was required to pay 40 per cent of the price of slaves in advance, whereas in Suriname slaves could be obtained on 18 months' credit. In Essequibo, often only planters with sufficient and readily available capital could purchase slaves, for the Dutch West India Company frequently sold them only on a cash-on-delivery basis. The Company was always very cautious about granting long-term credit to Essequibo and Berbice.[32]

The unavailability of such a facility to help planters to purchase slaves prompted Gedney Clarke in 1762 to recommend the establishment of a bank of credit in Demerara. Clarke told the Dutch metropolitan authorities that "there should also be a Bank of Credit formed to give a lifting Hand to the Inhabitants and enable them to purchase Slaves when they arrive."[33]

The British occupation of Demerara, Essequibo and Berbice in April 1796 ushered in an unprecedented period in the African slave trade to these colonies. For the first time British traders, who were dominating the Atlantic slave traffic, were able to supply these territories with slaves without restrictions over an extended period. The years 1796 to 1800 witnessed the zenith in the volume of British slave exports to the Americas. It has been estimated that in this period British slave traders landed there an annual average of 42,482 slaves, a figure which is nearly seven times as large as the highest annual figure for Dutch slave exports in the peak period in the 1770s.[34]

This extensive trade served to meet the increased demand for slaves which British occupation produced in Demerara, Essequibo and Berbice. The coming of British rule not only encouraged resident British planters to extend their plantations, but also was followed by a new influx of British settlers who purchased land and immediately sought to establish cotton, coffee and sugar estates. Within three years, the area under cultivation in Demerara and Essequibo increased by 10 per cent and by 1800, the number of plantations there had grown from 392 to 490.[35] The high prices being offered in Britain for coffee, cotton and sugar were an inducement to seek to maximise production partly through the acquisition of additional slave labour. The demand for slaves was also stimulated by a stipulation of the land grants which required the beneficiary to secure at least 10 slaves within 18 months.[36]

To meet this growing demand, a number of new firms, such as

McInroy and Sandbach, specialising in the slave trade to Demerara, Essequibo and Berbice, were established and some absentee proprietors purchased ships and despatched them to West Africa to secure slaves for their plantations.[37] Within five years, at least 28,000 slaves were landed in Demerara and Essequibo, while the imports into Berbice were so massive that its slave population doubled by 1802. By 1803, an average of about 8,000 slaves was being supplied each year to Demerara and Essequibo where many plantation proprietors now enjoyed long-term credit from British metropolitan merchants.[38]

Planters, especially new settlers, looked forward to a long duration of this flourishing trade. They were therefore bitterly disappointed when the British Government in 1805 prohibited the trade for the cultivation of new land and finally in 1807 outlawed the trade completely for all British subjects and possessions. This ban brought a virtually effective end to the African slave traffic to Demerara, Essequibo and Berbice, for only a small number of slaves were smuggled into the colonies after its introduction. In 1805, the last year of the unrestricted trade, Demerara alone received an estimated 6,631 slaves, a figure which exceeded the highest average annual supply of slaves by the Dutch to the entire Americas. This is clear evidence of the marked difference in the scale of the African slave trade to Demerara, Essequibo and Berbice during the Dutch and British periods of rule.

The limited scale of the African slave trade had a significant impact on the history of Guyana. It had a marked influence on the economy, being largely responsible for the underdevelopment which a recent work has rightly contended was the major characteristic of the economy of Demerara, Essequibo and Berbice during the period of Dutch rule.[39] It resulted in an insufficient labour force which compelled most proprietors to cultivate only a part of their land grants. The shortage of labour almost invariably prevented them from taking advantage of the offer of "second depths", to which they were eligible only when they succeeded in bringing all the land in their initial grant under cultivation. In short, it ensured that a significant proportion of the plantations remained small and that few large estates emerged. Thus, according to one estimate, as late as 1782, about 250 of the 637 plantations in the three colonies had fewer than 15 slaves and none seems to have had more than 300 slaves.[40] Not surprisingly, the production of the colonies lagged far behind that of Barbados and Jamaica which had a far more adequate labour force. It was only after British occupation in 1796 that Demerara, Essequibo and Berbice, mainly as a result of a substantial influx of labour and capital, experienced significant economic growth. There was a marked increase in agricultural production, especially in cotton and coffee. In fact, there was such a remarkable transformation that, by 1800, these colonies, whose economic growth had been stifled for so long, had become the second largest producer of sugar in British West Indies, the largest producer of coffee in the British Empire, and the greatest producer of raw cotton in the world.[41]

The low volume of the Dutch slave trade not only influenced the rate of economic growth but also its nature. The small size of the slave population helped to encourage the cultivation of coffee and cotton in the latter half of the eighteenth century in preference to the original agricultural staple, sugar, which required more labour and capital. It was widely agreed in Demerara, Essequibo and Berbice, that on the average, while one slave could cultivate one acre of sugar cane, he could cultivate one and a half acres of coffee and two acres of cotton. Consequently, proprietors, especially new settlers who possessed limited capital and labour, tended to establish coffee and cotton plantations rather than sugar estates. This consideration helps to explain why cotton and coffee eclipsed sugar in the late eighteenth century, relegating it temporarily to third place in importance among the staples being produced for export.[42]

The small size of the African slave trade to Demerara, Essequibo and Berbice seems to have influenced the attitude of slaveholders considerably towards the question of the loss of slave labour. It helped to make them reluctant to manumit slaves and to view with serious concern the problem of runaways and maroons and attacks on their plantations by French privateers and Spanish residents from the Orinoco region. Manumission in the Guiana colonies was rare because, until the late 1820s, it required the consent of the slaveholder who, largely because of the almost perennial shortage of labour, was usually extremely reluctant to free slaves. In these circumstances, usually the only slaves freed were women who had a relationship with the master, and their mulatto children. It was extremely rare for able-bodied males to secure their freedom.[43]

As a result of the low incidence of manumissions, the Guiana colonies had an extremely small free Coloured Ppopulation which was usually even more negligible than the tiny White population. For example, in 1798 in Essequibo there were an estimated 361 free Coloureds (68 men, 123 women and 170 children) compared to 701 Whites and 12,360 slaves.[44] Demerara, Essequibo and Berbice in fact had the lowest frequency of manumission in the British Caribbean, freeing, for example, only 44 slaves between 1808 and 1810 out of a total slave population of about 108,000.[45]

There seems also to have been a relationship between the small volume of the slave supply and the planters' deep concern about runaways and maroons. Guiana slaveholders manifested a strong determination to recapture runaways and to prevent the survival of maroon villages which would serve as a perennial magnet to the already small labour force on the plantations. Through the conduct of "Bush Expeditions" in which Amerindians played a crucial role, they were eventually able to reduce most maroon settlements and to recapture many of the fugitives, in spite of the size and forested nature of the terrain and the relative inaccessibility of most maroon villages. In contrast, slaveholders, especially in Essequibo, were unable to take any effective action to check the incidence of flight to Spanish territory in the Orinoco area. The Government of Demerara and Essequibo made repeated but ultimately unsuccessful attempts to persuade the Spanish authorities to extradite the fugitives.[46]

The limited slave supply also helped to intensify the concern of planters, especially in Essequibo, over the losses in slaves incurred as a result of periodic attacks on plantations there by Spanish subjects in the Orinoco. In an effort to avoid such losses, planters advised their slaves to flee into the hinterland of the estates in the event of Spanish incursions, which were particularly prevalent during the period of the Revolutionary and Napoleonic Wars.[47]

The inadequate volume of the slave trade also drove planters in Essequibo, Demerara and Berbice to seek to secure additional slave labour by other expedients. In particular, they resorted to smuggling slaves especially from the British West Indies and to the utilisation of Amerindian slaves. Almost throughout the period of Dutch rule there was a small minority of Amerindian slaves. In 1762, for example, Berbice had a slave population consisting of 3,824 Africans and 244 Amerindians. Although Amerindian slavery was a source of friction between the two peoples, the urgent need for labour prevented the Dutch authorities from prohibiting it completely until 1793. There was, however, a marked decline in the use of Amerindian slave labour after 1770, when the supply of African slaves increased.[48]

The increase in the slave supply in the late eighteenth and early nineteenth centuries not only led to a reduction in the use of Amerindian labour, but also made the *Deficiency Laws* unworkable. These laws, which required the maintenance of a certain proportion of Whites to Africans on a plantation as a security measure, were progressively modified to accommodate circumstances where planters encountered difficulty in recruiting enough Whites to keep pace with the growth of the slave population. In Berbice, for example, the ratio of one White to 15 slaves was modified to one White to 50 slaves in 1784 and further to one to 79 in 1810.[49] In Demerara, the ratio of one White to 50 slaves stipulated by an 8 June 1789 ordinance was altered to one to 75 in May 1805. The difficulty of recruiting enough White staff on the plantations was recognised to be so formidable that this 1805 ordinance stipulated that trustworthy free Coloureds could be considered as Whites for the purpose of the ratio required by the *Deficiency Laws*.[50]

Although the slave supply increased considerably after 1796, the Guiana colonies were still short of slaves when the British Government prohibited the traffic in 1807. The planters therefore protested strongly against the ban, but without success. The ban, however, was welcomed by planters in Barbados, where there was an adequate labour force as a result of an abundant supply of slaves since 1640. Barbadian planters viewed the ban as a means of putting a check on their increasingly formidable rivals in Demerara, Essequibo and Berbice whose interests would be jeopardised by the loss of their supply of African slaves. Some Jamaican planters, aware of the shortage of slaves in the Guiana colonies, also supported abolition of the slave trade for the same reason.[51]

Perhaps the most enduring effect of the small size of the slave trade to Demerara, Essequibo and Berbice was that it severely limited the population of these colonies. As late as the 1760s, the slave population of Berbice and Essequibo was only about 3,500 - 4,000 each, whereas that of Suriname was estimated at 74,500. Even at the time of abolition of the trade, notwithstanding its rapid growth after 1796, the estimated slave population of Demerara, Essequibo and Berbice (about 109,000) was modest compared with that of Jamaica (about 348,000) and negligible in view of their geographical spread.[52]

In spite of immigration in the post-slavery era, underpopulation has remained one of the principal features of the country, posing a formidable obstacle to its effective occupation, exploitation and development.

Notes

1. For an examination of the problems involved in assessing the volume of the trans-Atlantic slave trade and Caribbean slave populations, see P. Curtin, *The Atlantic Slave Trade : A Census* (Madison, 1969); B. Higman, *Slave Populations of the British Caribbean 1807 - 1834* (Baltimore, 1984); J. Inikori, "Measuring the Atlantic Slave Trade: An Assessment of Curtin

and Anstey", *Journal of African History, Vol. XVII, No. 2* (London, 1976), pp. 197- 223.

2. The best general accounts of the history of Guyana in the period examined in this essay are P. Netscher, *History of the Colonies Essequibo, Demerary and Berbice* - translated from the Dutch by W. Roth (Georgetown, 1929, originally published in the Hague in 1888); J. Rodway, *History of British Guiana from the Year 1668.* 3 Vols. (Georgetown, 1891-4); and A. Thompson, *Colonialism and Underdevelopment in Guyana, 1580 - 1803* (Bridgetown, 1987).
3. For the impact of the introduction of sugar cultivation elsewhere in the Caribbean in the seventeenth century, see R. Dunn, *Sugar and Slaves. The Rise of the Planter Class in the English West Indies, 1624 - 1713* (New York, 1972).
4. For Dutch involvement in West Africa in the seventeenth century, see K. Daaku, *Trade and Politics on the Gold Coast, 1600-1720* (Oxford, 1970); J. Postma, "The Origin of African Slaves: The Dutch Activities on the Guinea Coast, 1675 - 1795", in S. Engerman and E. Genovese, *Race and Slavery in the Western Hemisphere. Quantitative Studies* (Princeton, 1975), pp. 33 - 48.
5. A. Hopkins, *An Economic History of West Africa* (London, 1973), pp. 92 - 3.
6. J. Postma, "The Dimension of the Dutch Slave Trade from Western Africa", *Journal of African History*, Vol. XIII, No. 2 (London, 1972), pp. 237 - 348; Thompson, *Colonialism*, pp. 31, 33, 37, 39.
7. C. Goslinga, *The Dutch in the Caribbean and the Guianas 1680-1791* (Assen., 1985), p. 79.
8. H. Beckles, *African Rebellion in Barbados: The Struggle Against Slavery, 1627 - 1838* (Bridgetown, 1984), p. 127.
9. Curtin, pp. 94 -5 ; Goslinga, pp. 156 - 88.
10. K. Watson, "The Trans-Atlantic Slave Trade (with special reference to Barbados)" in A. Thompson (ed.), *Emancipation 1*, (Cave Hill, Barbados, 1986), p. 17.
11. Postma, "The Dimension", p. 238; Goslinga, pp. 156 - 188.
12. Netscher, p. 27; Postma, "The Dimension", p. 239.
13. Goslinga, pp. 312 - 20, 416 - 22; R. Van Lier, *Frontier Society* (The Hague, 1971), pp. 25-6.
14. National Archives of Guyana (N.A.G), 'Notes of the Shipping Arrivals', in the Kyk-over-al Diary.
15. Goslinga, p. 66.
16. *Ibid.*, p. 187.
17. Rodway, Vol. II, p. 31.

18. Goslinga, p. 49. See also Table 1.
19. Van Lier, pp. 26 - 7, 120.
20. *Ibid.*, p. 27; H. Lamur, "Slave Mortality in Suriname in the 19th century: The Role of Internal Factors", (Paper presented at the Thirteenth Conference of Caribbean Historians, Guadeloupe, April, 1981), p. 42; Netscher, p. 42; Thompson, p. 93.
21. Rodway, Vol. I, p. 111. Many of the plantations of new British proprietors in Essequibo and Demerara were initiated especially with labour from Barbados where, largely as a result, the slave population is said to have declined by 3,313 between 1740 and 1748 and sugar production decreased, much to the concern of the Barbadian Government. See F. Pitman, *The Development of the British West Indies 1700-1763* (London, 1967), pp. 96 - 7.
22. For copies of Gravesande's correspondences, see L. Storm Van's Gravesande, *The Rise of British Guiana*, 2 Vols. - translated and edited by C. Harris and J. de Villiers (London, 1911).
23. British Museum, London, E.G. (Egerton Papers) 1720, Douglas to Bentinck, 12 July, 1763.
24. *Ibid.*, Clarke to Bentinck, 16 July 1762, encl. Memorandum Concerning Rio Demerary by Gedney Clarke, 16 July 1762.
25. Rodway, Vol. II, p. 11.
26. *Ibid.*, Vol. I, pp. 242, 260.
27. Van Lier, pp. 31, 40 - 1, 125; Goslinga, pp. 329, 423 - 8.
28. E. Williams, *From Columbus to Castro. The History of the Caribbean 1492-1968* (London, 1970), p. 145.
29. British Museum, Add. *MSS, 42071*, Vol. 2, Sullivan to Grenville, 2 April 1802, encl. Observations on Dutch Guiana by Lord Seaforth, 5 Feb. 1801.
30. Public Record Office (PRO), London, C.O. III/I, Kingston to Townshend, 13 Jan. 1783 and enclosures.
31. For a more detailed examination of the developments mentioned in this paragraph, see W. McGowan, "The French Revolutionary Period in Demerara - Essequibo, 1793 - 1802", (Paper presented at the Thirteenth Conference of Caribbean Historians, Guadeloupe, April, 1981), pp. 1-12. For major documentary sources, see PRO, CO. 111/3, Hopkinson to Huskisson, 29 July 1795 and enclosures; Dundas to Hawkesbury, 22 September, 1795; Beaujon to Portland, 15 June 1799, encl. General State of the Produce of Demerary from the Year 1788 - 1799.
32. Rodway, Vol. I, pp. 61 - 2; Thompson, *Colonialism*, pp. 26, 56.
33. British Museum, E.G. 1720, Clarke to Bentinck, 16 Jul.1762, encl. Memorandum concerning Rio Demerary, 16 July 1762.
34. R. Anstey, "The Volume and Profitability of the British Slave Trade, 1761

- 1807", in Engerman and Genovese, pp. 7 - 10.
35. PRO, C.O. 111/3, Beaujon to Portland, 24 Jan. 1799 and enclosures; C.O. 111/4, Hislop to Turnbull, 12 Jan. 1801.
36. British Museum, Add. *MSS, 42071*, Sullivan to Grenville, 2 Apr. 1802, encl. Observations on Dutch Guiana by Lord Seaforth, 5 Feb. 1801.
37. PRO, C.O. 111/4, Hislop to Turnbull, 12 Jan. 1801; C.O. 111/6, Courher to ?, 1 Mar. 1806.
38. PRO, C.O. 111/4, Hislop to Turnbull, 12 Jan. 1801; *Ibid.*, Produce of Demerary and Essequibo for Six Years, as taken from the Customs House Books, n.d. (1803); Rodway, Vol. II, pp. 261.
39. Thompson, *Colonialism..*
40. Rodway, Vol. II, p. 11.
41. For a more detailed study of economic developments in the early British period, see McGowan, pp. 14-15.
42. PRO, C.O. 111/4, Hislop to Turnbull, 12 Jan. 1801; C.O. 111/5, Sayers to Sullivan, 21 Oct. 1803; Thompson, *Colonialism*, pp. 43, 52 -53.
43. See the record of manumissions which appears in the Minutes of the Court of Policy of the colonies.
44. PRO, C.O. 111/3, Beaujon to Portland, 9 April 1799 and enclosures.
45. Higman, pp. 380-1, 417, 692.
46. N.A.G., Minutes of the Court of Policy of Demerara - Essequibo (M.C.P.), 1 Nov. 1808. For a detailed study of Maroons and runways, see A. Thompson, *Brethren of the Bush: A Study of Runaways and Bush - Negroes in Guyana c. 1750-1814* (Cave Hill, Barbados, 1975).
47. PRO, C.O. 111/7, The Petition of Roger Leigh to Liverpool, 13 Jul. 1807; C.O. 111/8, Bentinck to Castlereagh, 28 Jan. 1808.
48. Netscher, p. 42; de Villiers, p. 237.
49. N.A.G., Proclamations of the Government of Berbice, 1796-1818, Proclamation by Governor Sam Dalrymple, 1 Oct. 1810; Rodway, Vol. II, p. 39.
50. N.A.G., Publications and Ordinances 1802-1810, Publication by His Excellency Governor Beaujon and the Honourable Court of Policy, 25 May 1805.
51. British Museum, Add. *MSS 42071*, Vol. 2, Sullivan to Grenville, 2 April 1802, encl. Observations on Dutch Guiana by Lord Seaforth, Feb. 1801; Watson, pp. 23-24.
52. Lamur, p. 42; Higman, p. 417.

Table 1 : Global Estimate for the Dutch Trans-Atlantic Slave Trade, 1630-1794

Period	WIC Trade	Rented Ships	Free Trade	Totals	Annual Average
1630-74	70,000	-	-	70,000	1,500
1675-80	18,302	-	-	18,302	3,050
1681-90	15,437	-	-	15,437	1,544
1691-1700	23,155	-	-	23,155	2,316
1700-10	23,822	-	-	23,822	2,382
1711-20	23,624	-	-	23,624	2,362
1721-30	25,424	3,000	4,215	32,639	3,264
1731-40	17,374	-	30,420	47,794	4,779
1741-50	2,259	-	52,984	55,243	5,524
1751-60	356	-	50,994	51,350	5,135
1761-70	-	-	62,921	62,921	6,292
1771-80	-	-	40,300	40,300	4,030
1781-90	-	-	9,695	9,695	970
1791-94	-	-	3,500	3,500	880
Overall	219,753	3,000	255,029	477,782	3,398

WIC trade=Dutch West India Company trade
Source: Goslinga, p. 49.

3: Slave Society during the Dutch Regime

by
Alvin O. Thompson

New World plantation slavery was an economic, social and intellectual prison.[1] It was the most draconian form of slavery known in the history of mankind, and the most absolute form of labour control ever witnessed. Under this system, labour was immobile, in the sense that the labourers were bound to a given plantation - that of their owner or the person to whom they had been hired. They could not sell their labour since it legally belonged to their master; its value was determined exclusively by the master class. At best, they had an indirect or negative say in the matter: by mutilating themselves or acquiring a reputation for intransigence they might depreciate the value of their labour. Whereas under a free labour system workers possess certain bargaining rights and can ultimately withhold their services, under slavery this was impossible, or at least only possible through absconding and revolting. But these forms of protest often met with their masters' full wrath.

Under slavery, the worker was regarded by the master class as essentially a unit of production. In the Dutch, as in the British, colonies his persona was overlooked and sometimes even denied. As James Pope-Hennessy says, he was regarded as "a kind of two-legged domestic animal".[2] To some planters, fresh or saltwater slaves were wild animals that needed to be broken in to domestic manners and, most of all, to the work regime on the plantations.[3] This view of the animal nature of Africans needs to be stressed. Contrary to what has often been asserted,[4] it had gained some currency in Europe before the heyday of trans-Atlantic slavery and might well have influenced the development of the Slave Trade.

Several European writers in the fifteenth and sixteenth centuries referred to Africans as "beasts", "savages", "monstrous folk", etc.,

The Demerara Maroon War, 1795: African Maroons ambush Dutch troops

having traits comparable with those of dogs, hogs and goats. They are said to have observed virtually no moral standard: they were "liars", "thieves", "great drunkards", "uncivil", "deprived of all knowledge of good", and "given over to vice".[5] One Dutchman, writing around 1600, declared that certain of them ate "raw dogs guts" and "also great store of stinking fish"; they stole like dogs; they were lecherous, great liars, and "much addicted to uncleannesse"; their children grew up like trees, and their women were given over to "Lust and uncleannesse".[6] Several Europeans also declared them to be physically repugnant. One Portuguese writer described some Africans on sale in Europe in 1453 thus:

> Among them were some well-nigh white, and were handsome and well made in body; others were black as Ethiopians, and so uncomely, as well in countenance as in body, that those who were guarding them thought they beheld the creatures of the lower hemisphere.[7]

This view of the physical repulsion, moral depravity and mental retardation of Africans gained general acceptance among the Whites in New World slave societies. Thus, slaves were branded, broken in, fed, housed, worked, sold, and sometimes made to breed like animals. A typical advertisement in the newspapers announcing a sale of Africans would list them along with other items on sale - boats, clothing, furniture, medicines, horses etc. In the early nineteenth century, Africans found their places on the ferryboat in Berbice among the sheep, goats, hogs and other animals, paying the same fare as the latter.[8]

Thus conceived of as beasts of burden, or "hewers of wood and drawers of water", slaves were barred from ownership or control of the means of production, distribution and exchange. Even the crops they grew in their 'kitchen gardens', their huts, and their families ultimately belonged to their masters. Thus positioned, they were completely divested of the means of upgrading their social and economic status, except on rare occasions when their masters allowed them to do so. But while slaves were on the periphery of the plantation system in terms of remuneration for their labour, they were at the centre in terms of their role as production units - they were the most important factor in the production of plantation staples.

While laws were imposed in most colonies limiting the authority of the master over his slaves and requiring him to give them certain basic necessities, in practice, the master was often a law unto himself. Slaves had no recourse to the law courts for redress of wrongs committed against them, not even when extremely harsh punishments were imposed on them. Therefore, the legal machinery, by giving the master almost complete control over his slaves, allowed him to exploit them nakedly and with greater impunity than under a free labour system.

Even in the late eighteenth century, when the law in the Guiana colonies sought to intervene to ensure the slaves certain minimal allowances of food and clothing, and to limit the coercive power of the master over them, the conception was not in terms of the rights of slaves, but rather the reduction of the incidence of insubordination and revolt, thus increasing the availability and efficiency of labour. Therefore, the law, by failing to recognise the slave as having certain imprescriptible rights, reduced him legally to a 'non-person' or a nonentity. From the late eighteenth century, when the institution of slavery was under attack in Europe, planters frequently asserted that they treated their slaves well, a viewpoint which still has some weight with some modern apologists for slavery. The humane or paternalistic view of the treatment of slaves is usually rationalised by pointing out that slaves were expensive personal property, and that masters were therefore committed to exercising great care over them and treating them well. This viewpoint is predicated on the premise that the institution of slavery was a rational one and that holding property in slaves can be a rational act, under certain circumstances. The view also fails to take account of the fact that people often abuse their own property, as was the case with the colonial plantocracy. It was blind avarice rather than enlightened self-interest which determined the day-to-day treatment of slaves by their masters. The raison d'être of the plantation was to produce profits, and slave labour was an essential element in doing so. The planters had no intention of allowing their profits to be eroded by spending even an extra penny on the maintenance of their slaves.

Economies might have been effected by more rational and scientific methods of cultivation and processing, but planters generally paid little attention to these aspects of production and concentrated on pressuring slaves for more labour. Thus, an irrational and lopsided agricultural economy developed, partly because of this circumstance. The plantation was the scenario for the daily round of violence, by which the mass of slaves was confined to a life of poverty, disease and lingering death. As Keller writes, "A widespread indifference or cynicism respecting the fate of the human working animal has prevailed; it has been regarded in general as an insentient factor in the accumulation of wealth".[9]

While a few planters treated their slaves less brutally than others, the 'good', 'humane', or 'paternalistic' planter was a chimera and it is time this ghost is laid to rest. All planters kept their slaves in bondage against the latter's will, allowed them to accumulate little if anything, exploited their labour for their (i.e. the planters') personal benefit, and treated them as persons with infantile minds. As we have stated elsewhere, the very act of enslaving a person is a dehumanising one both for the slave and the master.

Africans found it difficult to adjust to the new work ethic and regime of plantation America and to other aspects of the New World environment. Sylvia de Groot points out that, while the environment was similar in geographical features and the practice of agriculture, it was different in respect of the juxtaposition of African and European culture elements - especially the babel of tongues - social stratification, the dominance of the plantation system, and the features of plantation slavery.[10] Many contemporary writers argued that Africans were no better off than slaves in their home country and that many of them had been in the most abject form of slavery before capture. The debate still goes on concerning the nature and incidence of African slavery during the pre-colonial period.[11] Nonetheless, there appears to be a consensus that those areas which dispatched the majority of slaves to the New World had only a limited and much milder form of slavery up to the end of the eighteenth century than that of the New World.[12]

Planters recognised the need for slaves to adjust or become acclimatised to their new environment. This was expected to take place during the 'seasoning period', which could last up to one year. This period was a time of physical and psychological adjustment and also of healing for those unknowingly infected with various diseases at the time of purchase by the planters. Sheridan indicates that about one-third of all slaves imported into the West Indies died during their first three years of residence.[13] Many of them made a shadowy appearance on the scene, dying quickly of dysentery, ulcers and depression - the immediate aftermath of the Middle Passage. Fresh slaves were often placed with old ones to break them in and gradually initiate them into plantation work. The planters no doubt took great care to ensure that they were placed under 'faithful' slaves, who would indoctrinate them into the virtues of submission to planter authority; but this was a lesson not well-learnt as the high incidence of resistance and revolt testifies.

The production of a given crop involved a number of activities, which can be conveniently divided into two broad categories: those concerned respectively with the cultivation and the processing of the crop. While the labour force was also organised basically along these lines, during crop time the field slaves, or those involved in cultivation, were often required to put in extra time at the processing plants.

The field labourers constituted the largest section of the labour force, according to Craton, roughly seven-eighths.[14] They were divided into three or four gangs, depending upon age, sex and labour capacity. Theirs was the most exacting form of labour. The year was spent weeding, hoeing, digging and cultivating the land. The soil on the Guyana coast is much more intractable than that of Barbados or Jamaica, and turning it is extremely difficult when it is wet. It is therefore possible that slaves in

Guyana had a far more difficult time cultivating the land than those in the islands mentioned above. Of course, even before cultivating the land, work had to be done to empolder each estate and to provide the maze of irrigation channels, typical of Guyanese estates. This involved strenuous, back-breaking work - what Rodney refers to as "the steady work diet of mud and water".[15]

Artisan slaves were involved chiefly in the processing of the crop. This included the erection and maintenance of buildings, the manufacture of barrels (vats, casks) to contain the raw or semi-processed product, and the actual preparation of the product for export. The artisans were divided into specialist groups: carpenters, coopers, blackmiths, tinsmiths, boatbuilders, masons, etc. These were prized slaves on all plantations and fetched the highest prices. Several African artisans were transported as slaves to the New World and must have been included among the estate artisans once their skills were recognised.

Of course, both field slaves and artisans were sometimes assigned tasks not specifically related to the production process, but which had to do with the running of the plantation or the colony at large. Thus, among the multiplicity of tasks slaves were required to perform, were cutting grass for estate animals, building houses for the estate personnel, maintaining the section of the public roads coterminous with their plantation, erecting and maintaining the forts and other defence installations,[16] and assisting in the defence of the plantation or the colony.

Apart from field and artisan slaves, there were a number of others engaged in various plantation tasks. For instance, fishermen were expected to provide marine food for other slaves, to supplement that provided by the Indians. Others were assigned as hinterland traders with the Indians. These were mainly Dutch West India Company (WIC) slaves in Essequibo, referred to as creoles and considered among the most trustworthy slaves. (However, this did not stop them from absconding on several occasions.) There were also itinerant traders operating within the plantation area itself, plying their wares from estate to estate, and often spending several days away from home. Sedentary traders operated mainly in the urban centres, but since such centres did not exist before the late eighteenth century, it may be concluded that this trade was of relatively late origin. The range of tasks assigned to other slaves included acting as oarsmen, grooms, messengers, porters, cooks, seamstresses, wet nurses, midwives, doctors',[17] and drivers, almost all tasks requiring the use of manual labour and several requiring some degree of specialised skills. By and large, the various tasks referred to above were performed by the more healthy and vigorous slaves, but this did not mean that the aged ones and invalids (*manquerons*) were allowed to spend their twilight years free from toil for their owners. In fact, they played very important roles. In the early eighteenth century, several of them were WIC hinterland traders. There was, for instance, 'Big Jan' who was still involved in hinterland trade up to 1700; in 1706 he was said to be "blind through age",[18] and, as a result, was transferred from trading to salting fish in the Cuyuni, along with other *manquerons*. This category of slaves also performed such tasks as weeding, in addition to looking after their masters' poultry and crushing salt for the local fisheries. A slave had to be almost completely incapacitated before he/she was relieved of daily toil.

Slaves were rarely, if ever, assigned jobs such as bookkeepers, which required the use of literary skills. Teaching slaves to read and write was regarded as dangerous to the safety and integrity of plantation society, for these skills might be employed to plot conspiracies. Missionaries ran foul of the plantocracy in the nineteenth century when they attempted to introduce such skills to the slaves. While some slaves were literate, mainly in Arabic (which they learnt in West Africa), no notice was taken of this by the plantocracy. The freed Cuban slave, Juan Francisco Manzano, parodies the Cuban plantation overseer in words equally apt to the Guyanese situation:

> We purchase slaves to cultivate our plains,
> We don't want saints or scholars to cut canes;
> We buy a African for his flesh and bone,
> He must have muscle--brains, he need have none.[19]

The imperatives of the plantation system demanded that slaves work hard, accept graciously the minimal allowances granted them, and always show unquestioning obedience to those in authority over them. But the contradiction was that slaves were persons with needs, aspirations, feelings and reactions common to humanity.

No amount of indoctrination could change this situation, and so the planters' recourse was coercion. As Shahabuddeen puts it, " the kernel of the system was organised terror and coercion".[20] Physical coercion was intended to have two primary effects: first, to make the slave maintain a certain rhythm of work, and second, to cow him into respecting the authority of his master or overseer and, in fact, all Whites within the society.

Many of the punishments meted out to slaves had nothing to do with the regime of work, but rather with instances of so-called insubordination. This might involve such trivial matters as failing to give the appropriate salutation on meeting a White person on the street, or raising one's hand threateningly at a White. The reaction of the Whites to the slaves' failure to show fawning regard for them was born of fear that this might be the breach in the wall which might let in the flood-tides of revolution. This fear was always present in a situation in which Africans outnumbered Whites greatly in the colonies.

In Berbice, the ratio of the one to the other stood at 11 to 1 in 1762, 28 to 1 in 1785, and 46 to 1 in 1811.[21] The disparity on the plantations must have been much greater than the figures given above. It is known, for example, that of the 550 Whites in Berbice in 1811, 160 were soldiers (not counting commissioned officers). If the remainder is divided in half to take care of the number of women and children and the civil personnel in the colony, this would leave roughly 200 White adult males on the plantations, resulting in a African to White (adult male) ratio there of roughly 126 to 1.[22]

The Court of Policy was quite concerned about the great shortage of Whites in the colony. In 1797, Governor van Batenburg, speaking for the Court, stated that on average there was only one White adult male on each plantation.[23]

As elsewhere in the Caribbean, *Deficiency Laws* were passed from time to time to ensure a certain ratio of White adult males to Africans on each plantation. In 1732, the Berbice Government set the ratio at 1 to 15; by 1810 the situation was as follows:

Table 2: Stipulated African/White Ratios in Berbice in 1810

Africans	1-79	80-199	200-349	350-450	451 +
Whites	1	2	3	4	5

Source: N.A.G., *Minutes of Court of Policy of Berbice, Oct., 1, 1810.*

In that year, the Berbice Court of Policy prescribed stiff penalties for failure to abide by the *Deficiency Laws*. Each delinquent planter or manager was to pay an initial fine of *f*.500 and a further fine of *f*.100 for each subsequent month that he failed to comply with the law. Whenever a White should quit an estate, the owner or manager was to be allowed six months to fill the vacancy, save in the case of an estate having only one White on it, where the vacancy had to be filled within one month.

Efforts were also made in Essequibo-Demerara to cope with the problem of small White and large slave populations. The law of 1784 stipulated that at least one white was to remain on each estate at night, under penalty of *f*.300. In 1785, the prescribed ratio of White adult males to Africans was 1 to 50. The actual population in that year, according to van Houtte, was 14 slaves to 1 White.[25] No figures are available for the White adult population capable of bearing arms, but it must have been substantially smaller than the entire White population. It seems certain that, as in Berbice, the law stipulating the ratio of Whites to Africans on the plantation was breached regularly.

Writers on New World slavery often cite the great disparity in the African/White ratio as a major reason for the coercive machinery which the plantocracy established. In Guyana, where the disparity was unusually great, the need to coerce the Africans into submission was considered even more pressing and persistent.

The Dutch were unlike the Spanish and French, and more like the British, in that they did not enact or apply any slave codes to their colonies as a whole, nor, in the case of Guyana, were the slave laws codified until 1784 (i.e. for Essequibo-Demerara).[26] The Spanish applied their thirteenth century slave code, *Las Siete Partidas*, to their New World colonies and later on supplemented it with specific laws applicable to the various colonies. The French published the *Code Noir* in 1685, which provided the legal and theoretical framework for the management of slaves in their New World colonies. On the other hand, the *Constituto Criminalis Carolina*, or Imperial Criminal Code, of 1532, which the Dutch applied to their colonies was not a slave code, though in theory it was applicable to both slaves and free persons. It was left up to the proprietors of the various colonies to institute their own slave laws. This task was in turn delegated for the most part to the individual colonial legislatures, which institutionalised the slave system through a battery of coercive laws.[27] In 1784, when the WIC finally introduced a slave code for Essequibo-Demerara, it was in the face of strong opposition from the planter class who, like the British West Indians, saw this as unnecessary interference in their affairs, and likely to lead to a situation which might have pernicious consequences.

While the code attempted to stop the most flagrant abuses of the slave system, it was not revolutionary. In fact, it was vague on many aspects of master/slave relations, especially as regards the provision of food, clothing and other allowances. What the planters appear to have resented most of all was the initiative taken by the WIC to publish the laws. Since the members of the Courts of Policy were usually slaveowners, they were not in a position to look at the institution of slavery from a sufficiently objective viewpoint. Their overriding concern was with keeping the slaves in check.

Thus, slave laws tended to be characterised by a spirit of coercion and an attempt to regulate the lives of the slaves rather narrowly. The Africans must be kept in a position of subordination and subservience to the Whites at all cost. An important aspect of the situation was that there were few laws protecting the slave against his master, and where he was protected against another individual, it was purely in the context of his being regarded as the property of his master. Thus, in 1784 in Essequibo-Demerara, no one except the legally constituted authorities was allowed to punish another person's slave for insubordination with more than a single blow with a stick, and not in such a way as to injure him. Breach of this regulation entailed a stiff fine of *f*.600.[28]

The greatest number of laws, and certainly those which were repeated most often, were those circumscribing the movement of slaves off the plantations to which they belonged, and the congregating of slaves in large numbers. These laws were aimed at preventing slave desertions and revolts. The Berbice law of 1735 forbade slaves to leave their plantations without written passes from their owners or managers; this law was renewed in 1738. Other laws (in 1765, 1804 and 1806) forbade them to be out at nights "or other unreasonable times", except with their master's consent. They were to carry lights and written passes on such occasions.[29] Pass laws were also promulgated by the Essequibo-Demerara Court of Policy.

In all the territories, laws were passed regulating the hours and conditions under which slaves were allowed to dance, especially at nights. At least one White adult male was to be on the estate on such occasions, and no slave from another estate was to attend such dances. We do not know how stringently these laws were enforced but, in 1764, van Hoogenheim expressed the view that the facility with which slaves were allowed to roam about Berbice at night was probably one of the chief causes of the 1763 slave uprising.[30] To be sure, laws were passed threatening anathemas against delinquent planters. Thus, the Essequibo-Demerara law of 1784 stipulated a fine of *f*.30 for the first offence, *f*.60 for the second, and a summons before the Court of Justice for a subsequent offence.[31]

The laws restricting the movement of slaves were observed more rigidly both by the colonial authorities and the planters during periods of slave unrest or insurgency. In more relaxed circumstances, a watchful eye was kept mainly on the more recalcitrant slaves; still, they could never be sure that the so-called docile or faithful slave would not turn out to be a lion in sheep's clothing.

In any case, most planters felt that they knew their slaves best, the slaves were their property, and discipline and punishment their prerogative. They put more faith in their short but sturdy arms (or in those of their *bombas*) than in the long but feeble arm of the law. As van's Gravesande pointed out in 1770, the master had great freedom of action, as long as he did not kill his slaves: "if they but come from the stocks alive".[32] A similar situation prevailed in Berbice, at least up to 1764.[33] In 1784, in an attempt to prevent the wilful killing of a slave by his owner, the WIC prescribed that any person, White or slave, who should die suddenly "under suspicious circumstances" or "shortly after punishment", should not be buried until the proper legal and medical authorities had examined the corpse and certified the cause of death.[34] However, like others which sought to limit the planter's authority, this law turned out to be nothing more than a sterile injunction. The colonial judiciary was seen to have feet of clay when it came to enforcing the laws restricting the master's authority, which remained virtually unimpaired until the British period in the nineteenth century.

As it was, offences against slaves, which would have been regarded as heinous crimes if committed in free societies, were often either condoned, simply frowned upon, or resulted in a mild reprimand and/or a small fine. By contrast, acts which in free societies would hardly have been considered even misdemeanors, were treated as woeful crimes when committed by slaves. In each case, it was the social significance of the act (i.e. who committed it) that mattered. As Shahabuddeen observes:

> ...punishments were used primarily as a method of asserting and maintaining the authority of the planter

> and only very secondarily as a method of correcting wrong-doing in the sense in which punishment is understood in any modern system of criminal justice. It was a system based on the use of terror as a primary instrument of control. The slightest neglect of labour or infraction of discipline could call forth the most disproportionate response of power.[35]

Whipping was the most common punishment meted out to slaves for various offences. It was resorted to as the 'court' of first instance, while appeal was made to more brutal measures for what were considered particularly grave offences. Up to 1770 in Essequibo-Demerara, van's Gravesande (who had lived in the colony for some thirty-two years) could find no law on the statute books which limited the number of lashes a master or attorney could inflict on his slaves. It was only in 1784 that the WIC limited the number of lashes permissible by these persons to 25, and stipulated further that the blows were to be delivered "with reason and without cruelty or passion".

In order to avoid accidents, punishment was not to begin until the slave had been placed flat on his face and tied between four stakes.[36] In the case of Berbice, in 1810, private whippings were limited to 39 lashes and, in 1817, to 25. The colonial governments kept a free hand to deal with what they considered extraordinary situations. Thus, in 1752 some slaves were sentenced by the Berbice Government to 300 lashes each, for staging a minor revolt. Many Whites believed that the discipline of the whip was essential to keeping the slaves in due subordination; therefore, the whip was not spared nor used sparingly. The wife of a Demerara planter, on hearing the cries of a slave being whipped, exclaimed:

> Aha, it will do him good, a little wholesome flagellation will refresh him; it will sober him: it will open his skin, and make him alert. If Y-- was to give it [to] them all, it would be of service to them.[37]

For her, as for many others, this was an energizer to the slaves;

in reality it proved to be a death rattle to many of them. Slaves were commonly whipped either with a *meby* (liana) vine or a common cart whip used on animals. van Berkel stated that the *meby* cut deeply and tore off "whole flaps of flesh", while Pinckard, without describing the whip used, declared that he had seen a slave whose flesh had been torn "in a frightful manner" by it.[38] These whippings and other forms of punishment were usually administered by African slaves, called overseers or *bombas*. One way of doing so has been vividly portrayed in the following description of an incident which took place in Demerara in 1796:

> A poor unhappy slave was stretched out naked, upon the open street, tied down, with his face to the ground, before the fiscal's door, his two legs extended to one stake, his arms strained out, at full length, to two others in the form of the letter Y, and thus secured to the earth, two strong-armed drivers, placed at his sides, were cutting his bare skin, by turns with long heavy-lashed whips, which, from the sound, alone, without seeing the blood that followed, conveyed the idea of tearing away pieces of flesh at every stroke.[39]

The planters tried to bend the slaves to their will, and those whom they could not bend they tried to break. Sometimes this was literally the case, through two horrid instruments of torture known as the 'Spanish whip' (*Spaanse bok*) and the 'rack'. The Spanish whip has been described by Hartsinck, Nepveu and others. Nepveu described it thus:

> ...the hands tied together, the knees drawn up between them, and a stick inserted through the opening between the knees and the hands and fixed firmly in the ground, around which they then lie like a hoop and are struck on the buttocks with a guava or tamarind rod; one side having been struck until the skin is completely broken they are turned over to have the other side similarly injured; some use hoopsticks for this, although this is an extremely dangerous practice, as it generally results in the slaves' death, even

> though the chastisement is less than with the abovementioned rods.[40]

Thus excoriated, those slaves who did not die were often maimed for life. The rack or wheel was described by Bolingbroke as a horrid machine with recesses made for the principal joints to be placed in, upon which the criminals are laid out and extended, when they are broken by iron bars.[41]

Slaves were punished in several other ways for such acts as running away, revolting or striking a White person. For the first two 'offences', in addition to being whipped, they were sometimes put in chains and/or had iron collars placed around their necks, with long spikes protruding therefrom. Sometimes these spikes were bent at the ends to prevent the slaves from getting through the thick bushes which surrounded the plantations. The collars also prevented them from lying down comfortably. At other times, they were branded, and had their ears cut off or the sinews of their heels severed. In extreme circumstances, they were hanged with an iron hook inserted through their ribs and weights attached to their legs. They were also roasted over a slow fire, or burnt from the feet up, while having their flesh torn with red-hot pincers. For striking a White person, even in self-defence, their hands were often amputated, but a brutal whipping was deemed a more merciful treatment. One particular instance of brutality about which van Hoogenheim wrote was that of a slave who was punished by his master by having his back cut with a saw. van Hoogenheim actually witnessed the skin hanging from his back.[42]

The most horrifying punishment mentioned in the records consulted was that of a seven-year-old girl, who had committed acts which van Hoogenheim considered "only trifles and childishness, deserving only a child's punishment". However, Gerlach, her manager, had ordered that she be given 250 lashes and placed in the stocks, where she remained, without any food, save whatever was given her by slaves who sympathised with her plight. When van Hoogenheim saw her, on a visit to her plantation three weeks after the punishment had begun, her body had been "cruelly torn to pieces". It was only on his express orders that she was re-

leased from the stocks, in face of strong opposition from the manager who felt that she deserved greater punishment and who, according to van Hoogenheim, was probably going to keep her there much longer and give her another whipping. The Governor begged the Director of the Association to "give orders and laws by which all such atrocities [might] be prevented".[43]
Apart from the more extreme forms of punishment mentioned above, there were several other ways, of a less spectacular nature, of punishing slaves. Common punishments of this kind included confining them in the stocks, depriving them of allowances of rum, tobacco, food, clothing, etc., giving them additional tasks to perform, placing them in solitary confinement, and forbidding them to take part in evening dancing.

van Lier, like some other writers, argues that while the slave laws were brutal, the criminal laws in Europe were also brutal and reflected the thinking of men of a brutal age. He states further that the punishments meted out to slaves were "not prompted by racial antagonism or notions concerning the 'depravity' of the African, although doubtless these were aggravating circumstances".[44] However, his argument is unconvincing, and the examples he cites of brutal punishments occurring in Europe in the eighteenth and nineteenth centuries are trivial when compared with those he cites in respect of the slaves.[45] However, his own statements are somewhat contradictory, for he asserts that:

> the countless abuses, the numerous executions and mutilations, the severe sentences for what were often petty offences made the lot of the slaves exceptionally hard even in comparison with the practices in other countries.

We should also note that the edicts promulgated in the Dutch colonies (and in other European colonies), especially from the late eighteenth century, against the maltreatment of slaves, find no parallel in legislation in Europe at the time, suggesting that there was no need to do so. Also, the observations of several persons in the colonies - including Stedman, Pinckard, St. Clair and Bolingbroke - on the brutalities of the slave system make it clear that they found the punishments meted out to the slaves much harsher than those they had witnessed in Europe, or even among soldiers and sailors, who were supposed to have been severely punished for misdemeanors.

In Guyana, the criminal law treated Whites and Africans quite differently. For instance, Africans selling prohibited goods were to be "severely flogged on the plantation by sentence of the Court, according to the exigency of the case". On the other hand, Whites found receiving such goods were to be fined *f*.300 and if they could not pay the fine, they were to be put on bread and water for a few days.[46] van Lier himself admits that several laws were passed by the colonial legislatures, meting out unduly severe punishments specifically for slaves.[48]

The fact is that the legal and administrative machinery in the colonies was employed to maintain White domination through denying slaves access to the courts and allowing free Coloureds and free Africans only limited access to them. Normally, slaves were not allowed to testify against White persons and, in the few instances in which they were allowed to do so, it was only as ancillary witnesses.[49]

It was under this legal and social monstrosity that Africans were forced to work, live and die; and it is in the context of this failure by the legal authorities to protect the slaves from the excesses of their masters that the provision of food, clothing and accommodation for them must be viewed.

In most American plantation colonies the food provided for slaves was deficient in quantity;[50] in all it was deficient in quality. In Guyana it was deficient in both so that, while slaves were overworked, they were underfed. This combination of a surfeit of work and a dearth of food played havoc with their health, and was a major cause of the high mortality and morbidity among them. Fish was the slaves' main protein food, but the quantity provided was small. Theoretically, in the case of the WIC's slaves in Essequibo around the mid-eighteenth century, each adult was to receive 3lbs. of salted fish per fortnight.[51] This amounted to about 3.43 ozs. (or roughly 97.3 gm.) per day. However, 15 per cent or 14.6 gm. would have been waste, making the daily edible portion about 82.7 gm., containing about 32.8 gm. of protein.[52] The plantains they were supposed to receive would have added another 15 gm. of protein to their daily diet,[53] thus giving them a daily protein intake of some 47.8 gm.

Some authorities believe that the adequate protein requirement for an average adult is 1 gm. per kilogram (2.2 lbs.) body weight, especially if the protein is derived from a mixed diet (fish, cassava, plantain, peas, etc.), as distinct from a complete protein diet (egg, fish, beef, etc.). On this basis, the protein requirement was computed in 1945 by the USA National Research Council at 60 gm. for an average woman (132 lbs. body weight) and 70 gm. for an average man (154 lbs. body weight). On the other hand, the UK recommended daily allowance for 1975 was somewhat higher than 1 gm. per kilogram.[54] In any case, the slave's daily allowance of protein fell far short of the 70 gm. mentioned above, amounting to only about 68.3 per cent of it. We cannot simply attribute this deficiency to the colonial authorities' ignorance of what constituted an adequate daily supply of protein because, around the mid-eighteenth century, Government regulations provided that even petty White personnel should receive an adequate, and sometimes even a substantial surplus, allowance of protein.[55]

Fish was chosen as the chief protein food for the slaves for four main reasons. First, the Dutch, especially those of the northern maritime provinces, had built up a significant fishing industry there since the Middle Ages. In fact, Charles Wilson claims that for the Netherlands, the fisheries were the "germ of later maritime greatness".[56] It was natural, therefore, for the Dutch to carry over this tradition and knowledge of fishing into their new colonies. The second reason is closely linked with the first. The fisheries in Guiana offered the most readily available and abundant source of protein. Thirdly, it entailed much less effort to renew the supply than in the case of cattle, pigs or poultry. As one writer points out, "Fish is a unique food source in the sense that it replenishes itself without such efforts as are required to produce all other kinds of food".[57] Finally, and most importantly, it was the cheapest form of animal protein available to the planters.

If the ration of fish was bad enough in theory, it was worse in practice, for the slaves often had to do without it. According to van Berkel, Government Secretary in Berbice in the 1670s, slaves were given fish once or twice per year, or a cow or horse that had died of itself.[50] In Essequibo-Demerara, there was a critical shortage of fish during the second half of the eighteenth century, because the Atlantic fisheries around Orinoco and Trinidad, which formerly supplied the plantations with most of the fish they required, were frequently disrupted due to the escalation of border conflicts between the Spanish and the Dutch in Guiana. Nor could the fisheries within the colonies themselves offset this loss. Berbice depended mainly upon the Canje fishery, but this too offered only a very limited supply of fish. The failure to secure the required amounts of fish from the traditional fisheries forced the planters to purchase salted cod from the Americans at relatively high prices. However, as we have explained elsewhere, the large number of protested bills held by the Americans often hindered the trade. While the situation improved somewhat from the last decade of the eighteenth century, as late as 1810 the Governor of Berbice was complaining about the great shortage of fish in that colony, which was causing many slaves to abscond.[59]

Slaves also suffered from a deficiency in the supply of other foods. Plantains and cassava, and to a lesser extent yams, sweet potatoes and other ground provisions, were the staples provided for them. Apparently, neither rice, flour nor corn was given to them on a regular basis. As in the case of fish, the colonies were expected to be self-sufficient in supplying the staples. Thus, all estates were expected to cultivate plantain trees, or "succulent roots" as the ground provisions were sometimes called. However, planters regularly failed to grow adequate amounts of food. In the first place, it was apparently only in the nineteenth century that laws were passed specifying the exact quantity of food to be supplied to each slave. The Essequibo-Demerara code of 1784, for instance, simply stated that the provision grounds should be calculated on the ratio of "one acre for five negroes; allowing moreover a reasonable weekly allowance, according to the custom of the Colony "[60] The Berbice law of 1806 was somewhat more specific. Estates on the rivers, with lands capable of producing plantains abundantly, were to provide at least two full-grown 'bunches' of plantains weekly to each slave, except nursing children. As an alternative, each slave was to be given two common coffee baskets full of 'root'.

In order to ensure a sufficient supply of food on hand, each coastal estate was to grow 75 healthy plantain trees per slave, while the riverine ones (where the trees thrived better) were to grow 60. Estates providing ground provisions were to cultivate one acre of 'roots' for every six slaves.[61] The good intent of these laws was nullified by plant diseases, drought and simple neglect, and the slaves often experienced grave shortages of food. In 1806, the Court of Policy of Berbice noted the coastal planters' neglect to observe the laws and the dire consequences for the slaves. Some years earlier, van's Gravesande had noted a similar neglect by the planters of upper Demerara, who, for the sake of larger profits, had planted only cash crops, and had even refused to give their slaves the customary Saturday afternoons off. Instead, they depended upon food supplies from America, a situation which produced a grievous shortage in 1772, as the Director-General pointed out. [63]

Clearly, the neglect to cultivate adequate provision grounds was the main cause of food shortages in the colonies. Laws seeking to correct the situation had to be published frequently. Berbice passed laws on this matter on 12 and 31 July, 1787; 30 April, 1804; and 11 February, 1806. In the last instance, the Government specifically stated that the new law was occasioned by the planters' neglect of earlier ones.[64] Penalties were prescribed for failure to observe the laws. In Essequibo-Demerara, in 1784, delinquents were to be fined *f*.90 for each acre less than the stipulated amount, and *f*.1.50 for each slave who was not given his proper allowance. In Berbice, in 1806, the fine stood at *f*.1,000 for the first offence, *f*.2,000 for the second, and formal prosecution in the Court of Justice for the third offence.

These prescriptions of penalties made little difference to the planters because the inspectors of the estates were burgher officers, who themselves owned slaves and who were unlikely to take action except in the most flagrant cases of neglect. The colonial Governments often ruled by precept rather than practice. Around 1800, it was not uncommon to find slaves in Stabroek working in the colony's chain-gang "frequently with nothing but dry plantains to eat "[65]

Even if the planters had observed the letter of the law, the caloric value of the staples would have been significantly less than that required to sustain a healthy working adult. Plantains will be used here as representative of the lot, because they were the slaves' main diet and the quantities to be provided were stipulated in somewhat clearer terms than was the case with the other staples. Still, there is some difficulty in determining the actual weight of a 'bunch' of plantains. The Suriname Government, in dealing with the question of food for the slaves in that colony in 1851, estimated a 'bunch' at 9 lbs. If this estimate is used, the slaves' weekly allowance in Berbice in 1806 would have amounted to 18 lbs. (two bunches). Accepting a more liberal estimate to meet the stipulation of two full-grown bunches, this would have amounted to about 28 lbs.[67] On the basis of the latter estimate, the daily allowance would have been 4 lbs. or 1,816 gm. Allowing for waste (peel) of 31 per cent, the edible portion would have weighed 1,258 gm., having a caloric value of 1,654.[68] If we added another 218 calories derived from the daily allowance of fish,[69] the total daily caloric value would be 1,872. This figure is far from the 3,600 calories considered as the average intake required by a healthy, very active male, between 15 and 35 years of age.[70] It is therefore evident that the slave's diet was grossly deficient in both its protein and caloric content.

An interesting aspect of the Guyana situation is that slaves were fed mainly on plantains, roots and tubers, whereas in the Caribbean islands they were fed mainly on flour and corn. Several possible factors account for this difference. Guyana did not grow corn extensively in the pre-colonial period. Yet, corn gives one of the highest yields of calories per 100 gm. (around 360), about three times the caloric yield of an equivalent weight of plantains. Rice gives just about the same caloric yield as corn, but it was never cultivated to any extent by the Dutch planters,[71] though they knew that it thrived in certain parts of the colonies. However, both of these staples were much less bulky than those grown for the slaves, and the planters were concerned mainly with weight and cheapness, not caloric content. As one modern writer states about the roots and tubers, " when hunger arises the farmers often turn to these crops, since they can be raised in abundance rather quickly at relatively low cost".[72]

Other things being equal, an acre of land is likely to produce about the same weight of yams and plantains, and more than three times the weight of cassava, than it could produce in rice and corn.[73] The point is even more striking when viewed in relation to labour costs, or 'man days'. G. Geortay gives figures for the Belgian Congo per ton of each of the four crops mentioned in *Table 3*, when light forest clearing is involved.

Table 3: 'Man Days' per ton for Selected Crops in the Belgian Congo

Crop	Maize	Rice	Cassava	Plantain
Man Days	78	153	30	18

Source: B.F Johnston, The Staple Food Economies of Western Tropical Africa (Stanford, 1958), p. 136.

The precise situation in Guyana is not known, but it would hardly differ significantly from what obtains in the Congo. For South America generally, it is said that the method of cultivating plantains involved planting the suckers, then felling the tall forests on top of the planted area. The plantains sprout up between this felled mass and in the absence of major diseases are capable of producing fruit for 20 to 40 years, without replanting, tilling and manuring of any sort.[74] The facts above reveal that cassava, and especially plantains, require little manual labour in comparison with maize and rice, hence the greater attraction they held for the Dutch planters.

Cassava was indigenous to the Americas, whereas plantain was not. Some plantations, therefore, took to cultivating mainly the former in the early days. This crop, however, thrives best in sandy soil and so not every plantation found it economical to cultivate it. The WIC kept one or two bread (cassava) plantations in Cuyuni, but these became increasingly unproductive as time went by. The Indians supplied most of the cassava needed by the planters at the outset but, as the slave population increased, the Indian supply proved insufficient, forcing the planters to cultivate plantains.[75]

Fish, plantains, roots and tubers were the only foods which the slaves received regularly, apart from salt. They usually had to provide themselves with fruits and vegetables as best they could. In the early nineteenth century, St. Clair declared that these commodities were scarce in the slave markets. He stated that okra and peas were the only vegetables they cultivated, in order to obtain money to buy tobacco. On the other hand, writing a few years earlier, Pinckard declared that vegetables were in good supply in the Stabroek market.[76] The supply was no doubt seasonal, and this may account for the discrepancy in the two eyewitness accounts. Some slaves cultivated fruits; in Pinckard's time there was a good supply in the Stabroek market.[77] In one notable instance, that of the Berbice plantation, Anna Clementia, in 1781, fruit trees were provided for the slaves' use.

The Dutch planters may be forgiven for failing to provide fruits for their slaves. For centuries it was commonly believed in Europe that fruits gave rise to fevers and diarrhoea, resulting in deaths, especially in infants.[78] However, they cannot be forgiven so readily for failing to recognise the importance of vegetables. According to one writer, "Vegetable growing was a highly developed industry in Holland as early as the 15th century ".[79] The Dutch even played a significant role in the development of the English vegetable industry in the seventeenth century.[80] Nevertheless, in the case of Guyana, they imported the vegetables they needed for their own consumption - not for that of the slaves - from Europe and North America.

An issue which must necessarily arise from the discussion above is the extent to which slaves were allowed to supplement the food provided for them by their masters. On the basis of the evidence currently available, it appears that there was wide variation in practice, if not in theory, on different plantations at different times. While, in theory, slaves were given Saturday afternoons to cultivate their private plots, in practice this was sometimes denied them, especially since it was a matter of custom and not law. Likewise, Sunday was supposed to be their rest day, but they could be and were sometimes required to work, particularly during crop time.

Provision fields were cultivated either in communal or individual plots. According to Anna Benjamin, the Berbice Association employed the first method on its estates in the 1760s,[81] and it was still in operation during the British administration of the estates in the early nineteenth century. On some other estates individual plots were allocated, apparently in place of rations distributed by the planters. In fact, this appears to have been a prevalent, if not the main, method of feeding the slaves. van Berkel states that this method was employed in Berbice in the 1670s:

> [T]hey are allowed to make use of their own gardens and plantations, because they have nothing else on which they can exist, beyond the stinking salt fish [82]

Rodney says much the same thing of the situation in the late eighteenth century. Sometimes, however, both systems were in operation on a given estate, complementing each other. Higman states that the private provision grounds in Guyana in the nineteenth century were small, for planters preferred communal cultivation of the grounds.[83]

Slaves were also sometimes allowed to keep livestock, but it appears that this was not common practice, from references to the great scarcity of meat in the colonies, and also from St. Clair's comment that poultry was among the scarce commodities in the Sunday slave markets in Stabroek.[84] Bolingbroke, however, mentions the case of an old female slave in Essequibo, who left a legacy of £300 for her children - money she had acquired from selling feathered stock.[85]

The produce derived by slaves from their private gardens went to supply a number of needs, apart from food, such as extra clothing, household utensils and tobacco. But the absence of roads linking the plantations together, and the lack of urban communities, before the eighteenth century, limited severely the development of slave markets and thus the facility of slaves to barter or sell their goods. At the same time it must be noted that the efforts of slaves to supplement their diets and provide other basic necessities must have been a severe burden when added to the daily round of work. Even so, persistent hunger was a marked feature of slave society, as can be inferred from the fact that food was the commodity most commonly pilfered by them.[86] This practice was so common that by the late nineteenth century the plantocracy had passed laws to prevent them from doing so.[87] As a rule, slave diets were notorious for their monotony and vitamin deficiency. Sheridan states that:

> As with their counterparts in North America, Caribbean slaves had diets that were low in calcium, deficient in vitamins A and B_1, and lacking in bovine milk. Unlike their counterparts, their diet was high in vitamin C and low in fat content. Whereas their low-fat/high-carbohydrate diet required much thiamine or vitamin B_1, it is highly doubtful that Caribbean slaves received sufficient thiamine. Because of these and other deficiencies, Caribbean slaves suffered from eye afflictions, dirt eating or *mal d'estomac*, beriberi, endema or dropsy, and infant tetanus.[88]

While Sheridan only looks at Guyana during the British period in the nineteenth century, it is clear from what has been said earlier that his findings are also applicable to the Dutch period.

Before leaving this aspect of slavery it should be mentioned that those slaves, who through illness or old age were no longer able to function in a productive capacity, were treated with utter callousness by the master class. This even happened to those belonging to the WIC in Essequibo, who were given no rations and rarely any clothing during the annual distribution. Instead, they had to depend upon their children and friends for these necessities. Thus, according to van's Gravesande, they were "driven like old horses (as it were), naked and uncared for, from pillar to post ".[89] The private planters treated their unprofitable slaves with even less consideration. In the latter part of the eighteenth century, they used to banish them to their abandoned plantations farther upriver, ostensibly to retain the title to those lands. The attitude of the master class towards the *manquerons* emphasises the inhumanity of the system. Slaves who were no longer profitable to their masters were cast into outer darkness and dense oblivion. This treatment of the aged contrasted sharply with the situation in Africa, where they were respected and even revered.

Not only were slaves underfed, they were also under-clothed. Their clothing consisted mainly of a coarse linen, called *osnaburg* (to which Pinckard referred as "a coarse canvass"), or a cotton cloth known as *salempore*. While laws were passed enjoining masters to provide adequate clothing for their slaves, the actual quantity was not spelt out in these laws. The Essequibo-Demerara code of 1784 simply stated owners were to provide their slaves with "proper clothing".[90] Apparently, this state of affairs continued until 1830, when the actual quantities of clothing and other personal allowances were determined by law.[91]

Long before that time it had become customary to distribute clothing annually to the slaves, usually during Christmas. However, the amount distributed was usually inadequate and supplied with the greatest reluctance. For instance, in the 1670s in Berbice, according to van Berkel, the *osnaburg* provided was only long enough to make a pair of trousers for a man or a skirt for a woman.[92] As usual, the Directors of the WIC were among the chief delinquents; in 1760 van's Gravesande was moved to complain that the clothing provided by them was barely sufficient for the able-bodied slaves, leaving nothing for the old ones. In 1771, he declared that the slaves were without linen because the Company had not sent any supplies for the last 18 months.[93] Several years later, Bolingbroke had cause to comment that several Government slaves in Stabroek were "destitute of clothes, with only a coarse rag around their middle".[94]

Some slaveowners went beyond the boundaries of common decency and refused to give their slaves any clothing whatsoever. van Berkel pointed out that slaves often had nothing more for a covering than "their own black skin"; Pinckard observed a chaise being drawn by "six naked slaves", with two Dutch ladies in it; St. Clair noticed four naked African girls serving at a function on Plantation Vrede-en-Stein in Demerara. According to him, they were "as naked as they came into the world".[95]

It seems, then, that the Dutch proprietors, even in the seventeenth and eighteenth centuries, when the textile industries of Haarlem and Leiden in Holland were manufacturing cloth on a large scale, had scant regard for clothing their slaves. A few female slaves did have more than the usual amount of clothing to 'show off'. Pinckard described some of them as being arrayed on festival occasions in "gaudy trappings and decorated with a profusion of beads, bits of riband, and other tinsel ornaments".[96] However, these were usually domestics who sometimes received the clothing no longer wanted by their mistresses.

Slave lodgings were in keeping with their food and clothing - modest and inadequate. There were two modes of accommodation: individual huts and barrack-like dwellings. We are uncertain which was the more common method but available evidence suggests that huts were more prevalent. Most of these were small, makeshift, thatched-roof dwellings, ill-ventilated and provided with a modicum of furniture and household utensils, most of which were the result of the slaves' own efforts rather than the master's generosity. A few masters did provide more substantial dwellings, and at least one planter in the eighteenth century provided stone huts. Dwellings designed for single slaves often had to house several of them, especially when families were involved. While slaves were supposed to be given hammocks in which to sleep, these were often in short supply, forcing them to sleep on the floor. "Their lodging is a hard board," was the laconic remark of van Berkel.[97]

Slave compounds were usually unhygienic, and it was not uncommon to find deposits of garbage, and animal and human faeces around these dwelling places. These provided fertile ground for disease organisms to thrive. Many slaves, already the victims of various diseases contracted during their enslavement in Africa or the Middle Passage, were exposed to further hazards on the plantations. 'Micro-parasites', such as dysentery, whooping cough, pleurisy, measles, smallpox, yaws, elephantiasis, leprosy, tetanus, venereal diseases and dropsy, were common on slave plantations, and took heavy toll of human health and life.

Slaves chafed under the material and social burdens imposed upon them and made their disgust with the system evident in a number of ways. Some planters put this down to the 'brute' nature of Africans, which could only be harnessed, but not tamed. Others recognised that the degradation of slavery was exacerbated by the despotism of the plantation system, but were prepared to live with an uneasy conscience in order to realise the kind of profits which would allow them to maintain their lavish lifestyles.

At the same time, they deemed it necessary to offer periodic relief to the slaves through small material and social indulgences. This would act as a vent for pent-up emotions and surplus energy, and would ultimately redound to the benefit of the plantocracy. Slaves were therefore periodically given a little rum (known as *kiltum* or 'kill devil', because of its exceedingly poor quality), some tobacco, or a slightly larger allowance of food. Christmas was regarded as a time for merry-making, and on such occasions, they were given an extra portion of meat and fresh clothing. They were allowed to dance and sing with greater freedom than at other times. On this occasion, too, they might even be allowed to mimic their masters with impunity. On rare occasions, they were feted at Government House. Some planters might well have viewed their actions towards their slaves at this time as a form of penance which, however, did not last long. Nor could the slaves be duped by such ephemeral acts of goodwill, for the new year usually saw the rebirth of old planter attitudes and actions.

Of course, slaves might escape the trammels of slavery by obtaining manumission. Broadly speaking, there were two ways in which this might be achieved: either by purchasing their freedom, or obtaining it from their masters or the colonial Government for meritorious service. In 1807, the Berbice Court of Policy stated that "little formality and expense" were involved in obtaining the manumission of a slave.[99] The average manumission value of a slave there is unknown, but in Demerara and Essequibo around that time it stood at *f*.2,000, while the average price of a male slave was between *f*.900 and *f*.1,200.[100] In the early nineteenth century, the regulations for manumission were tightened up in all the territories, making it much more difficult than formerly for slaves to obtain their freedom. This is not to suggest that there was a large group of freemen during the Dutch period - quite the contrary. In 1797, van Batenburg stated that there was only a small number of free Africans in Berbice,[101] and the same seems to hold good for Essequibo-Demerara.

The small size of the free African population was due to the fact that slaves had to receive their masters' consent in order to be manumitted, few slaves possessed sufficient money to purchase their freedom, and the scarcity of slaves on the plantations made the planters reluctant to manumit them. But while the number of freed persons was small, the significance of their manumission looms large, because many of them were collaborators in one way or another with the master class. Some of them betrayed slave revolts, while others participated in 'bush-expeditions' against maroons and earned rewards for killing and capturing fugitive slaves. In 1764, ten slaves were granted their 'freedom' for important service to the Whites during the Berbice Slave Revolt in the previous year.[102] Likewise, in 1781, Ariantje, a Berbice slave woman, was set free for 'good conduct' during a revolt there and granted an annuity for life.[103] These and other slave collaborators helped to buttress the system of slavery.

The vast majority of Africans eked out a precarious existence on the plantations, with little if any hope of manumission. They were 'marginalised' in terms of their ownership of the means of production, distribution and exchange, and their lack of formal participation in the political life of the colonies. They were subject to a daily diet of contempt, abuse and wrong. Ironically, the planters killed a host of them in order to make a 'killing'. It was this draconian system that paraded under the banner of paternalism. It was a system reinforced by the myth of 'the lazy African' - a myth by which planters, principally the wealthy ones, tried to mask their own laziness as they lived off the sweat and blood of their slaves. Generally, the slaves viewed them as objects of execration, the ones who rubbed salt into their wounds and their noses into the ground.

But slaves did not simply mope and whine, or consume themselves with hatred against their oppressors. They sought various ways of liberating themselves from the physical and psychological fetters of slavery.

Notes

1. See Stanley Elkins, *Slavery: A Problem in American Institutional and Intellectual Life. 3rd ed.*, (Chicago, 1976) for a comparison of North American slavery to life in the German concentration camps, pp. 103-115.
2. James Pope-Hennessy, *Sins of the Fathers. A Study of the Atlantic Slave Traders, 1441-1807.* (London, 1967), p. 47.
3. This view of the African slaves still lingers in myth and legend. For instance, Goslinga, writing in 1985 about some slaves newly-imported into Berbice in 1763, referred to them as "strong, half-wild Africans" (*Dutch in the Caribbean and Guianas*, p. 466).
4. For example, Eric Williams in his well-known work, *Capitalism and Slavery*, asserted that the reasons for the trans-Atlantic slave trade were 'economic not racial," and that the derogatory comments on the features of Africans were later rationalisations to justify a simple economic fact (pp. 19-20). While it is true that the economic value of Africans was the prime motivation behind the trade, it can also be demonstrated that social, moral and intellectual 'justifications' for this trade were in existence, if not preva-

lent, in Europe before 1600.

5. See A. Thompson, "Race and Colour Prejudices and the Origin of the Trans-Atlantic Slave Trade," *Caribbean Studies*, 16(3-4), 1976-77, pp. 43 - 48.
6. S. Purchas (ed.). *Purchas: His Pilgrims* (1905 reprint), vi, pp. 251 - 73.
7. Eannes de Azurara, *Conquest and Discoveries of Henry the Navigator* ed. Virginia de Castro & Almeida, (London, 1936), p. 169.
8. The fare for Africans and animals was five stivers; that for Whites was ten stivers (N.A.G., M.C.P., Berbice, Apr. 19, 1808).
9. Keller, *Colonisation*, p. 11, cited by van Lier, *Frontier Society*, p. 6.
10. "Slaven en marrons; reacties op het plantagesystem in de Nieuwe Wereld. Een Schema," *OSO. Suriname. Slavernij, Abolitie en Nasleep* (special issue), 2(2), 1983, pp. 174 - 75.
11. See, for instance, S. Miers & I.Kopytoof (eds.), *Slavery in Africa* (Wisconsin, 1977); C. Meillassoux (ed.), *L'esclavage en Afrique Precoloniale* (Paris, 1975); W. Rodney, "Slavery and Other Forms of Social Oppression on the Upper Guinea Coast in the Context of the Atlantic Slave Trade", *JAH.*, 7(4), 1966, pp. 431 - 43; M. Klein & P.E. Lovejoy, "Slavery in Africa," in Gemery & Hogendorn, *Uncommon Market*, pp. 181 - 212.
12. For instance, Klein and Lovejoy assert that the ideology of slavery in West Africa was conceived of primarily in terms of "kinship structures," and that "We can accept this view as the fundamental tenet in the ideology of slavery [there] " ("Slavery in Africa," pp. 182, 184). In West Africa, at least up to the end of the eighteenth century, second-generation slaves did not suffer from economic and social disabilities which distinguished them sharply from freeborn commoners. In some societies such as that of the Oyo, certain high offices were traditionally reserved for the monarch's slaves. Usually also, second-generation slaves could not be sold, except for serious crimes. Slaves were allowed to maintain families, own property, and sometimes even acquire wealth. The tendency in African slavery was towards assimilation of the slave into the wider society. In all these respects, African slavery differed sharply from New World slavery. In any case, the vast majority of Africans who were transported to the New World as slaves were freeborn persons, who had never been reduced to slavery. The fact that they were acquainted with slavery in their own societies (by observation rather than experience) did not make their enslavement in the New World more palatable.
13. Richard Sheridan, *Doctors and Slaves. A Medical and Demographic History of Slavery in the Dutch West Indies, 1680-1834.* (Cambridge, 1985), p. 188.
14. M. Craton, *Testing the Chains. Resistance to Slavery in the British West*

Indies (Ithaca, 1982), p. 46.

15. W. Rodney, *A History of the Guyanese Working People, 1881-1905* (London, 1981), pp. 3-4.
16. A custom developed in Guyana whereby the wealthy planters were required to assign some of their slaves free of cost to the Government for maintenance of the forts, when called upon to do so.
17. Pinckard states that female drivers were fairly common in Demerara in the late eighteenth century and that they "often corrected the stoutest slaves with no feeble arm" (p. 230).
18. *BGBV*., App. i, pp. 216, 218, 221, 228. For further references to old traders, see: *Ibid*., pp. 214 - 19; USC., ii, pp. 149 - 51; Harris & De Villiers, i, p. 357.
19. *Poems by a Slave in the island of Cuba Recently Liberated*, cited by P. Foner, *A History of Cuba* (New York, 1962), i, p. 195.
20. M. Shahabuddeen, *From Plantocracy to Nationalisation. A Profile of Sugar in Guyana* (Georgetown, 1983), p. 129.
21. van Houtte, viii, p. 387; C.O. 111/78, Statement Relative to the Colony of Berbice, Oct. 7, 1811.
22. 25,169 slaves were in the colony at the time C.O. 111/78, Statement Relative to the Colony of Berbice, Oct. 7, 1811.
23. C.O. 111/73, van Batenburg to Graham, Sep. 15, 1797.
24. N.A.G., M.C.P., Berbice, 1 Oct., 1810.
25. van Houtte, viii, p. 388.
26. No comparable code seems to have been promulgated in Berbice which, as will be recalled, was governed by the Berbice Association at that time.
27. The Directors were not always aware of what slave laws were in force in the colonies. For instance, in 1735 the WIC, addressing itself to the problem of slaves deserting to Orinoco, suggested that "it would be useful if the Proclamation against desertion, if one exists, were renewed and amplified" (*BGBV*., App. ii, p. 19).
28. C.O. 111/44, "Regulations for the Treatment of Servants and Slaves," Oct. 1, 1784.
29. See N.A.G., M.C.P., Berbice, Feb. 11, 1806; van Lier, "African Slavery in Surinam," *Caribbean Historical Review*, 3 - 4, 1954, p. 119; "The Berbice Slave Revolt of 27th Feb. 1763," in W. McGowan & I. Velzing, "Resistance and Revolts" (mimeographed), 1980, pp. 4, 17, n.6.
30. *Journal of van Hoogenheim*, Mar. 22, 1764.
31. C.O. 111/44, "Regulations," Oct. 1, 1784.
32. Harris & De VIliers, ii, p. 638.
33. *Journal of van Hoogenheim*, Jun. 23, 1764.
34. C.O. 111/44, "Regulations," Oct. 1, 1784.

35. Shahabuddeen, *Plantocracy*, pp. 134-35.
36. C.O. 111/44, "Regulations," Oct. 1, 1784.
37. Pinckard, pp. 18-19.
38. *Ibid.*, pp. 18-85; van Berkel, p. 98.
39. Pinckard, pp. 22-23.
40. Cited by van Lier, *Frontier Society*, p. 130; see also R. Price, *To Slay the Hydra. Dutch Colonial Perspectives on the Saramaka Wars* (Ann Arbor, Michigan, 1983). pp. 7 - 8; Hartsinck, p. 916.
41. Bolingbroke, pp. 71-72.
42. *Journal of van Hoogenheim*, Apr. 16, 1764.
43. *Ibid.*, June 23, 1764.
44. van Lier, *Frontier Society*, p. 136.
45. *Ibid.*, pp. 133, 136-38.
46. *Ibid.*, pp. 138.
47. C.O. 111/44, "Regulations," Oct. 1, 1784
48. van Lier, *Frontier Society*, p. 130.
49. A search of the Dutch records by the British in 1824 revealed only one instance of a White in Essequibo-Demerara being convicted on the evidence of slaves. Even so, there was corroborating evidence by a White person. The case in question is that Pieter Callaert, who was convicted in 1774 of instigating and aiding a slave uprising in the previous year (C.O. 111/44, Convictions of Whites and Other Free Persons on Slave Evidence Between 1774 and 1824).
50. Kenneth and Virginia Kiple, basing their findings on the quantity of food prescribed by law, support the viewpoint that slaves in the British Caribbean received an adequate caloric intake - roughly 3,000 per day. Nonetheless, they note that slave diets suffered from many nutritional deficiencies (K.F. Kiple & V.H. Kiple, "Deficiency Diseases in the Caribbean," *Journal of Interdisciplinary History*, 11, 1980, pp. 197 - 215). For other studies on slave diets see R. Sheridan, "The Crisis of Slave Subsistence in the British West Indies During and After the American Revolution," *William and Mary Quarterly*, 33, 1976, pp. 615 - 41; R. Sheridan, *Doctors*, pp. 154 -64, 206; B. Higman., *Slave Populations*, pp. 205 - 18.
51. Harris & De Villiers, i, pp. 225 - 26; ii, p. 625. The discussion here is concerned mainly with the provision of food for slaves by their masters, as prescribed by law or custom. The private efforts of slaves to supplement their diets is a subject which still needs to be researched. The present discussion also focuses attention almost exclusively on protein and caloric requirements. A comprehensive treatment of the subject would need to consider also vitamin, niacin, thiamine, riboflavin, calcium and other nutritional requirements in greater detail than could be done here.

52. This calculation is based on the assumption that the fish was always semi-dried cod, estimated as containing 39.7 gm. of protein per 100 gm. of the edible portion (*Food Composition Tables for use in the English-Speaking Caribbean*, Kingston, 1974, p. 38). A less liberal estimate is 29 gm. per 100 gm. (B.K. Watt & A.L. Merrill, *Composition of Foods - Raw, Processed, Prepared*, USA Dept of Agriculture, 1973 edn., p. 25).
53. This is based on the estimate of 1.2 gm. of protein per 100 gm. of the edible portion of plantains (*Food Composition Tables*, p. 15). The allowance of plantains will be discussed in greater detail later.
54. See *Chambers Encyclopedia*, iv, 1955, p. 505; *Encyclopedia Brittanica*, xiii, 1975, p. 419. Estimates of protein requirements vary, but there is no doubt that 70 gm. would be the absolute minimum requirement for the kinds of work most slaves performed.
55. According to the regulation in Essequibo-Demerara, ordinary soldiers were to receive a monthly allowance of 28 to 30 lbs. of meat (beef). In protein terms, this meant a daily allowance of 62.5 to 66.7 gm. White artisans were entitled to receive 24 ozs. (100.5 gm. protein) of meat daily (Harris & De Villiers, I, p. 273; I, p. 514). This estimate is based on a deduction of 16 per cent for refuse and a protein value of 17.5 gm. per 100 gm. of the edible portion of medium, commercial-grade beef *(Food Composition Tables*, p. 33; see also *Chambers Encyclopedia*, v. 1955, p. 769).
56. Wilson, p. 2.
57. *Encyclopedia Britanica*, ix, 1964, p. 560.
58. van Berkel, p. 132. Richard Dunn states that "The custom in all the English islands was to give the carcasses of diseased cattle and horses to the Negroes" (*Sugar and Slaves*, p. 278).
59. C.O. 111/78, Gordon to Liverpool, Dec. 16, 1810.
60. C.O. 111/44, "Regulations," Oct. 1, 1784.
61. M.C.P., Berbice, Feb. 11, 1806, G.N.A.
62. *Ibid.*
63. Harris & De Villiers, ii, pp. 657, 661, 662.
64. M.C.P., Berbice, Feb. 11, 1806, G.N.A.
65. Bolingbroke, p. 39.
66. van Lier, "African Slavery in Surinam", p. 138. What was obviously meant here, as in the Berbice regulation of 1806, was a 'hand'. A good bunch usually comprised nine or more hands, weighing between 50 and 125 lbs. in total. Dalton, however, states that the average bunch in 1855 weighed between 25 and 35 lbs. (ii, p. 179). The view that the Berbice regulation was not intended to mean a bunch in the strict sense of the word is reinforced by the stipulation that, for each slave on the estate, 60 plantain trees had to be grown. Since these could only have yielded 60

bunches annually, at the most, and since each slave was to be given 2 'bunches' weekly, another 44 'bunches' would have had to be found from elsewhere. If, however, the term 'bunch' is interpreted to mean 'hand', the regulation would make much more sense.

67. *Encyclopedia Britanica*, ii, 1964, p. 73. This estimate is based on the calculation of a good bunch at 125 lbs., containing nine hands.
68. *Food Composition Tables*, p. 15. This work gives the estimate of calories at 132 per 100 gm. of the edible portion. Watt and Merrill, however, estimate them at 119 per 100 gm. (Watt & Merrill, p. 46). In 1855 Dalton stated that only about half the weight of the plantain was edible - a refuse content of 50 per cent (ii, p. 180).
69. *See Food Composition Tables*, p. 38.
70. *Encyclopedia Britanica*, xiii, p. 419. Stanley Engerman and Robert Fogel, on the one hand, and Richard Sutch, on the other, assert that during the last years of slavery in the south United States slaves were given more than the minimum protein and caloric requirements. Sutch, however, contrary to the other two, argues that the real issues related to the monotony of the slave's diet - largely pork and corn - and the inadequacy of essential nutrients (vitamins, minerals, etc.) See S. Engerman & R. Fogel, *Time on the Cross*, (Boston, 1974); P.A. David *et al.*, *Reckoning with Slavery*, (New York), 1976, pp. 231-301.
71. The maroons in Guyana cultivated it on a large scale.
72. *Encyclopedia Britanica*, ix, 1964, p. 559.
73. See B. Johnston, *The Staple Food Economies of Western Tropical Africa* (Stanford, 1958), p. 126.
74. *Chambers Encyclopedia*, ii, 1955, p. 90.
75. If Schomburgk is to be believed, an acre of land was capable of producing 70,000 lbs. of plantains, sufficient to feed a slave 45 lbs. weekly for 666 weeks, or 13 slaves for almost a year! (*Travels*, I, p. 65; see also *Encyclopedia Britanica*, ii, 1964, p. 73, for comparable estimates of production in other parts of South America).
76. St. Clair, p. 14; Pinckard, p. 13.
77. Pinckard, p. 13.
78. *Chambers Encyclopedia*, v, 1955, p. 771.
79. *Ibid.*
80. *Ibid.*
81. A.J. Benjamin, "The Background to the 1763 Berbice Uprising" (mimeographed), 1978, p. 7.
82. van Berkel, p. 132; see also Hartsinck, pp. 91 16.
83. Higman, p. 208.
84. St. Clair, p. 14.

85. Bolingbroke, p. 76. The rearing of livestock by slaves might have become more common under the British. In 1819, the missionary John Smith wrote that very many slaves raised livestock which they disposed of to itinerant traders. See E. Wallbridge, *The Demerara Martyr*, (orig. pub. 1848, reprint, New York, 1969), p. 53.
86. Sheridan, *Doctors*, pp. 178-79.
87. C.O. 111/44, "Regulations," Oct. 1, 1784.
88. Sheridan, *Doctors*, p. 206.
89. Harris & De Villiers, ii, p. 377.
90. C.O. 111/44, "Regulations," Oct. 1, 1784.
91. The 1830 law concerning Essequibo-Demerara stipulated that all slaves were to receive the annual allowances given to Government slaves in that colony. For working adult males, these were jacket, a shirt, a pair of trousers, two caps, a hat, a razor and a knife. Adult females were to receive a gown, a petticoat, a check shift, a hat and a pair of scissors. Each adult of either sex, in addition, was to receive a blanket every two years (N.A.G., M.C.P., Essequibo & Demerara). Apr. 17, 1830, see also C.O. 111/39, Amount of Clothing Received Annually for Slaves of the Civil Government of Essequibo and Demerara, Dec. 25, 1823.
92. van Berkel, p. 15; see also Pinckard, p. 242; Hartsinck, p. 913.
93. Harris & De Villiers, ii, pp. 377, 649, 654.
94. Bolingbroke, p. 39.
95. van Berkel, p. 132; Pinckard, p. 238; St. Clair, pp. 244, 247, 248. By the early nineteenth century, it was somewhat unusual to witness such a circumstance, but St. Clair was informed that it had been a common practice in early days.
96. Pinckard, pp. 242-43.
97. van Berkel, p. 132.
98. Sheridan, *Doctors*, pp. 188 - 89.
99. N.A.G., M.C.P., Berbice, Jan. 13, 1807.
100. Bolingbroke, p. 82; Pinckard, pp. 79, 308; St. Clair, p. 75.
101. C.O. 111/73, van Batenburg to Graham, Sept. 15, 1797.
102. This freedom was neither apparent nor real, because they were informed by the Government that, as a condition of their freedom, they would have to do paid work for the Association and would not be allowed to work for private planters (*Journal of van Hoogenheim*, Nov. 14, 1764).
103. Pay List of Annuities for the District of Berbice: Quarter Ending June 30, 1836, in N.A.G., M.C.P., British Guiana, 1836, ii.

The Berbice Revolt, 1763

4: The Berbice Revolt, 1763-64

by
Alvin O. Thompson

> I find if I talk with my rifle in my hand the White man pays more attention to what I say.[1]

These words, spoken by a Ndebele chief at the time of the European invasion of Zimbabwe in the late nineteenth century, echoed the sentiments of the slaves in Berbice, who took up arms against their sea of troubles in 1763. The revolt erupted with explosive energy, temporarily breaking the bonds of slavery and creating pandemonium among the Whites. It lasted for a little over a year and was unquestionably the most noteworthy slave uprising (as distinct from maroon wars) in the history of slavery in the Dutch Caribbean. It ranks with other major slave revolts in the Caribbean, such as those in the Danish island of St. John in 1733, Antigua in 1736, Jamaica in 1760 and 1831, Barbados in 1816, and Demerara in 1823. It was perhaps exceeded in length of time and intensity only by the Haitian revolt of 1791.

The slaves, attempting to shake off the thraldom of slavery, decided to beat their ploughshares into swords and exact their pound of flesh from the master class. The fact that the revolt was ultimately unsuccessful was not due simply to the ineptitude of the slaves but to the overwhelming odds they were up against. The revolt demonstrated that, while the imperialist powers might quarrel among themselves, they were prepared to provide a solid phalanx against the African onslaught and even offer military assistance to their imperialist counterparts. Thus, apart from assistance from their Dutch colleagues in Suriname, Demerara, Essequibo and St. Eustatius, the Berbice colonists received help from the British (a situation quite similar to what had happened in St. John, where British, French and Dutch forces assisted the Danes). By contrast, the Berbice insurgents remained isolated from their brethren in Suriname and Cayenne on the east, and Demerara and Essequibo on the west. It was this combination of assistance on the one side and isolation on the other which ultimately brought about the defeat of the freedom fighters. Nonetheless, for a while the backs of the Whites were up against the wall and by the end of the revolt the colonial foundations had been visibly shaken in Berbice, and to some extent in Demerara.

The Whites always feared slave revolts which were the nemeses of the plantation system. But on a number of occasions they were militarily and psychologically unprepared to deal with them at the outset, as they most certainly were in the case of Berbice. They placed faith in their ability to preempt revolutionary violence by the paradox of stiff coercion on the one hand and limited concessions on the other. Although dark clouds were on the horizon in Berbice for all who cared to see, the plantocracy looked upon these as passing ones which at the worst would only produce scattered showers, in the form of minor slave uprisings. They no doubt reminded themselves that in times like this the slaves had often found a vent for their grievances in desertion; and even this, in the case of Berbice, had always been small-scale by comparison with Suriname and Essequibo.

The few wiser and more far-sighted among them warned of the day of reckoning for the sins they had heaped upon their heads through their ill-treatment of the slaves, but they were usually dismissed as prophets of doom. Certain planters, in fact, had not only refused to let up on the treatment of their slaves but had initiated a new round of oppression, in response to the harsh economic conditions created by their failure to grow sufficient food locally, a dearth of supplies from Europe, and increasing impediments placed by the Spanish in respect of the Orinoco fishery.[2] The fairly consistent growth of the plantation economy since the 1730s seemed to give the lie to those who questioned the soundness of the economic system. A particularly good harvest had been reaped in 1755, and 1763 seemed to hold promise of another.[3] From their standpoint, there was no reason why their profits should not continue to increase once humanity continued to pay homage to materialism.

Thus the slaves were pressed out of measure in the drive for profits, and what hunger did not do the whip did. The harsh treatment meted out to the slaves was clearly the most immediate reason for the revolt, as the leaders of the insurgents themselves informed Governor van Hoogenheim. They even named eight of the most notorious planters and/or managers. Among these were Barkeij (Barkey), manager of Pln. Lilienburg; van Lentzing, manager of Pln. De Antonia and a lieutenant in the colonial militia; Dell, manager of Pln. Juliana; Wallenson, manager of Pln. De Vigilantie; and Waarneker, manager of Pln. De Velde.[4]

The growth of the slave population, though creepingly slow by comparison with that in Suriname or even Demerara, had meant more mouths to feed and, equally important, had increased the disparity in the African/White ratio in the colony. Officially this stood at around 11 to 1 in 1762, but it was perhaps higher due to the fact that several slaves were not included in the head count for the poll tax, which constituted the basis from which the ratio was derived.[5] Many of the slaves in the colony in 1763 were newly-imported Africans who had not been socialized in the system and who were therefore the most likely to seek to opt out of it. Historians agree that they formed a crucial element in the struggle for freedom and that some of them played important leadership roles.

The slaves considered the time propitious for a revolt because of two important circumstances: an epidemic which raged in the colony between 1756 and 1765, and a spate of servile unrest over the last few years. The epidemic - dysentery - seems to have originated among the Whites and was largely confined to them. It reduced their numbers and affected their health. By mid-1762 they were really in the grip of the epidemic, which continued throughout the period of the revolt with short phases of remission. It carried off several members of the Court of Policy, several managers of the Association's plantations, and dozens of soldiers and marines sent out to quell the revolt. At one stage, this circumstance was largely responsible for the Governor's decision to co-opt other persons as members of the Court of Policy and Criminal Justice.[6] The sickness also attacked both the Governor and Gerard Thielen, lieutenant of the regular forces in the colony and, though they recovered somewhat from it, they suffered from its aftermath for some time. The military personnel were so badly affected by the sickness that only ten soldiers at Fort Nassau were fit for duty at the onset of the revolt. Even the recall of others from various outposts could not bring the number of fit ones to more than thirty-five. In any case, the total number of soldiers in the colony before the outbreak of the epidemic did not exceed 100. The epidemic of war came in the midst of the epidemic of disease and together proved to be a two-edged sword which wrought havoc among the Whites.

The influence of recent minor insurrections on the minds of the slaves was also an important factor. Insurrections occurred in 1749, 1752 and 1762, the last of which threw the Whites into real panic. There were also rumours of insurrection or intended insurrection on Pln. Savonette in upper Berbice and at Fort Nassau towards the end of 1762; at least three notable incidents (1751, 1756 and 1759) of insubordination among the mercenary soldiers stationed in the colony, one of which was an attempt at desertion; the looting of an estate in the neighbouring colony of Demerara early in 1763; and the threat to the Akawois post around the same time by hostile Indians.[7] All these developments seemed to be reaching a climax in 1763, and it is indicative of the slaves' revolutionary consciousness that they did not let the hour of opportunity go by without striking a blow for freedom.

This raises the question of the extent to which the revolt was a thoroughly prepared and organised movement by the slaves to achieve mastery over the colony. Goslinga asserts that the evidence from the slave trials indicates that the Berbice insurgents had been planning a revolt for a long time, and that the Canje insurrection simply acted as a catalyst for the larger one in Berbice.[8] This point has not been proven conclusively. What is certain is that the first signs of revolt came from Magdalenenburg on the Canje on 23 February 1763. This revolt was apparently spontaneous, and initially involved the 73 slaves on that plantation and their brothers on Providence, the neighbouring plantation. The specific factors which prompted the revolt have not come to light but we know that the slaves on Magdalenenburg were treated cruelly.[9] This, plus the fact that the plantation was located in one of the most vulnerable parts of the colony from the military viewpoint, made it a prime target for insurrection.

Pln. Providence was supposed to spearhead the southern defence of the river and Jean Jolij, the manager of the plantation, was a militia captain. But his first recourse was to flee for his life, and so the insurgents, after looting, putting to death an African foreman - whom they regarded as a collaborator with the master class - and two Whites on the two plantations which they had overrun, and seizing whatever arms and ammunition they could lay their hands on, crossed to the other side of the Canje river and made off overland in the direction of Corentyne. Indications are that they were hoping to link up with, and become members of, the maroon communities in Suriname.[10] By 1 March, peace and quiet seemed to have returned to the Canje front, but this was an illusory calm for, two days later, the insurgents attacked the Corentyne post, causing its occupants to flee for their lives. Shortly after, several planters fled from the middle to the lower reaches of the Canje river because the slaves there had begun to "show inclination to rebel".[11] Their fears were not unfounded for, in the weeks that followed, Canje witnessed a fairly large uprising which almost completely devastated the estates and brought production to a standstill. In early June, a reconnoitring party reported that as far as the Corentyne post only a few buildings were left standing.[12]

Meanwhile, on 27 February, the slaves on several plantations along the middle reaches of the Berbice river had also decided to put an end to the untrammelled control of their masters and had wiped out several of them. The extent of the influence of the Canje revolt on that in Berbice is difficult to ascertain, but it must have been at least indirect, for the news of that revolt reached the ears of the slaves in Berbice. Some writers suggest that the influence was greater, that several slaves from Magdalenenburg crossed into Berbice and incited the slaves there to revolt. On 6 March, van Hoogenheim did express fears that the insurgents in

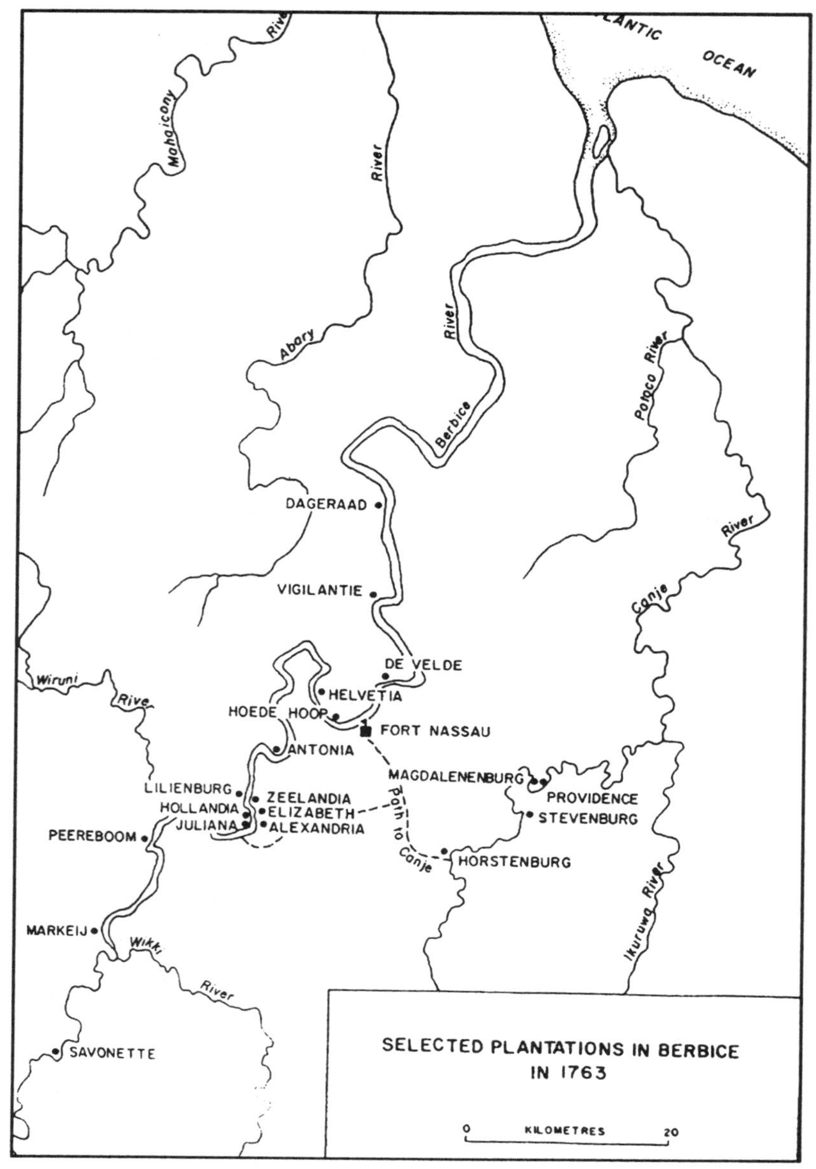

Map 3: Selected Plantations in Berbice in 1763

the two river areas would join forces.[13] This is precisely what happened, though we are uncertain at what time it actually took place.

The earliest available evidence that such a link was being attempted comes from van Hoogenheim on 31 March. On that day, he wrote that the two senior leaders of the Berbice insurgents had sent one of their colleagues to encourage the runaways in Canje to pursue the Whites to the coast. Some months later, he declared that he had been informed that the insurgents in Canje had sent to their brethren in Berbice for gunpowder, but that they could not provide it since they themselves were in short supply.[14] We also learn from the same source that Accabre and Paulus, two of the leaders in the latter part of the Berbice revolt, belonged to Pln. Stevensburg, on the Canje river; and that Fortuijn (Fortuin) of Pln. Helvetia in Berbice, and another of the main leaders of the revolt there, had a great following among the Canje insurgents.[15] According to Velzing, a recent writer on the subject, Kofi (Cuffy), the 'maximum leader' of the Berbice insurgents, had sent him to Canje as Governor, with a force to drive out the Whites.[16] The evidence is more than sufficient to confirm that the Canje and Berbice revolts became merged, possibly by late March 1763.

The plantations usually associated with the early phase of the Berbice revolt are Lilienburg, Juliana, Hollandia, Zeelandia, Elizabeth and Alexandria.[17] The first four of these have been variously put forward by different writers as the eye of the storm, but the evidence on this score is quite patchy at present. There is little doubt, however, that Lilienburg played a major role, contributing four of the main leaders of the revolt, including Kofi, and Akara (Accara), his second in command.

The insurrection in Berbice initially followed a pattern similar to that in the Canje - looting, burning, putting to death of Whites, and seizing the available arms and ammunition found on the estates. However, the insurgents on the Berbice river, unlike those on the Canje at the outset, had no intention of retreating into the forests. Rather they were bent upon a war of liberation and driving the Whites completely out of the colony. The new direction thus given to the insurrectionary movement had a highly beneficial effect upon the insurgents in Canje, because they reoccupied the estates from which they had retreated and carried the war of liberation further downriver. Within less than a month after the commencement of the revolt the vast majority of estates in the colony had been captured by the insurgents. The Whites, whose estates in upper Berbice had been taken, initially made an attempt to entrench themselves on Pln. Peereboom, lower downriver but, finding it impossible to hold out against their besiegers, they made a desperate bid for safety. However, in their attempt to reach their boats located in the river many of them were killed, while several others were captured and put to death. Few lived to tell the tale lower downriver.

As a result of the capture of Peereboom by the slaves, the way to Fort Nassau lay open. Here, van Hoogenheim, along with refugees from many plantations and his small military force, had taken asylum, hoping to put a stop to the escalation of the revolt but, on a survey of the fort, it soon became evident that it could not withstand a serious African offensive.[18] In the circumstances, both the military officers and the civilians agreed that further retreat downriver was absolutely necessary, if they hoped to save their lives.

The action thus became centred for a while on Dageraad, one of the Association's estates, which became the new place of refuge for the Whites. The slaves on that estate, said to be mainly creole, had remained on the whole extremely quiet and loyal.[19] The place was also much more defensible than Fort Nassau. An attack from the land side would be difficult because of the deep swamps and the low-lying lands which were under water for a considerable part of the year, while on the river side the few ships at the disposal of the Governor could easily shell the insurgents in the event of an attack from that quarter. In addition, the estate offered good drinking water facilities and provision grounds, and these could easily be supplemented by the estates lower down, which so far had not fallen into the hands of the insurgents.[20]

In spite of these advantages, the Whites did not remain long at Dageraad for, buoyed by their initial successes, the Africans were propelled into further action and were rapidly closing in on the estate. This produced such bedlam among the Whites that many of them fled on board the ships in the river and forced van Hoogenheim to quit that estate and retreat to Fort St. Andries, located at the confluence of the Canje and Berbice rivers. Meanwhile, the Whites had completely lost control of the estates along the Canje river and had also taken refuge at St. Andries, where they experienced a precarious existence.

The fort was completely indefensible as it stood at the time. Some effort was now made to improve it by erecting a battery and mounting three or four small pieces of cannon on it, but its defensibility was neither apparent nor real. There was also a chronic shortage of food and drinking water.[21] The Whites were consequently reduced to the nadir of despair, and not a few of them found relief from their physical privations through death, occasioned by dysentery and other diseases.

The situation in which the Whites found themselves reflected their inability up to that point to rationalize their actions. Had the Whites in upper Canje and upper Berbice been relieved by military assistance from the estates lower down, the revolt might have been contained, at least for a while. But the military weakness of the colony made such assistance impossible. van Hoogenheim was able only to dispatch a merchant vessel with about a dozen sailors to protect Pln. Stevensburg, the southernmost estate on the Canje, which was being threatened by insurgents. Not even this minimal assistance was forthcoming for Peereboom.

Indeed, the early stages of the revolt betrayed a spectacle of complete disunity and cowardice among the Whites. The first and perhaps the only thought of the ordinary civilians who were supposed to form the militia of the colony was to seek safety in flight. This is precisely what they did. Several of them made their way to Demerara, others fled to areas lower down the rivers, always a step or two ahead of the insurgents; still others crowded the decks of the merchant vessels in the river. According to van Hoogenheim, those who had initially sought refuge in Fort Nassau began "shouting and screaming", and engaged in "woeful lamentation and consternation" at the approach of the insurgents.[22]

The militia officers and the members of the colonial Government, without any compunction, considered their personal safety above their obligations to the colony. Among those culpable of dereliction of duty were van Lentzing (a militia officer), the Fiscal and the Chancery Master, all three of whom took refuge on merchant ships in the river, and also two members of the Court of Policy who fled to Demerara.[23] This lack of commitment to the system by the colonial officials was verbalized by Harkenroth, the Government Secretary, at the onset of the revolt: "I can't get enough for myself and my wife, and don't feel bound to stand here and be shot at for twenty guilders a month."[24]

If the colonial officers felt little if any obligation to maintain the colonial system, it is hardly conceivable that the captains of the four merchant ships in the harbour at the time would have been favourably disposed to doing so. van Hoogenheim attempted to requisition the services of these vessels and their crew, but he received cooperation from only one of them. The others refused to sail any considerable distance upriver or go to the assistance of the refugees at Peereboom.[25]

Thus, in their hour of travail, the Whites who had closed ranks so effectively against the Africans now engaged in scenes of disunity, confusion and panic. The Governor temporarily lost control of the situation and had to put up with instances of insubordination from all classes of Whites. His patience wore thin. But, on the other hand, contrary to the picture usually presented of him, the impression is gained that he was irascible, jumpy and not always as resolute as he depicted himself in his diary. This is perhaps understandable in the circumstances, for it is a superior soul who can maintain his equanimity when things begin to fall apart around him.

Nevertheless, the Governor adopted various measures to prevent the complete takeover of the colony by the insurgents. He sent whatever forces were available to relieve the colonists who were hard-pressed, called several extraordinary meetings of the Court of Policy, and made a careful assessment of the capacity of the colony to defend itself. He also wrote several letters to the Directors of the Berbice Association, the Governor of Suriname, the Director-General of Essequibo-Demerara, and the States General of the Netherlands, seeking urgent assistance. But up to the middle of March no such help was forthcoming for reasons detailed below, and on the whole the measures adopted by the Whites to contain the revolt had proved feeble and futile up to that point.

But the initiatives taken by the slaves to promote their own liberation were also highly conducive to this state of affairs. The revolt on the Berbice river took on the character of an organized movement within the first few weeks of its commencement. Revolutionary leaders of some calibre came to the fore. Kofi, a cooper of Akan origin on the Lilienburg estate (recognized by the insurgents as "Governor of the Negroes of Berbice"), along with Akara and Atta, who were both apparently also of Akan origin, formed the inner core of leadership. Nonetheless, it appears that at first there was a fair degree of unity or cooperation between the Akan and Central Africans (Kongolese and Angolans); at least there seemed to be no major conflicts among them. At this point, the vast majority of slaves paid more than lip service to the cause, while the others were in no position to withstand the insurgents.

The leaders took care to guide the insurrection along military lines. They adopted European military ranks and sought to equip their followers with weapons and achieve some degree of discipline. They obtained some guns from those estates which were managed by militia officers, such as De Antonia on the Berbice river and Providence on the Canje. In addition, several estates had small caches of weapons, the location of which the slaves knew, as in the case of Magdalenenburg. Rodway states that they possessed 400 muskets and quite a large quantity of ammunition, besides other weapons such as cutlasses, and that this gave them a clear advantage in weaponry over their opponents.[26]

In the early stages of the revolt strict discipline and sentinels constantly on guard were prominent features of life among the insurgents, according to the testimony of a White woman who had been held captive by them for a while.[27] Thus, in spite of several deficiencies in the organization and conduct of the revolt, the factors outlined above were, on the whole, favourable to the cause of the insurgents. They had driven the colonists almost completely out of the colony, confining them by mid-March to the swampy and malaria-infected area at the mouth of the Canje river.

The revolt also affected the neighbouring Dutch colonies. The possibility of a link-up between the insurgents and the maroons in Suriname was more than a remote one, while a link-up with the slaves in Demerara and Essequibo was an even greater possibility. In fact, the first news in Demerara and Essequibo of the outbreak of the revolt was accompanied by rumors that the insurgents were threatening to spread it to those areas. These rumours were not altogether unfounded for, around April, 200 rebels were dispatched to Demerara to overthrow the slave system there. Unfortunately, this coalition between the Africans of the two territories was never achieved because the force sent from Berbice found the paths to be impassable at that time of the year.[28] Still, the Whites had cause to worry. van's Gravesande thought that he detected signs of unrest among the slaves in Demerara and a state of tense expectancy prevailed throughout the territory and also in Essequibo. The planters in upper Demerara fled down-river for safety.[29]

The officials in Demerara and Essequibo took all possible precautions. They called meetings of the Court of Policy and the militia officers, and issued orders against able-bodied men leaving the colony. The women and children were transferred to Essequibo and St. Eustatius, and a few of the soldiers were dispatched from Essequibo to Demerara, which was more vulnerable to attack from Berbice. But these soldiers could offer no more than token resistance to the insurgents, since the total number of troops in Essequibo and Demerara could not have been more than 50. van's Gravesande also sought help from Gedney Clarke, a Barbadian planter with large investments in

Demerara. He requested the Indians in upper Demerara to mobilize and to go to upper Berbice to block the paths to Demerara. It took some time to put these last two measures into effect and it was only in late April that Demerara and Essequibo felt secure, with the arrival of two brigantines and 300 soldiers and sailors from Barbados. van's Gravesande was also assured of further help from the Governor of Barbados.[30]

Suriname was in a much better position than Demerara and Essequibo to prevent the spread of the revolt into that colony, due partly to the fact that the number of insurgents in upper Canje was much smaller than in upper Berbice, and partly to the presence of a much larger military force in Suriname than in the other colonies. Nevertheless, the situation produced some jitters throughout the colony, largely through fear that the revolt might cause disquiet and even insurgency among the local slaves. Therefore, in order to insulate the colony from the effects of the revolt, the colonial administration published a curious edict "prohibiting the spread of dangerous rumours", on pain of the rumour-mongers being punished as "agitators".[31]

More effective action was also taken. A force of about seventy soldiers was dispatched to Corentyne to protect the western section of the colony, and another hundred to relieve the beleaguered Whites at St. Andries.[32] These troops arrived in Berbice on 28 March, due to the lack of ships to transport them earlier, but their arrival marked an important event in the story of the slave revolt. van Hoogenheim took the decision two days later to leave a small part of this force at St. Andries and return upriver to Dageraad with the rest. His reasons for doing so appear to have been the greater all-round security which that estate offered as compared with St. Andries; the provision grounds which could be cultivated by faithful slaves, thus providing badly-needed food supplies; and the need to carry out a counteroffensive against his opponents. The decision gave the Whites a tactical advantage over the insurgents and led to the retreat of the latter from the estates between Dageraad and St. Andries. This was the first time that they had been forced to yield ground, and this event must therefore be seen as a significant setback for them.

An issue which has confounded historians and which seems inexplicable up to this time is why the insurgents did not continue the onslaught on the Whites around mid-March, when almost the entire colony lay prostrate at their feet. All that was needed was a single strike on Fort St. Andries to give the *coup de grâce* to achieve a glorious act of self-liberation. However, the cue was fluffed and this proved to be the single most important mistake in the entire conflict. The insurgents must have known that the fort was vulnerable to sustained attack and yet they seem to have made no effort to capture it. In trying to explain the strange action, or inaction, of the insurgents, Goslinga has put forward the view that, at that critical moment, Kofi came to the conclusion that the Africans could not run the colony without the Whites. Perhaps we should cite Goslinga more directly here:

> Being the man he was, probably always aware of his own social backwardness, he saw the world in which he lived suddenly collapse with the disappearance of the hated ruling class. Somehow he began to realize the unreality of his attitude towards his former masters. They had something Berbice needed and which the Africans did not have, or at any rate, not yet. He became somehow convinced that Berbice would collapse and fall into decay without the benefits of the White presence.[33]

Goslinga obviously had the Haitian situation in mind when Toussaint L'Ouverture was the head of the revolution for we have absolutely no proof that Kofi thought along these lines at all, nor can we logically infer that even in his wildest soliloquies he voiced such sentiments. At no time in his correspondence with van Hoogenheim did he suggest joint participation of Whites and Africans in a single Government, though he did suggest partitioning the country. More soberly, but almost as an afterthought, Goslinga suggests that centrifugal tendencies might have begun to nibble away the unity displayed by the leaders up to that point. This explanation is more plausible, but again evidence to substantiate it is lacking.

In the absence of any firm evidence on the subject, two other explanations are hazarded. The leaders might have decided to proceed with caution, since the merchant vessels had moved downstream, close to St. Andries, and might have been used against them to good effect. They might also have felt that hunger, fear and disease would prove to be a threefold cord around the necks of the Whites, and that there would be no need to expend African lives on what seemed virtually a *fait accompli*. Whatever the reasons for declaring a halt to military action, the result was that two vital weeks were wasted, allowing the Whites to make some repairs to the fort and obtain the necessary reinforcements to reoccupy Dageraad.

Despite this blunder, the situation still hung in the balance for the Whites. But van Hoogenheim immediately set to work improving the fortifications on the plantation, in an effort to resist the impending attack by his antagonists, who were entrenched in large numbers on Vigilantie, the adjacent plantation. The Africans carried out an ill-concerted attack on 2 April and followed it up with a more formidable one on 13 May.

The second encounter had perhaps as crucial a significance for the ultimate suppression of the revolt as van Hoogenheim's decision to reoccupy Dageraad. The Whites were in a much better position to resist the Africans than on any previous occasion because, a few days before, about 146 soldiers, besides sailors, had been sent in two well-armed barques from St. Eustatius to help them.[34] The African forces were also numerous. They were divided into three columns and were estimated by their antagonists at between 2,000 and 2,500 men. The fight lasted for about five hours and the Africans suffered an estimated casualty of 50 men, as against 8 on the part of the Whites.[35] More important than the physical loss sustained by the insurgents was their considerable loss of morale. The abortive attack might also have led to, or increased, the disagreement within the leadership, as may be noticed more specifically later on.

During the next five months, several petty skirmishes occurred between the two forces but no important encounters, and neither party was forced to quit further territory. The failure of the two forces to come to grips with each other can be partly explained by the fact that the rainy season began around this time. But this season would only have lasted for about three months, and therefore other factors must have been of great and perhaps of crucial importance.

The colonists at Dageraad began to experience another virulent attack of dysentery, which had abated temporarily and by the end of May this sickness had made inroads among the newly-arrived sailors and soldiers. Though on 7 July another ship anchored in the colony from St. Eustatius with 40 soldiers, these also quickly fell prey to the dreaded disease.

Up to this time no military assistance had arrived from the Netherlands. It was only in late May that the report of the insurrection in Berbice reached that country, through private sources, and was confirmed a few days later by the receipt of an official dispatch to the Directors of the colony. They immediately decided to send out a small relief force of 50 soldiers in two ships and to request further assistance from the States General. This body decided to send out initially three well-armed naval vessels, having 56 guns and 410 men. This force was to be reinforced shortly by another, comprising about five vessels and 600 men, to be raised from volunteers. The two forces sent out by the States General arrived in Berbice around November and December respectively.[36]

In the meantime, the colonists once again had been reduced to a state of despair by 10 October, with only a little over 42 men being fit for military duties. Moreover, during the five months' stalemate not much reliance could be placed upon the soldiers sent from St. Eustatius and Suriname, composed as they were of mercenaries from various European countries. Although van Hoogenheim had placed relatively large bounties upon the heads of Kofi and Akara, and smaller ones upon those of the other insurgents and, although he had agreed to pay compensation to those injured in action, he doubted that this would evoke much enthusiasm among the soldiers. Growing insubordination among them became evident, yet in the circumstances he had to deal lightly with them. However, he felt obliged to send two of them back to Suriname.[37] To make matters worse, in September Captain Hattinga, the military officer in charge of St. Andries, left his post in a drunken stupor and sailed up the Canje with some of his soldiers, shooting at everything and everyone in sight.

But even this event did not give as much cause for alarm as the mutiny and desertion which occurred in July among the troops from Suriname on the Corentyne river. About 42 of them tried to make their way to Orinoco but, on coming up against a group of insurgents on Magdalenenburg, they sought asylum with them and offered them military assistance against their enemies. Naturally, the insurgents viewed them with grave suspicion because they could not fathom why such a large party of Whites, armed with weapons, would seek to embrace their cause. This would clearly not be a marriage of love and might not be one of convenience either. The insurgents became convinced that the deserters were really spies and commandos secretly dispatched among them to subvert the revolution. No kiss of life was extended to them; instead, 28 of them were executed, others were put to toil on the estates, and three sent to Kofi who was resident at Fort Nassau at the time. Presumably, they were able to convince him that they possessed special skills as gunsmiths and 'medicine men' - skills greatly needed by the insurgents. These were therefore put to cleaning and repairing firearms, teaching the insurgents to use them effectively, and looking after the sick, no doubt under the watchful eyes of African guards.[38]

The natural and human disasters encountered in the White camp meant that they were in no position to take the offensive against the Africans in the five months under discussion. As disease and death etched their way into the White body politic, the Governor became increasingly unsure of his capacity to hold out at Dageraad. For one brief moment he bared his soul, declaring on 4 October that the Whites were like "sitting ducks".[39] It was only because he realized that the alternative to remaining at Dageraad was quitting the colony that he remained at his post.

But the Africans were also having their problems and had obviously become quite confused when van Hoogenheim's return to Dageraad forced them on the defensive. They knew that they could continue to fight and perhaps chip away at the Whites' defence, but some of the leadership were now unsure that they could 'make a revolution'. Had they known that by mid-August the White defence had become like a hollow reed, there might have been a different story to tell on the pages of history. However, it is doubtful that they were aware of this, for van Hoogenheim had taken care to maintain a show of strength by making improvements to the fortification on the estate.

Apart from their lack of knowledge of the true circumstances of the colonists, many of them also suffered from what Goslinga pithily referred to as "victory disease".[40] The first flush of success had thrown many of them into a euphoric mood before the task of liberation was fully accomplished. The result was that they became careless and discipline became a major problem. The provision grounds were neglected and the leaders had to coerce many of them, including those who had refused to side voluntarily with the insurgents, to grow food. Some of them became sullen and resentful, partly because they misunderstood what the revolution was about and thought of it mainly in terms of freedom from agricultural toil. The initial reaction of these slaves is understandable when we consider that they had been toiling in this way for a long time without any respite. They had understood that the revolution would bring about the death of slavery, but now it seemed that the institution was being resurrected in its old burial shroud. This attitude to work persisted for too long and created untold problems, which the leaders never fully resolved. As it was, famine followed in the wake of war and neglect of food crops. The Whites were informed that many of the insurrectionists were forced to eat horses, dogs, cats and the like to survive.

The coercion of the Creole slaves (apparently resident mainly on the Association's estates) and some African-born slaves to join the revolt did not help the cause of unity and in fact indicated that unanimity of views and action had never prevailed in the first place. There was little love lost between the Creoles and the African-born slaves, and the former chafed under the 'burden' of having to work for, and obey the commands of, the latter. This resentment manifested itself at times in the Creoles' seeking to return to their masters' fold, and threatening to assassinate the African-born leaders.[41] When the opportunity came later in the year for them to make their peace with the Whites, many of them did so willingly. There were also some Africans who, for various personal reasons, did not wish to join the revolt and these also sought opportunity to divorce themselves from the ranks of the insurgents.[42] These cleavages in slave society therefore did nothing to promote the cause of liberation and were important factors in destroying the revolt.

A more disturbing aspect than the disunity among the rank and file of the slave population was the growing antagonism among the hard-core leadership, which in turn produced further cleavages at the lower levels. The precise reasons for the friction among the leadership have not come to light, but we know that they were partly due to strategic/organizational factors, partly to ethnic ones, and perhaps also to personality clashes. While we cannot unravel the tangled web of relationships at the leadership level, we can be reasonably sure that dissension first manifested itself among the Akan leaders, between Kofi and Akara, and later between Kofi and Atta, leading eventually to Kofi's death and the assumption of power for a while by Atta. We also know that the Akan (Gold Coast) and 'Kongo' (Central African) groups ran foul of each other, causing an ethnic split later on.

Naturally, tensions ran high from around April when the first reverses were experienced. Eventually, the tenuous unity among the leadership snapped like a spring wound too tightly. The disagreement between Kofi and Akara started in early April. Apparently, the offensive against Dageraad on 2 April was carried out at the instigation of Akara and without the knowledge or approval of Kofi, as can be inferred from the latter's letter to van Hoogenheim shortly after. Akara wanted to go for the kill. Kofi, on the other hand, while by no means eschewing war to the death against the Whites, looked upon it as a last resort and thought that a negotiated settlement was possible. In pursuit of this, he began to dictate letters to van Hoogenheim from around 8 March, and about eight letters in all were dispatched by him.[43] These letters were written by Whites and Coloureds whom he had captured, and an educated African called Prins, who had been a foreman on Pln. Helvetia. They were ostensibly sent by Kofi and Akara, but the latter might not have been too keen about the correspondence.

The correspondence between Kofi and van Hoogenheim lasted for several months and is important for three main reasons. It allowed van Hoogenheim to play for time while he awaited reinforcements from Europe. This was expressly stated by him on at least three ocasions.[44] He had no intention of coming to any agreement with the insurgents, but at the same time it reinforced Kofi's view that the 'paper palaver' might eventually lead to a peace treaty with the Governor. It also caused him to temporize at times when military action might have been more appropriate and effective. For example, on one occasion a planned attack by the insurgents was called off because the day before it was due to take place Kofi had received a letter from van Hoogenheim which gave him hope that his negotiations would succeed.[45] Finally, it allows us to trace his dramatic shift from his early position of total abolition of White rule in the colony to one of allowing the Whites to resume control of a large part of the colony. His shift in position reflected his growing uncertainties about the ultimate success of the revolt.

A careful look at five of the letters he dispatched will bear out the point about his change of heart. In his first known letter, written in early March when all was going well for the insurgents, he advised van Hoogenheim to quit the colony or prepare for further military action. At the same time, he made it clear that he would not allow the Whites to take any slaves with them when leaving. However, by 3 April, when the Whites had already resumed control of a few estates, the African offensive against them on the previous day having failed and dissension having increased between him and Akara over the execution of this attack, he wrote the Governor offering a compromise. The Whites would be allowed to occupy lower Berbice and the Africans at the time on board the ships in the river were to remain slaves. He offered a further compromise in a third letter dated 9 May. This time he proposed restoring the estates to the Whites but without the Africans thereon. He must have encountered stiff opposition to this proposal from among the leadership, and this might have been the reason why he reverted to the compromise offered on 3 April, when he resumed correspondence on 27 July,[46] after a break of about one and a half months. On 2 August, he offered yet another compromise which would have allowed him to retain only four estates: Savonette, Markeij, Oostburg and Peereboom.[47]

The protracted correspondence which Kofi carried on with van Hoogenheim raises several questions about his leadership capacity. He comes across on paper as a poor tactician, especially since the advantages he hoped to gain by the negotiations are not obvious, while the correspondence gave the Governor the opportunity of practising cunning bordering on deceit, and using diversionary tactics to keep the insurgents away from a military course of action.

One should, not judge Kofi too harshly however, until more is known about the thinking which informed his decision to negotiate. The majority of the revolutionary council might well have considered it an astute move initially, especially when we recall that an important treaty had been made between the colonial Government and the maroons in Suriname only two years earlier, a treaty about which the slaves in Berbice must have known. Kofi might also have felt that even if they should succeed initially in driving the Whites out of the colony, the latter would return with new and more powerful engines of war, and consequently that the time for negotiating was while the insurgents held the upper hand.

Whatever the reasons for the negotiations, the fact is that while these were transpiring, the divisions within the leadership were becoming deeper, particularly between Kofi and Atta. The last letter known to have been sent by Kofi was dated 7 August, while the last report of him by the Governor as leader of the insurgents, was on 12 August. Matters came to a head over the leadership issue between this date and 19 October, when the leader's death was first recorded by van Hoogenheim.[48] Kofi, no longer able to retain the leadership, decided to commit suicide, but not before burying a large quantity of gunpowder.[49] Atta, the new leader, appointed several new officers, among them Goussari and Accabre. As for Akara, he was reduced to menial work once again, and later sold his soul to the Whites for a pardon.

One aspect of the leadership struggle, as intimated above, was the ethnic rivalry which eventually led to the 'Kongo' group separating itself from the Akan. Ethnic antagonisms were not unknown in slave society and many planters tried to ensure an ethnic mix among their slaves precisely in hope that this would help to keep slave society weak and divided. Unfortunately, in the case of Berbice we know almost nothing about the ethnic composition of the slave community. We may conclude, however, from the fact that at a given point in the revolt it split so clearly along ethnic lines, that ethnicity was a prominent feature of slave society before the onset of the revolt. The lack of ethnic homogeneity was always a threat to the success of the revolt and this contradiction in slave society was pathetically revealed when the insurgents were put under strain by untoward events late in the year. Nevertheless, the split did not occur at the time of Kofi's overthrow, for Atta and Accabre, two of the main leaders of the new order, were of Akan and 'Kongo' origin respectively. The evidence suggests, however, that the Akan continued to dominate the leadership.

The news that the movement had split along ethnic lines and that the Akan were attempting to lord it over the rest first broke in late November, through a White fugitive once held prisoner by the insurgents. While the reasons for the split remain obscure, we know that a large number of Central Africans hived off and gave up the primary task of defeating the Whites. But the insurgents dissipated their energies further by actual, and at times bitter, fighting between Akan and Central Africans.[50] Not even at the time of the White counteroffensive towards the end of the year did they see it in their interest to bury the hatchet. The Whites were therefore able to defeat them separately. This is one of the saddest commentaries on the revolt.

Quite apart from the disunity in the ranks of the insurgents was their failure to deal ruthlessly and uncompromisingly with every White and free Coloured whom they had captured. Several of these people whose lives they spared, but whom they kept as prisoners, managed to escape or were sent as emissaries to van Hoogenheim. These gave valuable information to the Whites lower downriver. For instance, the Governor received eyewitness reports from Whites: Rev. Famring, Mrs. Schreuder, Mrs. van de Broek, and Madam George; and also from the free Coloureds, Charbon and Paulus. As a result, he was kept fairly up-to-date with information about the shortage of provisions and ammunition among the insurgents, their disunity, their military defences, and the like. Even when considering the services which the mutineers from Suriname rendered the Africans, we should note that these did not prove a vital asset to the revolt. Moreover, one of the mutineers, the surgeon Mangemeister whom the Whites captured in November, gave vital information to them concerning the plans of the Africans and the discord that reigned among them.[51] But the intelligence corps of the Whites was not confined to those just mentioned; it also included faithful Africans and Amerindians.

The Amerindians also played an important role against the Africans by acting as the military auxiliaries to the Whites. From the early days of the revolt, the colonial Government sought the assistance of those of the surrounding regions to quarantine the Africans and thus prevent their departure from Canje and Berbice to Corentyne, Demerara and Essequibo, or into the far interior. Several skirmishes occurred between Amerindians and Africans during the early and middle stages of the revolt, and these deflected much of the insurgents' attention away from the Whites.

It seems therefore that during the five months, June to October, though on the surface a stalemate had been reached in the confrontation between the colonial and the insurrectionary forces, in reality the latter were slowly losing ground. Their temporising was ultimately their undoing. By early December, a large part of the military and naval reinforcements sent out from Europe had arrived in the colony. These consisted of about 460 men, besides three men-of-war and two merchant ships.[52] The arithmetic of power was now decidedly in favour of the Whites, who soon took the offensive. It was precisely from this time that the hopeless divisions among the Africans became apparent.

The colonial administration now put into effect a plan of action which they had thoroughly worked out some months before. The plan entailed establishing buffers along the Corentyne and upper Berbice and Demerara rivers in order to prevent the retreat of the insurgents to those places. The importance of this strategy, underlined by van's Gravesande in respect of the Demerara river, held good for the other two rivers:

> If their retreat in this direction is unhindered the rebels will be able to form settlements everywhere in the upriver lands and so continually disturb us, becoming also a refuge for our malcontent slaves, as the experience of Suriname testifies.[53]

The quarantining of the insurgents within a relatively narrow area was therefore the first objective, and soon they were beleaguered on all sides. A detachment was sent in November to capture Horstenburg, Stevensburg, and other estates in upper Canje. Simultaneously, another detachment was sent via the Demerara river to link up with a small force supplied by van's Gravesande and some Indian auxiliaries. This detachment was ordered to capture Pln. Savonette in upper Berbice and to establish a White military presence there. The two detachments accomplished their tasks with relative ease.

The second phase of the counteroffensive began around mid-December. Its main thrust was along the Berbice river but, at the same time, the Canje operations were stepped up. The Africans in the Canje had initially reacted to the White counter-attacks by burning whatever buildings and other equipment had been left on the estates and making off into the neighbouring forest or fleeing overland to Berbice. However, when the colonial forces achieved control over the path which ran from Fort Nassau to the Corentyne via the Canje, the insurgents' last hopes of retreating to the Corentyne were dashed. This, coupled with the loss of their provision grounds, forced them to submit in relatively large numbers to the Whites.

A similar situation prevailed in Berbice. The Africans concentrated on retreating, after setting fire to the estates. But many of them, especially those who had been coerced into joining the revolt, willingly submitted to the Whites. On the whole, therefore, little fighting took place. Nevertheless, some Africans refused to submit and instead retreated from the estates into the adjacent forest and established maroon communities, the entrances to which were camouflaged and studded with caltrops. The most important of these groups were led by Accabre at the head of 600 followers, and Atta at the head of 1,200 to 1,500.[54]

Mopping-up operations, which were conducted by the colonial forces from January with the arrival of the main force of 600 men and six transport vessels from Europe, saw the ferreting out of several small pockets of resistance. The task was rendered easier through the assistance of Goussari and Akara, who secured amnesty on the condition that they would aid in the final suppression of the revolt.[55] Still, it took a major expedition of over 100 soldiers to dislodge and capture Accabre.

The capture of Atta proved to be an even more formidable task. Three expeditions sent against him failed to do so and the first two suffered the loss of several officers in the process. The third expedition was sufficiently large to scare the majority of Atta's followers who, by now, were reduced to a state of despair through the want of provisions and ammunition, and the submission of hundreds of their former comrades-in-arms. Many of these therefore left Atta's ranks and surrendered or tried to survive as best they could in the forest. But Atta himself was only finally taken through the treachery of Goussari and Akara, who ambushed and captured him in April 1764, after an Indian had betrayed his hideout.[56] With his capture, the revolt can be said to have come to an end. A preliminary census taken by the Governor of the slave population in March 1764 gave the number as 2,600, and the number appears to have increased to about 3,370 in the next few months.[57]

As was to be expected, the suppression of the revolt was followed by the punishment of its major participants. This provided an opportunity for many Whites to pander to the psychosis of violence which was so much a part of slave society. There is no need to spell out the many gruesome details of the punishments inflicted on the slaves, but many of them suffered broken and mangled bodies. Some 124 to 128 of them were condemned to death, in spite of the admonition of the Governor to the Court of Justice to temper vengeance with mercy. Atta and a few others came in for special treatment. He himself was tortured for about four hours by having pieces of flesh torn from his body with red-hot pincers every fifteen minutes, after which he was burnt at the stake. He endured this torture without flinching for a moment.[58] Colonel de Salve, one of the principal officers dispatched from Europe to quell the revolt, was of the opinion that it would have been better:

> to shut the ring-leaders in iron cages and keep them confined there on show for the rest of their lives, giving them too much food to die and too little to live.[59]

With few exceptions, those who did not die the quick death of execution returned to the slow death of slavery. Sixteen Africans and Coloureds, who had identified themselves with the interests of the master class and who had played significant roles in suppressing the revolt, were compensated by being granted their freedom by the Directors of the Association on van Hoogenheim's advice. Akara and Goussari were among this number. However, it was considered inadvisable to keep them in the colony, in view of the role they had played in the early stages of the revolt. They were therefore sent to the Netherlands where they became drummers in the metropolitan army, and later joined Colonel Fourgeoud in fighting the maroons in Suriname.[60]

The revolt ultimately collapsed because of a number of factors: disunity, shortage of ammunition, lack of careful planning, famine, disease, outside assistance to the colonists; each made its contribution to the sad *dénouement*. But, for a brief moment in the history of slave society in Berbice, the Africans had assumed control over the colony in a scene of violent, explosive action. They had hoped to forge a revolution out of this crucible of violence, but the rock which their ambition struck proved to be too durable.

As it was, while they were able to visit recriminations and retributions upon several of their masters, they were unable to overturn the status quo. Many of them suffered, bled and died in pursuit of a dream and in so doing helped to write the history of African struggles with their blood.

The revolt itself inflicted deep wounds on the body politic of plantation society and ruined several planters.[61] Its echoes reverberated in the neighbouring Dutch colonies and into the vast hinterland which surrounded the plantation.

Notes

1. Cited by T.O. Ranger, *Revolt in Southern Rhodesia* (London, 1967), p. 248.
2. Pieter M. Netscher, *History of the Colonies: Essequibo, Demerara and Berbice* (orig. pub. 1888; trans. by W.E. Roth. Georgetown 1929). pp. 88 - 89.
3. *Ibid.*, pp. 87, 90.
4. *Ibid.*, pp. 90, 91, 93; A.J. Benjamin, "Background to the 1763 Berbice Uprising" (mimeo. Guyana, 1978), p. 10.
5. New planters were exempted from the poll tax for ten years; others avoided paying the tax by failing to declare the exact number of slaves they owned.
6. Netscher, pp. 87, 89.
7. *Ibid.*, pp. 87, 90; Jan J. Hartsinck, *Beschrijing van Guiana of de Wilde Kust in Zuid America* (Amsterdam, 1770), pp. 365 - 68.
8. Cornelis Goslinga, *The Dutch in the Caribbean and Guianas*, 1680-1791 (Assen, 1971), p. 466.

9. A.J. Benjamin, "Some Notes on the Origins of 1763," *Release, 1,* 1979, p. 44.
10. Hartsinck, pp. 371-72.
11. Wolfert J. van Hoogenheim, *Journal of van Hoogenheim, 1763-1764.* (Trans. By Barbara L. Blair; mimeo. University of Guyana Library). 3 & 6 Mar.1763.
12. *Ibid.*, 8 Jun. & 2 Jul., 1763.
13. *Ibid.*, 6 Mar., 1763.
14. *Ibid.*, 31 Mar. & 15 Nov, 1764.
15. *Ibid.*, 26 Mar., 19 Apr, 4 Jun., 1764.
16. "The Berbice Slave Revolt of the 27 Feb. 1763," in W. McGowan & I. Velzing, " Slave Resistance and Revolts" (mimeo., Guyana, 1980), p. 9; see also pp. 11, 14.
17. *Journal of van Hoogenheim*, 28 Feb., 1763.
18. The dilapidated condition of Fort Nassau has been described elsewhere.
19. Netscher, p. 94; Hartsinck, pp. 383-88, 391.
20. Netscher, p. 97; Hartsinck, p. 391 .
21. Netscher, pp. 94, 96; Hartsinck, pp. 396-97.
22. *Journal of van Hoogenheim*, 1 & 8 Mar., 1763.
23. *Ibid.*, 1 - 8 Mar., 1763; Netscher, pp. 92-93.
24. James Rodway, *History of British Guiana from the Year 1688.* 3 vols., (Georgetown,, 1891-94). I, p. 182.
25. Netscher, p. 91.
26. Rodway, *History*, I, p. 191. According to Netscher, they obtained many firearms from planters who fled, leaving behind all their weapons (pp. 90, 95). See also *Journal of van Hoogenheim*, 9 & 14 Mar. 1763.
27. Hartsinck, pp. 381-82.
28. *Ibid.*, pp. 409-10; *Journal of van Hoogenheim,* 4 & 9 May, 1763.
29. C.A. Harris & J.A.J. de Villiers, II, p. 419.
30. *Ibid.*, pp. 417-24.
31. R.A.J. van Lier, *Frontier Society,* (orig. pub. as *Samenleving in een Grensgebied*). (The Hague, 1971). p. 57.
32. *Journal of van Hoogenheim,* 28 Mar. & 17 Jun. 1763.
33. Goslinga, *The Dutch in the Caribbean and Guianas*, p. 474.
34. *Journal of van Hoogenheim*, 3 May, 1763.
35. Netscher, p. 99.
36. *Ibid.*, pp. 102-06.
37. *Ibid.*, p. 104.
38. *Ibid.*, p. 101; *Journal of van Hoogenheim*, 7 & 9 Aug. 1763; Hartsinck, pp. 424-8.
39. *Journal of van Hoogenheim*, 4 Oct., 1763.

40. Goslinga, *The Dutch in the Caribbean and Guianas*, p. 472.
41. Hartsinck, p. 459; *Journal of van Hoogenheim*, 11 & 19 Jun. 1763.
42. *Journal of van Hoogenheim*, 12, 14, 29 May; 19 June, 12 Aug. 1763. The dates of the various letters were 8 Mar., 3, 4 & c.27 Apr. 9 May; 27 Jul.; 2 & 7 Aug. 1763. Barbara Blair states that nine letters were sent by Kofi ("Wolfert Simon van Hoogenheim," *Bijdragen tot taal-, land- en volkenkunde*, 140(1), 1984, p. 74, n.15).
44. *Journal of van Hoogenheim,* 3 Apr., 29 & 31 Jul.1763.
45. *Ibid.*, 3 - 4 May, 1763.
46. J. Voorhoeve, *Suriname: Spiegel der Vaderlande Kooplieden* (Zwolle, 1958), pp. 81 - 82.
47. *Ibid.*, p. 84.
48. *Journal of van Hoogenheim,* 12 Aug. & 19 Oct., 1763.
49. Hartsinck. pp. 422 - 23.
50. *Journal of van Hoogenheim*, 1 Mar., 1764. The Akan dominated many of the Caribbean slave revolts (see M. Schuler, "Akan Slave Revolts," *Savacou,* 1(1), 1970, pp. 8-1; *idem.*, "Ethnic Slave Rebellions in the Caribbean and the Guianas," *Journal of Social History*, 3(4), 1970, pp. 374 - 85; see also B. Kopytoff, "The Development of Jamaican Maroon Ethnicity," *Caribbean Quarterly*, 22(2 - 3), 1976, pp. 35-50.
51. Hartsinck, pp. 458- 9.
52. Netscher, pp. 102, 105.
53. Harris & De Villiers, II, pp. 439-40.
54. Hartsinck, pp. 494, 500; Netscher, p. 109.
55. Benjamin questions the view that it was the same Akara, who had been Kofi's captain, who later became a traitor ("The Background to the 1763 Berbice Uprising" (mimeo., Guyana, 1978, p. 13). However, the *Journal of van Hoogenheim* makes it clear that it was the same person playing two different roles (17 & 18 Feb., 15 Apr., 14 Jun. 1764); see also Hartsinck, p. 516.
56. Netscher, p. 111.
57. *Ibid.*, Williams, *Dutch Plantations*, p. 7; J.A. van Houtte, *et al.*, eds. *Algemene Geshiedenis der Nederlanden.* Vols. 6 - 8, (Antwerp. 1943), viii, p. 387.
58. Hartsinck, pp. 505-06.
59. Cited by Goslinga, *Dutch in the Caribbean and Guianas*, p. 491.
60. *Ibid.*, John G. Stedman, *Narrative of Five Years' Expedition Against the Revolted Negroes of Surinam in Guiana on the Wild Coast of South America from the Years 1772 to 1777.* 2 vols. (orig. pub. 1796). (Reprint, Massachusetts, 1971), p. 71; Blair, "van Hoogenheim," pp. 74-75, n.17.

The Demerara Revolt, 1823: British troops massacre African rebels on 20 August, 1823 at Pln. Bachelor's Adventure

5: The Demerara Revolt, 1823

by
Winston F. McGowan

Sixty years after the ultimately abortive revolt by slaves in Berbice, another major slave insurrection took place in the neighbouring colony of Demerara-Essequibo. This insurrection in Demerara-Essequibo in 1823, like the one in Berbice in 1763, was staged by predominantly African slaves, for there were relatively few mulatto slaves in the population of the united colony. The 1823 rebellion, though also unsuccessful, was in many ways different from the earlier revolt in Berbice. It was numerically more massive, but did not engulf the whole colony or involve almost all the slaves as the Berbice uprising. Rather, it was restricted to one area, the East Coast of Demerara, and involved an estimated 11,000 to 12,000 slaves from about 55 plantations. This was about one sixth to one seventh of the entire slave population of the colony of Demerara-Essequibo which in 1823 was estimated at 74,978.

This 1823 revolt was the first massive slave uprising in the history of Demerara since its foundation as a European colony in 1746, 77 years before. Although knowledge of the revolt in Berbice in 1763 and the successful revolution in Saint Domingue in the 1790s and experience of a fairly serious revolt on the West Coast of Demerara in 1795 had made slaveowners in Demerara very fearful of the prospect of a massive slave rebellion, such an event was not really expected.

The predominantly British slaveholders in Demerara, which was occupied by the British in 1796, prided themselves in believing that they were more humane masters than their Dutch predecessors whose management of slaves they regarded as savage, brutal and likely to provoke slave resentment and rebellion.[1] They boasted that they had abolished the Dutch practice of torture and the use of the wheel or rab rack and had replaced them with

Enslaved Africans on a plantation, 1823

more humane forms of punishment which would make the slaves less prone to rebellion. Their views and attitude seemed justified by the fact that, in the first two decades of the nineteenth century, the colony experienced only a few spasmodic minor slave conspiracies and revolts which were either nipped in the bud or easily suppressed. Although these incidents disturbed slaveowners, they did not anticipate the occurrence of any major slave uprising.

This attitude was completely destroyed by the 1823 revolt. Much of the early, and some of the modern, historical writing on this revolt has focussed on a White man, Rev. John Smith, an English clergyman who was accused by slaveholders of being its main instigator, to the relative neglect of the slaves who planned and executed it. This misplaced or distorted focus is reflected especially in four works, all written by authors preoccupied with Christian missionary enterprise.[2] It, has been corrected in more recent historiography, however especially in two more academic publications,[3] which rightly present the revolt as an event where Africans occupied the centre stage.

The causes of this revolt are far more complex and debatable than those of the 1763 Berbice uprising. The most basic cause the 1823 revolt was probably the natural human desire of the rebels for freedom. This was no doubt particularly the case of the African-born slaves, who had been born free, but had lost that cherished freedom when they became victims of the trans-Atlantic slave trade and understandably longed to regain it. It is not known what proportion of the slave rebels in 1823 was born in Africa but, in the entire slave population of Demerara-Essequibo at that time, 34,773 or 46 per cent were Africans and 40,205 or 54 per cent were Creoles, i.e. individuals born in the colony or elsewhere in the Caribbean. Of Demerara-Essequibo's male slaves who were mainly responsible for the outbreak of the rebellion, 21,768 or about 52 per cent were African-born and 19,457 or 48 per cent were Creoles.[4]

Apart from the slaves' natural desire for freedom, they were prompted to rebel in 1823 by their wish to be free from the increasingly severe system of bondage which had developed on the East Coast of Demerara especially during the preceding ten years. This severity was reflected above all in excessive overwork, which was probably the most bitter single specific grievance shared by the majority of slaves on the East Coast in 1823. As Rev. John Smith observed a few days after the revolt broke out, "a most immoderate quantity of work has, very generally, been expected of them, not excepting women far advanced in pregnancy".[5] This excessive overwork, to which field and factory slaves in particular were subjected, was the result of a number of factors.

Firstly, it stemmed from the decline in the size of the labour force owing to the cessation of the importation of slaves from Africa which had been declared illegal for British subjects in 1807 with effect from 1 January 1808. Demerara, like most slave societies in the Americas, had always depended primarily on this trans-Atlantic slave trade to maintain and increase its slave population. In its absence after 1807, slaveowners discovered that the slave population could not maintain itself numerically by natural reproduction. This inability was due partly to the gender imbalance in the slave population in which there was a preponderance of males over females, resulting in comparatively low birth rates. It was also the result of high infant and adult mortality rates among slaves caused by the rigorous labour regime, inadequate diet, unhealthy working conditions in the fields and factories, and poor medical care.[6] Consequently, the slave population of Demerara-Essequibo declined from an estimated 77,376 in 1820 to 74,978 in 1823. This decline would have been much greater if the Demerara planters had not resorted to smuggling slaves especially from the French West Indies and the more or less legal importation of about 8,000 slaves from other British West Indian colonies, especially Berbice, Dominica and the Bahamas.[7]

As slave numbers declined, slaveholders resorted to a variety of expedients to deal with the problem of insufficient labour. They became more reluctant than ever to manumit slaves. Those who could afford it purchased expensive labour-saving machinery, especially steam engines and other equipment used in the manufacture of sugar and rum.[8] Above all, they began to require slaves to work much harder than before, especially the most productive or prime slaves, i.e., able-bodied slaves, particularly males, between the ages of 20 and 40. Not surprisingly, slaves in general, and this special category of slaves in particular, began to complain bitterly about the growing severity of their lot.

To make matters worse, especially for the field slaves, their masters demanded more work to increase productivity in an effort to counteract a decline in profits which they were encountering owing to a fall in the market price of cotton, coffee and sugar, the three main staples produced in the colony. For example, the price of sugar, the most profitable of these crops, fell from about 75 shillings a hundredweight in 1815 to less than 30 shillings a hundredweight by 1823 in the British market.[9]

Overwork on the East Coast of Demerara was also a consequence of a growing switch by plantation owners from the cultivation of cotton to sugar production, especially since 1815. This change was prompted by a marked fall in cotton prices in international markets and the increasingly effective competition which Demerara cotton was encountering from cotton grown in the southern United States of America.[10] The work in both the field and factory on sugar plantations was not only more onerous physically than that required in cotton cultivation but also of much longer duration. In particular, it required longer hours of work at night - often up to 10:00 or 11:00 o'clock - for a greater part of the year (normally 6-8 months because of the two crops of sugar harvested each year) compared to the 3 months of night work demanded for the production of the one crop of cotton grown each year. According to John Smith, the change from cotton to sugar cultivation meant that the amount of work needed to be done on a plantation doubled at a time when the labour force was at best stationary and on most plantations was shrinking.

In these circumstances, slaves were subjected to a number of new abuses by their masters who resorted to a variety of expedients to extract additional labour. On some plantations they were required to begin to work earlier (at 05:00 a.m. instead of 06:00 or 06:30 a.m.) and/or their lunch period was drastically cur-

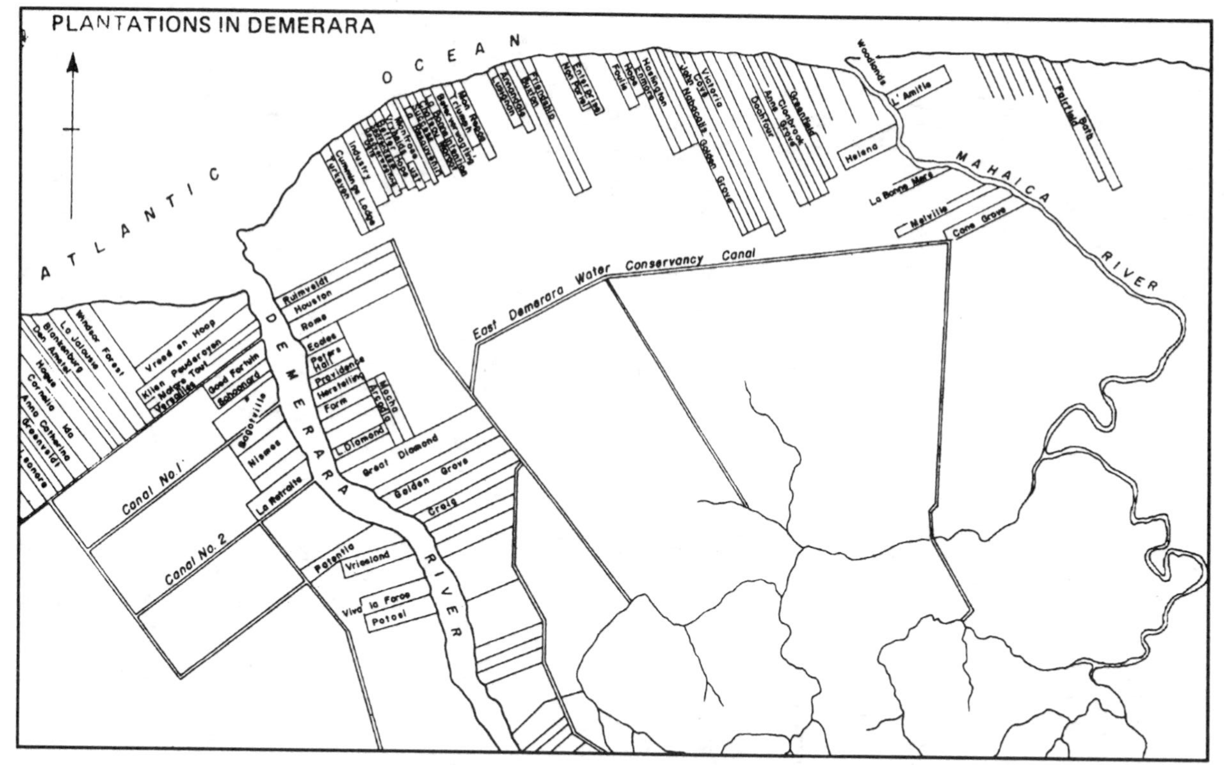

Map 4: Selected Plantations in Demerara in the Nineteenth Century

tailed.[11] On many estates, they were forced to work long hours into the night as well as on Sundays, legally a free day and the only day of leisure they were usually allowed. Planters could be fined *f*.600 under the colony's laws for making slaves work on Sundays, but this penalty was seldom imposed.[12] Consequently, by 1823, one of the main grievances of slaves on the East Coast of Demerara was the paucity of free time, making them unable to cultivate their plots of land essential to their subsistence. Some slaves complained that they did not have sufficient time even to prepare meals and so were forced to eat raw yellow plantains.[13]

Slaves who had been imported from Berbice and other British Caribbean colonies and those who had been accustomed to the less demanding labour regime on cotton estates in particular were greatly distressed by the change to sugar production which required longer hours of harder work. Captain Croal, an officer in the Demerara Rifle Corps which helped to suppress the rebellion, reported that Jack Gladstone, one of the main leaders of the uprising, told him that "he thought it very hard to work all the week and have no time for himself". In fact, slaves on Pln. Success, where the revolt began, in particular complained of overwork with the transition from cotton to sugar production. As early as August 1817, John Smith noted in his journal: "The Negroes of Success have complained to me lately of excessive labour and very severe treatment. I told one of their overseers that I thought they would work their people to death".[14]

The degree of overwork to which slaves were subjected was probably partly a result of the high level of absentee ownership on the East Coast of Demerara. At least one-third of the plantations there in 1823, including Pln. Success, were run by attorneys and managers employed by proprietors who resided for the most part in the United Kingdom. Many of these proprietors were formerly creditors who had acquired the property through confiscation when the planters failed to pay mortgages or other debts. It is generally accepted that attorneys and managers tended to be unduly severe in their treatment of slaves so as to increase productivity which determined the level of the commission which they received for their services.[15]

By 1823, virtually everywhere on the East Coast of Demerara, tired, slow, reluctant and recalcitrant slaves were being compelled to work harder by the use of the whip, resulting in a marked increase of physical brutality. This was a source of great dissatisfaction especially at Pln. Success where cruelty was particularly severe. In September 1817, a new overseer on this estate complained to John Smith of the cruel treatment meted out to the slaves there by the manager, Mr. Steward. According to Smith, the overseer "complains of Mr. Steward's conduct towards the Negroes : says that he (the manager) often gives them 100 lashes : that the Negroes work excessively hard, and have but little to eat".[16] Smith himself observed at the time of the rebellion that "their punishments have been frequent and severe... the whip has been used with an unsparing hand".[17] This situation understandably caused great discontent and distress among the slaves, making them more prone to flight and rebellion.

While almost all the slaves who participated in the 1823 uprising seem to have been affected by the increasing severity of the slave system, many of them were also prompted to revolt by religious considerations. One of the distinctive features of the uprising was the prominent role played by Christianised slaves, especially deacons, class teachers and other committed members of Bethel Chapel, the London Missionary Society (LMS) church located at Pln. Le Resouvenir, about eight miles from Georgetown. The Chapel had been built in 1808 when the LMS sent its first missionary, John Wray, to Demerara in response to a request from Hilbertus Hermanus Post, a Dutchman who owned Pln. Le Resouvenir, for a clergyman to instruct his slaves in Christianity. Slaves and a few Whites from plantations in the extensive area between Georgetown and Mahaica attended services at Bethel Chapel.[18]

The main specific religious grievance which these Christianised slaves on the East Coast of Demerara had in 1823 was the imposition of restrictions on the practice of their religion. In the opinion of John Smith, this was the principal cause of the rebellion. In a letter which he penned in August 1823 three days after the outbreak of the revolt explaining its causes, he wrote: "It was their religion that in general occasioned them the most vexatious treatment".[19] This Demerara revolt was in fact the first major slave rebellion in the history of the British Caribbean where religion and Christianised slaves played a prominent role.

Christianised slaves were annoyed that some masters who were opposed to the religious instruction of their slaves placed them in the stocks on Saturday evening or Sunday morning and kept them confined there so that they could not attend Sunday services at Bethel Chapel. They also resented the more common fact that illegal compulsory labour on Sundays often made it impossible to attend church then, while their late return home from field work at the end of the day or night work precluded their attendance at evening meetings during the week. In addition, particularly pious slaves sometimes suffered for their devotion to Christianity, being subjected by their masters to special punishment in the form of increased work, whippings, deprivation of food allowances and placement in the stocks.[20]

Christianised slaves were even more incensed by new obstacles which were placed in their way as a result of their masters' erroneous interpretation and application of a circular which was issued on 16 May 1823 by Major-General John Murray, the Governor of the colony of Demerara-Essequibo. This circular, which was a special source of irritation and discontent to Christianised slaves, was designed to tighten the pass laws. It required slaves to obtain written permission to leave their estates to go to Bethel Chapel and, to cater for the reservations and diffidence of some slaveholders, suggested that slaves could proceed there accompanied by an overseer or some other White person. It also made the master's consent necessary for slaves to conduct and attend religious meetings on their own estates at night.[21]

According to Governor Murray, he was prompted to issue this circular:

> ...In consequence of his having become acquainted with the existence of a misconception of a very serious nature, which appears to prevail amongst the Negroes in some districts, and more particularly on

> the estates on the East Coast leading them to consider the permission of their masters unnecessary to authorise their quitting the estate on Sundays, for the purpose of attending divine worship.[22]

He urged slaveholders to allow their slaves to receive religious instruction, however strongly recommending "that nothing less than a very urgent necessity should induce the planters to refuse passes to such of their slaves as are disposed to attend divine worship every Sunday".[23]

Contrary to the Governor's intention, however, many slaveholders used the circular to withhold permission from slaves who wished to attend Bethel Chapel or to conduct or attend religious meetings on their plantation at night. Managers on several estates prohibited such meetings or broke them up. Many slaves complained that passes to go to Bethel Chapel were refused or were difficult to obtain. Some masters gave only a limited number of passes, while others refused to give them until about 11:00 a.m. on Sunday with the result that the slaves arrived at the midday service very late. Slaves who went to the Chapel without permission were severely punished, often being whipped and then placed in the stocks until their wounds were healed.[24]

Religious instruction also affected some of the rebellious slaves in 1823 in other ways. For example, some of the doctrines of the Christian faith, especially those of the equality of man in the sight of God and Christian brotherhood, made certain slaves have an enhanced view of their self-worth which seemed to them no longer compatible with the inequality and subordination which distinguished slavery. In short, such teaching reinforced these slaves' view of the injustice of slavery. This was evident in a conversation which Governor Murray had with a group of rebels on the Lower East Coast of Demerara shortly after the uprising commenced. When the Governor asked them what they wanted, they replied "Our right". He then proceeded to explain to them that measures were about to be introduced to improve their condition, but their response was totally negative. According to Murray, they replied that "these things were of no comfort to them. God had made all men of the same flesh and blood. They were tired of being slaves".[25]

Some of the rebels were also influenced by their application to their condition of several features of the history of the Jews as recorded in the Old Testament of the Bible. In particular, they were affected by the accounts of the deliverance of the Jews from slavery in Egypt and the numerous wars which the Jews, apparently with divine sanction, undertook against their oppressors and other enemies.

The immediate cause of the rebellion, however, was the slaves' erroneous belief that the British metropolitan Government had granted them their freedom, but that this liberty was being illegally withheld from them by the local Government and their masters. This gross misconception stemmed from a major recent development in the long struggle over the question of slavery which was taking place in England. On 15 May 1823, the House of Commons there passed resolutions calling for the immediate introduction of a policy of amelioration of the conditions of slaves in the British Empire with a view ultimately to emancipation. On 7 July, the circular from Lord Bathurst, the British Colonial Secretary, forwarding these resolutions arrived in Demerara. Bathurst recommended strongly the immediate introduction by the Court of Policy, the local legislature, of two measures. The latter were the total outlawing of the flogging of female slaves and the absolute prohibition of the presence and use of the whip in the field, where it was customary for drivers to use this instrument as an emblem of authority as well as a stimulus to labour.[26]

On 21 July 1823, Governor Murray presented Bathurst's dispatch to the Court of Policy, but deferred discussion on it because of the absence of the First Fiscal, whose presence he felt was vital. The Court subsequently discussed the dispatch at two meetings, dragging its feet on an unwelcome matter. On 7 August, it finally agreed to implement the two recommendations and to frame a bill to this effect. No immediate action, however, was taken to implement this decision.[27]

The proposed implementation of this policy of amelioration was resented greatly by most slaveowners in Demerara for several reasons. They were opposed to the unilateral interference of the British Government into what they regarded as the internal affairs of the colony. They felt that they should have been consulted on the matter and that any regulations about improving slave conditions should emanate from them.[28] Furthermore, they regarded the policy of amelioration as an unjustifiable violation of their right of property and as a breach of the Articles of Capitulation under which Britain had assumed rule of the colony in 1803. They also viewed it as a likely cause of greater slave resistance and as a blow at the authoritarian control which they exercised over their slaves and considered crucial for the stability of slave society.[29] They had the sympathy of the Governor.

Instead of the ameliorative measures recommended by the imperial Government, some planters out of anger treated the slaves more cruelly than before, subjecting them to more demanding tasks and more severe punishment. Instead of the whip disappearing from the field, on some plantations it was used with greater severity. Some indignant managers gave their drivers a cat-o'-nine tails in addition to the normal whip. Under these circumstances the slaves' dissatisfaction with servitude increased greatly and their desire for freedom intensified considerably.[30]

Many slaveholders discussed the amelioration proposals with intemperate language in their homes, often indiscreetly in the hearing of domestic slaves. A few of them shared the news with slave mistresses. Everywhere on the East Coast of Demerara slaves received the news of the British Government's intervention with great excitement. Some masters, especially those who were aware that their slaves had heard something about Bathurst's dispatch, wished to explain his intentions to their slaves, but refrained from doing so out of fear that such unauthorised action would incur the Governor's displeasure. In the absence of any public announcement about the ameliorative proposals, a rumour soon spread among the slave population that freedom had been granted by the imperial authorities, but that the Governor, the other members of the Court of Policy and the planters were acting in collusion to deprive the slaves of their liberty.[31] This sense of injustice was the final impetus which drove the already very discontented slaves to resort to a rebellion, designed to force the local Government and their masters to concede what they concluded was their 'right' and the British Government's desire. Thus, at the outbreak of the revolt, some rebels told the Governor that "their good King had sent out orders that they should be free, and they would not work any more".[32]

Admittedly, not all the slaves who rebelled were convinced that freedom had been granted. Some of them were revolting merely to secure whatever benefit the metropolitan Government had granted them, even if it fell short of freedom. In fact, the rebels had different aspirations. Some of them wished 2 or 3 days each week for themselves as well as Sunday to attend Bethel Chapel, while others were rebelling to secure complete freedom. The abolition of slavery and total freedom, however, seem to have been the goal of all the leaders of the rebellion.[33]

Governor Murray, the Court of Policy and the planters certainly erred in not publishing and explaining what ameliorative proposals were intended. This was understandable for as planters they, including Murray, could hardly be expected to be enthusiastic initiators of the ameliorative programme. The difficulty which they faced could have been avoided if Bathurst had decided to effect the reforms in the slave system by means of an Order-in-Council. He deliberately refrained from this approach, however, for he preferred the reforms to seem to proceed or originate from the Court of Policy rather than to have been sent out from London as commands.[34]

The slaves' basic natural desire to be free, their hatred of the increasingly severe slave system, religious considerations and misunderstanding of the ameliorative proposals were important factors in the origin of the slave rebellion. These considerations were reflected in the answer which a slave gave to a White military officer who asked him why he had rebelled. The slave's reply was:

> Massa treat arl we too bad, make we work Sundays, no let we go Chapel, no give time for work in we garden, lick arl we too much. We hear for true great Bukra [the King of England] give we free, and Massa no let we hab nothing.[35]

There were also other causes of the rebellion such as the special personal grievances of the slaves, especially leaders of the uprising. For example, Jack Gladstone, the principal rebel leader, was influenced partly by the fact that he was peeved over the loss of one of his women who had become the mistress of John Hamilton, the White manager of Pln. Le Resouvenir, as well as over a severe punishment which he had recently received for seducing another slave's wife. Another leader, Telemachus of Pln. Bachelor's Adventure, was affected by the unwelcome prospect of being sold separately from his wife and child and away from his home and accustomed position by the family of his master who were about to divide the family property.[36] Furthermore, the participation of another leader, Sandy of Pln. Non Pareil, was due partly to his annoyance over the fact that Mr. Pollard, the estate's attorney and manager, "had taken away a Bible of his, and kept it for a considerable period".[37]

The slaves were also driven to rebel because they had seldom been able to gain redress for the wrongs which they had suffered when they made peaceful representations to the appropriate authorities. As John Smith observed during the rebellion, "Redress they have been so seldom able to obtain, that many of them have discontinued to seek it, even when they have been notoriously wronged".[38] For example, the burgher officers on the East Coast of Demerara were well-known for their aversion to the religious instruction of slaves. Furthermore, representations made to the Governor and the Fiscal about abuses to which slaves were subjected had almost invariably proved unfruitful.[39]

In the opinion of many slaveholders on the East Coast of Demerara, however, the main cause of the rebellion was not the grievances of the slaves, but rather the influence exercised over them by Rev. John Smith. They accused Smith of being the main instigator of the rebellion and as a result he was charged with inciting the slaves to revolt. They greatly exaggerated the influence and role of Smith, however, wrongly blaming him for a revolt which the slaves had planned and carried out.[40]

John Smith had assumed responsibility for Bethel Chapel, the LMS congregation at Le Resouvenir, from his arrival in Demerara in February 1817, nine years after the church had been founded by John Wray, the first LMS missionary to the Guiana colonies. Wray had encountered much opposition from slaveowners who feared that the evangelisation of the slaves would make them more discontented and rebellious. By the time of Smith's arrival, however, much of this opposition had subsided, though many slaveholders continued to express the view that instruction in Christianity, if not checked, would eventually have an adverse effect on the slaves, subverting order and subordination.[41]

From the beginning, John Smith was conscious of the difficulties and dilemmas which he faced as a clergyman working in a slave society. He was required to proclaim a gospel of spiritual liberty within a context of servitude, without preaching anything subversive which might offend the slaveholding class or suggest rebellious ideas to the slaves.[42] This proved to be an extremely difficult task for Smith, a man of strong convictions who was personally opposed to slavery and psychologically and emotionally disturbed by its extreme cruelty, of which his residence on a plantation enabled him to have first-hand experience. Thus, in March 1819, he wrote: "My heart flutters at hearing the almost incessant cracking of the whip".[43] In July 1823, one month before the outbreak of the slave insurrection, in response to the proposals of the British Government to ameliorate slavery, he observed: "The rigours of Negro slavery, I believe, can never be mitigated. The system must be abolished".[44]

By 1823, the relationship between Smith and the slaveholders on the East Coast of Demerara had become quite bitter. Apart from his general opposition to slavery, a very rare attitude by a White person in Demerara and one which made him become a special friend of, and sympathiser with, slaves, there were at least four major causes of conflict between the clergyman and slave-owners. Firstly, Smith objected strongly to the utilisation of slave labour on Sundays. He was opposed to Sunday labour not merely because it was illegal and adversely affected attendance at services at Bethel Chapel, but more fundamentally because in his opinion it was a serious violation of the fourth commandment, "Remember to keep the sabbath day holy". The planters, on the other hand, felt slaves should work on Sundays for several reasons, such as their failure to finish sufficient work during the normal working week, as punishment for alleged transgressions and because, at harvestime in particular, the considerable amount of work to be done required continuous labour.[45]

Secondly, Smith became embroiled with the slaveowners over his refusal to cease holding evening services at Bethel Chapel, especially during the week. His attitude was in marked contrast to that of Methodist missionaries at Mahaica further up the East Coast who, because of planter opposition, thought it prudent by March 1822 to discontinue week-night services.[46] Many slaveowners on the East Coast objected to such services partly because they wished slaves to work at night. Furthermore, they claimed that their slaves returned home very late and tired from these meetings, adversely affecting their ability to work effectively the following day. Finally, the planters feared that slaves would use the opportunity of absence from their plantation at night, especially without White supervision, to plan revolts.[47]

Smith felt that the planters' complaints and misgivings about night meetings were exaggerated and that nothing subversive of order happened on these occasions. He regarded the planters' complaints as opposition or an objection to religion itself, not to week-night meetings. He probably also resented the idea that missionary work was dependent on the goodwill of the planters.[48]

A third source of conflict between Smith and slaveowners was the question of access to members of his congregation in fulfilment of his pastoral responsibilities. He was annoyed because he was often not allowed to visit them without special permission from their masters, except on Pln. Le Resouvenir where he resided.[49]

Finally, the relationship between Smith and slaveowners was embittered because of their belief that he and other missionaries were spies sent out by the leaders of the increasingly militant and influential abolitionist movement in England and that his secret and ultimate objective was the emancipation of the slaves. This erroneous but understandable belief grew stronger after November 1818 when the London Missionary Society in London somewhat indiscreetly published in one of its magazines a letter from Smith attributing poor attendance at Bethel Chapel to the fact that many planters were forcing their slaves to work on Sunday.[50]

Although Smith was a strong-willed individual who felt strongly that the religious instruction of slaves should not rest on the goodwill of the planters, he made some efforts to conciliate them. For example, by November 1822, he abandoned the practice of ringing the church bell announcing the imminent start of the week-night services which the planters detested. He also ceased singing certain hymns and reading certain passages from the Bible during services at Bethel Chapel, especially hymns and passages which dealt with spiritual freedom, because he felt they could be misunderstood by slaves. For example, he refrained from using some of Watts's hymns which contained lines such as:

> "We would no longer lie
> Like slaves beneath the throne".
> and
> "We will be slaves no more
> Since Christ has made us free."[51]

Nevertheless, Smith's relationship with the planters continued to deteriorate and eventually he was accused of inciting the slaves to rebel. In fact, he may be considered to be partly responsible for the occurrence of the revolt, but not anywhere near the extent which the planters believed. His detestation of slavery must have strengthened the feeling of resentment which the slaves had and encouraged their opposition to servitude. He may also have helped to develop a spirit of insubordination by encouraging his class teachers to continue classes on the plantations contrary to the wishes of the estate authorities. Certainly, his teaching, especially the doctrine of the equality of man in the sight of God, served to reinforce the slaves' view about the injustice of slavery.[52] It does not seem, however, that Smith deliberately promoted discontent and dissatisfaction in the minds of the slaves towards their masters, managers and overseers, as he was charged. Nor did he excite them to revolt or to resist their masters. In fact, he tried, admittedly with only limited success, to convince Quamina and other slaves in his congregation that they were misled in their belief that the British Government had granted them freedom but that liberty was being withheld illegally by the local authorities and their masters. It seems, however, that Smith had some knowledge or suspicion of the impending slave insurrection shortly before it erupted, but for reasons which are not clear he did not communicate this to the authorities.[53]

The rebellion may have been prevented if Governor Murray had not underestimated the degree of dissatisfaction existing among slaves on the East Coast of Demerara. Two months before the outbreak of the rebellion, Rev. Austin, an Anglican clergyman, had informed Murray of the great discontent existing among these slaves especially over interference with their religious life as a result of the Governor's circular of 16 May 1823. The Governor, however, does not seem to have taken the matter seriously. In fact, as late as the morning of the day of the outbreak of the revolt, when Murray heard about the slaves' alleged plan of rebellion, he did not attach much credit to it.

The grievances which the slaves on the East Coast of Demerara had in 1823 may also not have resulted in a rebellion were it not for the existence of influential leaders who translated dissatisfaction into insurrection. The question of leadership, especially the role played by Quamina and John Smith, was at the time one of the most controversial aspects of the revolt and remains so in historical literature. Most leaders of the rebellion derived their importance and influence from at least one of two sources. These sources were the privileged position which they occupied on the estates as artisans or skilled slaves and the status which they had, in Bethel Chapel, where missionary work had resulted in the creation of an elite of deacons and class teachers, some of whom were prepared to take the lead in the rebellion.

The mastermind and principal organiser of the revolt seems to have been Jack Gladstone, the son of Quamina, the chief deacon at Bethel Chapel, but his position was not as dominant as that of Cuffy or Atta in the uprising in Berbice in 1763. Jack Gladstone was the head cooper at Pln. Success and in 1823 he was about thirty years old. His dissolute life disqualified him from membership of Bethel Chapel, though he attended services there periodically. The influence which he was able to exert over the other rebels stemmed from several factors, including his relationship to Quamina, his status as a privileged artisan, and his commanding physical appearance, for he was a tall, handsome young man. His involvement in the revolt was due largely to the influence of his friend, Daniel, a free African, who was a domestic servant of Governor Murray and had convinced him that Bathurst's letter to the Governor dealt with emancipation not amelioration.[54]

The two other principal leaders of the rebellion were Joseph of Pln. Bachelor's Adventure and Paris, a boat captain of Pln. Good Hope, whose duties included the transport of plantains from his estate to Georgetown for the Sunday market. Joseph was a class teacher on his plantation, whereas Paris, a man of intelligence and great physical strength, was not a member of Bethel Chapel, although he sometimes attended services there. Paris used his occupation to communicate plans for the uprising to slaves on several plantations on the East Coast. Other prominent leaders of the revolt included Telemachus of Bachelor's Adventure, a class teacher, Manuel of Pln. Chateau Margot and Seaton of Pln. Success.[55]

The leaders of the rebellion could be divided into two broad categories, namely, the radicals and the moderates. The radicals, such as Joseph, Paris and Richard of Pln. Success, were strong advocates of the use of force. They urged the seizure of guns from the Whites, an armed march to Georgetown, the overthrow of the Government, and the establishment of an African state, allegedly with Quamina as the king and Jack Gladstone as Governor. The moderates, on the other hand, recommended the pursuit of more modest goals and the use of less aggressive methods more in keeping with the modern concept of passive resistance. They proposed resort to strike action - "laying down their tools", as they put it - rather than violence to force the Governor and their masters to implement "the new laws" which had come out from England and which they believed granted them their freedom. Many of them were prepared simply to obtain their freedom within a colony ruled by Whites. In short, they wished civil liberty, not political independence.[56]

Among the slaves who advocated this essentially peaceful, moderate approach was Quamina, the head carpenter of Pln. Success and father of Jack Gladstone. Quamina was one of the most highly respected members of the slave community in the eyes both of his fellow slaves and free Africans. He was one of the earliest and most devoted slave converts to Christianity and in 1823 was the chief deacon of Bethel Chapel, the highest position which an African person could occupy in Smith's congregation. He was the slave who was closest to Smith in terms of personal friendship.[57]

Quamina was considered by the slaveholders, who were eager to attribute the rebellion to the influence of Smith and Christianity, as one of the main leaders, if not the chief leader, of the rebels. This view is also shared by some modern scholars, one of whom has described Quamina as "the chief and noblest of the rebel leaders".[58] This belief in the prominence of his role in the uprising and a desire to withdraw recognition from the Governor who arranged for its suppression prompted the Government of Guyana in 1985 to change the name of a street in Georgetown from Murray Street to Quamina Street. It seems, however, that the role which Quamina played in the rebellion has been greatly exaggerated. Although in the earlier phase of planning and preparation for the revolt he was actively supporting it, Smith's counsel appears to have made him become increasingly unsure about the alleged grant of freedom to the slaves by the British Government. Consequently, by the time the revolt started, he was not deeply committed to it. In fact, on the day when the rebellion began, he tried, albeit unsuccessfully, to postpone, if not to prevent, its outbreak. He does not seem to have been actively involved in the course of the rebellion. Certainly he did not arm himself or take part in the fighting.[59]

The leaders of the rebellion used church organisation to discuss grievances and to plan the uprising, religious activity being employed as a cover for political discussion. Several of the meetings where the rebellion was planned took place immediately after the conclusion of church services at Bethel Chapel. For example, the final such meeting occurred on the middle walk of the neighbouring plantation, Success, after the midday service at Bethel Chapel on Sunday, 17 August 1823, the eve of the outbreak of the uprising. This service was attended by a far greater number of slaves than usual, obviously in anticipation of the planned rebellion. Furthermore, under cover of religious meetings on the plantations, many of the rebels were required to swear an oath on the Bible in relation to their participation in the revolt.[60]

The revolt broke out at Pln. Success between 17:00 and 18:30 hours in the late afternoon of Monday, 18 August 1823. In the following two days it spread up the East Coast, engulfing almost all the plantations as far as Mahaica and several in the other direction between Success and Georgetown. Slaves on some estates only joined the rebellion after they were subjected to taunts that they were cowards or threats of violence on their life from the rebels, especially the leaders.[61]

For at least one of several reasons, slaves on about five plantations between Georgetown and Mahaica refused to join the rebellion. Some of them did not believe that freedom had been granted by the British Government as was alleged and, if it was, they were prepared to wait until they were given it. Furthermore, some slaves felt that rebellion was not justified because they had considerate managers or masters. The slaves of at least one plantation, Felicity, which was the residence of a prominent officer of the local White militia and a base for the troops which helped to suppress the revolt, were overawed by White military strength. Some slaves were also fearful that the rebellion would fail just as the one in Barbados in April 1816 and that the rebels would suffer many casualties and incur severe punishment.[62] Others feared the aftermath in the event of a successful revolt. For example, one of the slaves of Pln. Nabaclis, which refused to join the rebellion, although urged to do so by Telemachus, explained their action thus:

> I answered him [Telemachus] we were very well treated by our master, and allowed to go to church, and that, if they intended to do this, we would not join them; for that, even if we gained the country, it would be of no use, as we should begin to fight among ourselves.[63]

Another plantation where the slaves refused to join the uprising was Better Hope. In fact, they opposed the rebels by force, drove them away from the estate, but were finally overpowered after the rebels returned with reinforcements. The slaves of Better Hope desired freedom, but they felt that it should be obtained, not by means of African rebellion, but rather by waiting until it was granted by the Whites.[64]

From the outbreak of the revolt, the action of the rebels assumed a general pattern. They seized the Whites - proprietors, attorneys, managers and overseers - and placed them in the stocks without hurting them to prevent them from escaping to raise an alarm or to join the militia and as an act of revenge, giving them a taste of their own medicine. They also took possession of their arms and ammunition, burnt some estate buildings and canefields, and destroyed some bridges to hinder or prevent access by troops from Georgetown.[65] This action was rendered quite easy because of the overwhelming numerical preponderance enjoyed by the slaves who outnumbered the Whites by as many as 50 to 60 to one on many plantations. On a few plantations where the rebels were opposed with firearms, they resorted to the use of guns in return. These encounters resulted in the death of two and the injury of three or four White plantation personnel in defending their estates.[66]

The most remarkable feature of the course of the revolt, however, was that the slaves hardly offered personal violence to anyone, especially where they met no resistance. They had the opportunity, especially during the initial two days of the uprising, to kill most of the White personnel on the plantations, if this had been their desire or intention. Instead, they demonstrated a remarkable degree of restraint, self-control and humaneness. This virtual absence of the shedding of the blood of Whites during the uprising was attributed by the slaves to the influence exerted on them by religious instruction which they had received at Bethel Chapel. They explained: "We will take no life for our pastors have taught us not to take that which we cannot give".[67]

This situation benefited Governor Murray who had the responsibility of suppressing the revolt. If he had acted promptly, he might have been able to nip the insurrection in the bud. He first heard definitely of the imminent revolt at about 10:00 hours on 18 August, i.e., seven or eight hours before its outbreak, from Alexander Simpson. Simpson, the owner of Pln. Le Reduit, an estate on the East Coast about five miles from Georgetown, was informed of the impending rebellion by Joseph Packwood, a mulatto domestic slave.

It was only several hours later that the Governor, "being desirous to ascertain personally the nature and extent of the designs of the slaves",[68] proceeded up the East Coast as far as Le Resouvenir accompanied by some officials to investigate the report. Eventually he met a group of rebels near a bridge and engaged them in a dialogue. He tried to explain the real nature of the dispatch from Lord Bathurst about the amelioration of slavery, but the rebels were exasperated and too convinced that the British Government had granted them freedom to believe him and abandon their plans for rebellion. According to Murray, they "claimed from him immediate and unqualified freedom for themselves and fellow slaves".[69] Finally, one of them fired his musket at the Governor, but missed the target.

Murray, alarmed, returned hurriedly to Georgetown to implement action to suppress the uprising. He immediately dispatched up the East Coast all the regular troops which he could muster and some of the militia.[70] The Governor also declared martial law and all White persons capable of bearing arms were required to enrol in the forces which were being assembled to suppress the revolt. Additional detachments of soldiers - both regular troops and civilian volunteers - were dispatched to the scene of the rebellion with specific instructions. They were required to reconnoitre, to rescue Whites who were besieged in the plantation houses or placed in the stocks on the plantations, or to reinforce the small military post at Mahaica. Their progress was hindered by the broken bridges and by the presence of large groups of rebels with whom they had several minor encounters.[71]

The slaves achieved some success in these initial clashes. For example, on Monday evening they fired on a small party of regular troops and forced them into a skirmishing retreat all the way back to Georgetown. Furthermore, on Tuesday, about 700 or 800 of them drove Lieutenant Brady and his small garrison of 12 soldiers from Pln. Dochfour back to Mahaica.[72]

The decisive military engagement in the rebellion occurred on the following day, Wednesday, 20 August 1823, at Pln. Bachelor's Adventure. There, a large body of slaves, numbering about 3,000-4,000 according to one estimate, armed mostly with cutlasses and pikes, i.e., knives fastened on poles, met 300 well-armed regular soldiers under the command of Colonel Leahy. Leahy tried to persuade the leaders of the rebels to end the rebellion and to ask their followers to lay down their arms and return to their plantation and work. However, they refused, declaring that they would fight for freedom. Eventually, Leahy ordered his troops to open fire much to the surprise of some of the slaves who were so misguided that they expected the British troops not to fire on them. An estimated 200 of the rebels were killed and the others, dispersed in confusion, fled.[73] This massacre at Bachelor's Adventure was the turning point in the uprising. Within a few days of this battle, the rebellion was suppressed and public peace was virtually restored.

In short, within a week of its outbreak, the East Coast Demerara revolt, in striking contrast to the insurrection in Berbice in 1763, can be said to have ended, in the sense that there was no further resistance from the slaves. In the following weeks, however, the local Government and the planters sent several expeditions into the forested hinterland of the plantations to capture fugitives. It was during one of these expeditions on 16 September 1823 that Quamina, for whose capture an attractive financial reward had been offered, was shot and killed by an Amerindian in the bush behind Pln. Chateau Margot as a runaway.

There were many reasons for the failure, especially the quick collapse, of this massive uprising in which the slaves had the valuable advantage of a decisive numerical preponderance over the Whites. Firstly, the slaves lacked a carefully conceived and well-concerted overall plan and strategy. This weakness was reflected in the lack of agreement among their leaders as to the method to be adopted to secure the freedom which they believed had been granted by the British Government. While some leaders wished the slaves to proceed, armed, in a body, to Georgetown to claim freedom, others were in favour of remaining on the plantations, withdrawing their labour and forcing their managers to go to Georgetown to ensure that the slaves were granted freedom. Furthermore, some leaders believed that a strike would force the managers to inform them of their new rights.[74]

The cause of the slaves also suffered from inadequate military preparation. They had made no preparation for war and as a result at the outbreak of the rebellion they had no guns, gunpowder or bullets. Their military training and experience were also inadequate. Unlike the White troops, they were not trained for military service. Many of them were Creoles who had never handled a gun and therefore were not skilful in its use. Moreover, the rebels were deficient in military tactics. As a White soldier noted when they were decimated at Bachelor's Adventure, "they soon fell into confusion for want of method".[75]

The possibility of success in the rebellion was rendered more difficult by the failure of the slaves to extend the uprising to other areas of the colony apart from the East Coast of Demerara. Their plans and efforts to persuade slaves in Georgetown and West Demerara to join in the rebellion failed. Consequently, Governor Murray was able to focus all his attention and resources on the East Coast rather than being faced with the much more frightening prospect and demanding task of having to suppress a rebellion on several fronts simultaneously.

The slaves' defeat was also a result of their lack of ruthlessness. The remarkable moderation and restraint which they demonstrated towards the Whites during the uprising could not win what ultimately was a war. The slaves' attitude was in striking contrast to the extreme ruthlessness of their White opponents, facilitating the latter's victory. As Wallbridge correctly observed:

> No mercy, however, was shewn to the Negro. With regard to them, there was a tremendous slaughter - under the influence... of an ill-judged and unwarrantable severity, it was deemed necessary to make terrifying examples of not a few, by killing them on the spot. Many were wantonly shot by the Militia soldiers for mere sport.[76]

The treatment of the rebels by Colonel Leahy in particular was marked by such severe cruelty that it horrified civilian volunteers who served under his command.[77]

Another crucial factor responsible for the defeat of the uprising was the inferior armament of the rebels, most of whom were armed with cutlasses and pikes. The only firearms which they possessed were the small quantity which they seized from the planters. The tremendous advantage which the Whites had in firing power, easily compensating for their numerical inferiority, was clearly demonstrated in the decisive confrontation at Bachelor's Adventure. There, the 300 well-armed White troops suffered only two casualties - one bugler killed and one rifleman wounded - whereas the 3,000 odd rebels, who had less than 100 muskets, quickly experienced 200 fatalities.[78] This crushing defeat at Bachelor's Adventure had a dramatic and permanent effect on the morale of the rebels. It struck great terror in the minds of many slaves, prompting some to flee into the bush, while the greater part returned to their respective plantations and resumed work.[79]

The abortive rebellion had numerous consequences, especially for the slave population. It caused the rebels, especially the leaders, to incur severe punishment, initially at the hands of the victorious White troops. From as early as 26 August, by which time armed resistance by the slaves had ended, Colonel Leahy began marching with his troops from plantation to plantation, conducting what he called courts martial which sentenced to death leaders and other slaves who were believed to have participated in the revolt. Later, other slaves were subjected to less arbitrary and less summary justice administered by special courts established by the Governor.[80]

As a result of these proceedings, between 23 August and 8 October 1823 about 47 slaves were hanged publicly and 25 others who were sentenced to death were reprieved. Several slaves were decapitated and their heads mounted on poles on the public road on the East Coast of Demerara and in Georgetown both as a punitive measure and as a means of creating fear among slaves which, the Whites hoped, would serve as a deterrent against future rebellion. Many slaves also received severe whippings, in some cases as many as 1,000 lashes, and were sentenced to work in chains.[81] As a further and general penalty, by a 16 December 1823 proclamation from the Governor and the Court of Policy, all the slaves on the East Coast were forbidden to have their customary Christmas dances and other festivities which they normally enjoyed annually during that season.

The rebellion had calamitous consequences for John Smith. On its third day, the clergyman was arrested and later charged with several offences, including complicity in the revolt. At his trial, prejudice and ill-will, more than concrete evidence of his complicity, resulted in a verdict of guilty being returned against Smith, who was sentenced to death by hanging. This sentence was referred to the British metropolitan Government for confirmation. In February 1824, however, Smith died from illness in prison in Demerara, while a response was on the way from London granting him a reprieve, but ordering his deportation to England.[83]

Ill feeling against the London Missionary Society was so intense in Demerara that the Society, acting on the advice of the attorney of Pln. Le Resouvenir, decided not to appoint a missionary to replace Smith. In fact, the colonial authorities in Demerara sequestrated Bethel Chapel and entrusted it later to missionaries sent out to Demerara from England by the Church Missionary Society, an Anglican body which, as an arm of an established church, the planters deemed more trustworthy than the nonconformist LMS Bethel Chapel was never returned to the L.M.S, which, owing to planter hostility, never resumed its mission there. In 1835, the building was removed to Montrose, another plantation on the lower East Coast, where one Rev. Wyatt had begun to work on behalf of the LMS[84]

The rebellion also served to stimulate strong local White opposition to the interference of the British metropolitan Government into what the colonists in Demerara-Essequibo considered the colony's internal affairs. Owing to resistance from the Court of Policy and the metropolitan Government's reluctance to override the Court's decisions, two more years were to elapse before any concrete action was taken in Demerara-Essequibo for the amelioration of the conditions of the slaves.[85]

The uprising in Demerara-Essequibo also had a significant impact on other countries. It caused considerable tension in many colonies in the British West Indies, stimulating unrest among slaves, fear among planters of slave revolts, and White opposition to missionaries. In October 1823, a Methodist chapel was burnt down in Barbados. Missionaries throughout the West Indies found themselves under suspicion and felt very threatened. Some of them made serious attempts to allay the fears of slave-owners and the colonial authorities. In Trinidad and St. Lucia, for example, missionaries sought interviews with the Governor to solicit his support and protection.[86]

The rebellion had serious repercussions especially on Britain. In its wake, the British Government felt compelled to have a royal proclamation, dated 10 March 1824, issued and sent to the West Indies. The proclamation was designed partly to correct the misconception about the amelioration proposals - i.e., the erroneous belief that the Crown had freed the slaves which had helped to cause the uprising in Demerara. It expressed the King's "highest displeasure against slave insubordination in Demerara", requiring slaves to render entire submission as well as dutiful obedience to their masters. It also urged Governors "to enforce by all the legal means in their power, the punishment of those who may disturb the tranquillity and peace of our said colonies and possessions".[87]

Of greater importance, however, was the impact which the slave rebellion in Demerara had on the anti-slavery campaign in Britain. Two hundred petitions about slavery were submitted to Parliament in April, May and June 1824 and there was a long acrimonious debate in Parliament about the rebellion and West Indian slavery. For some time, the insurrection proved to be a serious blow to the abolitionist cause. Wilberforce and Buxton in particular, and the abolitionist movement in general, were accused by the Demerara slave-owners and their supporters of being responsible for the outbreak of the rebellion by their demands for the abolition of slavery. In the face and wake of this strident criticism many supporters of the abolitionist cause left the movement, which, in the circumstances, was forced to adopt a somewhat cautious approach.[88]

But this setback to the abolitionist cause proved to be only temporary. In the long run the 1823 Demerara revolt, especially the treatment and fate of Rev. John Smith, helped the abolitionists to triumph, particularly after the occurrence of an even more massive slave uprising in Jamaica in 1831 which resulted in the persecution of Christian missionaries and the burning down of their chapels by slave-owners and their White supporters. Memory of the 1823 rebellion, especially the death of the English clergyman, helped to attract attention in Britain inside and outside Parliament to the necessity of abolishing slavery. This played a part, along with other humanitarian, economic and political factors, in influencing the momentous decision of the British Parliament in 1833 to abolish slavery in British Guiana and elsewhere in the British Empire with effect from 1 August 1834.[89]

In short, the abortive 1823 East Coast Demerara revolt served eventually to enable the slaves to gain their objective, liberation, although none of the rebels who survived was likely to have anticipated this in the wake of the failure of the uprising. After serving four years of what was called apprenticeship, these African-Guyanese became completely free on 1 August, 1838.

Notes

1. H. Bolingbroke, *A Voyage to Demerary, 1799-1806* – orig. pub. in 1807 (Georgetown, 1941-reprint), pp. 23-24, 71- .
2. E. Wallbridge, *The Demerara Martyr : Memoirs of the Rev. John Smith, Missionary to Demerara* (London, 1848); D. Chamberlin, *Smith of Demerara, Martyr-Teacher of the Slaves* (London, 1923); S. Jakobson, *Am I Not a Man and a Brother? British Missions and the Abolition of the Slave Trade and Slavery in West Africa and the West Indies, 1786-1838* (Uppsala, 1972); C. Northcott, *Slavery's Martyr : John Smith of Demerara and the Emancipation Movement* (London, 1976).
3. M. Craton, *Testing the Chains : Resistance to Slavery in the British West Indies* (Ithaca, 1982); E. Da Costa, *Crowns of Glory, Tears of Blood. The Demerara Slave Rebellion of 1823* (New York, 1994).
4. Slave population statistics presented in this chapter are derived from the following sources: P.P., 1831-2, Vol. XX, Report from the Select Committee on the Extinction of Slavery throughout the British Dominions, 11 Aug. 1832, evidence given by Hugh Hyndham, 4 Feb. 1832, encl. Summary of the Slave Population of the United Colony of Demerara and Essequibo, agreeably to the preceding. Returns for the Year 1817, 1820, 1823 and 1826, including the Registry for the 31 May, 1829; encl. List of

the Slave Population of the United Colony of Demerara and Essequibo for the Year 1817 to 1829 at intervals of 3 years; P.P., 1833, Vol. *XXVI*, Return of the Numbers of the Slaves in each of the West Indian Colonies, 18 Jul. 1833; Da Costa, *op. cit.*, especially pp. 48-56.

5. Smith to Burder, 21 Aug.1823, printed in London Missionary Society, *Report of the Proceedings against the late Rev. J. Smith of Demerara* (London, 1824), pp. 183-4.
6. B. Higman, *Slave Populations of the British Caribbean, 1807-1834* (Baltimore, 1984), pp. 76-7, 311, 339, 342; Da Costa, pp. 52, 55-6.
7. D. Eltis, "The Traffic in Slaves between the British West Indian Colonies, 1807-1833", *Economic History Review*, 25 (1972), pp. 55-64; Higman, pp. 79-85.
8. P.P., 1831-2, Vol. XX, Report from the Select Committee on the Commercial State of the West Indian Colonies, 13 Apr., 1832, especially the evidence of Peter Rose.
9. The best account of the economic history of Demerara in this period is R. Farley, "Aspects of the Economic History of British Guiana, 1781-1852", (Unpublished Ph.D. Thesis, University of London, 1956).
10. Farley.
11. *Ibid.*, L.M.S. Papers, School of Oriental and African Studies, London, Smith's Journal.
12. Smith's Journal, 17 Nov.1821, 29 Sep., 1822; L.M.S., British Guiana-Demerara Box 2/ Folder 2/Jacket A/, Smith to Burder, 7 May, 1817.
13. Smith's Journal.
14. *Ibid.*, 30 Aug. 1817.
15. See D. Hall, "Absentee Proprietorship in the British West Indies, to about 1850", *Jamaican Historical Review*, 4 (1964), pp. 15-34.
16. Smith's Journal, 7 Sep. 1817.
17. Smith to Burder, 21 Aug.1823, printed in London Missionary Society, *Report*, pp. 183-4.
18. On the early history of the L.M.S. work in Demerara, see W. Mc Gowan, "Christianity and Slavery : Reactions to the Work of the London Missionary Society in Demerara, 1808-1813", in K. Laurence (ed.), *A Selection of Papers presented at the Twelfth Conference of the Association of Caribbean Historians* (1980) (Bridgetown, 1985), pp. 23-44.
19. Smith to Burder, 21 Aug. 1823, printed in London Missionary Society, *Report*, pp. 183-4.
20. Smith's Journal; Wallbridge, pp. 90, 145.
21. P.P., 1825, Vol. XXV, Copy of Major General Murray's Circular Instructions to the Magistrates of the Colony of Demerara, dated the 16 May 1823.

22. *Ibid.*
23. *Ibid.*
24. Smith's Journal; Wallbridge, p. 172.
25. C.O. 111/39, Murray to Bathurst, 24 Aug., 1823.
26. N.A.G., M.C.P., 21 Jul. 1823.
27. *Ibid.*, 21 July, 4, 7 Aug. 1823.
28. L.M.S., Notebook entitled "Missions John Smith".
29. *Report of the Trials of the Insurgent Negroes* (Georgetown, 1824), p. 159.
30. Wallbridge, p. 105.
31. *Report of the Trials*, pp. 4, 25, 159.
32. C.O. 111/39, Murray to Bathurst, 24 Aug. 1823.
33. *Report of the Trials*, pp. 45, 159.
34. N.A.G., M.C.P., 21 Jul., 1823, encl. Bathurst to Murray, 28 May 1823.
35. L.M.S., Cheveley's Journal, p. 20.
36. Wallbridge, p. 245.
37. *Report of the Trials*, p. 69.
38. Smith to Burder, 21 Aug. 1823, printed in London Missionary Society, *Report*, pp. 183-4.
39. Smith's Journal, 18 Mar. 1821.
40. Wallbridge, p. 50; McGowan.
41. L.M.S., B.G. Demerara, Box 2/Folder 2/Jacket A/, Smith to Burder, 17 May, 1817.
42. L.M.S., B.G. Demerara, Box 2/ Folder 2/Jacket A/, Smith to Burder, 7 May, 1817.
43. Smith's Journal.
44. *Ibid.*
45. *Ibid.*
46. *Ibid.*; L.M.S., Missions John Smith.
47. *Ibid.*
48. L.M.S., Missions John Smith.
49. Smith's Journal; Wallbridge, p. 53.
50. L.M.S. B.G. Demerara, Box 2/Folder 2/ Jacket A/, Smith to Burder, 7 May 1817; L.M.S, Missions John Smith.
51. L.M.S., Missions John Smith; *The Evangelical Magazine* (Aug. 1824).
52. *Report of the Trials*, p. 76.
53. *Ibid.*, pp. 180, 188; Smith's Journal.
54. *Report of the Trials*, pp. 71-2, 156, 164-5.
55. *Ibid.*, pp. 3-4, 23-5, 55-64, 180, 221-3.
56. *Ibid.*
57. *Ibid.*, p. 192.

58. Craton, p. 269. According to Governor Murray, "Quamina, was undoubtedly the principal ringleader in the revolt". See C.O. 111/44, Murray to Bathurst, 14 Feb. 1824.
59. Smith's Journal, 25 Jul. 1823 and subsequent entries; C.O. 111/45 Browne to Murray, 24 Jan. 1824.
60. *Report on the Trials*, pp. 159, 163-4.
61. *Ibid.*, pp. 14, 32, 37, 39, 40- , 44, 63, 66.
62. *Ibid.*, pp. 59, 160, 165.
63. *Ibid.*, p. 59.
64. *Ibid.*, pp. 4-6, 42.
65. *Ibid.*, pp. 21, 58, 62.
66. *Ibid.*
67. Wallbridge, pp. 118-9.
68. N.A.G., M.C.P., 19 Aug. 1823.
69. *Ibid.*
70. *Ibid.*, L.M.S., Cheveley's Journal, p. 14.
71. *Ibid.*
72. Cheveley's Journal, p. 14.
73. *Ibid.*, pp. 19-21; Hispanic Society of America, New York, MS entitled "Gibraltar, Africa, West Indies from the Journal of Rev. W.R. Payne, Chaplain of H.M.S. Forte and Iphigenia, 1822, 1823, 1824, 1825.
74. *Report of the Trials*, pp. 45, 164; Wallbridge.
75. Cheveley's Journal, p. 20.
76. Wallbridge, p. 120.
77. Cheveley's Journal, pp. 23-30.
78. *Ibid.*, p. 21.
79. *Ibid.*
80. *Ibid.*, pp. 21-30.
81. Payne's Journal; Wallbridge, p. 121.
82. N.A.G, Proclamation by His Excellency Major-General John Murray, Lieutenant Governor and Commander-in-Chief in and over the United Colony of Demerary and Essequibo, 16 Dec, 1823.
83. C.O. 111/44, Murray to Bathurst, 27 August 1824; Wallbridge. London Missionary Society, *Report of the Proceedings*.
84. Jakobson, p. 365.
85. C.O. 111/39, Murray to Bathurst, 31 Aug. 1823; C.O. 111/45, D'Urban to Bathurst, 9 Dec. 1824; N.A.G., M.C.P., 5, 6 Sep., 1825.
86. Jakobson.
87. N.A.G., Proclamation by Governor Murray, 22 April 1824, encl. Bathurst to Murray, 18 Mar. 1824.
88. Jakobson.

89. *Ibid.*; M. Turner, *Slaves and Missionaries : The Disintegration of Jamaican Slave Society, 1787-1834* (Urbana, 1982), pp. 179-91.

Part II

Post-Emancipation Period

6 : The Social and Economic Subordination of the Guyanese Creoles[1] after Emancipation

by

Brian L. Moore

Emancipation was as much a challenge to the ex-slave as to the ex-master. For the former, it promised to offer increased opportunity for political, social and economic advancement with a view to taking full control over his future. For the latter, it threatened to undermine his entire way of life and his dream of returning to Britain wealthy. In short, Emancipation brought to the fore the divergent and contradictory interests of these two 'ethnic groups' or 'classes'[2] which in the post-slavery colonial society seemed irreconcilable.

A struggle for supremacy was thus bound to occur. If the ex-slave had numbers on his side, the planter had the political and military power of the imperial state on his. Although a physical confrontation was feared, that never in fact materialized. The conflict was fought out mainly in the economic and social arenas. The key was control of the economy and that, in large part, turned on the availability of land and good drainage.

It will be shown in Chapter 9 below that the planters were able to preserve their control of the political system until the last decade of the century and, with the active support of the colonial officialdom, managed to seize control of the administration of the African villages as well. This political power was of critical importance in determining the outcome of the struggle for economic supremacy after Emancipation, for it was used to restrict Creole access to land and credit, and to impose burdensome taxes and licences in order to restrict independent Creole economic activity.

Almost from the moment of their Emancipation, the Creoles made clear their intention to seek some measure of independence from the plantations. This was vividly demonstrated by their vigorous efforts to purchase land, favoured by bankruptcy of several planters during the depression years of the 1840s. They bought lands both as communities and as individuals and, by 1850, had spent over $1 million in acquiring 16,850 acres, thus enabling about 80 per cent of the ex-slave population to relocate themselves off the estates.[3] This process of land acquisition offered the prospect of Creole economic independence, but the key lay in the continued control over the vast resources of remaining land in the colony by the planters and the Government. This determined how much land (and where) the Creoles could acquire, and thus, to a large extent how independent of the plantation sector they could become.

The debate between Green and Bolland[4] is thus very pertinent here. Although there were vast acreages of unused land in Guyana, the Creoles increasingly found themselves fettered by a growing unwillingness of the planters to sell after 1850 and by restrictive Crown lands regulations. A few hundred did opt to squat along the rivers in the hinterland, but they were ferreted out by the superintendents of rivers and creeks. Furthermore, the price of Crown lands was progressively raised to prevent the Creoles from settling or working in the interior. Set in 1839 at $4.80 per acre for a minimum parcel of 100 acres, it was raised to $10 per acre in 1861.

Successive Governors made no bones of their intention to restrict Creole settlement to the coastal plantation belt in order to limit their economic activities and to maintain political control over them. But even within that belt, Creole efforts to acquire private lands were frustrated by legislation designed to prevent group purchases. In 1852, joint purchases, one of the prime methods by which the ex-slaves had acquired land, were restricted to twenty persons; and that figure was reduced to ten persons in 1856.[5] Thus, as in Belize, low population density (Green) had very little to do with the availability of land for the ex-slaves after 1850. It was the control of land by the planters and the Government, largely through their control of the political power structure (Bolland), which was the principal determining factor.

What this meant was that Creole land acquisition more or less dried up during the second half of the nineteenth century and, consequently, their efforts at building an independent agricultural (peasant) economy became solely dependent on those plots which they had purchased in the first decade after Emancipation. These, however, became increasingly uneconomical as they were subjected to subdivision, poor drainage, and diminishing fertility and crop yields. The problem of subdivision in the communal or joint-stock villages was initiated by the practice of allotting plots to each shareholder in different parts of the estates, and made worse by inheritance. By 1850, many of these estates were already fragmented into uneconomic units.[6] Adamson shows that during the second half of the century the majority of Creole village landholders owned less than one acre.[7] These landholdings could hardly support individual families let alone produce profitably for the market.

The fragmentation and miniaturization of Creole landholdings exacerbated an already bad drainage situation in the villages. As the plots became uneconomic, their owners increasingly abandoned them, as well as the canals and dams so necessary to proper flood control and drainage. The village economy also became too impoverished either to generate the capital required to pay for modern, efficient steam drainage pumps, or to borrow (for that purpose) from the commercial banks which charged them ruinous rates of interest of between 40 and 50 per cent. The result was that the villages literally became inhabited swamps during the rainy seasons with great loss of whatever crops and livestock there were, and in the process presented grave health hazards to surrounding communities. This is what prompted the central Government to step in and take political control of them.[8] Besides, unscientific and inefficient farming techniques (e.g., little use of fertilizers, poor agricultural equipment, etc.) combined with the periodic flooding to promote the further impoverishment of the peasant village economy.

As we have seen, even while purporting to assist the villagers, the central Government added to their economic burdens by imposing burdensome rates on their properties to meet the cost of loans imposed on them for village improvements. Those villages which 'benefited' from these schemes incurred enormous debts which their agricultural lands, even when drained, could not repay. Moreover, the majority of villages (and villagers) were not included in any of those Government schemes; and it was rare that a plantation would offer assistance to neighbouring villagers to drain their flooded lands. For the most part, therefore, the villagers were left to sink in the floodwaters, for it meant that as the village economies became increasingly uneconomic, more Creole labour was released for plantation work and at reduced wages. By the 1860s, village lands became so worthless that it suited some villagers to rent drained plantation lands at $24 per acre rather than cultivate their own.[9] In less than a generation after Emancipation, therefore, the dream of economic independence harboured by the ex-slaves had turned into a nightmare, and they were once more dependent on the plantations either as tenant farmers or as full- or part-time labourers.

This renewed dependency of the Creole villagers enabled some planters to foster a new paternalistic relationship with them, and some villagers were encouraged to cultivate sugar cane for sale to the plantations. This, of course, was born more out of self-interest than altruism on the part of the planters because they could expand the supply network of sugar canes to increase sugar manufacture. Thus, in 1872, the villagers of Beterverwagting entered into such an agreement with the proprietor of Pln. La Bonne Intention, William Russell, which enabled them to earn over $42,000 in the next twelve years.[10] But these arrangements depended entirely on the continued goodwill of the planters, with the villagers having very little leverage as regards the disposal of their canes or the prices which they received. Attempts by some to construct their own mills to bypass the plantations generally proved ineffective because they lacked the requisite engineering technology.[11]

Creole economic subordination was also effected by taxation. It was the planters and merchants who, through their majority in the Combined Court, fixed the colonial taxes, and they made sure that the greater burden fell on the ex-slaves by a system of indirect taxation on articles of common consumption. The rationale was simple: the more taxes the Creoles had to pay on basic consumer products, the more money they would need to earn; and as the village economy proved increasingly incapable of providing them with sufficient income to meet their basic needs, they would have to turn to plantation labour. Thus, from the very first tax ordinance after Emancipation until the end of the century, consumer goods were heavily taxed — wheat flour, cornmeal, codfish, beef, pork, rice, salt, lard, soap, candles, cloth fabrics, hardware, confectionery, tobacco, wines, beer, etc. Generally speaking, over 90 per cent of the total revenue was raised by taxes on consumer goods. By contrast, plantation supplies such as bricks, machinery, manures, lime, hay, staves, steam engines and ploughs, etc., were exempt from taxation.[12] This kind of discriminatory taxation bore very heavily on the Creole working people and played no small part in their impoverishment and renewed dependency on plantation labour.

Taxation also took the form of licences which were required for portering, huckstering and shopkeeping, as well as for boats, cabs, and mule and donkey carts operated by the working people for hire. Once again, the boats, horses, mules and carts operated by plantations were exempt from taxation.[13] More sinisterly, however, the huckster and shop licences were calculated to hinder the Creoles from engaging profitably in the lucrative retail trade to accumulate wealth and thus become relatively independent of the plantation sector. Successive Governors recognized that these licences discriminated against the Creoles in favour of the Portuguese, but did very little about them since the planters and merchants controlled the Combined Court. Since the primary objective of most Creoles after Emancipation was to save money to buy a plot of land, the outlay of $10 or $20 for one of these licences was very often a major deterrent to engaging in the retail trade.[14]

On the other hand, the Portuguese immigrant's sole ambition was to acquire sufficient money to pay for his trading licence, stock a pack and turn peddlar; so the licences had no deterrent effect on them.[15] In fact, the Portuguese themselves recognized that the licences gave them a competitive advantage over the Creoles. Thus, when in 1848-49 a dispute between the planters and the Government caused the former to refuse to set the taxes, the Portuguese petitioned the Combined Court, calling for the reimposition of the trading licences.[16] Moreover, the practice of the merchants to grant Portuguese traders goods on credit while denying same to the Creoles further enabled them to out-compete the Creoles in the retail trade.[17] By the 1850s, therefore, this very lucrative sector of the economy was dominated by the Portuguese who in turn contributed further to the impoverishment of the Creoles by overcharging and other fraudulent practices (e.g., short weights and measurements).[18]

Such malpractices by Portuguese traders aroused the animosity of the Creoles and led to repeated attacks on Portuguese shops during the nineteenth century.[19] It was in the wake of one of these disturbances in 1856 that perhaps the most oppressive tax was imposed on the Creole population. This was the registration or 'poll' tax designed to raise revenue to compensate the Portuguese shopkeepers for their losses. Although payable by the entire adult population, it intentionally bore most heavily on the Creoles. This tax was a levy of $2 per annum for males and $1 for females for a period of five years; and non-payment was a criminal offence punishable by fine and/or imprisonment with hard labour.[20] Because of the great hardship generated by this impost, it aroused considerable hostility not only towards the Portuguese, but also towards its chief architect, Governor Philip Wodehouse, against whom the Creoles vented their anger by stoning him on his way to the Stabroek wharf in July 1857. This punitive tax was mercifully repealed in 1858 after much orchestrated protest from the missionaries and other local pressure groups, as well as from the Anti-slavery Society in Britain.[21]

The combination of land restrictions, poor drainage, decay of the peasant village economy, discriminatory taxation, and marginalization in the retail trade, reduced the Creoles to a state of chronic poverty and renewed dependence on the plantation sector during the second half of the nineteenth century. Even though the plantations welcomed such dependence, it did not guarantee jobs for the Creoles who found themselves competing against indentured immigrants at reduced wages. Since the terms of indentured contracts bound the plantations to provide the immigrants with five full days' labour each week before hiring extra labour, many Creoles found that, particularly in times of recession, they were made redundant or their wages were reduced. And, as time went by, even those specialized and well-paid heavy field tasks or skilled factory jobs, for which the Creoles were previously favoured, were increasingly performed by indentured immigrants. In short, as their dependence on the plantations grew, so they became more and more marginal to the production process.[22]

This depressing state of affairs left few alternative options in the hands of the Creoles. Migration to the sparsely populated extremes of the coastal belt, e.g., the Pomeroon region in Essequibo and the Corentyne coast of Berbice accounted for a few hundred. Some even ventured across the eastern border into the Dutch colony of Suriname after the emancipation of slavery there in 1863. But emigration was looked upon with disfavour by the planters who feared a drain of local labour resources and increased wages: hence they imposed restrictions.[23] Still others, prevented by stiff Crown lands regulations from obtaining licences of occupation, opted to work as the hired labourers of elite grantholders and engaged in woodcutting, balata-bleeding, and gold-and diamond-prospecting. If lucky, they could earn decent sums of money from these occupations.[24] But they were relatively few and the physical dangers were very great.

Many Creoles, however, moved from their villages to the urban centres of Georgetown and New Amsterdam in search of better jobs and an improved way of life. This migration began at Emancipation and continued throughout the century. Thus, the urban Creole population increased from about 20,000 to 50,000 between 1841 and 1891 and comprised 80 per cent of the total urban population by the end of the century. In the towns, they worked as porters, stevedores, domestics, seamstresses, coalwomen, artisans and craftsmen, tram-drivers and conductors, railwaymen, teachers, dispensers, policemen, clerks, parsons, etc. Skilled white-collar jobs were greatly sought after but, because they conferred higher social status, they were very difficult to obtain. At first, even jobs as store clerks were denied the Creoles, although that changed later in the century when the pool of White competitors declined.[25]

The most prestigious and sought after positions were appointments in the Civil Service and, not surprisingly, obstacles were erected to limit the number of Creoles who were admitted and how far up the ladder they could advance. In a way the Creoles used the Civil Service as an index of their social progress and constantly pressured the colonial authorities to appoint more of them to its ranks. In 1842, for instance, a small group of Creoles formed the British Guiana African Association to agitate for fairer employment practices in the Civil Service, and they published the *Freeman's Sentinel* to articulate their views.[26] This sort of pressure (though not as organized later on) was maintained for the rest of the century by the middle-class Creole press, although successive Governors were at pains to deny that race and colour played any role in public appointments. Instead, they claimed that ambitious Creoles generally aspired to positions for which they were not qualified or competent, and that they used the race/colour card as an excuse for their inadequacies.[27]

Yet, there was abundant evidence to the contrary. When, for instance, in 1857 a Creole clerk named Oudkerk, with twenty years experience in the Civil Service, was bypassed for the post of financial accountant in favour of a White Barbadian, the reason given was that it was done for the good of the public service since he lacked influence with the merchants. But of course the only way a stranger from Barbados could have more influence with the Guyanese merchants would have been on account of race since they were mainly White. Such instances of discrimination against Creoles were quite common in nineteenth century Guyana.[28]

It was no secret that appointments and promotions in the Civil Service were made through patronage, family connections, and social standing based on race/colour and class. The prominent

Creole, E.N. McDavid, observed that "merit, if associated with a sable complexion, is not recognized, or, if called into play at all, is made to fulfil the drudgery, while the lucrative positions are bestowed upon others".[29] Young White lads graduating from the élite boys' school, the Queen's College, automatically found well-paid, responsible positions in the Civil Service over the heads of long-serving, experienced Creoles who invariably had then to teach them how to do the work. This not only generated enormous discontent among the Creoles, but also led to all forms of incompetence in the Civil Service.[30]

Further discrimination could be found in the fact that most White civil servants were appointed 'staff officers' on the permanent establishment, thereby offering them job security and entitling them to such benefits as leave of absence and pensions which (through contributions to the Widows and Orphans Fund) their families continued to receive after their death. On the other hand, most Creole civil servants were employed on a year-to-year basis as 'supernumerary officers' without job security or any of the other benefits. Thus, after working many years, they often retired without a pension or died leaving their families without any form of economic support.[31]

Ultimately it was only by qualifying as a lawyer or doctor that Creoles could grudgingly earn respect and significant social advancement. But, as this was a slow and expensive process requiring tertiary level training abroad, relatively few Creoles were in a position to achieve this. Nevertheless, with considerable sacrifice, most of the lawyers and doctors in the colony by the end of the century were Creoles, and were recognized by independent observers to be as good as any of their White counterparts.[32]

In the socio-economic climate of nineteenth century Guyana, where even unskilled jobs on the estates were increasingly difficult to find as more immigrant labourers were imported, there were many unfulfilled dreams and ambitions among working-class Creoles. For many of them, un- and under-employment became a way of life. To some of these, therefore, crime seemed to offer a way out of their miserable existence and a means of 'getting back' at society. By the 1860s, burglary, street robbery ('choke-and-rob'), shoplifting, and violence became fairly prevalent especially among Creoles in the depressed urban ghettos. Unemployed youths roamed the streets and wharves, brawling, gambling, swearing, and stealing. The backstores of merchants and shopkeepers were prime targets for these delinquent youths. Young working-class Creole women were reduced to prostitution.[33] In the countryside, praedial larceny became prevalent, with both plantations and peasant farmers suffering.[34]

The later nineteenth century thus witnessed a significant surge in crime among working-class Creoles and increasingly the press, both White and Coloured middle-class, urged draconian methods such as flogging hardened criminals with the 'cat-o-nine tails'. However, neither this nor the erection in 1877 of a reformatory school for juvenile delinquents at Onderneeming, Essequibo, served as a deterrent to criminal activity,[35] for the fundamental social and economic conditions which caused working-class Creole youths to lose hope were not addressed by the colonial authorities.

The most pervading problem that Creoles of all classes continuously faced in post-Emancipation Guyana was White racism. It was this which to a large extent determined the parameters within which they were allowed to operate in the colonial system, and which blinded the colonial authorities to their plight. Racist theories became very fashionable in Britain and Europe in the later nineteenth century, the most influential of which was Social Darwinism which purported to provide (pseudo-) scientific proof that African people had not evolved to the same level of human development as Whites. Not that Creole Whites needed any proof, since these ideas had been alive in the West Indies ever since the slave period.

But in the later ninetenth century many British people (including colonial officials, plantation owners and managerial staff, merchants, army and police officers, magistrates and judges, priests and missionaries, etc.) started out from Britain with pre-conceived racist prejudices about African people as a result of these pseudo-scientific race theories. This was clearly reflected in the literature which they generated (travel books, letters, diaries, newspapers, official documents, church records, etc.) during this period, not least of all the two major contemporary 'historians' of Guyana, Henry Dalton and James Rodway. Pejorative racial stereotypes about African people abounded. 'Quashie' (the typical Creole) was childlike, improvident, worthless, shallow, lazy, excitable, and loved to sing and dance.[36]

What this meant was that it almost certainly precluded the ex-slaves and their descendants from getting a fair chance to make good. Classic proof of this came from Magistrate Hewick who in 1885, half a century after the abolition of slavery, sentenced an African man for loitering on an Essequibo estate with the following observations:

> Blacks would neither work nor starve; instead they stole someone's plantains and lay in the sun everyday after eating them. The heads of the blacks were so thick, it was no use telling them anything, and it was useless doing them a good turn; the only way to make the black man work was by use of the lash ... If the black man wished to be their lords and masters, let them go to Hayti ... They seemed to think that White people only lived to put food in their (the blacks') mouth ... as a race, the Africans were the laziest on the face of the earth, and were there no White men they would soon starve; ... they did not appreciate acts of kindness shown to them, and were most ungrateful ...
> (as reported by the *Royal Gazette*[37])

These racist attitudes hardened as the nineteenth century wore on and as White urban society became more stable with the growing presence of White women. Except in the rural areas where White women were few, the old practice of White men cohabiting with African or Coloured women declined after Emancipation and social distance between the 'races' increased.[38] Kirke pointed out that among White colonists in the later nineteenth century there was "objection to the Negro taint, the 'touch of the tar brush' as it is locally called ...".[39] But, long before that, Richard Schomburgk had observed that it was a brave man indeed who would marry a Creole woman:

> If in isolated cases the European disregards these prejudices and still marries a coloured woman upon whose reputation even the most stinging envy can find no stain, the blot of birth indelibly remains: all the aristocratic circles are open to the husband, but to the wife they are impenetrably closed.[40]

Yet, in spite of such deep-seated racial prejudices, some Creoles managed by dint of hard work and great sacrifice to achieve some measure of upward social mobility. By the end of the century, there were lawyers, doctors, priests, civil servants, teachers, and even some plantation managers among the Creole population. But such social advancement was often accompanied by a denial of their Afro-Creole cultural roots as many sought to acquire the attitudes, airs and graces, beliefs, customs and values of the White colonial élites in order to prove that they had arrived socially. Some became unbearable with conceit and even referred to Britain as 'home' and boasted about their English family traditions, coats-of-arms, sports crests, etc. The ultimate symbol of their newly attained social status was marriage to a White woman.[41]

It is important to stress, however, that only a small minority of Creoles achieved significant upward social mobility, notably the lawyers and doctors. Those who became civil servants, teachers, priests, policemen, clerks, dispensers, nurses, etc., entered the middle-class, with skilled artisans and craftsmen, seamstresses, etc., a peg or two below. But the vast majority of Creoles remained working-class, eking out an existence as best they could. Many, however, simply did not survive the hardships of life in the racist colonial society.

This was clearly reflected in the population statistics for the post-Emancipation period. Although the Creole population increased by 58 per cent from about 92,000 in 1838 to 144,619 in 1891, much of that increase was due to the inflow of 55,077 immigrants from the West Indies and Africa.[42] If one excludes those, the number of Creoles would actually have decreased by 1.7 per cent. So the Creole population owed its increase after Emancipation almost entirely to immigration rather than to natural increase.[43] This had all the makings of a potential demographic catastrophe, and was the direct result of the colonial Government's policies, nurtured in a climate of racism, which systematically discriminated against the Creoles. Thus, by the end of the nineteenth century, not only were they subjugated within the colonial polity, increasingly marginalized within the colonial economy, and subordinated within the colonial society, but they were literally becoming an endangered species unable to increase their numbers naturally.

What is striking, however, was the apparent inability of the Creoles to react to these disastrous policies and pressures with any degree of cohesion and unity as an ethnic group. This was largely on account of two factors. First, they were deeply divided along colour-class lines. Colour distinctions and phenotypical features assumed such great significance among the Creoles that, in general, the lighter the hue and the more European the features, the higher was the perceived class status. These physical attributes were very jealously guarded, and great care taken to ensure that one's progeny improved the stock ('lightened their darkness', as they were taught to pray by the Anglican Church). Coloureds who ranged from *fustee*, through *mustee*, to *mulatto* kept their distance socially from people of darker complexion, e.g., the *cob* and *Negro*, even though some of their close relatives might fall into the latter categories. To be called a 'nigger' was the greatest insult imaginable to any Creole regardless of colour.[44] There was little common cause, therefore, between people at the two poles of this colour-class continuum, and very generally their social interests differed accordingly.

These Colour-class differences were reinforced by the second element of Creole disunity - culture. After generations of indoctrination, most Creoles unquestioningly accepted the idea of the inferiority of Afro-Creole culture and the superiority of White culture; and the higher up the social ladder they aspired to be, the stronger were their efforts to 'Europeanize' themselves. Socio-cultural divisions thus existed among the Creoles depending on the extent of their acculturation to the dominant White norms; and although there was a viable Afro-Creole cultural tradition in nineteenth century Guyana, it was so depreciated in the minds of its primary bearers that it could not provide them with a positive sense of ethnic identity to resist cultural imperialism, White racism and colonial domination.[45]

The Creoles, therefore, remained a disparate social category, lacking the sort of group cohesion and ethnic pride so necessary for overcoming the obstacles (social, economic and political) that were placed in their way. It is not surprising, therefore, that even the few dark-skinned persons who dragged themselves out of poverty literally by their 'boot-strings' should have sought to distance themselves from their roots, because they felt this was necessary in order to earn social respectability. The price of social advancement in the colonial society was thus cultural self-denial, and there were many Creoles during the nineteenth century who were quite prepared to pay it.

Notes

1. The term 'Creole' is here used to mean an African or Coloured(mixed African-White) person born in Guyana.
2. Neither term, 'ethnic group' nor 'class', suffices to classify the Creoles. While the majority were, and remained, working-class throughout the century, some made social advances to enter the middle and upper-middle classes with widely different interests from the majority. As an 'ethnic group', the Creoles again were very diverse. All shared a common Afro-Creole cultural heritage, but the more upwardly socially mobile they were, the more 'Europeanized' they became and thus sought to shed as many of their Afro-Creole cultural roots as they consciously could. They therefore lacked a sufficiently distinct cultural identity to constitute a cohesive 'ethnic group'.
3. P.P., 1851., XXXIX, Encl. 3 in Barkly to Grey, 121, 15 Aug. 1850.

4. O. Nigel Bolland, "Systems of domination after slavery: the control of land and labor in the British West Indies after 1838", *Comparative Studies in Society and History* (hereafter *CSSH*), 23, 1981, pp. 591-619; *idem*, 'Reply to William A. Green's "The perils of comparative history", *CSSH*, 26, 1984, pp. 120-25; William A. Green. 'The perils of comparative history: Belize and the British sugar colonies after slavery', *CSSH*, 26, 1984, pp. 112-119. Green argues that in the British Caribbean sugar colonies, population density was the main factor which determined the availability of land for the ex-slaves. Bolland, however, is of the view that demographic factors alone were not enough to account for land availability, but also (and more importantly) the system of domination maintained by the planters which enabled them to control the disposal of land.
5. Brian L. Moore. *Race, Power and Social Segmentation in Colonial Society: Guyana after Slavery 1838-1891* (New York, 1987), pp. 96 and 111-113.
6. *Ibid*., pp. 94-96.
7. Alan Adamson, 'Monoculture and Village Decay in British Guiana 1854-1872', *Journal of Social History*, 3, (4), 1970.
8. Moore, pp. 95 - 97.
9. C.O. 111/336, Hincks to Newcastle, 140, 28 Jul., 1862.
10. *Creole*, 3 May 1872; *Colonist*, 12 Sep. and 2 Nov. 1883; *Argosy*, 15, 22, and 29 Mar., 1884.
11. Encl. in Kortright to Kimberley 140, 4 Aug. 1881; *Argosy*, 4 Dec. 1880, 22 Apr., 23 May and 25 Oct. 1884.
12. See the annual tax ordinances.
13. *Ibid.*
14. 111/227, Light to Stanley, No. 70, 7 April 1845; C.O. 111/277 Barkly to Grey, 173, 31 Dec. 1850; and *Colonist*, 26 Feb. 1851.
15. C.O. 111/280, Encl. 4 in Barkly to Grey, No. 12, 20 Jan. 1851.
16. *Official Gazette* for 1852.
17. *Royal Gazette*, 30 Oct. 1843.
18. Moore, pp. 145-46.
19. The Portuguese commercial community was attacked on three occasions after Emancipation: 1848 in Berbice, 1856 in Demerara and Essequibo, and 1889 in Georgetown. On each occasion, it was their shops and stock in trade which were looted and destroyed, not their persons. But in 1856, in order to encourage continued Portuguese immigration into Guyana in order to boost the White population, the Government thought that they should be compensated for their losses out of the public revenues.
20. C.O. 111/311, Wodehouse to Labouchere, 83, 23 Jun.1856; *Creole*, 22 May 1858.

21. C.O. 111/317, *Creole*, 21 Feb. 25 Jul., and 8 Aug. 1857; *Berbice Gazette*, 30 Jul. 1857; C.O. 111/320, encl. 2 in Wodehouse to Labouchere, 140, 6 Nov. 1856; C.O. 111/317, Wodehouse to Stanley, 68, 7 Jun. 1858.
22. Moore, pp. 120-21.
23. LMS 99/1, Scott to Tidman, 18 Feb. 1865; L.M.S. 8b/4 (Dem.), Scott to Mullens, 8 Mar., 1867, (Dem.); Adamson, pp. 58 - 59; LMS 10/l Pettigrew to Mullens, 22 Feb. 1868, and Munro to Mullens, 21 Feb. 1870, (Ber.); C.O. 111/345, Hincks to Newcastle, No. 60, 18 Mar. 1864, *Creole*, 19 Aug. 1868.
24. SPG/E1O, Tanner to Hawkins, 18 Jan. 1862; C.O. 111/345, Hincks to Newcastle, 84, 26 Apr.1864.
25. Moore, pp. 122-23.
26. C.O. 111/193, Light to Stanley, private, 1 Nov. 1842, and C.O. 111/200, private and confidential, 13 Mar. 1843.
27. *Ibid.*; C.O. 111/316, Wodehouse to Labouchere, 29, 24 Feb. 1857; C.O. 111/419, Kortright to Kimberley, 229, 21 Jul. 1881, C.O. 111/438, Irving to Holland, 76, 19 Feb. 1887.
28. *Creole*, 18 and 22 Jul. 1857; W. Rodney, *A History of the Guyanese Working People 1881-1905* (Baltimore: 1981), p. 113.
29. E.N. McDavid, *The future prospects of the Creoles of the Colony* (Georgetown, 1900).
30. R. Duff, *British Guiana* (Glasgow, 1866), p. 315; H. Bronkhurst, *Among the Hindus and Creoles of British Guiana* (London, 1888), p. 191; *Echo*, 13 Jul. 1889.
31. *Echo*, 3 Aug. 1889.
32. D. M.D. Comins, *Note on Emigration from India to British Guiana* (Calcutta, 1893), p. 8 - quoted comment made by the American consul in Georgetown; see also McDavid, *loc. cit.*
33. The local press was full of reports of crime in the city in the later nineteenth century. See also C.O. 111/301, Wodehouse to Grey, 41, 21 Jul. 1854; C.O. 111/383, Scott to Kimberley, 25, 23 Feb. 1871; C.O. 384/103, encl. in Longden to Carnarvon, No. 188, 7 Oct. 1874, C.O. 114/44, Report of the Inspector-General of Police for 1888,.
34. C.O. 111/252, Light to Grey, separate, 3 May 1848, L.M.S 7/1 (Ber.), Roome to Tidman, 30 Jan. 1850; *Berbice Gazette*, 17 Feb. 1864; *Colonist*, 26 Jan., 19 Jul. and 5 Aug. 1867, and 19 May 1874; *Royal Gazette*, 20 Feb. 1879. See also the Blue Books of Statistics, C.O. 114, for criminal statistics for the later nineteenth century.
35. See the newspapers of the 1860s and 1870s. Also C.O. 111/415, Young to Hicks Beach, No. 241, 4 Nov. 1879.
36. Henry Dalton's work was entitled *The History of British Guiana*, 2 vols.

(London, 1855); James Rodway's, *History of British Guiana*, 3 vols. (Georgetown, 1891-94). The contemporary 'literature' of nineteenth-century Guyana and the Caribbean is riddled with overtly racist comments and stereotypes of the Creole population. It was extremely rare to find a White observer who did not harbour such race prejudices, and at the very least he/she certainly thought that the Creoles were culturally inferior and uncivilized. Thus, even 'do-gooders' embraced the notion that they had a moral obligation to 'civilise' these poor unfortunate African beings. At worst, Whites felt that the Creoles had to be subordinated permanently to their will.

37. *Royal Gazette*, 18 Apr. 1885.
38. Overt White-African sexual relationships declined in the two major towns during the 19th century. But there was still a considerable amount of clandestine activity taking place ('under covers', so to speak). In the rural areas, however, the old practice of relatively open 'concubinage' between White males and non-White women persisted largely because of the paucity of White women; but the number of Creole women in such relationships declined as more and more Indians were imported to work on the plantations [see the author's *Cultural Power, Resistance and Pluralism: Guyana 1838-1900* (Kingston, 1995), chapter 3].
39. H. Kirke, *Twenty-five years in British Guiana* (London, 1898), pp. 45 - 46.
40. Richard Schomburgk, *Travels in British Guiana*, vol. 2 (Georgetown, 1922), pp. 45-46.
41. Kirke, p. 40.
42. A total of 41,027 West Indians (1834-90) and 14,060 Africans (1834-67) went to Guyana (see G.W. Roberts and M.A. Johnson, "Factors Involved in Immigration and Movements in the Working Force of British Guiana in the 19th Century", *SES*, 23(1), 1974).
43. Moore, *Cultural Power*, chapter 2.
44. Moore, *Race*, pp. 110-11.
45. See chapters 5 & 6 in Moore, *Cultural Power.*

7: The Strikes of 1842 and 1848

by
James G. Rose

The Strike of 1842

At the beginning of 1842, the labourers on most of the sugar plantations in Demerara and on the Essequibo Coast[1] refused to accept certain "Rules and Regulations"[2] which the planters sought to impose on the work force. Because the new "Rules..." were harsh and unjust, as well as arbitrarily conceived and imposed, the labourers withheld their service from the plantations. Apart from sporadic instances of plantation unrest, this strike was the first open confrontation between the two groups since Emancipation.[3]

Labour relations between the planter and the work force had in the main been poor in the three and a half years since freedom, but the planter had nevertheless been able to harvest his crop and to produce sugar for the fragile export market. This is not to suggest that African labour had been given freely, or, that it had been given in adequate supply or, for that matter, without rancour.

One of the dominant features of post-Emancipation Guyana had been the problem of labour. Accustomed to slave labour, the planter found it difficult to become reconciled to wage labour. On the other hand, the work force, realizing its full worth and potential, consciously regulated the supply of labour to the plantation, while consistently demanding competitive wage rates. Neither position was achieved by chance. It was the product of pre-Emancipation class antagonisms and the continuation and escalation of soured relations in the immediate post-Emancipation years. Slavery had been abolished, but it had always been intended that the plantation system should continue. Its survival depended on the continued availability of a servile and cheap labour force. As a result, strenuous efforts were made to keep African labour bound to the system.

The labourers had protested in various ways. They had mobilized themselves into task gangs offering their labour to the most competitive employer and by deliberately creating an artificial shortage of labour, they fabricated conditions encouraging the payment of competitive wage rates. The planters responded aggressively by arbitrary ejectments, punitive rents and the denial of gardening and grazing rights on plantation lands. These responses produced periodic work stoppages aimed at consolidating the new limits of power and influence in the ongoing conflict, but the work force had never combined in such a determined show of solidarity before. Both the combination and determination frightened the planters. The planters had from time to time been forced to come to terms with their altered circumstances in a free society, but this was the first time that they had found themselves so completely at the mercy of their work force.

During the years just prior to Emancipation, particularly during the Apprenticeship period, some planters had repeatedly complained of major labour problems consequent on Emancipation.[4] They had anticipated the complete withdrawal of the labour force from the plantations. This migration, though not in mass, was nevertheless in progress. To stem the tide of this movement, coercive practices had been invoked and, because of the punitive nature of some of the accompanying Ordinances, the Colonial Office had rejected them. This, however, did not erase the aggressive attitude which had given birth to such measures and the practices persisted even though overturned by the Colonial Office. There were other planters, however, who felt that coercion was not the best policy, preferring instead to offer attractive wage rates and other inducements. This latter group succeeded in retaining adequate labour where the former more aggressive recourse had succeeded only in alienating it.

In the final analysis, both policies proved almost equally injurious to the sugar industry. The former ensured that conflict between the classes persisted, while the latter enabled the freedmen to earn enough so quickly, that it was possible for them to offer their labour to the estates at times convenient to them and not necessarily when most needed by the planters.[5] More importantly, however, the freedmen were able to earn and save enough to buy properties which considerably reduced their dependence on, and consolidated their freedom from, the plantation system.[6]

The result of the first development was that labour continued to be virtually scarce and expensive, the cost of the commodity produced was high and therefore increasingly uncompetitive and the bankruptcy of plantations continued at an accelerated pace. In these altered circumstances, conflict persisted and because the planter was capitalist-oriented, he attempted to cut the cost of production to avoid financial ruin, and because he was yet to accept the notion of free/wage labour, whatever steps he adopted to cut the cost of production were detrimental to the welfare of the labourer. On the other hand, since 1838 the labourer had grown in confidence. He had witnessed the panic responses of the plantocracy and had not been fooled by its transparent policy of seduction. He was conscious of the true worth of labour to the plantation system and was determined that this new worth should not be subverted.

Whatever the planters' reservations or incapacities, the labourers were confident that the survival of the plantation system in British Guiana depended on the manner in which labour was courted. They therefore insisted on wage rates that were reasonable, as well as improved gratuities and allowances. For many planters, the entire exercise became prohibitive and they were ruined.[7] The closure of these plantations was not altogether without its advantages because it reduced the sources of competition and made more labour available to those who persisted. Some commentators even suspected that, should the trend continue, the supply of labour would soon outstrip the demand and wages would then come down.

By 1841, however, even some of those plantations which had enthusiastically embraced the policy of inducements came face to face with the harsh economic realities of the times. The artificial shortage of labour created the need for an immigrant labour force, the cost of which further inflated production costs. By May 1841, most planters had begun to grumble.[8] An attempt to cut the cost of production by either limiting or withdrawing altogether plantations perquisites proved abortive when the labourers refused to work on those estates which had abandoned their plantain walks.[9] The planters re-examined their position and in particular the system by which their labour needs were supplied and were mostly dissatisfied. They conceded that:

> a labouring man should work for whom he chooses and ought to receive wages for his work. He should live where he pleases and pay rent for his occupancy, then he and his employer are equally independent of each other.

They concluded that it was "impolitic to have permitted (the Negro) occupation of huts and provision grounds rent-free".[10] The freedmen shared similar sentiments but had been forced to fight for a very limited realisation of such hopes. Indeed, such freedom and responsibilities were always their ultimate conception of true Emancipation and so they had resisted planter machinations to restrain labour in servile conditions on the plantation.[11]

Yet the emergence, growth and development of an independent labour force were not perceived by members of the planting community as being in their best interests. The economic imperatives of the 1840s, however, were forcing them to revise their strategy.[12] Even so, considerable caution must be exercised when interpreting the planters' definition of an 'independent' labourer. In its real sense, the concept of an independent labour force, acceptable to the planter, would have implied revolutionary thinking on the part of the plantocracy. But the plantocracy had always been reactionary employers. What the planter now sought to achieve was freedom from the additional expenses which allowances, gratuities and higher wages entailed. In the process, he sought both to inflate the labourer's cost of living and reduce his earning capacity at the same time.

It was not without significance that, just at this time, efforts were being made in the metropole to resolve other issues fundamental to the solution of the planters' perceived labour problem. Lord Russell and the Colonial Office were formulating a comprehensive scheme of immigration "to solve the problem of labour shortage."[13] Almost coincidental was the notice of a motion by Mr. Labouchere, aimed at 'the removal of those restrictions which bore on the trade of the colonies with foreign countries, and of the duties on the food for maintaining labourers."[14] Admittedly, the real cause of the planters' problems stemmed from the cumulative effects of a number of problems, not necessarily all related to labour, which had been developing over the years. Some of these had become chronically entrenched in the plantation system, but the successful implementation of the measures contemplated in Britain would nevertheless have brought some relief to the planters. The effective salvaging of the plantation economy called for fundamental reforms in the functioning of society and a radical restructuring of the economy. But, in the interim, Russell's initiative coincided favourably with the planters' desire for a new supply of labour to 'set off' against what they deemed 'a recalcitrant African labour force'.[15]

Buoyed by such support, the planters embarked on a programme of open confrontation with the labour force. To this end an Ordinance was proposed in the form of a petition to the Governor and Court of Policy requesting a "change in the system at present in the management of Estates at least in so far as occupancy of grounds and tenants by the labourers is concerned."[16] Not surprisingly, and in keeping with their new intentions, the petition noted that:

> The houses, grounds, allowances free of rent are remnants of a system which the good of all ranks and conditions among us are desirous to forget, and as long as they are continued the idea of full and complete freedom cannot be realized; neither can that Independence of spirit and action necessary in a free people, be universally obtained.[17]

To assume here that the plantocracy had, at long last, been converted to a recognition of basic rights of the work force would be a serious misconstruction. The intention of the planters was to deceive the public in general, and the labour force in particular, into accepting a plan that was as sinister as it was devious. Rather than an improvement in the lot of the labour force, the real purpose was to increase their dependency on the plantation, to effect a deterioration in their condition and a deprivation of some of the freedoms they had fought for and won in the years since 1838.

The plantocracy was seeking both to curtail the growing independence of the labourer and redress what they saw as the serious economic ills caused by this new assertion. In the pursuit of these objectives they had prepared a new set of import duties to inflict punitive taxation on the labouring class to the benefit of the plantocracy.[18] The necessities of life were to be heavily taxed to raise large sums of money (£104,000) to defray the cost of immigration and a canal excavator. As early as 1839, Governor Henry Light was forced to admit that the labourers had been embittered by the heavy and one-sided taxation system.[19] The Government Secretary, Henry Young, on this occasion noting the bias and oppressive nature of the measure, remarked that "the appointment of the taxes (was) no less unequal and oppressive than the exclusive character of the Committee by which they have been framed was unjust and unconstitutional."[20] Interestingly enough, the nature and purpose of the taxes were not lost on the labouring population either.

It was an unrefuted fact, though unpalatable to the planters, that innovations in a taxation system skewed against the working-class and taxing the indispensables of their life, inevitably created demands for high and higher wages.[21] The planters had begun to complain against the high wage rate, but the Government Secretary pointed out that "the necessaries of life are burdened with duties which tend to increase prices and thus maintain wages at a rate high to the employer but only nominally so to the labourer."[22] Even so, the inequality in the system clearly demonstrated that taxation was a potent weapon in the hands of the plantocracy. In the first instance, they used their preponderance in the Combined Court to relieve themselves of taxation. At the same time, they shifted this burden unto the unrepresented classes.[23]

The 'Capitation,' 'Land' and 'Produce' Taxes were typical examples. The first was abolished, while the second was considerably reduced.[24] At the same time, consumer items (flour, beef, pork, malt liquors and clothing), favoured by the labourers, were repeatedly taxed.[25] This oppressive bias repeated itself in the 1841 'Colonial' Taxes which were increased by £74,000 solely for a purpose, immigration, which benefited the planter class alone. Yet the labourers were the ones taxed for it. Small wonder, therefore, that when the planters complained of high wages, the labourers pointed to the high level of taxation and the rising cost of living. The labourers were quite aware of the fact that as revenue accumulated and import duties grew larger, the planters' contribution to the national revenue became smaller and smaller.[26]

But there was still another side to taxation other than the mere raising of revenue to pursue projects which benefited the planter class alone. The planters knew that taxation, skewed as it was, possessed the ability both of reducing the purchasing power of the labourer, even as it paid back to the planter community, some of the money paid out in wages. This was achieved by creating areas of expensive compulsory expenditures (high-priced necessities) and by the payment of high rates. (Horses, mules, carts, huckstering and the portering trade were also taxed).

The need for increased quantities of local currency was thus created which induced the labourer to work more regularly on the sugar estates and in some cases to put in longer hours. In short, the conditions making for greater reliance on the plantation system were subtly but inevitably created. As the marginality of the labourer's position increased, his ability to establish himself as an independent peasant or small farmer correspondingly decreased. What the planters tried to ignore, and what seemed to save the situation for the labourer, was his early and accurate assessment of the planters' designs. What was achieved therefore was increased personal bitterness, social tension and the ongoing polarization of the two groups.

By November 1841, the planter community was sufficiently incensed by their problems and their apparent inability to cope that they convened a meeting, the object of which was "to ascertain and discuss whether the rate of production throughout the colony was ruinous".[27] After determining this most important fact, a public meeting was to be convened to discuss plans to effect a reduction of the cost of production. At this first meeting, attended by all the local notables from among the planter class, a committee was appointed to investigate the central problem. Its terms of reference included specifically the task of eliciting information on the actual cost of production, or the average cost of the previous ten months' production, and secondly, to ascertain the proportion of the cost and the value of the article produced with a view to devising measures to reduce the cost of production.

The Committee took evidence from 60 estates which had produced 10, 343 hogsheads of sugar and found that the cost of production was $98.81, while the selling price of the staple was $86.40, per hogshead. The planters, like Adam Smith, argued that "the cost of production was the grand regulating principle of price" and, since they recognised their inability to effect changes in the selling price of the commodity, they recommended that immediate efforts be made to equalise 'the rate of wages and production'.

The Committee's report identified a number of causative factors purported to be responsible for the planters' problems. As expected, labour was the first. The Report noted its irregularity, its unreliability, its inadequacy, its indifference, its uncaring performance and its high price. The practice of paying for unfinished work was stoutly condemned, as was the granting of gratuities and medical and educational facilities, all of which were immediately discontinued. Free housing , grazing land and the provision plot were deemed anachronisms, while the engaging of task gangs was considered much too expensive an expedient to be further practised. These factors were set up as the principal causes of the planters' distress and were treated as such during the course of the deliberations. In the end, it was decided that overseers were to insist that tasks undertaken be properly executed or payment withheld. Labourers who performed indifferently and inefficiently were to be dismissed. Gratuities and allowances were to be abolished and for every day that a labourer absented himself from estate duties, a fine of two bits was to be charged for the occupation of his cottage. The burning of cane was to be discontinued or, where the practice persisted, the wage rate was to be reduced by 25 per cent. Finally, the employment of task gangs was to be brought to an end.

It has already been noted that while the planters considered the rate of wages excessive, the labourers felt that the cost of living made such a rate reasonable. Since Emancipation, they had been at pains to ensure the receipt of just wages. The work force considered themselves in full control of the labour situation. They were conscious of their worth and not in a mood to be underpaid.[28] On the question of task gangs, it was observed by the planters that generally they earned from $1.00 to $3.00 daily but, on occasions, they had earned as much as $4.00 per day. It was felt, however, that expensive as they were, such gangs represented an expertise and strength not to be had elsewhere, and because of this, higher wages were a necessity.[29]

What the planters chose to ignore was the fact that as task gangs they were essentially itinerant work groups and estates therefore paid only for the particular task and nothing else. There were no perquisites attached to their employment.[30] Gratuities and allowances were not a part of any pact between the two groups and as a consequence the wage rate had to be higher than normal. Even more important, however, was the further consideration that tasks gangs were specialized work units which performed a task undertaken better than any other available work force. Their normal assignments were larger than that which was allocated to others and their rate of completion was faster.

The truth was that, initially, the planters thought that the task gang was advantageous. They had been averse to offering day work which, according to their way of thinking, would pander to the 'indolent' nature of the labourers.[31] Since both the extent of the task and its rate were set by the planter, he considered himself in full control of the situation and so the task gangs were encouraged. The labourer's expertise and the self-confidence came later and with it a shift in the virtual control of the situation. The planters therefore found themselves caught in an expensive arrangement of their own construction.

As far as fines and eviction were concerned, the law had clearly stipulated a grace period and certain conditions of tenancy which incurred obligations on the part of both groups but which had been observed by neither. In the days immediately after Emancipation, similar efforts had been undertaken to remove the labourers forcefully from their 'homes'. Using their strong bargaining position, the labourers had succeeded in frustrating these efforts. As late as the early 1840s, eviction was used punitively and as an instrument of coercion. Governor Light had always favoured this expedient,[32] but, on occasion, even he was appalled by the callousness of the planters' exercise of this facility.[33]

When news of the planters' deliberations became public, it was immediately pointed out that the course of action contemplated was fraught with danger, much of which was unnecessary.[34] The planters were reminded of the withdrawal of an allowance of rum in August which resulted in a strike by some workers and of the immediate capitulation of the planters involved. Further, when the withdrawal of some allowances was attempted in the districts of Couva and Tacarigua in Trinidad, the labourers there went on strike as well,[35] and when attempts were made to reduce the wages of the Trinidad labourers, another strike ensued.[36] The withdrawal therefore of all gratuities and allowances, a reduction of wages, eviction and the threatened destruction of crops and livestock from a working force, quite conscious of its strength, was certain to result in strike action.

Were the planters prepared to adopt a firmer stand than the weak showing of their colleagues earlier in the year? Many doubted their ability to withstand a strike. Indeed, the planters were conscious of this weakness and had cautioned their ranks about disloyalty and a lack of solidarity. Planter Young, speaking on behalf of the Governor, noted "that combinations of planters (always ended) in disappointment if ever formed for a purpose other than the communicating of ideas".[37] The editorial of the *Gazette* commended the withdrawal of all gratuities, but felt that wages should have been left to the vagaries of market forces.[38] This, no doubt, was the result of a silent belief among some planters that the labourers would accept the general reform proposal, except for the cut in wages, to which they would object most strenuously. The earlier attempt to withdraw rum and plantains had resulted in strike action and so it is difficult to accept, with any degree of seriousness, such a belief, silent or otherwise. Even so, unity of purpose and action would still have been prime requirements. There was no record of such a unity among the planters and in this instance, two planters, Porter and Pearson, had already expressed grave misgivings about the so-called 'action plan'.[39]

The planters chose to ignore the allegation of past disunities and developed their plan further. Two motions were presented to the Combined Court on 13 December 1841: one to effect the recovery of possession of lands, tenants and houses and the other for the speedy recovery of rents.[40] Meetings of planters were held throughout the cane-farming districts of Demerara and Essequibo during the month of December. These meetings concentrated on drafting new rules and regulations for the employment of labourers on all the estates from 1 January 1842.[41] Copies of the new 'Rules and Regulations' were in circulation from about 20 December 1841.[42] In circulating the 'Rules and Regulations,' the planters stipulated that all those who refused to accept the new arrangement would be required to leave the estate by 1 January 1842 and anyone still in residence after that date would be considered as having accepted the new conditions of employment.

The work force neither accepted the 'Rules' nor left the estates. They deemed the new arrangement oppressive, withheld their labour and demanded that the new arrangement be withdrawn. Milliroux remarked that "more than twenty thousand labourers answering coalition with coalition, very coolly folded their arms; and nearly two months thus passed away in inaction".[43] From the moment the labourers rejected the new 'Rules', the planters, who felt they held the initiative, lost it and never recovered. The labourers, in their organisation and mode of operation, outclassed their employers and easily out-manoeuvred them. The strike action crippled the industry in both the counties of Demerara and Essequibo. This clearly demonstrated the unity, organisational ability and militancy of the workers just four years after Emancipation. Labourers reported for duty on some estates but these were estates which had not adopted the 'Rules', and even so, production was rapidly brought to a halt.[44]

The behavioural response of some planters indicated their state of disunity and disorganisation.[45] They had hoped for an immediate capitulation and acceptance from the labourers.[46] They had obviously underestimated the militancy and resolution of the work force. Barton Premium, a prominent member of the planter community, argued that the planters expected a strike, but if this was so, then they did not expect the type of solidarity with which they were confronted.[47] They had planned, not from a position of dependency or even mutual dependence, but from the arrogant power base of the superiority of the old plantation, for Milliroux noted that "they drew up and caused to be adopted a resolution... in each line of which one perceived the reminiscences of pure slavery".[48]

In spite of all the evidence which they themselves had adduced over the years, they persisted in seeing the work force as a group of dumb, driven cattle, — chattell — still expected to cower before them because of the ascribed superiority of the Victorian cultural tradition, European brain power and technological advancement. Their fundamental mistake was in not acknowledging how far and by how much their power as a group had been eroded since 1838. Conversely, they failed to realise, until it was too late, the significant evolution in the African psyche that had taken place. Further, they could not assess the spirit of self-determination which drove the Africans relentlessly to rebel against the plantation and its innumerable symbols of inhumanity and oppression.

Unlike the Europeans who continued to consider them as so many cyphers or mere chattel, the Africans seemed to have come to terms with reality at a much earlier date. Having realized the current inevitability of the plantation system and their inability to destroy it, they sought to exercise some measure of effective control over the terms of their relationship with the power structure. At a more profound level, however, they were determined not to have the plantation reassert that dominance over their existence which had been the central feature of pre-1838 relations.[49]

As soon as strike action was taken, workers' delegations from various parts of the affected counties began seeking audience with the Governor.[50] (Between 4 and 5 January alone, the Governor had seen or caused to be seen no fewer than 20 delegations, some of them as large as 20 persons). Their reasons were several. They wanted to ascertain the legality of the planters' actions, to find out if these actions had the blessings of the Governor and of the Queen, to state their case and to make plain their intention to reject the imposed conditions. But underlying all of this was the labourers' desire to win the support of the Queen's chief servant to their cause.

Militant though the labourers were, the protest action was relatively peaceful.[51] There were instances of aggressive behaviour but these were not significant enough to destroy the overall exemplary conduct of the labourers, in spite of tremendous provocation. On one occasion more than 20 labourers were evicted and the manager supervised the destruction of their personal belongings.[52] In another instance, the manager ordered all the personal effects of strikers destroyed.[53] Stringent efforts were made to block entry to provision plots, to restrict grazing rights, to prevent fishing and to destroy crops and stock. To these several acts of provocation, the workers held their ground stoically, knowing that any form of retaliation would be seized upon by the colonial administration to let loose the coercive arms of the colonial state against them.

Nevertheless, the proprietor of Blankenburg claimed he had been molested, threatened and assaulted, while a Justice of Peace who attempted to investigate the incident himself was nearly attacked.[54] Members of the Police Force and Justices of the Peace claimed obstruction in the lawful execution of their duty,[55] while prospective strike breakers reported incidents of threats and obstruction.[56] The most profound testimony of the peaceful nature of the strike, however, was the fact that no one was arrested and not a single shot fired.[57]

On his first contact with the new 'Rules', the Governor immediately referred them to his Attorney and Solicitor General noting that in his opinion, Rules 1, 9, 12 and 13 sought to 'divest the labourers of their right to earn the value of their labour, subject them to a fine for not working on the estate, infringe the ordinary rights of property, and presumed that the labourers agreed to such unusual deprivation under penalty of the mere act of continuing to reside in their accustomed habitations after the notice given ...[58] After a perusal of their law books, the learned gentlemen concluded that the Rules in question did, in fact, 'contemplate the commission of acts inconsistent with the laws in force'. They also disclosed that the manner of communication with the labourers was not sufficient to render them binding on the labourers. It was further pointed out that the new 'Rules', if permitted to go into operation, would seriously infringe the 7 September 1838 *Order-in-Council* governing the relations between the contending classes.[59]

In short, therefore, the 'Rules' were an infringement of the Constitution and their mode of implementation illegal. This information was communicated to the Governor on the third day of the strike yet he claimed repeatedly to the delegations an inability to intervene on their behalf.[60] Rather, he advised that the peace be kept and that the Stipendiary Magistrates redress any wrongs committed by the planters. It is significant that Governor Light should adopt such a stand when the Constitution was being violated and a major illegality was being perpetrated. What was more, he not only sent police reinforcements to protect the planters' rights and properties[61] but he himself visited plantations and sought to have the workers return to work even before a resolution of the conflict.[62] Further, when he failed to get the workers to return to work, he wrote, recording his regret. What he said was particularly significant:

> ... when the people become thoroughly convinced that they cannot remain in their cottages without working for the estate and being assured that the law would force them to quit their cottages, if they persisted in refusing to come to reasonable terms with the proprietors, they will resume work.[63]

It is quite clear that in spite of the unconstitutional and illegal nature of the course of action adopted by the planters, the labourers were being put in the wrong. Light, while not deeming the strike action illegal, nevertheless was sanctioning the use of his coercive forces against the labourers. Strangely enough, his attitude conflicted with that of the Government Secretary who openly recommended that the 'Rules' be withdrawn immediately, if the further 'excitement and discontent' they generated were to be effectively curtailed.[64] Young warned that the persistence with 'Rules' which contemplate "the Commission of acts so extremely harsh, illegal and impolitic ..." would inevitably "operate injuriously to the exports of the Colony".[65]

What is also very interesting is the fact that even before his referral of the 'Rules' to his law officers, Light had found them "of too offensive a nature ... which even if lawful, the movers of them must have known would create disaffection".[66] In spite of this, however, Young disclosed that the Governor "was disposed to spare the planters the further publicity to which in contrary event His Excellency would be compelled for the protection of the labourers to give to his own opinions and those of the Law Officers of the Crown" pertaining to the Rules.[67]

This was a typical administrative cover-up. But even stranger was the attitude of the planters towards the Governor. A Mr. Blair, accused him, in open court, of thwarting the constitutional endeavour of the planters to save themselves from ruin.[68] They saw his seeking the advice of his legal officers, along with his former reluctance to support unrestricted immigration, as a stand against the planting interest.[69] What bothered them most, however, was the fact that the labourers 'did not hesitate to say that the Governor supported them in resisting the measures of the proprietors'.[70] It would seem also that the Governor did not make as freely with his coercive powers as the planters would have liked.[71] A deeper insight into Light's dilemma could be had from one of his letters. In refusing planter Sandbach's request for executive intervention, the Governor observed that:

> To threaten to remonstrate, or, even advise labourers to acquiesce on Rules pronounced illegal by the law officers, and which if legal are of unusual stringency would be against, instead of keeping them on the side of the Government.[72]

The truth of the matter was that Light very early realized that the planters were in the wrong.[73] How wrong he soon found out from his law officers. Having thus verified the extent, he sought to keep it from coming out into the open. He no doubt suspected the worst, if the labourers ever became privy to this information. He did not openly support the labourers and indeed sought at every opportunity to get an assurance of peaceful protest. Light went further when he tried to get the labourers to return to their jobs and to undermine their right to strike action. As the Chief Administrator of a colony, faced with a difficult problem which could have escalated so easily, causing irreparable damage to the colony and to his reputation, he sought to save the economy which was synonymous with sugar. His conduct was much to the advantage of the planters, being not openly supportive of the interest of the striking work force. In the circumstances, if criticisms were in order, as indeed they were, they should have been forthcoming from the labourers and not the planters.

The efforts of the planters were thus doomed to failure from the beginning. Premium observed that the labourers were always aware of the planters' purpose and plans and never considered giving in to the new conditions. Premium, himself a planter, learnt of this from his foreman:

> Massa remember I told you before that if White people don't gib money African won't work. Da so he stand (so it is) Nigga will not work in dis here country for little money. I don't care who know it me say so.[74]

The same point came out in a letter they wrote in which they pointed out that;

> During our slavery we were clothed, rationed, and supported in all manner of respects. Now we are free mens (free indeed), we are to work for nothing. Then we might actually say, we becomes slaves again. We will be glad to know from the proprietors of the estates, if they are to take from us our rights altogether.[75]

Here is one of the ironies of the African-White relationship. The Whites have always considered themselves superior and more civilised, yet they invariably failed to read the African man's mind. The mystery of the African man's thinking was forever beyond the unraveling of the Whites. The Africans knew long in advance what the planters had been planning and had prepared effective counter measures. These responses found the planters' position indefensible. The labourers could afford to wait the planters out. But in January, "a season of the year favourable to every department of agriculture", the planters could not play out a waiting game.[76] Canes needed constant care and, once ripe, could not be kept waiting in the soil. If a delay occurred, myriad ancillary problems resulted and these were very often extremely expensive and injurious to the future of the enterprise. Premium's description of the planters' dilemma is enlightening. The planters had to give in, he argued, and:

> ...when one remembers the destructive effect of time on tropical cultivation intended by the hand of man, the dreadful anxiety with which a planter beholds his cane fields, week after week, assuming more and more, the appearance of so many patches of ground in a state of nature (then) it will at once be understood.[77]

It was an appreciation of this vulnerability which prompted planters such as McTurk, Austin, Bagot, Croal and Retemeyer to reject the 'Rules'.[78] Once their ranks had been broken, however, the planters' cause was further weakened.[79] For not only did the labourers take heart from such a turn in events, they became more resolute in their intentions. The planters on the other hand were affected in an opposite manner. They lost heart and "dispirited and worn out... gave way". One after the other they 'resumed their labourers at the old rate of wages'.[80]

What is of further significance was the solidarity lent to the striking labourers by the immigrants, especially those from Sierra Leone. These workers promptly demanded repatriation in consequence of the proposed altered conditions of labour. From one estate alone, Pln. Lima, with which Peter Rose had very close connection, 21 immigrants sued for a return to their native land.[81] This type of support was heartening since in the event of any work being done on the estates, all of it had to be done by immigrants. When, therefore, these chose to identify with the Black labourers, the planters' position was made even more hopeless.

By March, the situation had resumed some semblance of normalcy with the labourers once again in receipt of the old gratuities and allowances. Of the planters, it was prophesied that of the 220 plantations affected not more than perhaps 20 would show a profit.[82] While the strike had cost the planters dearly, the cause they pursued had eluded them.

This 1842 strike was important not only because the labourers by resolute and concerted action had forced the planters to reverse a plan aimed at inhibiting the growth of an independent labour force but also because it was a triumph of a free spirit which gave new meaning to the Emancipation Act. It represented as well the fulfillment of the African's dream of freedom from the dominance of the plantation system. The planters were also affected in an important way. They had always feared the weakening of their hold over the subordinate group and this was confirmed beyond their wildest imaginings. Not only was the newly freed population capable of combining in a determined manner to challenge the plantation system, but the contempt with which this was successfully achieved was a frightening experience.

This experience coupled with the arrogance of an emerging peasantry and the unreliability and inadequacy of an indifferent labour force, questioned the notion of which group held the advantage on the plantation. If it had not moved in its entirety, the locus of power seemed to be shifting away from the plantocracy.

To save themselves, the plantocracy had to devise ways and means of freeing themselves from their dependence on an African labour force in the shortest possible time.

The Strike of 1848

The abortive attempt of the plantocracy to impose a reduced wage rate, and the resolute opposition of the African labour force, during the early months of 1842, indicated quite clearly to the plantocracy that they could either come to terms with the demands of the labour force or recruit an alternative that was cheaper and more malleable. The planter community conceded that such a force was needed as much to offset the "inadequate and capricious" African supply as to lower the existing rate of wage.[83] They concluded that an alternative supply was necessary "to sustain the cultivation, to arrest the fearful depreciation in value of landed property, and to prevent the abandonment of the colony".[84] Significantly, no mention was made of lowering the cost of labour when, especially after 1842, this must have been as important a motive.

Immigration actually began before full and final Emancipation, although even then, it was a response to the impending freeing of the slaves. William Hillhouse had suggested recourse to an imported labour supply and, as early as 14 February 1835, ten Germans arrived in the Colony consigned to a planter named Bumbury of Devonshire Castle. Between 1835 and 1838, about 5,726 labourers were brought into the colony.

It is helpful to note two important points about the first batch of immigrants. In the first instance, exposure to a new environment and the rigorous, demanding and brutalising routine of the plantation severely decimated their ranks.[85] Secondly, each initiative was undertaken by a private individual. The failure of these efforts to make a real impact on the labour situation was also significant. It has to be admitted, however, that this was not because of the inferior quality of persons recruited nor the restricted quantity imported. Rather, it was because of the inability or the reluctance of most of the immigrants to adjust to the rigorous labour regime. Of those immigrants who arrived in 1835, 236 died. The Madeirans in particular proved vulnerable, and Governor Light admitted that "they died so fast that common humanity would not let us do it".[86] Their importation was discontinued for a while.

The prohibitive nature of the financial aspect of immigration prompted joint ventures.[87] The Court of Policy passed a Bill seeking permission to raise £400,000 by issuing bonds in the name, and on the security, of the Governor and the Court of Policy.[88] This measure encountered severe opposition both in the Court of Policy and from the Colonial Office.[89] The latter agency thought it both "unwise and unjust" to use public revenue to enable the planters to shore up their own economic interests.[90] But there was also the deeper fear of which Lord John Russell made mention. The Colonial Office was "not prepared to encounter responsibility of a measure which may lead to a loss of life on the one hand or, on the other, to a new system of slavery".[91]

Permission to organise, and subsequently finance, the scheme of immigration, was not the only problem which the planters had to resolve with the Colonial Office. The question of contracts proved just as thorny an issue. It was one thing to procure labourers but, given the rigours of the plantation system, it was another to make them work, or even stay on the sugar estates.

The planters and the West Indian lobby in London, demanded that arrangements be made for the "efficient control of newly introduced immigrants." Lord Glenelg was fearful lest a new system of slavery evolve and this fear, and a corresponding determination to safeguard the welfare of immigrant labourers, seemed to inform Colonial Office policy over the next few years.[92]

The disallowance of their efforts led to a struggle between the planters and the Colonial Office and, in the end, through a gradual process of small concessions, the planters secured the sort of scheme they desired. This turn about was in some measure influenced by the Pakington Committee which proposed "the immigration of a fresh labouring population to such an extent as to create competition for employment".[93]

Between 1842 and 1848, the mechanics for the funding of a less restrictive scheme were worked out and some 24, 848 immigrants were introduced between 1846 and 1848 alone. It is important to note that, by this time, public funds amounting to £232,100 had been spent on immigration for the years 1846 to 1848 alone, and all of this had been raised by taxation. The rate of taxation, and the manner in which the revenue was being spent, produced fertile ground for growing discord between the African and planter communities.

Just as the planters seemed on the verge of a solution to their most crucial problem, they experienced a serious setback when in 1846, the *Sugar Duties Act* was reintroduced and passed. This *Act* signalled the imminent termination of the preferential treatment on the British market to which the planting community had become dependent. Earl Grey, a staunch advocate of free trade, reasoned that it was time to free British industry and commerce from impediments which had been constructed mistakenly for their benefit.[94] Preferential treatment had been conceded to West Indian planters to aid their industry but, to judge by the planters' own persistent cry of 'ruin', it had failed. Not only had prosperity not been assured but protection seemed to have contributed to the distressed state of the industry. High wages, it was claimed, were encouraged and maintained simply because the planters were assured of a protected market. Grey concluded, "I cannot admit the justice of a system which imposed a heavy tax upon the English labourers".[95] Protection had to go.

As far as the planters were concerned, Britain was abandoning them and it was obvious that she was doing so in preference to slave societies. The planters had always felt that one of the principal causes of their distressed state was Emancipation. They therefore felt betrayed when Grey announced that the *Sugar Duties Act* was about to bring an end "to the distinction established by a previous *Act*, between foreign sugar, the product of countries in which slavery does or does not prevail".[96] At the end of 1846, therefore, the planters were faced with grave problems. The cost of labour was high, in spite of the gains of immigration. Successive years of drought, 1842-45, had substantially reduced the annual yield. Production was declining, while the cost of the product remained high and uncompetitive. Then there was this final invasion of their once secure market, by slave-produced competition, critically increasing their vulnerability and threatening the viability of the local product.

But there was more to come. There was a serious financial crisis in 1847 from which the interests of sugar suffered heavily. The bankruptcy of more than a dozen West Indian houses of long standing had concentric effects throughout British Guiana. Subsequently, even the banks which maintained some semblance of solvency refused to make loans available to the estates. When Hamilton House of Dublin fell, no fewer than 12 estates folded with it. The West Indian body in Britain issued strict instructions prohibiting the usual drawing rights of planters.[97]

Confidence in local institutions was undermined and when public officials began making heavy and conspicuous demands locally, a run on the banks had begun.[98] Small business concerns on Water Street followed, and before long, the African labour force began refusing bank notes as payment. Those who had paper money, whether at home or in the banks, hastened to the City to convert to specie. Shrewd Portuguese businessmen encouraged the panic among the African population and were able to buy up bank notes at as much as 20 per cent below par. Cries of ruin were heard everywhere as "universal panic prevailed and the most sanguine despaired of continuing to grow sugar so as to pay."[99] The gloom was shared by Governor Light who, in his final despatch for 1847, declared that, "As affairs now stand, one half of the sugar estates will not be able to carry on the cultivation..."[100]

Beset as they were by problems on all fronts, the planters convened a meeting on Friday 29 September 1847. There, it was resolved to construct and forward to the British Government a memorial of the planters' predicament. A committee made up of the more notable planters was delegated to draft the memorial.[101]

It was also decided to hold another meeting on 15 October 1847. This second assembly was chaired by Peter Rose, and a series of measures aimed at alleviating the local situation were proposed. Among these was a request for a loan to finance immigration from Africa, another loan for the drainage of the cultivable portion of the coastlands, the admission of local sugar, molasses, insipidated cane juice, and spirits to the British market under favourable terms of trade, and the manufacture of refined sugar in the colony.[102]

It was noted that the 1842 House of Commons-appointed committee had reported that "the distress now prevailing in the colonies is very great and required immediate attention".[103] Since then, the distress had been aggravated but the call for remedial action continued to be ignored. Instead, Britain had, by her insistence on free trade, contributed to a deepening of the crisis. The 1842 Pakington Committee had also noted the part played by the African labour force in the early stages of the distress. Yet Britain had continued to be difficult where really liberal labour contracts were concerned.[104] Lord Bentinck, leader of the Anti-Free Trade Party had concluded that the implementation of the

Sugar Duties Act "without any accompanying remedy for the difficulty of production by free labour has precipitated ruin by aggravating previous pressures".[105]

Not long afterwards, the Governor was requested by the proprietary body represented in the Court of Policy to have the Government Secretary instruct the Stipendiary Magistracy to explain to the African labour force the dire straits of the planters and to urge them "to accept a lower rate of wages", or to perform an increased task for the same wage rate.[106] If they did not, it was intimated, cultivation would cease and the labourers thrown out of employment. Whatever might have been the intentions for bringing relief to their distressed state, the planters knew they were attempting an explosive expedient. They had ample experience of this in the recent past. They had been informed of the disastrous attempt of their Jamaican counterparts, who, experiencing the same disabilities as the Guianese planting community, had unsuccessfully attempted an almost similar course of action.[107] In British Guiana, where relationships were acrimonious, not surprisingly, the labourers immediately struck work.

In preparing the labourers for a 25 per cent reduction in the rate of wages, the Stipendiary Magistrates alerted them to the designs of the planters. In 1842, when the planters had attempted to reduce wage rates, Africans had withdrawn their labour. The same thing occurred in 1846 when the workers in Leguan went on strike after a renewed assault had been attempted on their wages.[108] In 1848, the response to a pay reduction was a colony-wide strike. Cane fields were set on fire; estate properties destroyed, acrimonious and confrontational relations were generated between the Africans and immigrant populations, and the ongoing soured relations between planters and labourers were further aggravated.

The problem of a reduced wage rate has always been a sore point between employer and employee, and this was so even where there were enlightened relations between the two groups. In the 1830s, the relationship between the planter and the labourer was antagonistic. What was more, the policy pursued by the planters since 1842 had done nothing to dissipate the antagonism. Within recent years, the budgetary provisions for immigration had expanded rapidly and created disaffection. Independently, taxation or immigration was by itself an explosive issue. Taken together, confrontation was inevitable. Throughout the 1840s, taxation, which had become oppressive, was the subject of bitter attacks.[109] In 1846, the *Tax Ordinance* became the subject of a petition which a Committee was appointed to investigate.[110] The petition noted among other things:

> ...the comparative inequality of the share of taxation to be borne by the separate classes and the injurious effects of both on the standard of living of the labouring population.

If there was widespread disaffection with taxation, there was even greater discontent over the disbursement of the revenue collected. It was alleged that in the midst of their distress, the "Combined Court recklessly saddled the taxpayers with an enormously increased amount of taxation, voting away among other extravagances no less than $10,000 of taxes for the erection of an ice house in Georgetown."[111] Such indiscretions did not escape the notice of the labourers. It was not difficult for Governor Light to confirm charges that the "temper of labourers is soured".[112] He admitted that it was "not at all uncommon for remarks not of the civilist kind being made by groups of Creoles on meeting carriages and horses of officials to the effect that they the people were taxed to pay (for) such luxuries".[113] This admission accepted that discontent was rife, widespread and openly vented.

Even so, the 1847-48 withdrawal of labour stemmed from an even greater sense of outrage and injustice. The labourers could not escape the knowledge that immigration was financed by the taxes they were forced to pay. The Committee appointed in 1846 tried to ignore the widespread:

> ...discontent in the minds of the labouring population ... that the Combined Court and the constituted

> authorities of the colony showed a total disregard for their interest and welfare and that they combined for the purpose of opposing them by levying on them excessive taxation.[114]

Africans were also aware that one of the fundamental aims of immigration was the reduction of wage rates.[115] This objective was openly announced repeatedly by the planters and so suspicion on the part of the African community had grown into conviction. When in September 1846 disturbances broke out at Leguan, Governor Light was forced to admit that the labourers were convinced that "The influx of immigrants is to reduce their wages to a greater extent than can ever occur and I believe gave rise to the beginning of the unrest".[116] It was only logical therefore, that when, during a period of heightened immigration activity the Africans were approached about a considerable reduction of wages, they should resist.[117]

On the first day of 1848, fire destroyed a 500 foot long megas logie at Pln. Palmyra. By the end of the month, there were six such fires and incendiarism became a much feared feature of the dispute.[118] Several properties were destroyed and quite a few lives endangered, though only one was lost.[119] Fire was a particularly potent weapon against the planters and the source of these fires was never convincingly established. The planters, in a petition of 17 January 1848, noted that "several fires have taken place of megas logies whereby these costly and indispensable buildings have, with their large stock of fuel for manufacturing the product of estates, been entirely consumed".[120]

The attitude of the labourers to these incidents of fire was another source of concern to the planting community. They reported that "a bad feature of the case was the indifference of the people of the estate. They were seen standing with folded arms, laughing and refusing to move an inch to arrest the progress of destruction."[121] So bitter did the situation become that the Governor was induced to issue a proclamation on Tuesday, 18 January 1848 and another, three days later, on Friday, 21 January. Several inviting rewards were offered for information leading to the arrest, or for the apprehension, of anyone connected with acts of incendiarism but invoked no serious response from the labourers.[122] The proclamations were in themselves very interesting. In the first instance, Governor Light warned all persons, but Africans in particular:

> ...against the tendency of such combination or agreement and to point out to them the immediate results of each atrocious conduct both as affecting their own character, their interest and possibly their lives.[123]

In speaking of a "combination or agreement", Governor Light alluded to the deep-seated fear of the plantocracy of a united, angry African group in open confrontation with them. In the days of slavery, the fear of such a combination was a constant nightmare; the 1842 strike, peaceful though it was, more than justified that fear. The Governor was convinced that such a combination, with a particularly odious design, was in operation. He declared:

> ...the fires (were) not accidental but the result of wilful and deliberate design, and connected with some plan or combination for the general destruction of plantation property throughout the colony.[124]

Revolutionary though this was, it was on this occasion far from the truth. For it was not the entire African population that had gone on strike and the intention might reasonably have been to further reduce the influence of the plantation to negatively impact on the lives of the labourers, but it certainly was not to destroy the system.

For quite some time previous to the conflict, some planters had not been paying wages to their labourers.[125] This was not an act of malice: some planters simply could not meet their wage bill. On these plantations, and the indications are that there were quite a few of them, the labourers continued to give service in the hope that with the in-coming crop, they would be paid. This was not an indication of mutual trust or cordial relationships.[126] The planters might have been embarrassed by summary proceedings, but two things need first to be understood. The first was that since the planters were in arrears to the labourers, they could not think of lowering the wage rate. Secondly, they were hardly in a position to regulate the level of production and productivity of their labourers who were consequently more or less in command of the estate operations. Further, there could be no hope of saving these plantations by not going on strike. Estates which were so badly off that they could not pay wages were already bankrupt.

All the labourers hoped for, therefore, was to ensure payment for services already rendered and at the same time to oversee the eventual closure of the estate. It was not surprising therefore that Governor Barkly could have observed that "even where the labourers had not struck they still seemed bent on witnessing the bankruptcy of the estates".[127] It was also pointed out that sequestered estates continued to pay the normal wage rates, a factor which generated considerable bitterness among the planters.[128] Finally, there were some planters who ignored the agreement of a lowered wage rate and persisted with the old. These estates secured labour and continued to produce sugar.[129]

In general, however, all operations were affected, but some were harder hit than others. These planters concluded that "the Negroes (believed) that as soon as the ruin of the planters here is completed they will get possession of the estates upon their own terms'.[130] While Henry Barkly, who was to become the next Governor of the colony, observed that:

> ...they (the Creoles) are beginning to take it for granted that the country is to be their own, in which notion they have been confirmed by emissaries from Demerara, urging them to hold out, and consequently in the West Coast they now give out that they will not work at all even if a Guilder is offered them: that they will go to their own grounds.[131]

Interestingly enough, these men had gained an insight into the true dimensions of the struggle which was taking place. The plantation, the old symbol of oppression, was under the threat of destruction and the plantocracy, the oppressors, were to be driven out of the colony.

The strikers soon came to the conclusion that they could not count on the support of the immigrants. They had refused to withdraw their labour and were working for a reduced wage rate. This was unlike 1842 when even the immigrants from Sierra Leone had withdrawn their labour.

On this occasion, the immigrants sided with the plantocracy. What was more, since 1842 the immigrant working force had swelled by the infusion of some 32,000 more agricultural labourers who had a significant effect on the state of the economy during the course of the strike. Governor Light conceded that, "whatever is done and very little is doing - is performed by the Portuguese and Coolies".[132] Inevitably, therefore, conflict between the two groups was generated. A small number of Africans was imprisoned for threats to, and ill-treatment of, immigrants who accepted lower wages, but the imported labourers continued to give their services and the intimidation persisted.[133]

The Inspector General was instructed to exercise "every diligence in arresting the process of intimidation". He was directed to use force and despatch "to support the peaceable and well inclined, against their more turbulent comrades".[134] Such directions stemmed from a realisation that it was the immigrants who stood between the planters and ignominious defeat. As one newspaper conceded, "were it not for the immigrants nothing else would at the moment remain for the planter but the alternative of either entirely abandoning his property or submitting to the merciless exactions of the emancipated peasantry".[135] But even so it was noted that the reduction of the work force resulted in "neglect to the cane cultivation in every district".[136] This point is significant since, while harvesting continued to be attended by immigrant workers, neglect in important aspects of cane culture was still evident. Neglect of this nature always had expensive consequences.

The planters were no doubt happy that their makeshift arrangements in the plantation buildings were kept supplied with cane, and hence the sugar mills were kept going. This ability to produce sugar in spite of the withdrawal of African labour had an encouraging effect upon the planters, and helped them to hold out against the labourers on strike.

Unlike the 1842 strike when his mills had ground to a halt, in 1848, there was always the healthy sign of his chimney billowing smoke, indicating that his cane had been harvested and was being converted to sugar. In March, the newspapers still bemoaned the fact that:

> ...the settled determination of the creole peasantry of the colony to withhold their labour from the cultivation and manufacturing process of sugar estates, continues to be the theme of complaint in almost all the accounts which reach us from the rural districts.[137]

The fact was that African labour was withheld and African labour was still crucial to the manufacturing process. But the factories had not been brought to a standstill and, in the circumstances, that was the most important consideration. A strike that did not cripple the industry could not be considered as effective. An ineffective strike action did not supply the essential bargaining power needed by the African labourers to enable them to force the planters to withdraw their oppressive demands.

Unlike the 1842 strike, it was the planters rather than the strikers who were in command of the situation. Very early in the year, the planters, in a petition, pictured the situation as "highly alarming", portending at no distant period to "a dissolution of the bonds by which society is held together".[138]

It was characteristic of the planters to exaggerate the problems in order to receive speedy amelioration. Even so, it is none-the-less necessary to interpret such a statement in the light of the attitude of the striking African labour force to the planter class.

This makes it clear that the fabric of plantation society was never closely knit in British Guiana, consisting as it did of an exploiting planter class, a disaffected African group, and disparate immigrant groups. The segmented nature of such a society was beyond question.[139] When conflict of a profound nature escalated into open confrontation of all the groups in such a society, its fragmentation was always a distinct possibility.

The disunity of the working-class was the most crucial factor in the final resolution of the 1848 conflict. The contest between the planters and the African labourers was as old as their relationship, but with the introduction of an alternative work force in substantial numbers, another dimension had been added to the struggle. Immigrants had been recruited to undermine the African command of the labour market. By 1848, the inflow of immigrants was to a large extent sufficiently numerous to undermine African control of the labour force as the statistics below indicate.

Table 4: Immigration to British Guiana, 1842 - 1848

Years	1842	1843	1844	1845	1846	1847	1848	Total
Influx of Immigrants[140]	2,967	550	918	3,631	11,519	7,784	5,542	32,911
Exodus of Creoles[141]	15,906	-	18,511	-	-	29,000	44,443	-

The actual number of immigrants on the estates, as distinct from the number imported, was seriously affected by vagrancy, escapes and deaths, all of which were relatively high. In spite of these, however, there was still a high percentage of the immigrant population resident on the sugar estates. Of even greater significance was the fact that this resident group, in 1848, still perceived its interest as being bound up with that of the plantocracy.

The Portuguese had already exhibited their commercial inclination but their role in the 1847 financial crisis aggravated relationships with the African community. They may not have started the run on the banks, but they sold to the African labourers the idea that the bank notes were of little value, and were thereby able to purchase the hawked bank notes at a considerably reduced value.[142] Further, they pressed the labourer into an acceptance of the lowered wage rate and when things were bad, refused credit to them in an effort to get them to go back to work.[143] Feelings between the two groups quite naturally ran high and the clash between them on the West Bank of Berbice in 1848, serious as it was, was but a dress rehearsal for the more bitter encounter eight years later.[144]

At the end of April, Governor Light announced that "after three months of opposition to a reduction of wages, the Creole population are beginning I believe to see the necessity of yielding to the pressure of the times and are pretty generally working on Estates at reduced wages".[145] He inferred that the strike had come to an end and that the issue had been resolved in favour of the planters. While this was denied by Mr. White, on behalf of the planter class,[146] there could be no doubt but that African labourers were returning to the fields. In their June reports, most stipendiary magistrates attested to this fact.[147] The indications were that African labourers accepted a lowered wage rate, but by the end of the year, the rate had returned to what it had been before the strike.[148] The cause for this was not difficult to determine. The resolution of the strike increased African disaffection with the plantation system. The result was a serious escalation of the exodus.[149] But the significance of this increased movement is heightened, many times over, when it is realised that in 1848 only 5,542 immigrants were imported into the colony. This sudden reduction in the labour force, at a time when the estates were still suffering from the debilitating effects of the strike, would almost certainly have pushed the wage rate upwards once again.

When an attempt is made to determine the factors which made the African labourers abandon their strike action and return to the estates at the reduced rate they had earlier rejected, a number of interesting possibilities emerge. For instance, even before the contest, some plantations were in arrears of payment of wages for several months.[150] This indicated a genuine inability to meet the wage bill rather than an attempt to lower the rates normally earned by the African labourer.

Further, there were instances in which offers were made to the labourers on certain estates to take off the "standing crop at half the produce,"[151] and in Leguan, planters were forced to hold out an offer of the *metayage* system to the labourers.[152] Both these offers were made in lieu of payments which planters were unable to meet.[153] Such overtures were initially rejected but, in the face of the general depression which became manifest throughout the commercial sector and the consequential credit squeeze,[154] the labourers became convinced that the planters' plight was not a ruse to attack their standard of living or their freedom. They therefore accepted the terms offered. In Berbice, for instance, the labourers acknowledged the planters' plight but refused to permit a reduction because the sequestered estates continued to pay normal wages.[155] What is extremely important to realise, however, is that while Africans recognised the planters' plight, they did not concede the planters' right to attack their living standards and the freedom for which they had fought and won.

But this was what the planters had done and what the labourers had protested against. In the circumstances, the planters' plight could not have been a significant determinant in calling off the strike. What was more, the labourers' desire to destroy the plantation system would not have been significantly affected by a conviction of the planters' distress. This might well have inspired a greater determination to carry the struggle to the bitter end. The strike came to an end because first, it was not as effective as it needed to be. Secondly, the strike ended because a section of its leadership withdrew support for its continuation.

When the strike was first called a newspaper was established[156] and leadership, from without the class and ethnic grouping, organised, articulated and guided the protest action.[157] One significant agency from which the Africans drew much inspiration was the Church. On previous occasions, the Church had championed the Black man's cause.[158] This was not the case in 1848 and Light boasted of this.[159] In 1846, the Church supported the planters' protest against the *Sugar Duties Act.*[160] From this point onwards, it was committed to supporting the planters' cry of distress. The Church's dilemma was how to hold to this stand and support strike action for a continuation of the recognised wage rate.[161] An important distinction had to be made and the holy men failed to do so. The planters' distress could not be resolved by a 25 per cent reduction in the wage rates.[162] But even if this were in fact possible, the planters could not usurp the right to alleviate their distress by creating a class of distressed African labourers.[163]

This type of redress could not be divorced, and was in no way different from the ongoing policy of planter oppression of the African population, a factor which increased the uneasiness of the clergy. Barkly spoke of "emissaries from Demerara" encouraging the Africans to continue the strike. These "emissaries" did not include, within their ranks, the highly respected and influential members of the clergy. The role of the clergy was of a different nature. It adopted a position supporting the planters and used its influence to get the labourers to accept a reduced wage rate while returning to their jobs.[164] This betrayal of working-class interest was crucial and, apart from the role of the immigrants, it was the most significant contributor in the defeat of the Africans in the 1848 contest.[165]

The year 1848 marked an important turning point in the affairs of the African labouring population in British Guiana. It was the year in which their past triumphs in the struggle to keep the dominance of the plantation in check suffered a most serious setback. The programme of immigration, which was yet to reach its peak, had begun to achieve its aims of lowering wages and breaching the African monopoly of the labour market. This was the most important lesson of the 1848 defeat. The immigrants had been used to frustrate the strike effort. In the future, immigrants would be used to make the planter completely free of his dependence on the African labour force.

The planters' position had not improved significantly, but the resolution of the 1848 contest was an important victory nevertheless. The succeeding years would see them gradually re-establish and consolidate their ascendancy over the African labour force. The balance of power had shifted once again. The options still available to the African labourer were very limited indeed. They could either migrate into the villages, as many had been doing over the past decade, or remain on the plantations on terms dictated by the plantocracy.

It was true that those who remained, soon after, received their former wage rates, but essentially, and this was all important, the African labourer was now only marginally important to the estate and would be made increasingly so as the years went by.

Notes

1. The planters in Berbice were not involved.
2. See Appendix "A".
3. There had been several instances of isolated protest action before but this was the first time that the entire work force had combined to achieve a common goal.
4. See Dr. McTurk's speech, MCP, 4 Jul. 1838.
5. Governor Henry Light to Lord Glenelg, 46, 4 Sep. 1838. See also Light to Glenelg, 22, 20 Fe., 1839.
6. By 1842 there were about 15,000 labourers living in villages.
7. M.F. Milliroux. *Demerara: The Transition from Slavery to Liberty* (Paris: 1843), translated by J.R. Mac Farlane, (London: 1877) p. 20.
8. The *Royal Gazette,* Saturday, 2 May 1841.
9. Ibid., Saturday, 2 Mar.1841.
10. *Ibid.*, Tuesday, 11 May 1841.
11. *Ibid.*
12. *Ibid.*
13. Extract - *London Journal of Commerce*, 27 Feb. 1841. Reprinted in *The Royal Gazette*, Thursday, 13 May 1841.
14. *Ibid.*
15. Light to Glenelg, 61, Oct. 1838. John Gladstone coined the term in 1838 when he argued that Coolies would be used as a 'set off' which 'when the time came will make us, as far as possible, independent of our Negro population', in John Scoble, *Hill Coolies* (London: 1840).

16. Published in The *Royal Gazette*, Saturday, 29 May 1841.
17. *Ibid.*
18. No. 11 of 1841. Colonial Taxes published in *TheRoyal Gazette*, Tuesday, 22 Jun. 1841.
19. M.C.C. Monday, 7 Jun. 1841 reported in The *Royal Gazette*, Tuesday, 8 Jun. 1841.
20. Light to Glenelg, 78, 2 May 1839.
21. The *Royal Gazette*, Thursday, 17 Jun. 1841. See also Government Secretary, Henry Young's Speech in M.C.C., Monday 7 Jun. 1841.
22. *Ibid.*
23. Light to Glenelg, 78, 2 May 1839.
24. Young's Speech, M.C.C. Monday, 7 Jun. 1841.
25. Editorial comment, The *Royal Gazette*, Tuesday, 8 Jun. 1841.
26. *Ibid.* See also Young's Speech, M.C.C., Monday, 7 Jun. 1841.
27. This meeting did not receive general press coverage and only a very general reference to it could be found in The *Royal Gazette*, Thursday, 9 Nov. 1841. The second meeting held on 1 Dec. 1841 received comprehensive coverage and the information herein presented was gathered from this release in The *Gazette*, Thursday, 2 Dec.1841.
28. Milliroux, 20.
29. The *Gazette*, Saturday, 4 Dec. 1841.
30. The *Guiana Times*, 14 Jun. 1841.
31. H.D. Dalton, *History of British Guiana*, 2 vols (Georgetown, 1855) Vol. 1., 12.
32. M.C.C. Tuesday, 19 Feb.1839; Light to Normanby, 3 Jun.1839; Light to Genelg, 55, 18 Sep. 1838.
33. Light to Russell, 99, 11 Jun. 1840.
34. Article by "Viator". The *Gazette*, Saturday, 4 Dec. 1841.
35. Reported in The *Gazette*, 14 Sep. 1841.
36. Lord Stanley to Light, 29 Nov. 1841, referred to in Light to Stanley, 4, 6 Jan. 1842.
37. See proceedings of Meeting of Planters reported The *Gazette*, Thursday, 2 Dec. 1841.
38. Editorial comment, The *Gazette*, Thursday, 2 Dec. 1841.
39. Proceedings of Meeting, The *Gazette*, Tuesday, 14 Dec. 1841.
40. Published in The *Gazette*, Tuesday, 14 Dec. 1841.
41. Light to Stanley, 4, 6 Jan. 1842.
42. J.A. Allen to H.E.F. Young, 30 Dec. 1841.
43. Milliroux, 53.
44. Light to Stanley, 9, 13 Jan. 1842.
45. A number of planters had not adopted the New Rules, while others

amended them to remove the offending clause and still offered even greater incentives. The results were the same; the labourers refused to work because of distrust.

46. Light to Stanley, 33, 2 Feb. 1842.
47. B. Premium. *Eight Years in British Guiana, 1840 - 1848* (London : 1850), p. 100.
48. Milliroux, 23.
49. The Governor noted that '...it is difficult to persuade them that the rules were not a prelude to greater encroachments on their liberty. Every variety of interpretation has been put on them, according to the proportionate intelligence of the parties, the least enlightened ascribing to them a return to slavery'. Light to Stanley, 37, 5 Feb. 1842.
50. H.E.F. Young to George Bagot, 5 Jan. 1842; also Light to Stanley, 4, 6, 9, 13 Jan. 1842 and 4, 6, 9, 13 Jan. 1842.
51. Lockhart Nurse to H.E.F. Young, 6 Jan. 1842.
52. Henry Young to Captain Coleman, 3 Jan. 1842.
53. Light to Stanley, 4, 6 Jan. 1842.
54. A. Grant and C. Flemming to George Bagot, 5 Jan. 1842.
55. Light to Stanley, 31, 2 Feb. 1842 and S.M., W.H. Wolsely to Bagot, 5 Jan. 1842.
56. *Ibid.*, 33, 2 Feb. 1842.
57. *Ibid.*
58. Governor's Minute to Attorney General H. Glouster and Solicitor General, W. Furlonge, 2 Jan. 1842, contained in Light and Stanley, 14, 6 Jan. 1842.
59. Glouster and Furlonge to Governor Light, 3 Jan. 1842, contained in 4, 6 Jan. 1842.
60. Light to Stanley, 4, 6 Jan. 1842.
61. J.O. Lockhart Nurse to George Bagot, 6 Jan. 1842; Wolsely to Young, 6 Jan. 1842 and Governor's Orders issued on 6 Jan. 1842.
62. Light to Stanley, 23, 26 Jan. 1842;.31, 2 Feb. and 33, 5 Feb. 1842.
63. *Ibid.*, 25, 26 Jan. 1842.
64. Young to Bagot, 5 Jan. 1842, also Light to Stanley, 37, 5 Feb. 1842.
65. Young to Peter Rose, 3 Jan. 1842.
66. Light to Stanley, 4, 6 Jan. 1842.
67. Young to Peter Rose, 3 Jan. 1842.
68. Premium, 115.
69. *Ibid.*, pp. 90-100.
70. *Ibid.*, pp. 116 and 99.
71. Light to Stanley, 37, 5 Feb. 1842.
72. *Ibid.*

73. Young to Bagot, 5 Jan. 1842.
74. Premium, 96.
75. Labourers of Pln. Walton Hall to Stipendiary Magistrate in pp., Vol. 13, 1842. No. 479, pp. 656-657.
76. Light to Stanley, 9, 13 Jan. 1842.
77. Premium, 114.
78. Light to Stanley, 9, 13 Jan. 1848.
79. A.R.F. Webber, *Centenary History and Handbook of British Guiana* (Georgetown, 1931), p. 210.
80. Premium, p. 114.
81. Light to Stanley., 14, 6 Jan. 1842.
82. Premium, p. 115.
83. C.O. 111/232, Governor Henry Light to Earl Grey (received on 6 Aug. 1846); C.O. 111/224, Light to Grey, 29 Jun. 1846; C.O. 111/237; Light to Grey (received on 25 Jan. 1847) and "Resolutions of House of Commons Committee on The East India Colonies" (P.P., 1842, XIII).
84. M.C.P., Wednesday, 19 Jun. 1850.
85. John Scoble, *Hill Coolies: A Brief Exposure of the deplorable conditions of the Hill Coolies in British Guiana and Mauritius* (London: 1848). See also The *Royal Gazette*, Tuesday, 9 Nov. 1841, and Saturday, 20 Jul. 1844; *The Colonist*, Friday, 1 Dec. 1844.
86. Light to Russell, 125, 30 Sep. 1841.
87. Light to Glenelg,. 58, 21 Mar. 1839.
88. M.C.P., 18 Jun. 1839.
89. *Ibid*., see also Light to Normanby, 195, 26 Jun. 1839.
90. C.O. 112/27, Normanby to Light,. 70, 15 Aug. 1839.
91. C.O. 112/21, Russell to Light,. 56, 15 Feb. 1840.
92. See Hill to Aberdeen, No. 12, 20 Mar. 1834 and Spring Rice to Hill, No. 26, 2 Nov. 1834, cited in K.O. Lawrence. "The Evolution of Long Term Contracts in Trinidad and British Guiana", *Jamaican Historical Review*, 5, 1 (1965), p. 9
93. "Resolutions of House of Commons Committee". (P.P., 1842, XIII).
94. Earl Grey, *The Colonial Policy of Lord John Russell* (London: 1852) pp. 5 - 9.
95. C.O. 112/249, Grey to Light, 324, 10 Apr. 1848.
96. Grey, *The Colonial Policy...*, p. 51.
97. C.O. 111/249, Light to Grey,. 25, 18 Jan. 1848.
98. For a complete analysis of the pains in British Guiana, read "Observations on Effects of Tax Ordinance Dec. 1847. Monetary Affairs in Colony 1846-1848". Robert R. Craig to Light, 1 Jan. 1848, enclosed in C.O. 111/249, Light to Grey, 18 Jan. 1848.

99. C.O. 111/289, Barkly to Pakington, 21, Apr. 1852.
100. Light to Grey, 223, 31 Dec. 1847.
101. The *Guiana Times*, Monday, 27 Sep. 1847. Among those who served on the Committee were Messrs. P. Rose, J. Croal, A. Mc Rae, C. Sampson and P. Watson.
102. The *Guiana Times*, Friday, 15 Oct. 1847.
103. Resolutions of House of Commons Committee.
104. *Ibid.*, see also The *Guiana Times*, 18 Oct. 1847.
105. P.P. 1847-8, 23, Pt. 3 (361), 459.
106. M.C.P., Wednesday, 22 Dec. 1847; William Walker to Stipendiary Magistrates, Friday, 24 Dec. 1847, and C.O. 111/249, Light to Grey, 224, 3 Dec., 1848.
107. See C.O. 111/236, Light to Grey, 192, 18 Sep. 1846 for "Report on Disturbances in Leguan, Essequibo, 1846".
108. Reprints of the *Morning Journal* and The *Times*, 18 Oct. 1847, in the *Guiana Times*, Monday, 29 Nov. 1847.
109. C.O. 111/236 Light to Grey, 192, 18 Sep. 1846.
110. M.C.C. , Monday, 7 Jun. 1841 for speech by Government Secretary, Mr William Walker. See also Light to Glenelg, 78, May 1839.
111. C.O. 111/234, "Report of Committee appointed to investigate Petition - Tax Ordinance of 1846"; M.C.P. 29 Jun. 1847.
112. Editorial Comment, The *Guiana Times*, Monday, 18 Oct. 1847.
113. "Planters Memorandum" C.O. 111/249, Light to Grey, 25, 14 Feb. 1848.
114. C.O. 111/249, Light to Grey, 25, 14 Feb. 1848.
115. C.O. 111/234, "Report of Committee appointed to investigate Petition - Tax Ordinance".
116. This had become obvious as early as 1839 to the Creoles who complained that the immigrants had "come bring wages to nothing". The *Royal Gazette*, Tuesday, 5 Feb. 1839.
117. C.O. 111/234, Light to Grey, 192, 18 Sep. 1846.
118. It was clear therefore that the labourers were in no mood to countenance any reduction of their wages. They chanted "Massa we can't live on three bits". Further, the plantocracy had the experiences of their Trinidadian and Jamaican counterparts. Governor Light had his warning from Stipendiary Magistrate Ross which he chose to ignore, claiming he saw "no reason to apprehend that the reduction of wages which would seem inevitable is likely to be followed by acts of violence or a general strike". They all knew what to expect and yet they sought to effect such a reduction. The *Guiana Times*, Monday, 3 Jan. 1848. C.O. 111/237, "Critique of Outlines on a Scheme for Rural Polity" (Received at the Colonial Office on 25 Jan. 1847).

119. C.O. 111/249, Light to Grey, 31 Jan. 1848.
120. On 16 Mar. 1848, one labourer named Daniel, was shot and killed, while another, Abraham Innis, was wounded, both by Joseph Corria, a Portuguese, who owned several shops in and around Sisters Village on the West Bank of the Berbice River.
121. "Planters Petition", C.O. 111/249, Light to Grey, 25, 1 Feb. 1848.
122. The *Guiana Times*, Wednesday, 2 Feb. 1848.
123. *Ibid.*, Wednesday 19, and Friday, 21 Jan. 1848.
124. *Ibid.*
125. C.O. 111/249, Light to Grey, 18 Jan. 1848.
126. C.O. 111/249, Light to Grey, 82, 18 Feb. 1848. Also Letter by "Verax", The *Guiana Times*, 8, and 13 Mar. 1848.
127. Light to Grey, 32, 18 Jan. 1848.
128. P.P. 1847-48, 23 Pt 2 (206), p. 7.
129. Letter by "A Canje Planter", 18 Jan. 1848. The *Guiana Times*, Friday, 21 Jan. 1848.
130. Letter by "Forbes", The *Guiana Times*, Monday, 27 Mar. 1848.
131. P.P. 1847-48, 23 Pt 2 (184), p. 75.
132. *Ibid.*, 23 Pt 2 (206), p. 7.
133. C.O. 111/249, Light to Grey, 18 Jan. 1848.
134. *Ibid.*
135. C.O. 111/249, "The Proclamation", 30 Mar. 1848.
136. The *Royal Gazette*, Tuesday, 4 Mar. 1848.
137. *Ibid.*
138. The *Guiana Times*, Monday, 30 Mar. 1848.
139. C.O. 111/249, Planters Petition, 17 Jan. 1848.
140. M.G. Smith, "Social Structure in the British Caribbean About 1820", *Social and Economic Studies 1*, No. 4 (Aug. 1953).
141. Dwarka Nath, *A History of Indians in British Guiana* (London: 1958), p. 219.
142. Alan H. Adamson, *Sugar Without Slaves* (New Haven: 1972), p. 37. These figures represent the number of persons living in the villages at the particular times specified.
143. C.O. 111/234, Report - Tax Ordinance 1846. M.C.P., 29 Jun. 1846. See also The *Royal Gazette*, Thursday, 27 May 1847.
144. C.O. 111/254, Report of Stipendiary Magistrate Edward Carbery, 30 Mar. 1848.
145. C.O. 111/252, "1848 Riots in Berbice". Reports to William Walker, Government Secretary, 29 Mar. 1848.
146. M.C.C., 26 Apr. 1848. The *Guiana Times*, Friday, 28 Apr. 1848.
147. *Ibid.*

148. C.O. 111/254 Stipendiary Magistrates' Report, 30 Mar. 1848. See also The *Guiana Times*, Friday, 23 Jun. 1848.
149. P.P. 1847-48 (749), 235.
150. *Ibid.*, 46 (749), 235.
151. The *Guiana Times*, Wednesday, 15 Mar. 1848. See also C.O. 111/249, Light to Grey, 32, 18 Feb. 1848.
152. C.O. 111/249, Light to Grey, 32, 18 Jan. 1848.
153. *Ibid.* See also letter by "Verax", The *Guiana Times*, Monday, 13 Mar. 1848.
154. The *Guiana Times*, Wednesday, 15 Mar. 1848.
155. C.O. 111/254, Report of Stipendiary Magistrate Edward Carbery, 30 Mar. 1848.
156. Letter by "A Canje Planter", The *Guiana Times*, Friday, 21 Jan. 1848.
157. *Freeman's Sentinel* and *Emery's Journal* were the most articulate.
158. Among the more notable figures were John Emery, Edwin Wallbridge and J.M. Vries.
159. The London Missionary Society was in the forefront and its local representatives were very often very unpopular among the plantocracy.
160. C.O. 111/249, Light to Grey, 18 Jan. 1848.
161. See Letter by Rev. Francis Forbes, Pastor of St. Luke, The *Guiana Times*, Monday, 3 Apr. 1848.
162. *Ibid.*
163. Earl Grey, *The Colonial Policy,* p. 146.
164. The *Guiana Times*, Monday, 31 Jan. 1848.
165. The *Guiana Times*, Wednesday, 5 Apr. 1848. Reprint of Sermon preached by Pastor of St. Luke's parish. See also C.O. 111/249, Light to Grey, 18 Jan. 1848.

APPENDIX 'A'

Rules And Regulations For The Employment Of Labourers On Plantation... West Coast, Demerary, From And After 1st Jan., 1842.

1. Every field labourer is expected to turn out at 7 o'clock; and any labourer not present at the work by 8 o' clock, without good cause to the satisfaction of the Manager, shall be deemed absent without leave, and should any labour be performed by such party, it will not be paid for; and every labourer employed in the manufacture of sugar will be at work at 5 o' clock; and any person who shall not be at the buildings by 6 o'clock, shall forfeit half a day's wages.

2. No labourer shall be paid for less than an agreed daily task, except in cases of sickness or other valid cause to the satisfaction of the Manager.

3. Nothing in the shape of allowances or gratuities will hereafter be given.

4. No labourer, not employed by the Estate, shall be allowed or permitted to occupy apartments thereon, without a special agreement with the Manager.

5. Any Labourer refusing, or not performing the work as ordered, will not be paid for the performance of any other description of work, and shall be considered as absent without leave.

6. For the due and faithful performance of each and every Field Task hereunder mentioned, the sum of 4 bitts or 32 cents will be paid in cash, on demand, except when canes have been burned, when the sum of 3 bitts, or 24 cents, will be paid per task for cutting canes, or relieving such land.

7. Any labourer performing more than one Task will be paid at the same rate as the amount fixed by Regulation No. 6, for any number of Tasks.

8. A Roster or List of the labourers will be kept in the Boiling House, by which all parties may ascertain their turn for Building duty.

9. Any labourer absenting himself or herself from work without leave or sufficient cause, will be required to pay 2 bitts or 16 cents for every such absent day.

10. The labourers are required to furnish themselves with all tools.

11. No Plantains or other produce will be sold to the labourers or others on this Estate, below the market price.

12. No person whomsoever shall be permitted, without special leave in writing from the Manager, to hunt, shoot, fish, cut grass, or to pick fruit on this estate.

13. Labourers employed on this Estate will not have any provision grounds allowed to them; if they choose to plant provisions, it must be only on sufferance, and at their own risk; and if they leave the Estate, or the Manager discharges them, any provisions they may have growing become the property of the Estate.

14. Every labourer who does not intend to submit to these Rules, is required to leave the Estate, on or before the 1st Jan. 1842, and every labourer who continues to live upon the Estate after that date, is understood thereby to signify that he agrees to the Rules.

8: The African-Guyanese Demographic Transition: An Analysis of Growth Trends, 1838-1988

by
Carl A. Braithwaite

Elections, public opinion polls, referenda and other exercises in political arithmetic invariably focus attention on demographic data to invigorate and otherwise elucidate the results. Such information concerning racial and ethnic composition, age and sex-ratios, their geographic distribution, fertility and mortality patterns, economic performance, social mobility and migration patterns are important statistics for pollsters, political analysts and party campaign managers. These data facilitate prediction of balloting clusters and correlations or variance between principal components of the population.

On the eve of full Emancipation, the sizeable African component about to be liberated was obvious cause for concern, not only among the political, economic and administrative interests, but also among the Amerindians of the Colony who had featured in the pre-Emancipation policing of Africans.

In the post-Emancipation era, political auditing along racial lines inevitably focused on the Africans, Mixed or Coloured and the East Indian components. Since 1911, the racial balance of the Guyana population has shifted towards a preponderance of Indians over Africans, culminating in a 20 per cent difference in the proportion of the total accruing to the two principal ethnic sub-groups.

Whether or not these actual statistics are known to the masses of African- and Indian-Guyanese enjoying universal adult suffrage since 1953 is academic. What is remarkable, and consequently the subject of myriad interpretations and polemics, is that, de-

A street scene showing social stratification and demographic diversity in a town

spite the relative decline in the proportion of Africans vis-a-vis Indians, the former have managed to realise social aspirations of self-determination, enfranchisement and political ascendancy.

This essay attempts neither analysis of the Guyanese political arithmetic nor critique of socio-political postures taken by various writers on the demographic factor in Guyanese politics. However, it attempts a rationalisation of some of the remarkable phases in the social demography of the African population over the period 1838-1988. Statistics are used in this essay to illustrate trends in the African demographic transition, some of which have been accounted for by socio-economic and political factors, whereas others remain unexplained or as errors in accounting.

The essay first identifies the principal problems of accuracy in enumerating the African population, particularly during the nineteenth century. Also, a brief description is offered of the enumeration difficulties regarding the mixed sub-group, to a large extent biologically connected to the African sub-group and, for part of the period under consideration, indistinguishable from it. The main body of the essay comprises a five-phase analysis of the factors affecting the growth of the African population. The five phases identified are: The African Village Movement; Immigration and Indentureship; Changing Sex-Ratios, Declining Mortality and Flagging Fertility; Malaria Eradication, Urbanisation and PhaseOne-Emigration; and, PhaseTwo-Emigration and Increasing Fertility.

Some degree of overlap between phases is soon apparent; for example, African immigration and indentureship began during phase one in the 1840s (Laurence, 1958), and the process of rural-urban migration began to develop momentum after the collapse of the early village movement in the 1850s. Another explanatory note concerns inclusion of the first-phase - The African Village Movement. Whereas there is no evidence to indicate that this phase was in effect one of noticeable growth in numbers of the African population, its significance lies in the spatial dimension; between the years 1842 and 1858, some 74 per cent of the former slaves moved off the plantations and established village communities and other forms of social organisation hitherto sanctioned. These spatial and cultural expressions of self-determination would have been a measure of social cohesion to these people which had all the psychological prerequisites for population growth. However, high infant mortality has been recorded in African villages during this period (Farley, 1964). Adamson (1970) refers to the 'demographic stagnancy' of the African villages of the nineteenth century.

Slave registration was officially enforced after 1807, but clandestine trading in slaves and deliberate attempts to hide slave mortality rates led to gross miscounting. Also, infant mortality and fertility statistics were not required for the audit of the 'stock of slaves', hence deaths of infants below 3 years were not reported and 'births' comprised all those 3 years and under at each enumeration. Sporadic and haphazard attempts at enumerating the African population in the pre-Emancipation years revealed accounts of 34,700 (1782), 101,712 (1817), 88,824 (1832) and 85,000 (1834). For the entire colony of British Guiana in 1838, the figure was 96,734.

There were several reasons why assessment of the African subgroup prior to the 1871 census of British Guiana had a high probability of inaccuracy. Among the reasons cited by Braithwaite (1979) was the fact that official registering of vital statistics (concerning Africans) only commenced in 1869 with the passing of the Registration of Births and Deaths Ordinance in 1868. Other reasons include inconsistency in classification of race at the various censuses, inconsistency of census and vital statistical records, and inept recording of migration in the mid-nineteenth century. According to Roberts (1957), 'except for indentured immigration, the British Government never took steps, as in the case of vital registration, to have a satisfactory system of recording migration adopted in the colonies'. This omission resulted in the 'unexplained loss' (Mandle, 1974) of numbers of Africans and others in the latter half of the nineteenth century. Also, the Mixed category, comprising children born to parents of different racial groups, posed problems because of what Roberts (1948) referred to as 'progressive miscegenation' in the Colony.

Beginning with the free Coloured sub-group comprising the offspring of concubinage involving African women and White men, the racial mix has become more complex with immigration of other Whites, e.g. Portuguese, as well as Chinese, Hindus, Madrasi and West Indian Creoles. The dire shortage of Indian females in the early stages of indentureship inevitably resulted in some miscegenation between these juxtaposed masses. Also, with increasing rural-urban movement of Africans, predominantly females, miscegenation with some Portuguese and Chinese took place. In the interior areas, African runaways, loggers and pork-knockers soon intermingled with Amerindians. The result is that today the Mixed group comprises several combinations and various permutations involving Africans, although the strain is not always discernible or acknowledged.

It is commonplace to find children with mixed parentage identifying themselves with the race of one particular parent. Sometimes the offspring of a mixed and racially (pure) parent may appear to resemble one of the grandparents, with no visible trace of the other race. These biological complexities have continued to bedevil enumerators since, in some cases, it is difficult to ascertain the true race of a respondent. Hence, since the inclusion of this category in the population censuses in Guyana, noticeable changes have taken place within the African sub-category. This has elicited the comment that the Mixed group grew at the expense of the African (Mandle, *op. cit*). Table 5 shows the recorded figures for the African population between 1831 and 1891.

The African Village Movement phase in the two decades immediately following Emancipation was a demographic process within the struggle for African self-determination and economic independence. The post-Emancipation movement into proprietary and communal villages had its roots in the system of slavery, wherein the sustained antagonism towards the plantocracy and the social conditions on the British Guiana sugar plantations had induced sporadic revolts and a steady trickle of runaway slaves who had established maroon settlements in the hinterland. However, the mass shift of the African population off the plantations in the post-slavery epoch was a reflection of the ensuing tensions between planters and ex-slaves with regard to wage negotiations. According to Rodney (1981:32), "planters were bitterly opposed to the untrammeled operation of free wage labour, while the former slaves were equally resistant to that aspect of the free labour system that demanded total alienation of the workers from land ownership".

In demographic terms, these postures ensured a significant exodus of ex-slaves from the plantations. Mandle (1974:19) notes that in 1834, out of a total population of 98,000, some 84,915 comprised the plantation population and only 13,015 the non-plantation figure. However, by 1851, the total non-plantation population reached 88,320 as compared with 39,375 persons still remaining on the plantations. The total population living in villages formed since Emancipation also trebled during the period 1842 to 1854. Table 6 shows that between November 1842 and June 1854 the number of Africans living in villages increased from 15,906 to 49,402.

The significance of this shift in population off the estates increases when other demographic features are examined. Adamson (1972) notes that entire families moved off the plantations, thereby disrupting a range of domestic, field and factory operations essential to the running of the estates.

Also, this period was one of high mortality among Africans. With fertility during slavery never having been very high, this extremely high mortality among both the local-born and immigrant population raised real fears of the decline in the Creole population during the 1850s. Between 1841 and 1851, over 43,300 immigrants entered the Colony, but the population increased by only 29,500 at the end of the decennium. According to Rodway (1887), "in 1847/48 there died an average of 1,639 in each year out of an estimated population of 24,000 immigrants". Up to 1861 there was an excess of 37,375 deaths over births, or 26 per cent in 20 years. Adamson suggests that had it not been for immigration, the colony would have soon been depopulated. And Roberts (1948) indicates that these deaths were occurring among the newly arrived population. Yellow fever, cholera, and other diseases were identified as the principal causes of death. With the deplorable health conditions in the early African villages, worsened by the almost permanent waterlogged conditions, it is no surprise that infant mortality was high.

However, there being no registration of births and deaths before 1871, no accurate data are available concerning the effect of this morbidity pattern on the African Village Movement. Indeed, despite economic hardships occasioned by the strikes in 1842 and again in 1848, the moving off the estates continued to rise. Also, the number of inhabitants of villages increased significantly between 1842 and 1858. Victoria Village increased from 827 to 2,370, Buxton from 881 to 2,107, Plaisance from 131 to 1,372 and Queenstown from 148 to 877 (Cruickshank, 1921). Eventually, by the late 1850s, the planters managed to regain hegemony of the labour force by a number of measures, including the previously sanctioned forced African immigration to offset losses being incurred. Other measures included:

- Inhibition of the African Village economy;
- Radical reconstruction of the plantation labour force; and,
- Massive injection of public capital into the sugar sector (Adamson, 1970).

These tactics eventually led to the demise of the Village Movement. Gradually, Africans left the villages for the towns and some sought jobs on the plantations. Others drifted to the interior, establishing squatter communities and working in the timber and prospecting fields.

The 'Immigration and Indenture' phase in the demographic history of British Guiana is perhaps the most important in terms of ethnography. It was marked by the immigration of peoples from more than ten countries of Asia, Africa, Europe and the Americas. These persons were differentiated in terms of race, caste, religion and language, as well as their status at the time of entry. Even among the African immigrants there were distinctions based on ethnicity (Wood, 1978) and status (Laurence, 1971). Laurence (p.14) describes how the treatment meted out to African immigrants differed markedly from that reserved for Liberated Africans. West Indians comprised a third category of non-Asia immigrants, thus making three separate categories of predominantly Black immigrants to add to the local-born (Creole) and other Africans already in the colony.

Before further examination of the dynamics within the African demographic mix, it is important to note the composition of the other immigrants to British Guiana in the latter half of the nineteenth century. In the decennium 1831-1841, a total of 9,018 immigrants entered the Colony, including 429 Madeirans (henceforth referred to as Portuguese) and 406 East Indians, who were labelled either Madrasi or Calcuttan. By the next decade, the number of immigrants had increased to 43,314, with the non-African component still predominantly Portuguese and East Indians. This census (1851) recorded the early signs of the change in the composition of the total population. Thus, after only 20 years, the Creole component had shrunk from 96 per cent (including Coloureds and Free Africans) in 1831 to 62.1 per cent (local-born Creoles) in 1851. Portuguese and East Indians now comprised 5.8 per cent and 5.6 per cent, respectively, Africans made up 10.4 per cent, West Indians 6.8 per cent and others (including Amerindians, seamen and the military) 6 per cent. Europeans (other than Portuguese) made up the remaining 1.5 per cent.

Subsequent censuses recorded significant numbers of Chinese immigrants after 1852, mostly from Canton. These totalled 3,283 (1861), 9,343 (1871), and 903 (1881). The result of these additions of Asians, Africans, West Indians and Europeans (the Portuguese immigrants came primarily from Madeira and the Canary Islands) was the peculiar vitality which still characterises the population of Guyana. However, in the first decennium after Emancipation, the Colony's population showed a slight reduction, despite the immigration statistics quoted above. The triple attack of yellow fever, small-pox and cholera outbreaks between 1851 and 1857, along with the ever prevalent malaria hazard, was largely responsible for mid-nineteenth century stagnation of the local-born population, as well as decimation of incoming indentured servants, including Africans.

African immigration to the West Indies and British Guiana began early in the 1840s, despite British efforts to avoid continuance of the enslavement of Africans by European colonists. Since Spain and Portugal still indulged in slave-trading, this was always difficult to enforce in British New World colonies.

Emigration of Africans to the British West Indies was officially supported during the lull in Indian immigration up to 1845 (Roberts, 1954). Hence, to make up for the loss of Indian immigrants who were being decimated by yellow fever and malaria, African immigrants were allowed into British Guiana in sizeable numbers (*Ibid*). Part of the strategy seemed to be to find permanent residence for Africans liberated from British ships engaged in illicit trading in African slaves and who were being held at St. Helena and Sierra Leone at the British administrative headquarters on the African coast. Slaves freed after the capture of enemy vessels in the New World also comprised the stock of liberated Africans who were sent to the British West Indies, including Guyana. Although there was supposed to be no coercion in obtaining immigrants for this new trans-Atlantic voyage, a degree of compulsion was soon instituted, as the colonies were depending heavily on this source of labour. (Roberts, 1954; Laurence, 1971).

However, history records a group of African immigrants who voluntarily came to the West Indies as contract workers. These peoples of the Kru (Kroo) tribe came largely to British Guiana between 1841 and 1856. Roberts (1954) and Wood (1978) estimate the Kru migration to British Guiana over the period to be between 500 and 1,000. A significant proportion returned to Africa at the end of their three-year indenture, but several stayed, some forming liaisons with Creole women. (Laurence, 1971: 15).

Roberts (1954) notes that this immigration of Africans continued after the resumption of Indian immigration in 1845 and the start of the Chinese in 1853. In this year, cessation of the Brazilian slave trade curtailed a large source of African immigrants. Cuba was another source of African immigrants which dried up after abolition of the Spanish trade to the USA. This meant that the main supply of African emigrants from Sierra Leone disappeared in 1866, bringing a curtailment in African immigration in the late 1860s. By this time, more than 39 per cent of the total number of African immigrants, approximately 13,970, had been working in British Guiana. (Roberts, 1954). Roberts claims that, given the small population in the Colony, African immigration contributed more to population growth in British Guiana than in Jamaica, although slightly less than in Trinidad. He calculates that between 1843 and 1867 some 6,792 Africans left Guyana. Laurence (1971) notes that some African immigrants established ethnically homogeneous villages rather than return to Africa. Some of these villages were established on the West Bank of Demerara, e.g. La Retraite, and also several in West Coast Berbice.

West Indian immigration began early in the post-Emancipation period. Inter-island movement of ex-slaves was widespread, as slaves sought to escape the hardships of survival in land-starved colonies. The drift to the larger British territories, e.g. Trinidad and Guyana, was inevitable, since opportunities for squatting were enhanced. Laurence (p. 15) notes a continuous flow of West Indians, particularly Barbadians, into British Guiana, amounting to some 40,656 between 1835 and 1893. This Creole immigration was linked to the 'bounty system', but many West Indians refused contracts, preferring to remain in the Colony, especially if lands were made available. It is also significant that in 1891 the Mixed Creole race-group was the only category of immigrants in which females exceeded males - 2,664 to 2,388. Mixed Creoles comprised 14.2 per cent of the total population, with a preponderance of females (13,138) to males (10,839).

Despite these statistics for immigration, the total population of Guyana grew relatively slowly during the period 1861-1881, the heyday of immigration. The decennial increases between 1851 and 1891 were 19,983, 27,584, 68,695 and 26,242. The corresponding increases in the African population are difficult to ascertain but between 1861 and 1871, the total number of Africans increased from 17,608 to 20,926, which excludes local-born Africans, who were not differentiated from other local-born during the tricennium. Table 7 gives the breakdown of the total population according to country of origin over the period 1861-1881.

However, it should be stressed that no system for recording emigration was in place. Thus, despite a record of more than 60,000 (26 per cent) increase in the total number of immigrants entering British Guiana between 1871 and 1881, there is an 'unexplained loss' of some 10,000 persons during this decennium. Although there was the slowing down of the African and West Indian immigration, the time period corresponds with a period of high mortality in the Colony as well as significant unrecorded African emigration to Africa (Daly, 1966).

In Phase Three: 1891-1931 - Changing Sex-Ratios, Declining Mortality and Flagging Fertility - and by the last decennium of the nineteenth century, certain demographic features were being manifested in the Colony: Births had begun to surpass deaths, thereby adding to the population growth without immigration; there was a significant Mixed sub-group of the population, comprising more than 10 per cent of the total; and, whereas Africans had maintained their position as the single most numerous group, their percentage of the total population had dropped to 41 per cent, while that of the Indian group had risen to 37.9 per cent. The 1891 census also reveals a change in the sex ratio of the African population. Here females for the first time outnumbered males, despite the three decades of immigration which tended to have a preponderance of youthful males. This meant that females were more numerous in the local-born population, with a greater number of live births and survivors to adulthood.

Of tremendous significance was the sizeable increase in numbers of Africans in the towns of Georgetown and New Amsterdam. Here, as always, females outnumbered males. In the case of Georgetown, the difference in numbers between the sexes was 2,554. Between 1911 and 1931 females proceeded to outnumber males in the country as a whole and moreso in the urban areas. The number of females per 1,000 males in the Colony in the first three decades of the twentieth century was 1,084, 1,102 and 1,108 respectively, with the figures for the urban areas being even higher — 1,441, 1,399 and 1,335 respectively. Males tended to exceed females in the rural areas. Table 8 gives a race and gender breakdown for the years 1891 and 1911.

By 1911, the Indian population had completely outstripped the African population. There was no recording of this event since no census was taken in 1901, the decennial year between 1891 and 1911. What was remarkable was the fact that the African population increased by only 17,713 over these two decades, or at a rate of 885.6 per annum. In attempting to explain this, it should be stated that the death rate and life expectancy for the Colony had been fluctuating during the last quarter of the nineteenth century. There was, however, a definite drop in the death rate and an increase in length of life by 1910-12 with a more favourable situation for females.

The 1911 census records reveal that the absolute number of males declined for every race group except for Indians and Mixed over the 20-year period. However, in the case of females, the Africans show an increase, which is slight when compared with Indian females. Births and deaths for Africans over this period were 74,421 and 73,861 respectively or 41.8 and 41.0 per cent, a net natural increase of 0.8 per cent. By comparison, the national rate was slightly lower than that of the African, but that of the Indian was higher by about 2 per cent. Also, among the Africans the female population increased at a much better rate than that of the males over this period. (See Table 9).

Despite the preponderance of males over females among the Indians, this group alone accounted for the relatively marginal rate of natural increase over this period. The Africans, despite having the second largest numbers, and indeed with significantly more females than the Indian group, had a rate of increase of only 0.25 per cent over the period 1891 to 1921. This group, with a more equable male-female ratio, should have been expected to lead the Colony's net natural increase by race but, in fact, the overall population grew only by substantial increments of Asia immigrants. Moreover, as Table 9 shows, Indian birth rates surpassed those of the Africans early in the twentieth century and continued to outstrip them thereafter, with the latter showing a steady decline between 1891 and 1946. Thus, even though Indian indentureship was to end in 1921, this sub-group had already established itself as the future dominant group.

The flagging African birth rate raised questions about the fertility status of Africans vis-a-vis Indians. It was observed that the Indians had a higher proportion of females in the fertile age class, compared with Africans and the Mixed group. Roberts (1948: 213) notes that 'the demographic position of the Colony (British Guiana) in 1911 was one of heavy wastage occasioned by high mortality from birth through the childbearing age'. In short, the replacement level was low. These statistics, obtained by calculating the number of baby girls born per 1,000 females, give the gross reproduction rate (GRR). Roberts further notes that by 1921 the Net Reproductive Rate (NRR) had increased slightly to 1.05, due primarily to the striking increase in fertility recorded for the Indians. By the next decade, however, Roberts suggests that the Colony had entered a phase of population expansion, with NRR of 1.36 (See Table 10).

With the Africans already having the most favourable mortality position during the first quarter of the twentieth century, this improvement in the prospects of progeny implied future expansion of the sub-group. Unfortunately, the African population, although being the least affected by the sex imbalance, did not have a clustering of females in the most fertile age group. It has also been posited that lower birth rates among Africans were due to their greater urban concentration which meant greater exposure to cramped, unhealthy housing conditions.

Nevertheless, life expectancy for Africans increased by 12.5 years between 1911 and 1931, particularly after 1921. Much of this was due to a drop in mortality of children under five years of age, since the period 1910-1912 had seen one-quarter of the cohort of African births perishing by the age 1.2 years, significantly below that of Indians and the Mixed group. This high infant mortality rate of Africans has been linked to their poor economic status, urban concentration, as well as the deplorable drainage conditions in their villages, which were repeatedly inundated as nearby estates were drained and also by inundation from the sea.

In summing up this phase of African-Guyanese demographic history, it appears that urbanisation, which began with the collapse of the village movement, picked up significantly during this phase, with a larger number of female migrants who probably found jobs in the towns easier to get than their male counterparts. However, this shift to towns on the part of Africans may also have been due to attempts at escaping the scourges of cholera, yellow fever and malaria affecting the coastal and outlying areas and the easier access to medical facilities in the towns. These diseases had continued to ravage the incoming migrants to the Colony and accounted, especially in the case of the Indians, for a continuous increase in death rates over births up to 1921. The Africans, by comparison, showed a decline in mortality, despite their poor showing with regard to fertility. Roberts (p. 214) notes that from 1921 to 1931 with regard to the number of years lived by women in the child-bearing phase (i.e. 15 to 49 years), the Africans showed the greatest improvement (21 per cent) for the decade, compared with 19 per cent for Indians. Thus, like the Indians, the African sub-group appeared poised for real growth in the second quarter of the twentieth century.

However, despite all these potentially positive signs, at the end of the third decennium of the twentieth century the overall trend regarding the growth of the African population remained unchanged. For instance, despite showing a slightly more favourable potential, compared with Indians, of increasing their proportion of the total population over the years 1911 to 1931, by 1946 the census records indicate an even greater proportion of Indians relative to Africans. More importantly, over these fifteen years the African proportion of the total population dropped from 39.95 per cent in 1931 to 38.17 per cent in 1946. This coincided with an overall increase of 4.9 per cent from 1931 of the percentage of Africans in the urban areas of the Colony. Furthermore, by this, time the sex ratio for the Indian sub-group had evened out, which meant that thereafter the gap between the two races would tend to widen.

Reference was made above to high mortality rates, especially among infants, that had affected net natural increase in the Colony, particularly among the Africans and Indians living on the coast. Deaths from malaria began to feature in medical and administrative reports of the Colony from 1900. For instance, the Registrar General's Report for 1905-06 indicates that deaths from malaria for the entire population doubled between 1900 and 1905 (from 216 to 475) and in 1907-08 stood at 1,148, peaking at 2,066 in 1910-1911. According to Potter (1974: 339), the actual number of deaths of adults from the disease was small, although the debilitating effect on the affected communities was considerable. Moreover, the impact on children and infants was devastating, accounting for some 22.5 per cent of all deaths among the 0-5 age group in 1911. Sporadic, short-lived malaria epidemics continued throughout the first half of the twentieth century.

In Phase Four - 1946-1960 – 'Malaria Eradication, Urbanisation, Phase One Emigration' the Malaria Eradication Programme (MEP) which was spearheaded by George Giglioli in the 1940s has been identified as one of the principal factors responsible for significant increases in population in the immediate post-war period. However, Sukdeo (1973) contends that several demographic trends already occurring in the population, particularly among the Indians, guaranteed an increase in numbers "even if endemic malaria were still prevalent in Guyana" (p. 5). He disputes Newman's (1964) contention that malaria eradication was the principal single factor accounting for 40 per cent of the accelerated growth in the Guyanese population. He identifies four phases of population growth in Guyana, including a stabilising phase up to 1945, in which local-born individuals outnumbered immigrants and there was the balancing of sex ratios for the major race groups and declining mortality. These developments created the conditions for rapid population increase in the post-war phase of the demographic transition. Thus, one year before the MEP began, the entire population for the first time in over a 100 years attained a normal sex and age distribution which are preconditions for an increase in birth-rate and decline in the death rate (Sukdeo, p. 18).

Giglioli himself, in 1948, declared that malaria struck at the very root of the population's vitality by reducing fertility and causing a decline in birth rates (Mandle: 107). These conditions were evident in the African component during the two decennia prior to 1946, which coincide with the period of endemic malaria on the coast of Guyana. Also, increased fertility rates among Africans have been attributed to improved medical and public health care. Moreover, vital statistics for the years immediately following the MEP indicate that deaths per thousand declined from 16.2 in 1945-47 to 13.0 in 1950-52 and dropped to 9.8 in 1959-61. The age at which the life-table cohort was reduced by a quarter increased from 33.2 in 1945-47 to 44.0 in 1950-52 and to 54.6 in 1959-61. The probability of dying decreased for all age-groups and the general improvement in mortality in the Colony shows direct effects of improvements in public health care during this period.

Rapid rural-urban migration was another feature of the post-war era. Africans in Georgetown increased in number by some 20,000 between 1945 and 1960. This increasing urbanisation reflected the unbalanced development of the country, whereby the concentration of job opportunities, education facilities, health facilities, housing , and entertainment exerted a tremendous 'pull' on rural Africans in particular - the so-called 'Bright Lights Syndrome' (Dumont, 1974). This group, better educated than rural Indians, found jobs easier to get in the teaching profession and the Public Service. Table 11 gives a breakdown of the population according to ethnicity and location.

Within these urban areas the sex ratio among Africans still showed a preponderance of females. The 1946 census figures show 5,169 widows to 2,189 widowers among the Africans, evidence that women tend to outlive the men by more than 2 to 1. By 1960, the male/female ratio in Georgetown and New Amsterdam was 14,947 to 18,189 and 3,443 to 4,135, respectively. Moreover, the age at which African women got their first child dropped from 24-25 to 20, indicative of an increase in fertility. Table 12 shows an age-breakdown of the African population 10 years and over, by conjugal status. It has been stated by several writers (R.T. Smith, M.G. Smith, Jaywardena, Robinson, Matthews & Lee) that differences between African and Indian family organisation, conjugal behaviour, attitudes to marriage and assimilation of European mores regarding the size of families are responsible for the wide variations in fecundity between the two major race-groups. (See Table 13).

A third aspect of the early post-war demographic phase in Guyana was the emigration of large number of persons, predominantly African, to such places as Aruba, Curaçao, Panama and the United Kingdom. This first phase of the post-war emigration phenomenon saw Africans outnumbering East Indians (Sukdeo, 1972). Migrants from both urban and rural areas left the Colony in search of betterment. Some sought jobs in Panama, Aruba and Curacao, but the majority went to the United Kingdom, where they found jobs as nurses, bus conductors, janitors, etc.

At the height of this exodus, the British Government passed the *Commonwealth Immigration Act*, effective June 1962, which brought to a trickle this mass egress of the Guyanese population. In the months and weeks before this *Act* was enforced, many Africans in Guyana made desperate efforts to secure finance and relevant documents in a last scramble to 'beat the ban' on British immigration. Between 1956 and 1960 some 233,000 British West Indians were numbered among the immigrant labouring population in the United Kingdom. Of these there were some 14,000 Guyanese, mainly of African descent, with a significant proportion of females among these mostly youthful (20-40 years) emigrants. This movement also absorbed many technicians, craftsmen and other semi-skilled and skilled persons, as well as a large number of aspiring students, many of whom never returned (Sukdeo, *op. cit.*).

In Phase Five - 1966-1986, 'Phase-Two Emigration and Increasing Fertility' the Guyana censuses of 1946, 1960, 1970 and 1980 returned figures of 143,385 (39.9 per cent), 183,980 (34.4 per cent), 218.461 (31.2 per cent) and 231,330 (30.4 per cent) respectively for the African component. One estimate (1986) returned a total African population of 229,844 (30.3 per cent), which is lower than the census of 1980 and well below a 1982 projection which estimated a total population of 803,000, with Africans comprising 31 per cent of that total. Nevertheless, the trend continues to be one of below 2 per cent decennial increase in the African population. Indeed, between 1960 and 1970, despite an increase of some 34,480, the African proportion dropped by 3.2 per cent. Between 1970 and 1980, the African population grew by only 12,869, or almost one-third of the previous inter-censal increase. More significantly, the Guyana Regional Demographic Survey (1987) suggests a decline of 1,486 in the African population between 1980 and 1986.

These statistics indicate a familiar downward trend, even in a period when improvements in health, housing and nutrition were being vigorously enunciated as part of the post-Independence development strategy. Guyana's 1972-1976 Draft Development Plan was described as a plan to 'Feed, Clothe and House' the nation. Allocations for new medical facilities in rural and hinterland areas were important tenets in the programme. However, these inter-censal developments did not result in significant increases in the population. These relatively small demographic gains in the inter-censal periods are due primarily to the perpetual expatriation of Guyanese since the 1950s, which ceaselessly whittled away at the net natural increase of the population. And Africans, according to Sukdeo (1972: 10), have been the group with the highest proportion of emigrants, although Indian emigrants have (since 1969) comprised the largest group in absolute terms.

Indeed, during the two decennia since Independence, there has been a continuous flow of migrants (including Africans) to Canada and the United States, with small numbers emigrating to Caribbean islands. Statistics for migration over the period 1969 to

1974 indicate net emigration for every year, fluctuating between 6,339 (1969) and 2,483 (1971) and increasing again to 5,215 (1974) (*International Migration Report, 1969-1974*).

GUY REDEM's household survey collated data on external migration over the period 1980-1986. The data revealed a steady upward trend in migration with peaks in 1983 and 1986. The statistics also reveal a distinct preponderance of females among those emigrating, with the highest returned in 1983 and 1986. Significantly, in 1983, males in the 20-24 age-group (the most likely migrants over the period) outnumbered females by 25 per cent, whereas in 1986 females outnumbered male migrants by 33 per cent.

The survey results also reveal that recent migrants are found within every age group, indicating that the current trend is for families to migrate. However, the most populous group of migrants are those in the 15-19, 20-24 and 25-29 age groups, with 65 per cent between the ages 15-34. According to the survey, an estimated 31,808 persons have emigrated over the six years, 1982-1987 or an average of 5,300 per annum.

Without available statistics for a racial breakdown of migrants it is impossible to discuss the trend within the African sub-group. However, Sukdeo (1972) and Enloe (1972) have discussed possible implications - social, economic and political - of the continued exodus of the most dynamic group of the population, i.e. 15-49.

This second phase of post-war emigration can be broken into two broad sub-divisions: the 1962-68 phase, which continued with the period of political unrest and electoral reform before and after Independence; and the 1980-88 phase, which coincided with the international recession and the prolonged malaise and economic retardation in Guyana.

The International Migration Report covered the intervening period (1969-74) which, despite showing significant annual net emigration, was perhaps the least traumatic phase both economically and politically, over the two decennia immediately after Independence.

Significantly, it was during these comparatively tranquil years in the country's recent history that a migration policy concerning Africans seemed to have a brief consideration. During the early 1970s, it was claimed that suggestions were mooted concerning settling West Indians in Guyana.

Enloe (1972) suggests that this may have been seen as an attempt to redress the racial imbalance in the electorate. However, the numbers of West Indians willing to live in socialist Guyana at any time over the 1970s decade would not have been significant to change the demographic structure for another 80 or more years. In any case, the small groups of Jamaicans, St. Lucians and others who might have emigrated to Guyana were 'unlikely to take on the 'dirty work' of Guyana's development for the Guyanese' (Enloe, p. 10).

Public policy concerning immigration was articulated through an ongoing programme of remigration. Moreover, the 1980-81 Guyana Volume of the census of the Commonwealth Caribbean contains a section on Immigration (Vol. I, pp. 128-34) in which a detailed breakdown of the foreign-born population according to country of birth and year of immigration before 1970 and for each year following was given in Table Three (3.3).

Of the total West Indian foreign-born population in 1980, the highest number (752) was from St. Lucia, 528 from Barbados, 353 from Trinidad and Tobago with 286, 183 and 180 from St. Vincent, Grenada and Jamaica respectively. The Guyana Regional Demographic Survey (GUY REDEM (1987) returns indicate 30 per cent or some 2,000 Caribbean immigrants among the foreign-born residents.

Finally, it is essential to comment on the fertility patterns of Africans at the end of the period under study. A World Fertility Survey in 1974 elicited valuable information for the two major race groups in Guyana. A brief analysis of some principal components tested in the Guyana Fertility Survey of 1974 indicates that whereas the trend of more favourable fertility status of Indians vis-a-vis Africans continued, there were signs that women (of both races) born after 1950 tended to enter unions around the same time and to have almost equal knowledge of contraception. The data revealed that where differences did exist, these were attributed to place of residence, level of education and union status.

Thus, whereas in 1946 the Indian women, who were predominantly rural and comparatively less educated, tended to have significantly larger families and entered unions (married) at an early age (15-16), by 1975 non-Indian women (predominantly African) tended to display similar differences in fertility based on place of residence and level of education. For instance, there is little difference in the number of children born to African women in rural areas, compared with Indians, and more educated African and Indian women tend to have greater knowledge of contraception and fewer children. Also, African women who were married, better educated and lived in urban areas tended to have fewer children than their rural, less educated counterparts. African women involved in visiting and common-law unions, however, tended to have fewer children, although they aspired for larger numbers. Table 13 gives statistics on the number of children ever born over the period 1946-1986. (See also Singh, 1979).

GUY REDEM's recent estimates indicate a decline in fertility of Indians to a level on par with Africans and the Mixed group. Moreover, they seem to indicate that emigration has perhaps affected East Indians more than Africans, bringing down their fertility and altering the ratio between the two major components of the population. Furthermore, a noticeable trend is the increase in teenage pregnancies among Africans, particularly in urban areas. Although statistics are not available, social workers, women's groups and parent-teachers' associations are already expressing their concern about the problem. This development may well bring about further lessening of the gap in fertility between Africans and Indians and possibly accelerate growth in the African population. The graphs at figures 1 and 2 show the growth of the African population with respect to the total and the changing relationship of Africans vis-a-vis Indians in the Guyana population over the period 1838-1988.

The dominant characteristics of the African population in the post-Emancipation period are undoubtedly its migratory behaviour and, for most of the period, its low fecundity. Having been, to a large extent, forcibly transplanted from the motherland of Africa, these people seemed to express a restlessness and mobility that have been fuelled by compelling economic, social and political forces. First they moved off the plantations - scene of their bicentenary of enslavement; they were then obliged by cruel political, economic and environmental conditions to drift to the towns. However, in these urban centres the socio-economic order still relegated Africans to the lowest stratum of society, with limited scope for upward mobility. These conditions eventually forced African-Guyanese to look outward for economic salvation, as their African brothers had opted to return to Africa in the nineteenth century. Ironically, initial expatriate salvation was sought in the inner cities of the home of their former colonial masters.

More recently, pressures have catapulted migrants to North America and the Caribbean. Disenchantment, dissent and disharmony with the orientation and administration of the national economy have resulted in the exodus of large numbers of Africans (as well as others) from Guyana over the decade 1978-1988. And, as with all previous migrations, the majority of migrants tended to be between ages 20 and 40 years, with a large proportion of females. Although statistics are currently unavailable, it is reasonable to anticipate a significant diminution in the African population, if and when these data are compiled. For, in addition to entire families, a significant number of single women of child-bearing age are among those migrating to North America. This could reduce the potential for Africans to improve their demographic performance in the last decennium of the twentieth century.

Other demographic features of the African population over the

150 years are subsumed within this overall trend. In the absence of vital registration before 1871, there are no vital records to account for the preponderance of deaths over births among the Creole population. Only after the first 80 years of Emancipation did African birth rates surpass the death rates. Hence the African population for more than a century had been increasing only by successive increments of slaves and, after Emancipation, immigrants from Africa and the West Indies. Apart from such causes as the passive resistance of female slaves, who some claim practised abortion and infanticide, as well as the known age-sex imbalance in the African population up to the late nineteenth century, several other reasons for this negative NRR have been posited. Among these are late motherhood, unstable conjugal unions, urbanisation, religion and education (particularly of women).

High mortality rates in the first half of the nineteenth century also contributed to negative growth in the Creole population. Infant mortality was high, life expectancy up to 1881 was only 30 years, and there were the ever-present ravages of cholera, smallpox, malaria and yellow fever. The decline in mortality rates among Africans preceded the increase in fertility by several years so that, for a long time, the African population was stagnant and later stable, but showed very little growth. After the mid-twentieth century, improved public health and medical care coincided with a general improvement on mortality rates. Also, by this time, evenness in the African age-sex ratio, the lowering of the age of motherhood, and inversely, raising the period of time and the number of women in the child-bearing age-group, all combined to improve the fertility status of Africans in the latter half of the twentieth century. However, these improvements in the growth parameters are being undermined by the pull of international migration, a phenomenon which affects a relatively high proportion of Africans, including women in the 15-35 age-group.

It is apt to end this essay with a reference to the African population in the Caribbean. Peculiarity of terrain and plantation conditions, and to some extent ethnic mix, have given the African population in Guyana a distinctive demographic history. However, there have been similarities with other West Indian territories, e.g., African and Asian immigration, emigration to the United Kingdom and North America, rural-urban migration, influence of White religious values, and the recent upsurge of teenage pregnancies.

These similarities all suggest that a broad reference base exists for future research into common problems associated with African populations in the Caribbean.

References

Adamson, A.H. "Monoculture and Village Decay in British Guiana", *Journal of Social History* (Sep., 1970).

______________ .*Sugar without Slaves : The Political Economy of British Guiana, 1838-1902*, (New Haven : Yale University Press, 1972).

Braithwaite, C.A. "The Growth of the African Population in Guyana 1871 - 1970". (Unpublished Research Paper, Department of Geography, University of Guyana, 1979).

British Guiana : *Census Reports/Abstracts* 1831, 1841, 1851, 1861, 1871, 1881, 1891, 1911, 1921, 1931.

Cruickshank, J.G. "The Beginnings of Our Villages," *Timehri*, 24, VII, (Aug., 1921), pp. 65-76.

Daly, V.T. *A Short History of the Guyanese People*, (Georgetown, 1966).

Dumont, R. *The State of Urban Planning in Guyana*, (Georgetown, 1974).

Enloe, C. *Guyanese Political Response to Migration*, (Clark University, 1972).

Farley, R.E. "The Rise of Village Settlements in British Guiana," *Caribbean Quarterly*, No. 1 (Mar. 1964), pp. 52-61.

GUY REDEM *International Migration Report.* GUY REDEM Conference, Preliminary Results. Statistical Bureau, Georgetown, 1987.

Jayawardena, C. "Marital Stability in two Guianese Sugar Estate Communities", *Social and Economic Studies*, Vol. 9, No. 1 (1960).

Laurence, K.O. *Immigration into Trinidad and British Guiana 1834–1871* (Unpublished Ph.D. Dissertation, Cambridge University, 1958).

Mandle, J.R. *The Plantation Economy : Population and Economic Change in Guyana 1838-1960*, (Philadelphia : Temple University Press, 1973).

Matthews, L. & Lee, S.C. *Two Forms of Matricentrality : The Matrilineal Ashanti and the Matrifocal Guyanese*, (American Sociological Association, 1975).

Newman, P. *British Guiana : Problems of Cohesion in an Immigrant Society*, (London : Oxford University Press, 1964).

Population Census of the Commonwealth 1970, 1980, Guyana.

Potter, L.M. *Internal Migration and Resettlement of East Indians in British Guiana 1870-1920* (Unpublished Ph.D. Thesis, McGill University, 1975).

Roberts, G.M. "Some Observations on the Population of British Guiana", *Population Studies*, Vol. 2 (1948), 185- 18.

____________ "Immigration of Africans in the British Caribbean", *Population Studies*, Vol. 7(3), (1954) 235-62.

Roberts G.W. *The Population of Jamaica* (Cambridge University Press, 1957).

Robinson, P. "The Social Structure of Guyana" in, *Cooperative Republic of Guyana* (Georgetown, 1970).

Rodney, W. *History of the Guyanese Working People, 1881-1905* (Baltimore : Johns Hopkins University Press, 1981).

Rodway, J. "Ruin", *Timehri*, 16, Vol. XI (Jun.1887).

Singh, S. "Demographic Variables and the Recent Trend of Fertility in Guyana 1960-1971," *Population Studies*, Vol. 33(2) (1979), 295-334.

Smith, R.T. *The Negro Family in British Guiana.* (London : Routledge and Kegan Paul, 1956).

Sukdeo, F. *The Impact of Emigration on Manpower Resources in Guyana* (Georgetown, 1972).

____________ *Malaria Eradication and Population Growth in Guyana* (Georgetown, 1973).

West Indian Population Census, Part C, British Guiana 1946, 1960.

Wood, D. "Kru Migration to the West Indies" (Seminar Paper, University of London, 1978).

World Fertility Survey, Guyana 1975.

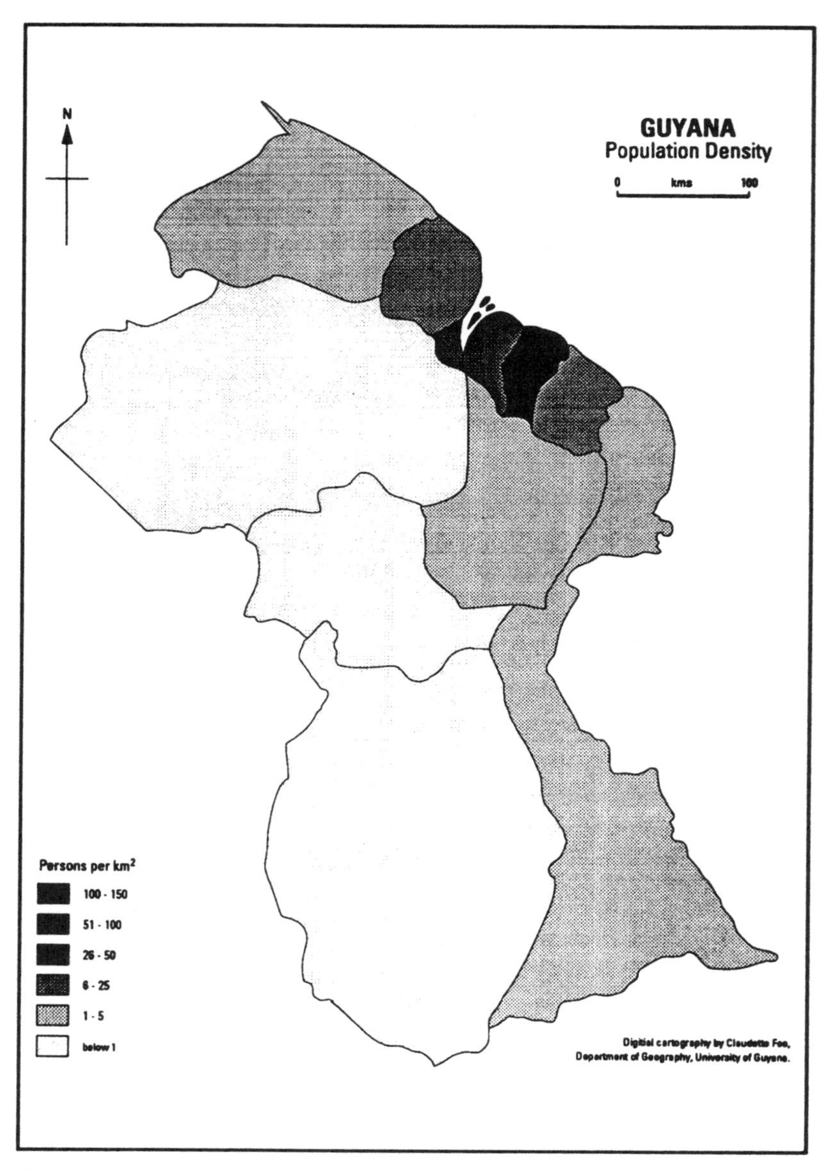

Map 5: Population Density Map of Guyana in the Late Twentieth Century.

Figures

Figure 1: Growth Of The African-Guyanese Population, 1841-1986

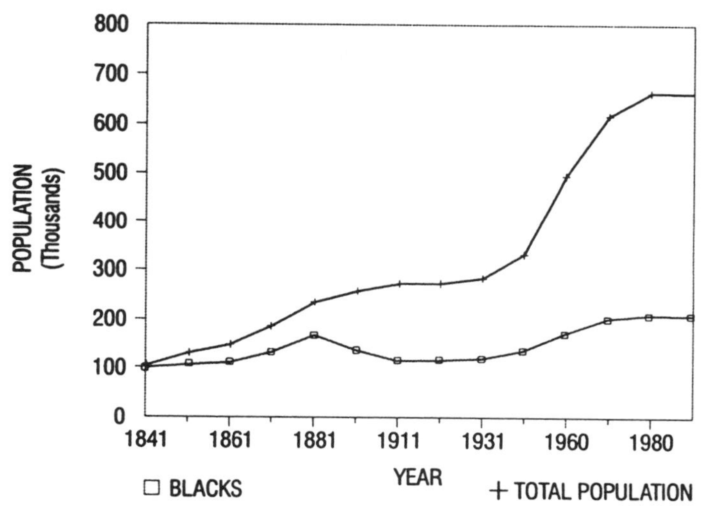

Figure 2: Africans and Indians as a Percentage of the Total Population, 1851-1980

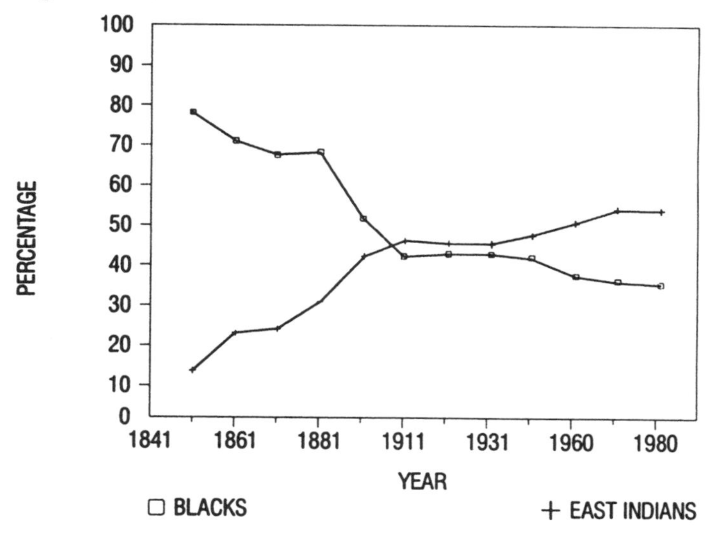

Tables

Table 5: Population of African-Guyanese, 1831-1891

Year	Local Born Africans	Free Africans & Coloured	West Indians	Africans or African	% Creole
1831	88,486	7,521	N.A.	N.A.	89.40
1841	N.A.	N.A. (5)	8,192	15,856	N.A.
1851	86,451 (2)	N.A. (5)	9,278	14,251	62.10
1861	N.A. (1)	N.A. (5)	8,309 (4)	9,299 (4)	60.10
1871	N.A. (1)	N.A. (5)	13,385 (4)	7,541 (4)	61.80
1881	N.A. (1)	N.A. (5)	18,318 (4)	5,077 (4)	59.20
1891	112,155	N.A. (5)	15,973 (3)	3,433	62.51

Notes

(1) Census records lumped all local-born - including those of Indian descent - thus making African enumeration impossible.
(2) Roberts (1948) p. 211-212 observes extremely high mortality among immigrants and local population between 1841 and 1851. See also Rodway, J. *History of British Guiana*, vol. 3 (Georgetown, 1894).
(3) Not included in 1891 Census figure; may therefore be a double count.
(4) Roberts (p. 211) estimates that up to about 1871 the high wastage of life among immigrants (69/1000 made hardly any natural increase possible. Secondly, he reckons that Africans and Portuguese, both immigrant and native, constituted a significant proportion of the unrecorded emigration, particularly after 1871.
(5) This category became superfluous after 1838. Also Coloured, Creole and later Mixed and Mixed Creole absorbed a significant proportion of this initial category.
(6) NA- Statistics not available.

Table 6: Population Living in Villages, 1842-1854

Month	Nov.	Dec.	Dec.	Dec.	Jun.-Dec.	Jun.-Dec.	Jun.-Dec.	Jun. - Dec.	
Year	1842	1844	1847	1848	1849	1850	1851	1853	1854
Village Pop.	15,906	18,511	29,000	44,443	40,038-41,303	42,755	46,368	47,265-48,991	49,402

Source: Adamson (1972), p. 37

Table 7: Population by Native Country and Geographical Distribution, 1861-1881

Areas	A	B	C	D	E	F	G	H	I	J	K	L	M
G/Town													
1861	19637	4168	2996	775	82	117	700	309	229	155	14	4	29194
1871	23608	7113	2960	652	139	118	417	371	905	253	19	7	36562
1881	30864	9723	2855	353	158	410	228	416	1112	492	30	8	46649
Demerara (1)													
1861	37997	2204	5025	343	28	72	4362	2360	8540	1247	5	12	62195
1871	46828	4000	3554	410	24	116	3455	1439	22366	3934	17	27	86250
1881	62037	5961	2952	379	23	156	2262	1549	34409	2470	41	29	112268
Esseq.													
1861	16743	1253	1099	179	19	31	1837	353	5775	661	7	2	27959
1871	20157	1240	785	149	22	18	1441	183	10073	1014	8	32	35122
1881	26013	1397	602	143	13	40	1069	249	15376	646	7	27	45582
N/Ams.													
1861	3640	328	296	106	7	21	102	9	35	33	1	1	4579
1871	4435	378	255	105	5	29	56	11	119	42	2	-	5437
1881	6316	657	247	91	9	49	61	20	488	175	3	8	8124
Berbice (2)													
1861	15844	356	443	99	10	57	2290	634	3837	533	1	15	24119
1871	18542	574	371	128	6	41	2172	531	6693	1052	-	20	30120
1881	24409	580	223	115	2	70	1457	618	10934	610	18	1	39037

A - Natives of British Guiana
B - West Indian Islands
C - Madeira, Azores & Cape Verde
D - Europe
E - North America
F - Places not mentioned
G - Immigrants from Africa
H - Immigrants from Madras.
I - Immigrants from Calcutta
J - Immigrants from China
K - Born at Sea
L - Not known
M - Grand Total

Notes:
(1) Demerara except Georgetown.
(2) Rest of Berbice

Source: British Guiana Census Abstract 1861,1871,1881.

Table 8: Population by Race and Gender, 1891-1911

Gender	Population	Africans	Indians	Mixed
Males				
1891	151,759	58,398	64,703	13,227
1911	155,717	55,139	75,027	13,417
Females				
1891	126,569	57,190	40,760	15,802
1911	142,324	60,347	53,490	16,834

Source: Census Reports 1891, 1911.

Table 9: Vital Rates (Births And Death) for Africans and Indians

Birth Rates		Period	Death Rates	
Africans	Indians	1891-1945	Africans	Indians
32.1	27.7	1891-1911	31.4	30.4
29.5	29.9	1911-1921	29.7	31.7
28.6	35.2	1921-1931	25.2	28.4
27.1	37.1	1931-1935	21.5	25.4
26.9	38.0	1935-1940	21.0	23.3
28.4	40.6	1941-1945	21.1	19.6

Source: Census of British Guiana, 1946

Table 10: Estimated Net Reproduction Rates and Probabilities of living to 30th Birthday (NRR/GRR)

Racial Group	1910-12		1920-22		1930-31		Per cent Increase in NRR	
	NRR	NRR/GRR	NRR	NRR/GRR	NRR	NRR/GRR	1910-1931	1921-1931
Indian	0.93	0.515	1.13	0.531	1.66	0.624	78.0	47.0
African	N.A.	N.A.	0.94))1.02	0.564)) 0.581	1.03))1.15	0.667)) 0.683	-	10.0))13
Mixed	N.A.	N.A.	1.30)	0.633	1.62	0.735	-	25.0)
All Races	0.91	0.508	1.05	0.564	1.36	0.666	49.0	30.0

Source: Roberts (1948), p. 213

Table 11: Geographical Distribution of the Population, 1891-1970

Year	Area				
	Georgetown	Demerara	Essequibo	N/Amsterdam	Berbice
African					
1831	10,984	35,279	29,465	2,230	19,049
1891	24,270	46,339	20,865	4,732	19,087
1946	50,432	45,334	16,907	5,958	27,754
1960	72,024	N.A.	16,194	7,578	N.A.
1970	83,860	62,914	N.A.	9,176	28,872
Indian					
1891	3,976	58,658	22,502	1,262	19,065
1946	14,547	70,825	19,671	1,694	56,697
1960	32,471	N.A.	29,212	3,476	N.A.
1970	41,333	92,695	N.A.	5,601	12,972

Notes:
(1) In 1831 Free Coloured and African are added to the Slave population for enumeration. In 1891, the separate Mixed category is not included in the enumeration of the African population.
(2) N.A. - Statistics not available.

Source: Census Reports 1891, 1946, 1960, 1970.

Table 12: Distribution of African and Indian Women ever in a Union by Current Age, Ethnic Origin and Union Status

Current Union Status And Ethnic Grouping	Number Of Women	Current Age						
		20	20-24	25-29	30-34	35-39	40-44	45+
All Types Of Union								
African	1,263	10	20	20	13	18	18	12
Indian	1,928	9	20	20	17	15	11	9
Married								
African	516	3	14	25	16	13	15	15
Indian	1,573	9	21	20	17	14	10	8
Common Law								
African	204	6	18	19	14	18	15	10
Indian	150	9	11	19	21	19	12	8
Visiting								
African	366	23	33	8		7	7	5
Indian	36	14	33	19	28	8	3	0
Single								
African	177	11	15	15	10	14	14	21
Indian	169	2	14	17	12	17	18	21

Source: Guyana Fertility Survey, 1975: Vol 1: Table 3.1.2

Table 13: Average Number of Children ever Born to Women ever in a Union, by Ethnic Origin and Age Group

Age Group	African		Indian	
	1946	1986	1946	1986
15 - 19	0.17	0.17	0.39	0.12
20 - 24	0.93	0.93	1.88	0.80
25 - 29	1.83	1.88	3.31	1.95
30 - 34	2.60	3.17	4.40	3.41
35 - 39	3.07	4.07	5.01	4.06
40 - 44	3.47	4.90	5.37	5.32
45 - 49	3.70	6.10	5.43	7.01

Ssource: West Indian Census, 1946: GUY REDEM, 1987

9 : African-Guyanese Political Disempowerment during the Nineteenth Century

by
Brian L. Moore

The political constitution of post-Emancipation Guyana made no pretence at seeking to disenfranchise the vast majority of ex-slaves. Although many of the latter had moved off the estates and acquired their own freehold properties, the qualifications for both the franchise and membership of the political institutions were deliberately fixed beyond the reach of most Africans.

In 1849, the franchise was granted to persons who owned at least three acres (valued at $96 per annum), or who leased six acres (valued at $192 per annum), of cultivated land in the country; or, in the towns, to those who owned property valued at $500, or leased same valued at $120, per annum. Alternatively, persons who paid taxes on an income of $600 per annum were also entitled to the vote.[1] Governor Henry Barkly was quite candid in noting that this franchise was intended, to prevent the ex-slaves from becoming a majority in the electorate.[2] Indeed, less than a third of the new voters in the rural areas qualified on the basis of the freehold qualifications and, until the 1890s, less than one per cent of the adult male population (mainly White) could vote.[3]

As regards membership of the political institutions, that too was denied the African majority. Under the old style Dutch *Constitution*, the electorate voted for members of the College of *Kiezers*, an electoral college whose members were responsible for nominating suitable candidates whenever vacancies arose in the colonial legislature, the Court of Policy. The sitting members of the legislature themselves made the final decision as to who would be selected to fill vacancies in that body. This convoluted system was originally designed to preserve a planter monopoly of the colonial seats but, after Emancipation, it became quite a useful mechanism for keeping Africans out of the legislature until the

Constitution was changed in the 1890s. Only one non-White person gained entry into the legislature during this period: Richard Haynes, a wealthy Coloured merchant and mayor of Georgetown during the early 1840s. He qualified as a 'planter' by purchasing an abandoned estate and was able to entice the more liberal Whites to back his nomination for a seat in 1850. But he was refused re-entry in 1855, and the nomination of 'undesirable' candidates was put beyond doubt in 1864 when the qualification for membership of the Court of Policy was by law made the ownership of 80 acres of land, of which at least half had to be cultivated.[4]

A third political institution made up the constitutional structure of nineteenth century Guyana. This was the College of Financial Representatives. The members of this body were, like the *Kiezers*, elected directly by the qualified voters, but were only required to sit with the members of the legislature in 'Combined Court' to determine the colonial budget. But the same landed qualifications as for the legislature were required for membership of both elected Colleges; and even the alternatives of leased property valued at $1,440 per annum, or earned income of $1,440 per annum, were way beyond the reach of all but a tiny minority of Africans and Coloureds after Emancipation.[5] All told, therefore, until the constitutional reforms of the 1890s, the African-Guyanese population of Guyana was effectively disempowered at the state level.

This reality thus made local government at village level all the more important as a battle ground. The extent to which the ex-slaves could exercise control over the political institutions in the villages was critical for establishing some measure of African political autonomy within the colonial state, and could provide them with the basis of corporate ethnic identity. On the other hand, if the merchant-planter interests were to reassert their unchallenged dominance within the colonial state, it was vital that any semblance of African political independence at the village level be subordinated and controlled by the colonial authorities. In this quest, they had the forces of nature on their side — in the form of the poor drainage of the coastlands where the largest African villages were established. As Guyana's coastline lies a few feet below sea level at high tide, an elaborate sea defence system is required. This involves dykes, dams, sluices and drainage canals.

In the middle and later decades of the nineteenth century, the drainage problem was made worse by the formation of shifting silt banks particularly along the East Coast of Demerara. In addition, two seasons per year of heavy tropical rainfall often meant that flooding of agricultural lands along the coast rendered necessary the acquisition of expensive steam draining engines to pump out the floodwaters. If the sugar plantations could barely afford these, it was even worse for the ex-slaves in the villages who were unable to obtain loans from the banks at reasonable rates of interest, or grants from the Government, to purchase such equipment. The drainage problem thus became an important matter around which the issue of the political autonomy of the villages was fought.

This issue was also influenced by the system of land tenure in some of the largest villages which the ex-slaves had purchased as joint-stock enterprises, e.g., Buxton, Plaisance, Victoria, etc. The joint ownership of land almost from the outset posed problems as each shareholder sought to establish claim to a specific portion of the estate. The tendency to allocate to each shareholder small plots of land in different sections of the village led to uneconomic parcels, made worse by further subdivisions among heirs. All this was done without recourse to law so that, in many instances, individual landholders never obtained legal titles for their plots; and even when they did, inheritance was complicated by the system of Roman-Dutch law which granted the widow and children each a specific but undivided share of the deceased's land. Further confusion was caused by the 'problem' of 'illegitimacy' and unregistered births within the African community which led to many property disputes among the villagers.[6]

This chaotic land tenure system and poor drainage not only undermined African ethnic cohesion and solidarity as villagers began to squabble among themselves, but rendered the villages the target of central Government intervention which ultimately destroyed any notion of village autonomy. The colonial authorities could in fact, with good reason, intervene in village affairs in order to deal with a clear health problem which flooded villages posed to the entire society and, perhaps, even with the support of some villagers themselves, to straighten out the legal problems relating to land ownership. But such intervention represented the thin edge of the wedge: for at stake was the critical issue of where political control of these substantial village communities would lie.

When, therefore, the villagers of Plaisance (of their own volition) sought Government help to put their affairs in order, it was clearly not their intention to hand over political control to the central Government. Instead, they demanded municipal powers which would vest them with the legal authority to take decisions affecting the whole community, to tax themselves, and to put in place the organizational framework which would enable them to request and receive financial assistance from the Government in the same way as the White-dominated Georgetown and New Amsterdam municipalities did. In 1850, a council of six commissioners was formed at Plaisance with the power to finance drainage and the public roads through local rates on village property, under Government supervision. But at the outset it was made clear that no financial grants for such public works would be forthcoming from the central Government; the villagers would have to meet those costs themselves.[7] This was to prove the basis on which the villagers would become financially overburdened and incapable of meeting those obligations and on which the central Government would intervene to take political control of the villages.

On the question of land tenure, the Government's initial intervention came at the invitation of the villagers of Buxton who sought to have that estate legally partitioned among the shareholders and proper titles bestowed to each. This was effected by a law of 1851 which was made extendable to other communal villages. Hereafter, individualization of land became one of the Government's principal policies as regards the villages. In 1852, the purchase of land by more than twenty persons was prohibited by law. This was reduced to ten persons in 1856, while at the same time the colonial legislature assumed the power to partition any estate owned by ten or more persons on the request of a single shareholder.[8]

Even more sinister, another law of 1856 made the first serious attempt to bring the political administration of villages under central Government supervision, although the element of 'choice' was given to the villagers. Partitioned villages could thus opt to be 'incorporated' by law under the authority of a district registrar appointed by the Government. Although there would be elected village commissioners and a salaried overseer, they would function under the district registrar. Furthermore, such villages were required to meet the full costs of public works, village partitioning, and the overseer's salary out of revenues raised by rates on assessed property. Because these requirements seemed 'punitive', only 17 out of about 200 villages sought legal incorporation.[9]

But as roads, drainage and public sanitation in the villages grew worse for want of adequate funding, the colonial Government felt it incumbent to intervene more forcefully and take full control of the villages. The principal mover in this direction was Governor Francis Hincks (1862-1868). Using the villages of Buxton, Friendship and Beterverwagting as guinea pigs, he initiated a pilot project in 1862-63 aimed at improving their physical condition. Comprising the district sub-commissary of taxation, an overseer appointed by the Governor, and four elected members, Special Improvement Boards were set up to administer each village. Although the elected members were a majority, in reality they served as the window-dressing to 'legitimize' the unpopular policies of taxation imposed by the central Government in order to raise the necessary funds for village improvements.[10] Under this system, these three villages did experience improved physical and sanitary conditions, and this encouraged Hincks to extend the system to other villages.

What Hincks chose to glean from his limited experiment was that a strong centralized political authority was necessary to improve conditions in the villages. Premised on the misguided notion that the ex-slaves were incapable of governing themselves, he was a firm believer in the 'White man's burden' - the idea that Whites had to teach the Africans what was good for them.

The poor state of the villages, therefore, was not attributed to the lack of resources but, rather, to African mismanagement. It thus required the strong and knowledgeable hand of the White colonial overlords to remedy the situation.

Thus, in 1866, a new system of village administration was set up which disempowered the African villagers. The Governor, members of the colonial legislature, and other persons appointed by the Governor formed a Central Board of Villages with the power to partition villages, make loans for village improvements from a fund of $60,000 voted for this purpose by the Combined Court, and to recoup this expenditure by the imposition of special rates on assessed property. Any, or all, of these actions could be taken without soliciting the consent of the villagers affected.

This was colonial authoritarianism *par excellence*. Even the Colonial Office in London expressed reservations about Hincks's high-handed methods. The local village boards with their elected officials remained in being, but they were rendered powerless. All appointments that mattered were made by the Governor, and the villagers had no say whatever.[11]

Historians have themselves been divided as to the motivation and intention of Hincks's scheme. Adamson, for instance, considers it well-intentioned in so far as it aimed to effect physical improvements in the villages.[12] But such improvements could have been made without imposing the heavy burden of taxation and debt on the villagers, and certainly without depriving them of their ability to govern themselves. Properly constituted village councils elected by the villagers themselves, vested with municipal powers, and supported financially by the central Government out of revenues collected mainly from the ex-slaves, could have achieved the same ends without the need for African political disempowerment. But this did not tally with Hincks's, or, for that matter, his fellow White élites' ideas. Autonomous African villages represented an unacceptable political challenge to total White domination in the colonial state at a time when the British were seeking to tighten their control in all their West Indian colonies. At any cost, therefore, these villages had to be brought under the political control of the colonial authorities.

The African villagers earned local political autonomy easily. They resisted every effort to compel them to acquiesce in Hincks's scheme. In 1863-64, the villagers of Buxton and Friendship refused to pay their rates on pain of levies on their properties. Because the colonial press, even that of the Coloured élite, was hostile, the villagers were forced to publish their side of the issue overseas - in an African-Barbadian newspaper, *The Liberal*. Rioting occurred at Ithaca, Agricola, Bagotstown and Friendship which was only quelled by the repeated interventions of armed police contingents.[13]

One should be careful not to interpret this action as simply a 'rates war', as Adamson does.[14] Certainly, the imposition of onerous rates on village property was an economic burden which not many villagers could endure. But it was not the first time the villagers were paying taxes. The elected councils of the first incorporated villages during the 1850s raised revenues solely through local rates. But those councils were representative of the village property-holders who approved of how the money was spent.[15] Hincks's scheme, by its highly centralized character, removed local government (and its supervision) from the very villagers that it was ostensibly intended to benefit. Taxation by this 'alien' and remote authority was interpreted correctly by the villagers as colonial oppression. The Americans went to war against Britain in 1776 on the same basis with the cry, "No Taxation without representation". Why should the African-Guyanese villagers of Guyana feel any differently? Hence they resisted forcefully.

They recognized that Hincks's and the colonial Government's main intention was to subordinate and disempower them in the one area where they had some control over their lives - the villages. This struggle, therefore, did not involve only the village property-holders, but all villagers: for it went far beyond the issue of whether or not the rates imposed were too high (as indeed they were). It went to the heart of an issue of grave concern to every ex-slave, not only in Guyana, but throughout the Caribbean: the issue of freedom. That is why the African-Barbadian newspaper printed the case of the Buxtonians.

In the long run, African political opposition to Hincks's scheme portended its failure. No system of administration could succeed in the face of resistance from the people it was intended to govern. In the end, therefore, the scheme failed largely because opposition in those villages where it was implemented so bogged it down that it could not be extended to the vast majority of villages in the country. In addition, the 'experts' appointed by the Central Board more often than not lacked knowledge of local conditions; and because they functioned in a highly autocratic system, they refused to listen to the 'ignorant' villagers and their elected councillors. Considerable sums of public money were thus spent on infrastructure which was ill-advised, ill-devised, and badly executed, resulting sometimes in more physical damage and loss of property than improvement; and, besides, the villagers were saddled with an increasing debt burden from what amounted to forced loans for village works which they neither sought nor approved of, but for which they had to pay through the rates.[16]

By 1873, the colonial Government was scrambling to salvage the whole local government administration from collapse and so reluctantly reverted to the pre-Hincks system. New village councils were thus set up with elected majorities under the district commissary of taxation. This, however, was merely sop to the villagers with very little substance as regards village self-government, for the Central Board could still act independently and above the heads of the councils in undertaking public works and imposing rates.[17] It therefore did nothing to restore local autonomy or to ease the debt burden of the villages. For that reason it was no more than plaster over a sore that was fast becoming gangrenous.

One of the great weaknesses of Crown Colony Governments throughout the British Empire was the lack of imaginative creativity. Most became inert and settled for doing as little as possible. In so far as they were motivated to act, it was generally in the direction of preserving the *status quo* and keeping the Africans 'in their place'. So it was in Guyana in the nineteenth century. Successive colonial administrations utterly failed to deal effectively with the physical and sanitary conditions of the villages because they were more concerned with establishing their political dominance over the villagers. This, however, meant that by the late 1870s the villages still presented a serious health hazard.

Something drastic was required but instead, in 1878, an inept colonial Government set up another clumsy bureaucratic authority in the form of the Central Board of Health. This body was assigned responsibility for the sanitary condition of the entire Colony, town and country, including the villages. The problem was that the old Central Board of Villages was retained.[18] This thus made the villages subject to two central authorities whose powers tended to overlap. Far from solving the problems facing the villages, therefore the new Board merely added to them and for the next five years the villages saw no material improvement either in their physical, sanitary or economic conditions.

Ironically, it was the villagers who bore the blame for the poor state of the villages, although the councils created by the 1873 legislation were largely powerless to implement schemes which the central authorities did not approve. By the 1880s, autocratic colonial officials were once more advocating a return to full central Government control over the villages. These ideas very largely were based on overtly racist premises. In 1881, for instance, the Inspector of Villages had the audacity to assert that still too much power remained in the lands of the villagers since they were insufficiently civilized to govern themselves. He further suggested that they had to be forced by a gentle pressure into the ways of civilized men, and that it was necessary to guide them in almost every action of their lives by rules of law. The solution, therefore, lay in passing legislation empowering him to force the proprietors either to work on village lands, sea dams, drains and roads, or to provide the financial means for having these works done. Failure to comply should be a criminal offence punishable by imprisonment.[19] This sort of narrow, short-sighted thinking was typical of late nineteenth century British imperialism tinged with racism.

The notion that the African villagers were incapable of ruling themselves and that the colonial authorities should do it for them (the concept of imperial trusteeship) was shared by other colonial élites, not least of whom was Governor Henry Irving (1882-1887). But while espousing strong central Government control, he recognized that requiring the villagers to finance public works entirely out of their own diminishing resources (through Government loans) imposed enormous financial debt on them which in the long run proved counter-productive; for the loans became bad debts and whatever was recovered in rates hardly covered the costs of collection and management.

Irving thus determined to overhaul the entire system by ceasing to treat the villages as separate (almost alien) entities and bringing their drainage and sanitary affairs under the general law of the Colony. His first step, however, was to ask the Combined Court to write off the existing debts owed by the villages to the Government and to hand over to a newly established Public Works Department (PWD) all the equipment and drainage works for which those debts had been incurred. From there on, all expenditure on drainage, empolderment, and other public works in the villages would be done by the PWD and paid for out of the public revenues to which all villagers, not just property-holders, contributed through indirect taxes.[20]

Irving was one of those rare Crown Colony Governors willing to innovate. By the time he took office it was patently obvious that the entire system of village administration was in a shambles and that something radically new was necessary. Unlike his predecessors, he was willing to turn the system on its head. But if Irving was 'revolutionary' in his approach to the question of financing village works, he was decidedly conservative in his attitude to village Government and to African people. He wholly embraced the prevailing imperialist view that strong centralized Government control was necessary, ostensibly to ensure the prompt and efficient execution of critical public works.[21] In other words, the African villagers had to suffer further political disempowerment in order to benefit from debt relief.

These divergent aspects of Irving's new scheme did not go down well with either the planters or the villagers. The former could hardly be expected to go along with the idea of forgiving the debts of the villagers and adding expenditure on public works in the villages to the colonial budget. Since they had to maintain the polders and roads running through their estates, they saw no reason why those in the villages should be maintained at public expense. Consequently, their elected representatives who formed a majority in the Combined Court refused to support Irving's proposal. Instead, they were prepared to grant only a portion of the costs of village works and thus maintained the rates system to meet the rest. In practical terms, they provided funds to cover only 52 per cent of the estimated $48,000 required for village improvements.[22]

Thus, the African villagers remained saddled with a substantial financial debt burden. But at the same time, they were effectively deprived of the last vestiges of political control over their own affairs. The 1883 Ordinance repealed previous village laws and dissolved the old Central Board of Villages. All lands and property previously held by village corporations were vested in the PWD. Each previously incorporated village became a sanitary district, and the PWD assumed sole responsibility for the main drainage works and roads. Rates, fixed by the Central Board of Health (now the sole administrative body) at two per cent per annum on the appraised value of property, were to be paid to the Government.[23] For the African villagers, this system was an utter political disaster. Although it offered some relief with respect to the financing of village works, they still had to bear a substantial portion of the costs. In addition, they saw their corporate village lands expropriated by the Government without being offered any form of compensation. No less bothersome was their total disempowerment, as the entire machinery of village Government was now controlled exclusively by the central Government.

If this new system was intended to guarantee improved and efficient delivery of public works projects to the villages, in reality it was hardly more successful than its predecessors. First, only the old incorporated villages with an estimated population of about 80,000, which had in place a system for rate collection, really benefited. The rest, whose population was estimated at about 87,000, received virtually no financial assistance at all. So the majority of African villagers continued to suffer from poor drainage, poor sanitary facilities, and poor roads.

Secondly, as a result of the highly centralized system, and haughty and authoritarian colonial officials, the demands and complaints of the villagers were very generally ignored, leaving behind considerable resentment and dissatisfaction among them. The villagers were never told how much revenue was collected through the rates or how it was (mis)spent.[24] They often accused the PWD overseers and engineers of mismanagement and of paying insufficient attention to their needs. Such inattention from time to time resulted in disastrous flooding of village lands as, for instance, at Plaisance and Golden Grove in 1887. This style of administration so alienated the people it was supposed to serve that, by the late 1880s, they began to clamour for a restoration of the elected village councils with corporate municipal powers.[25] This call coincided with the growth of intense agitation for political change at the state level among the middle classes in town and country.

That agitation produced the first significant political changes in Guyana in the post-Emancipation period. Between 1891 and 1896, reforms of the colonial political *Constitution* led not only to modifications in the political institutions, but also to very modest extensions of the franchise and qualifications for membership of the political institutions themselves. The old College of *Kiezers* was abolished, thus permitting direct elections of members of the legislature. The qualifications for membership were lowered to include those persons earning $1,440 per annum or possessing immoveable property other than land valued at $7,500 per annum, or renting a house and land valued at $1,200 per annum. The franchise was extended to those persons earning $480 per annum, although a literacy requirement was retained.[26]

Together with the introduction of the secret ballot in 1896, these adjustments, modest though they undoubtedly were, brought about relatively significant change to the face of colonial politics in Guyana because, despite enormous obstacles, a fair number of Africans and Coloureds had risen economically to attain those requirements. So, although the number of registered voters still numbered less than one per cent of the population in 1896, the elections of that year saw not only the presence of non-Whites in the legislature for the first time since Richard Haynes in the early 1850s but, more importantly, produced the first African and Coloured majority in that body.[27]

This had important ramifications for the political administration of the villages. If Africans and Coloureds (albeit from the wealthier and educated middle class) were sufficiently 'civilized' to be admitted to a share of political power at the state level, then why not at village level (although generally of a lower class)? In any event, after nearly a decade it was obvious that the Irving system of highly centralized administration had not brought the expected benefits to the villagers. The year 1892, therefore, saw a return to partial democracy at the village level. New corporate village councils were formed with an elective majority of three to each member nominated by the Central Board of Health. The councils were granted substantial administrative powers which ensured a considerable measure of self-management. Still, the Central Board of Health not only retained overall responsibility for local Government, but could also dissolve any council ostensibly for failing to perform its duties. Besides, the principle of rate-paying by the villagers was retained.[28] Even so, these changes were a welcome move away from imperial authoritarianism and African political disempowerment, and together with the changes which took place at the state level marked a new era in African politics in post-Emancipation Guyana.

For most of the nineteenth century, however, the African-Guyanese majority in Guyana remained politically subordinate to the White (mainly planter) élite. Every effort was made to ensure that they remained disempowered both at the state and village levels. But if they acquiesced to a point in their 'fate' at central Government level, they mounted resolute resistance to enforced subordination at the village level. The village was identified with African freedom from the oppression of the plantation system, even though many villagers continued to work part-time on the estates. Any effort to deprive them of their political autonomy in the villages was interpreted as an assault on their basic human rights and freedom. Yet, while the village provided working-class Africans with a sense of corporate identity as a distinct social group in the post-Emancipation period, it is not clear if they perceived it as the foundation or basis of a challenge to the wider system of White political, social and economic dominance.

The colonial élites, however, seemed to see the villages in precisely that vein and this in no small way accounts for their attitude towards the idea of village self-government. If the African villagers were allowed to become successful in governing themselves, then what would prevent them from seeking even greater political rights at the colonial state level? In the middle decades of the nineteenth century, the notion of an African-dominated Colony was anathema to both the White colonists and the imperial Government.

Haiti, equated in their minds with African barbarism, always served as a warning. That is why after the Morant Bay disturbance in Jamaica in 1865, nearly all the colonial legislatures in the British Caribbean dissolved themselves in favour of direct imperial rule.

As a Crown Colony ever since it became British at the beginning of the nineteenth century, Guyana was not in immediate danger of becoming African-ruled (certainly not before the very end of the century); but successful self-ruled African villages could conceivably send the 'wrong' message. This in large measure accounts for the systematic measures taken by the colonial authorities to disempower the African-Guyanese villagers after Emancipation.

Notes

1. See *Ordinance No.* 15 of 1849.
2. C.O. 111/284 Governor Henry Barkly to Lord Grey, No. 164, 24 Nov., 1851.
3. Brian L. Moore, *Race, Power and Social Segmentation in Colonial Society: Guyana after Slavery* (New York, 1987), Appendix iv, p. 175.
4. *Ibid.*, 54 - 58.
5. *Ibid.*
6. J.G. Cruickshank, 'The beginnings of our villages', *Timehri*, 7, 3rd. ser., 1921, pp. 20-21; J.B. Cropper, 'Our villages and countryparts', *Timehri*, 2 (2), 1912, p. 253; P.P., 1847-48, XXXIII., Pt. 11, and C.O. 111/288 Barkly to Grey, 26, 10 Feb. 1852.
7. Hadfield to Young in Light to Stanley, 3, Jan. 1845.
8. C.O. 111/297 Allan Young, *Approaches to Local Self-Government in British Guiana* (London, 1958), p. 44; Walker to Newcastle, No. 102, 20 Oct. 1853,.
9. Young, *loc. cit.*; Attorney General's report in Wodehouse to Labouchere, 157, 24 Dec. 1856, C.O 111/313.
10. Young, pp. 50-56; *Royal Gazette*, 8 Apr. 1856.
11. Young, pp. 58-59; C.O. 111/340 Governor Francis Hincks to Newcastle, 66, 20 Apr. 1863.
12. *Creole*, 20 Dec. 1865; C.O 111/355; encl. in Hincks to Cardwell, No. 25, 22 Jan. 1866, A. Adamson, *Sugar without Slaves* (New Haven, 1972), pp. 76 - 77.
13. A. Adamson, 'Monoculture and village decay in British Guiana, 1854-1872', *Journal of Social History*, 3, 1970, p. 402.
14. See the newspapers for the period 1862 - 67, especially the *Creole, Colonist, Royal Gazette and Berbice Gazette.* Also C.O. 111/353; Hincks to Cardwell, 186, 23 Nov. 1865, and Hincks to Buckingham & Chandos, 159, 20 Dec. 1867, C.O. 111/364.

15. See appropriate references in notes 11 and 12.
16. Young, pp. 59-60.
17. N.A.G.Petitions from Craig village, 17 Jan. 1871, and Plaisance village, 10 Nov. 1871; letter by Robert Will in *Watchman*, 11 Nov. 1871; *Royal Gazette*, 23 Jul. 1872.
18. C.O. 111/398; Encl. in Rushworth to Kimberley, No. 126, 7 Aug. 1873; *Watchman*, 4 Jul. 1873; *Royal Gazette*, 29 May 1875.
19. C.O. 111/412. Encl. in Kortright to Hicks Beach, 52, 24 Feb. 1879.
20. C.O. 114/32 Report of the inspector of villages, 29 Mar. 1882.
    C.O. 111/425 Governor Henry Irving to Kimberley, No 285, 3 Oct. 1882.
21. *Ibid.*
22. C.O. 111/4274, 4 Jan. 1883, C.O. 111/427, Governor Henry Irving to Kimberley.
23. C.O 111/428 Irving to Derby, No. 125, 5 May 1883.
24. C.O. 111/457 Encl. in Governor Lord Gormanston to Knutsford, 248, 28 Jul. 1890.
25. *Echo*, 12 and 19 Feb., and 8 Dec. 1887; and 17 Oct. 1888.
26. Ordinance No. 1 of 1891.
27. Blue Books of Statistics for 1890 and 1891; C.O. 111/484, Minute of C.A. Pearson, 26 Feb. 1896; C.O. 111/485, Hemming to Chamberlain, 153, 27 Apr. 1896; C.O. 111/486, Same to Same, 198, 11 Jun. 1896, C.O. 111/487, Same to Same, and 282, 10 Sep. 1896.
28. C.O. 111/465 Encl. in Gormanston to Ripon, No. 384, 25 Nov. 1892; Adamson, *Sugar without Slaves*, pp. 92-93.

Part III

Pre-Independence Period

10: The Causes of the Protest of 1905

by
Kimani S. Nehusi

Not in bland ignorance, and certainly not only in Georgetown where most, but not all, of the action was centred, did the Protest of 1905 in British Guiana take place. The Protest itself began when workers, first at Sandbach Parker and Company, stopped work and demanded higher wages and improved conditions of work. They were opposed by intransigent shipping companies. The confrontation developed into rioting and bloodshed, and British troops were eventually summoned. This action by the group of workers at Sandbach Parker was the immediate cause of the Protest; but this action and its aftermath were merely the reaction to conditions which were present and had been building up in British Guianese society long before. It was largely against these conditions that the workers were protesting in 1905.

The story of the Protest of 1905 was one of the masses in action, and the reaction of the middle and upper classes to the events of November and December of that year; it was also a story of the slow process of the building up of latent tensions in the society. But if '1905' was a reaction to the 'pre-1905' era, then it is to this period that one must look to find its underlying causes.

An examination of the socio-economic formation of post-Emancipation British Guiana, particularly between the 1880s and 1905, will show a monocrop economy in recession, high taxes, a fast rising cost of living and declining wages.

It will also show the political and economic dominance of the planter oligarchy which maintained its position with the tacit connivance of the Colonial Office, and the indulgence of most of the local representatives of the imperial Government. This dominance, based as it was on strategies of restricting the political and economic participation of the masses through the use of legislation, bred increasing resentment not only among the lower classes, but also among members of the 'middle class' professionals and shopkeepers.

Since the days of the Dutch, the sugar industry had been the largest sector of the economy and provided employment for the major segment of the working population of the Colony.[1] In 1905, it was still by far the most important aspect of the economy, and was owned and controlled mainly by British capitalists through their local agents and subsidiaries.[2]

By 1882, the sugar industry of British Guiana, like its counterparts in other Caribbean territories, had shown signs of recovery from post-Emancipation problems, particularly the labour shortage. However, around this time, the sugar cane industry was suffering a world-wide decline. The industry in the British Caribbean did not escape uninfluenced and, by 1897, it was only in Grenada, where sugar was not by any means the major sector of the economy, and in Trinidad with its relatively well-diversified economy, that the likely effects of the depression were not being predicted as catastrophic.[3]

Governors, legislative bodies and other representatives of the sugar interests portrayed the industry in the British West Indies as being in a state of extreme depression, economically unviable, and contracting through the abandonment of plantations and consequent discontinuation of cultivation. The consensus was that, if the depression continued, the abandonment of many more sugar estates would become imminent. The consequences of this situation were held to be general distress for the lower classes and destruction of the colonies' general prosperity so as to make it impossible for them to discharge the responsibilities of Government and administration without external aid.[4] The problem in British Guiana was found to be one of 'extreme difficulty' and a very gloomy future was predicted for the Colony:

> ... it is clear that British Guiana is in the perilous position of being dependent on a single agricultural industry, the production of sugar, that industry be-

> ing in a state of extreme depression and threatened with possible extinction, while it is difficult to see how it can survive or even be maintained under present conditions.[5]

Widespread abandonment of estates was a very real possibility if prospects did not improve, and it seemed that any further fall in the price of sugar, or a few bad seasons, would have occasioned a general collapse of the industry. Worse, it was extremely doubtful if increased economic efficiency or improved machinery would have staved off the crisis. The injection of capital, though not necessarily a remedy, was discounted because the uncertainty in the industry made it impossible to attract capital.[6]

The general depression in the industry was indicated by the constant depreciation in the value of sugar properties. For example, Plantation Hamburg on Tiger Island was valued at $434,400 in 1832 but, in 1897, it was sold for $6,075, even though by then its factory had been equipped 'with the best modern machinery'.[7] The price of sugar was also falling; in 1837 it was between $264 and $332 per ton; by 1877 it had fallen to $122, in 1887 to $67, and in 1897 it was $46. There were many fluctuaions in the price of this commodity but, during the 60 years before 1896, the price of sugar decreased by over 70 per cent of its previous value.[8] A fall in the prices of its by-products, rum and molasses, attended the fall in sugar prices. For example, in 1837, rum of 36° to 38° over proof was easily sold at $1 per gallon. However, in 1897, it was very difficult to sell rum at 40° overproof at even 25c per gallon.[9] Between 1891 and 1896, alone the price of Demerara rum fell from 2s. 4 ¾d per gallon to 1s. 0½d.[10] In 1896, investigators of British Guianese society were convinced that "... this depreciation in the by-products of sugar (had) contributed appreciably to the ... depression in the (sugar) industry".[11]

These conditions had a very grave effect on the Colony's export earnings. Between 1881 and 1885 the value of exports of sugar, molasses and rum was £12,038,699, but it fell to £9,305,880 in the years between 1886 and 1891.[12] Prices fell further between 1891 and 1892, and by 1895/96 the Colony's earnings from these sources were only £8,276,916. The average annual decrease in export earnings from the industry during this period was £1,655,383. Between April 1895 and March 1896 (one year of account), exports were valued at a mere £1,183,000. In the calendar year 1896, it was valued at £1,280,000. In contrast to these times, during the period before 1885, the average annual value of sugar products of British Guiana was well over £2 million, and it was over £3 million in some years.[13]

The value per gallon of rum exported fell 50 per cent between 1872 and 1896 (from 2s. 1d. to 1s. 0½d), while that of molasses decreased by 58.17 per cent from 1s. to 5d. In both cases, the actual volume of exports also fell during the interval: rum from 2,428,300 to 2,169,616 gallons and molasses from 1,108,300 to 811,500 gallons.[14] In effect, the per cent value of the Colony's exports earned by sugar and sugar products declined steadily after Emancipation. In the years between 1838 and 1840, sugar, rum and molasses earned 90.8 per cent of the total value of exports from British Guiana. The figures were:

1880/1882,	91.9%;	1883/1885,	91.9%;
1886/1888,	89.6%;	1892/1894,	71.5%;
1895/1897,	66.1%;	1898/1901,	58.2%;
1901/1904,	66.2%.[15]		

The slump in the sugar industry during this period was also indicated by decreases in the production cost, profit and revenue per ton of the commodity. In 1882/83, revenue per ton was £23. 16s. 0d., and production cost was £22. 10s. 0d. By 1894/95, revenue was £12. 10s. 3d., production cost £12. 15s. 2d. and the loss per ton was 4s. 11d. By 1901, the situation had improved slightly, and a relatively small profit of 6s. 6d. was made on each ton of the commodity produced.[16] But, despite the fall in its value and general profitability, the gross output of sugar was generally maintained. The same may be said of rum, while both the gross output and value of molasses decreased appreciably.[17]

Thus, in the period immediately before 1905, the situation in the British Guiana sugar industry was precarious and its future seemed uncertain. Most observers made gloomy predictions of imminent ruin and widespread destruction affecting the entire society. Governor Hemming felt that the very existence of the Colony was threatened.[18] This was a view advanced by many of the staunchest supporters of the sugar interests, for traditionally, they felt that the Colony meant the sugar industry, and the sugar industry meant the Colony.[19] One must note, however, that a ploy developed by many members of the plantocracy was to shout 'ruin' as loudly as possible in the hope of soliciting the sympathy, connivance and more generous aid from imperial authorities.

If the demise of the sugar industry seemed imminent during the post-Emancipation crises, by 1905 the planters had already evolved a strategy for successfully combating the problems which threatened their survival as the dominant group in the society. This was achieved through increased efficiency within the industry, mainly through the importation of technology, and a drastic reduction in the wage bill. But this was achieved only against the general background of the post-Emancipation period, in which one of the preoccupations of the planters was the retention of their traditional monopoly of the key factors of production - land, labour and capital. These were allocated only, or mainly, to themselves, while they placed a heavy tax burden on the masses and other perceived rivals. This promoted the rejuvenation of the sugar industry, stifled development within other sections of the economy and restricted the advancement of other groups in the society.

Yet, by 1905, sugar certainly did not "completely and entirely hold the field", as Governor Hemming postulated.[20] There were two other significant industries in the Colony, the gold industry and the rice industry. As yet, they were small, lacking the relative technological sophistication of sugar, and beset by their own internal problems. In addition, other problems were posed by a covetous, but sometimes reluctantly condescending, plantocracy which generally refused to recognise the growing importance of these two industries in particular, and the incumbent need for economic diversification in general.[21] The plantocracy viewed the

British Guiana gold industry as first and foremost a competitor for the labour resources available in the Colony. It was also seen as a form of economic activity — as it tended to perceive all forms of economic activity outside the sugar industry — which was to be heavily taxed to provide revenue for Government spending on essential work and the sugar industry; this discouraged growth outside the sugar industry, while promoting it within.

So much had the development of the gold industry demonstrated the intense preoccupation of the plantocracy with this strategy for self-preservation, that it may be said that the gold industry survived and grew 'in spite of' the obstacles placed in its way.[22] These obstacles were as formidable as they were vexatious. They eventually resulted in the alienation and hostility of the gold interest from the plantocracy. Restrictive legislation imposed a heavy tax burden of 90 cents per ounce of gold, plus payment for the necessary miner's licence, royalty on timber cut, and on silver produced. It also imposed many tedious duties upon the prospector. These, along with the absence of laws designed to promote the industry, and also the absence of Government spending for the same purpose, tended to restrict the expansion of the industry. In truth, the British Guiana gold industry suffered from a chronic lack of an informed policy on the industry and a positive unwillingness or inability of the local authorities to recognise its potentially great contribution to the economy and society which most observers recognized as being decadent.

In British Guiana, the laws and practice of the authorities were the converse of those of other gold-mining countries in which the regulations and usage aided gold production. The laws and usage in British Guiana were counter-productive and designed to retard the growth of the industry. This was essentially the same strategy employed by the planters against the peasantry, a nascent petit middle class and, indeed, any competitor or imagined competitor for land, labour and capital. The plantocracy had traditionally enjoyed the monopoly of them from the times of slavery in a society in which the mode of production was then colonial capitalism, and the Government, oligarchic.[23] In the Colony, the Government's policy on the gold industry was seen to be in direct opposition to that of other countries "both in principle and in detail", and that "it was perhaps not unnatural that planters should have sought, by means of stringent laws, to hamper an industry which would surely lessen the labour supply on the estates".[24]

A full examination of this question is beyond the scope of this study, but it is instructive to note that it was not merely the issues of competition for labour and finance for development which were at stake. Of wider significance and ultimate pertinence, was the question of the viable economic independence of the lower classes from the plantation and, thus, their ability to offer some effective challenge to the dominance of the plantation in the society. In a situation in which sugar traditionally dominated all aspects of society, and the planters had come to regard it as the beginning and the end, it was impossible, or at least infinitely difficult, for the planter-controlled local assembly to permit the development of an industry when, in its very conception and growth, it clashed with what planters commonly held to be the interests of sugar.

To make matters worse for the fledging gold industry, the post-Emancipation period was one in which the entire *status quo* which resulted from, and was indicative of, the old sugar dominance, was put on trial by new social and economic forces. This point was not lost on the sugar barons, who saw themselves as being beset by numerous problems, including labour and finance, two crucial factors in capitalist production. In fact, the public ear was constantly bombarded by convenient cries of 'ruin' and prophecies of doom from sugar representatives in post-Emancipation British Guiana.

By the 1890s, the decline in the world sugar industry gave real reason for alarm. To compound the fears of the plantocracy, and give substance to what had become their constant fear of labour shortage, the existence of the gold industry caused recurring labour crises in the sugar industry in 1891, 1892 and 1893.[25]

An important factor in the promotion of this crisis was the decline in the labour price and the general working conditions on the sugar estates. In 1884 and 1885, the wage rates for labourers on the estates were 24 cents to 80 cents per day for cane cutters and 24 to 32 cents per day for weeders; it was recognized that the estate authorities "had been leaning more to the lower rates".[26] The reduction in the wages of the individual worker was reflected in the total sugar estate bill for wages paid during the period 1882 to 1904. Beginning at the 1882 wage bill of $6,500,000, the total sugar estate wage bill had been reduced by 55.75 per cent by the latter half of 1896; by 62.3 per cent in 1904; and by an average of 60.5 per cent between 1901 and 1904.[27] By 1896, the ordinary man had to toil very hard to earn 48 cents per day as a field labourer. In comparison, miners in the gold industry were offered a higher wage of 64 cents per day, payable in a lump sum at the end of a three-month contract. Working conditions were also better, with food and sleeping accommodation being the responsibility of the employer.[28]

Available evidence suggests that the situation had not improved by 1905. Cane-cutters gave figures which showed that daily earnings were as low as 7 to 8 cents among women. Among the men, it ranged from 11 and 12 cents per day to 17 and 18 cents per day with hard work - from 04:00 a.m. to 6:00 p.m. Monday to Saturday. The pay of other males who were not cane-cutters varied from 13 to 24 cents per day. A reporter calculated that the average cane-cutter, leaving his home in time to arrive at the work-site at about 04:00 a.m. each day from Monday to Saturday, when he would cease work at 12:00, would have earned between 37 and 41 cents per day.[29] While this is far more liberal than the estimates of the cane-cutters themselves, the higher figure is still well below the 48 cents cited for 1896/1897, and far below the 64 cents per day then recorded by the workers in the gold industry.

This industry had a special lure for the African villagers whom the planters were inclined to look upon as their labourers. Not only did it hold out the prospect of getting rich quickly,[30] but it also offered a chance to establish an independent existence away from the plantation.[31] It is not too difficult to comprehend the

African-Guyanese villager making the choice he did. He chose the glitter of the goldfield rather then the dull drudgery of plantation labour. In 1896/97, about 6,000 were employed in the gold industry.[32] This represented an increase of about 3,356 or about 55.93 per cent from 1888.[33]

But, if the African villager had escaped the direct influence of the planter, he could not escape him indirectly, for the mining community suffered under the imposition of restrictive legislation by the planter-dominated local assembly. Mining regulations were passed in 1880, 1886, 1887, 1892, 1896 and 1897.[34] It was widely felt that these regulations severely restricted the expansion of the industry, which had much to contribute to the Colony's development. Indeed, so dim a view did one observer take of the regulations that by 1897 he felt that the complete stagnation of gold mining was imminent. He was obliged to portray the industry as:

> ...the bird with the golden eggs and not only has every egg been taken and none left to hatch, but the unfortunate fowl has been so hedged about with laws and regulations and so plucked of its feathers that it is likely to die, unless change of policy takes place.[35]

The miners themselves felt that the regulations were "too irksome, too restrictive, too oppressive", and contended that the method of collecting the royalty on the metal was "absurd, expensive, cumbersome and wasteful of time".[36] Persons involved in the industry also found to be repugnant, certain practices arising out of attempts to enforce the regulations, which made unfortunate anyone who located even a small placer mine; he was compelled "to load himself with a number of expensive forms and books irrespective of the fact that he probably (could not) write".[37]

Besides, "respectable men" who journeyed into the interior to prospect were subjected "to the indignity of an indecent search".[38] There were complaints and petitions over the system of registering gold miners.[39] Some gold diggers from West Demerara were so dissatisfied with the existing arrangement in which they had to travel to Georgetown to register, they petitioned the Government for magistrates on the West Demerara to be given powers to register labourers for the industry.[40]

The tax system in the Colony was another cause of hardship and anger of the majority. It functioned to circumscribe the growth of alternatives to the sugar industry, and generally to propagate the interests of the dominant planter oligarchy through the concentration of finance in the sugar industry while deforming other sectors of the economy through the promotion of capital starvation. After Emancipation, there was a need to create more revenue for the Government to cater for increased social services. This was achieved chiefly by legislation which shifted the burden of taxation on to the peasantry, the Indian immigrants as they became a permanent section of the society, and to a lesser extent upon the upcoming Creole petit-bourgeois class. This was achieved mainly by changing from direct to indirect taxation.[41]

The plantocracy made hardly any effort to hide the fact that it deliberately contrived to have import duties fall hardest upon the poorest segments of the population - the African peasantry and the Indian immigrants - while avoiding such duties themselves.

This policy was especially demonstrated by the articles exempted from duty which always included those used by the planters who, by virtue of their higher income, had the greater ability to pay taxes. On the other hand, the articles taxed always included those frequently used by the other classes. For example, corn, oatmeal, flour, pickled beef, pickled pork, dried fish, rice and tallow candles - all articles used by the Colony's poor - were severely taxed. As early as 1850, flour, rice, dried fish and salt pork were taxed for more than 50 per cent of all import duties. Although there was a reduction a year later, flour and salt-beef were still paying between 20 and 25 cent of their value as import duty.[42]

The tax on rum and the initial steady increase of retail spirit shop licences were attempts to circumscribe the Creole petit-bourgeois elements which had begun to develop slowly after Emancipation.[43] Duties on auctions, licences for porters, a tax on carts for hire, and licences for shop-keepers and hucksters were among those imposed. Meanwhile, those taxes which fell directly on the estates were greatly reduced. First of all, the poll tax on slaves went out with Emancipation. Income tax was reduced from two per cent to one per cent after 1842, and abolished in 1853. The income obtained from sugar, rum, molasses, cotton and coffee - the chief crops and exports of the Colony - had been exempted from taxation. The export duty on sugar and its by-products was given the same treatment - gradual reduction until abolition, in this case in 1856. Thus the plantocracy had almost exempted itself altogether from taxation, while imposing a heavy tax burden upon other sections of the society, particularly the poor.[44]

By 1899, these conditions had not changed, and many social groups were voicing their disapproval of "the grievous burden of taxation under which we labour ... a subject which has filled every mouth with murmur".[45] This tax structure remained `remarkably stable' over the period and by 1905 it had changed very little. The policy of the sugar barons of inflicting a heavy tax burden upon, while allocating little financial resources to, those they perceived as rivals, is also very well demonstrated in the case of the gold industry. When compared with the sugar industry, it was very heavily taxed to provide funds for the Government. In 1894, the sugar industry paid $108,873 as an acreage tax. Of this amount, only $18,145 were given over to the general revenue of the Colony.[46] This was the last year in which any part of the acreage tax was given towards the general revenue of the Colony. After then, the minimal taxes paid by planters were not handed over to the public treasury, but were appropriated to help pay for immigration, which benefited only the planters themselves. The only direct tax payable by sugar estate proprietors was an acreage tax of $1.35 for every acre of cultivated land and two cents for every acre empoldered, but not cultivated. Revenue from this source was then $94,554 and, even if it had been given to the Colony's treasury, revenue from gold would have contributed about $10,000 more. But it was not permitted to:

> Every penny of this sum was devoted to the payment of the expenses of immigration and thus the estates really took the money from one pocket and put it into the other.[47]

In comparison, there was a nominal tax of 90 cents on each ounce of gold. In 1894/95, $119,695 were collected from this source. In 1894, sugar and sugar products had a total value of about $6,933,555. Of this sum, the revenue the Colony received as direct tax was $18,145, or just over a quarter of one per cent. In the same year, gold produced in British Guiana amounted to $2,402,140. Direct tax in the form of royalty paid to the revenue of the Colony was $119,695 or just under 5 per cent. Thus, "roughly speaking ... gold paid direct taxation in the ratio of twenty to one as compared with sugar".[48] This observer appears to have been fully conscious of the way direct taxation was used against certain groups in the society, noting that it "... bears on one class of men and not the others, and is therefore a fit subject to be introduced as a vital element in the condition of any specific industry". The disparity in the levels of direct taxation on the two industries remained a stark testimony to the complete dominance of the planters in the politics of the Colony. It also remained a source of constant discontent among the gold interests.[49]

The existing conditions of increasing population, restricted importation of goods and lack of money in circulation seemed ready-made for the spread of discontent. This was particularly so when some sections of the plantation felt that these resulted from the preoccupation of the plantocracy with furthering the interests of sugar while neglecting the other industries.[50] However, the policy of the Government towards the villages, as reflected in finance allocation, did not help to alleviate increasing discontent. Between 1892 and 1896, the Government spent $589,386 of money it borrowed on water supply systems which benefited sugar estates, while merely $31,270 were allocated to water supply systems for villages.[51]

Yet, it was the villages which were in urgent need of developmental aid, and it was in the villages that most of the population resided. By 1905, the villages were in a pathetic state. Since 1897, about two-thirds of those which functioned under the *Village Ordinance* were not properly drained. Besides, flooding and crop destruction had severely disillusioned villagers on the East Coast of Demerara and in Essequibo. Their technique of shifting cultivation increased the cost of drainage by constantly increasing the area to be empoldered and drained. The depression in the sugar industry at this time also compounded their problems. Generally, work done for estates by African villagers decreased by half, and there was a consequent reduction in earnings from this source.[52] The reduction in the wage rate also contributed to this situation.

But, even those who found full-time work on the estates by 1905 did not escape the poor economic circumstances of the lower classes. For example, conditions on Pln. Ruimveldt, which was one of the centres of the Protest of 1905, were extremely harsh. They were in most ways typical of estate conditions at the time. Besides the low wages, the rent was also low, for workers were provided with rooms at a rent lower than was normal either in Georgetown or the suburban areas. But this low rent was only an illusion of low cost of living and good conditions; the rooms were given "to workers with the understanding that they worked on Ruimveldt at whatever wages the estates offered".[53] This most probably indicates that the wages offered were lower than the low pay received by the workers of other estates, whose wages were described as `miserably small' even after the Protest.[54] And it is to be noted that the conditions under which most of these estate workers laboured were aggravated by the seasonal nature of the employment which was available to most of them.

During most of the period between 1880 and 1905, the low price obtained for sugar precipitated a drop in employment and a corresponding reduction in business. Unemployment, low wages and high taxes combined to produce great hardship for the poor in both urban and rural districts. So difficult were their conditions of existence that, in 1897, Governor Sir Augustus Hemming decided that the masses had very little room to pay more indirect taxes.[55] Just before 1905, it was felt that "the impoverishment of the masses (was) increasing; their capacity to bear the heavy burdens of taxation (had) declined to a degree unparalleled in the annals of the Colony since Emancipation".[56] Even one member of the plantocracy, probably moved by the events of 1905, felt compelled to recommend that these conditions be alleviated.[57]

In Georgetown itself, the main focus of the Protest, the West India Royal Commissioners had reported in 1897 that even skilled artisans and mechanics, and persons above the labouring class, were experiencing much poverty.[58] For example, a conductor of an electric car - a respectable position in those times - received a wage of five cents per hour during the first year of his employment. After that, there was a rise of one cent per hour. However, by 1905, the wage no longer permitted conductors to cope with the rising cost of living in ways to which they were accustomed. They felt that they needed a rise of 25 per cent to meet the increased cost of living. One conductor reported that "working steadily, we can only earn 64 cents a day, and that is not enough for men of our class. If we could manage to earn 80 cents a day that would be fair and reasonable".[59] Conditions on the waterfront, where the Protest began, were at best difficult, even for those times:

> Our working hours were ten and one half. The system of quarter-day existed. There was no overtime for night work. We asked the employers to change these conditions. The reply was that we must take them or go.[60]

This intransigence of the shipping firms was evident among other sections of the ruling class, and added another dimension to the Protest. At this time, wages were 48 cents per day for truckers, who were called 'boys' but were really men, and 64 cents per day for men.[61] The truckers rarely got a full day's employment[62] for, when they accepted work, they often found that their services were needed only for a short while.

The shipping firms also combined to inflict a harsh penalty upon those workers who sought to protest by refusing work from one firm which disaffected them by this practice. When they took work from another firm, they were paid only three cents per half hour.[63] Casual workers were also very dissatisfied with their conditions of work. They were taken on at two guilders for each day's work of ten and one half hours' duration. If they worked past noon - i.e., worked for more than one half of the working day - but stopped before the end of the day, they were paid only for the half day up to noon. After that, they were paid an hourly sum, calculated according to the rate of the daily wage. Besides, puntmen were also feeling the squeeze of the worsening economic situation. They claimed that their wage rate was reduced by at least 25 per cent during the years before 1905.[64]

The social and political condition of the British Guiana masses was as bleak as their economic existence. The condition of the lower-class masses in the slums of Georgetown and elsewhere was definitely depressing during the era of the sugar crash. Housing was deplorable. Many of the inhabitants of the City resided in dilapidated old shanties. This existence was characterised by overcrowding, especially at night, lack of privacy and a consequent lack of self-respect, and an absence of common decency which might have been exacerbated by the communal standpipes which still evoke images of the Georgetown 'nigger yards' of this era. Within the houses, there was inadequate sitting room and ventilation, and this encouraged the widespread practice of sitting on doorsteps or on bridges. Yards and drains were usually littered with rubbish, thus providing the ideal conditions for diseases to thrive.[65] In these circumstances, it is hardly surprising that statistics show that by 1905 the life expectancy was shorter in Georgetown than in other parts of the Colony. Infant mortality was a high 201 per 1,000 children born in the Colony. In the City, it was higher still, being 232. The death rate tells the same story. Elsewhere in British Guiana, it was 28.3 per 1,000 in 1904; in Georgetown, it was 44.7 per 1,000.[66]

The poverty, disease and immorality of the Georgetown lower class proved conducive to crime, and spawned the self-styled 'centipede' boys and girls. They developed a pugnacious disregard for authority and middle-class morality and an abrasive propensity to pursue their own proclivities. 'Centipedism' was an entire reaction syndrome to the lower-class reality. By 1899, the yards of Georgetown lower-class folk were almost synonymous with rowdyism:

> The yards of the City, containing within their narrow limits many persons of evil reputation, are, with some few exceptions, hotbeds of vice, drunkenness, and rowdyism, and there is scarcely a street which does not have one or two yards which have obtained an unenviable notoriety for the blackguardism of its inmates, some of whom it is said (sic) to reflect, take an amount of pride in their profligacy and dissoluteness which would be difficult to get them to bestow on noble objects and laudable ambitions."[67]

In 1904, the growth of 'centipedism', which coloured the reaction of the lower class in the Protest of 1905 caused the Government to issue special legislation aimed against the adherents of this lifestyle.[68] But it was not only in Georgetown that crime was increasing. In 1885, there were 14,421 offences reported to the police or to magistrates. These were 2,029 more than the number reported during the previous year. In 1885, the number of prisoners committed was 7,195 as compared with 2,250 in 1884. The daily average number in prison also increased, from 701 in 1883 to 741 in 1884 and 880 in 1885.[69] By 1905, this trend towards increased criminal activity was still very evident. In 1903/04, there were 20,684 persons apprehended or summoned before magistrates. In 1904/05, the number was 24,578. Offences against the person and praedial larceny were again higher than in the previous year. There were 2,239 offences against the person reported in 1904/05, an increase from the 2,174 reported in 1903/04. During the same period, offences for praedial larceny increased from 212 to 379.[70]

These figures tell of the hard times brought to the population by the sugar crisis. So, too, do the statistics for the type of crime committed. As early as 1885, the authorities in the Colonial

Office felt that "the large increase in the number of convictions for praedial larceny is very significant of the hard times which were being felt by the labouring population of the country districts".[71] The socio-political relations of this time reinforced the economic situation in the Colony, and were themselves products of the historical development of that economic environment. What was said of the villagers was equally valid for the entire working-class:

> ... the views of the mass of the population were so rarely heard. The illusion of a consenting majority could be maintained partly because it was such a silent majority. And even when it was raised, the voice that spoke for the villager was hardly representative.[72]

It was only in times of mass protest that the voice of the majority was heard. This was invariably when conditions became unbearable and the masses, or sections of the masses, were forced to adopt 'unconstitutional' ways of making themselves heard because the *Constitution* did not permit them to participate in the legislature. At such times when they were not in protest, it was their class allies who spoke up for the poor. These ranged from the propertied petit-bourgeois (merchants, etc.) in 1871, to the 'small' Coloured professional middle class' in the 1890s and immediately after.[73] But always, they represented the working-class on issues in which their interests tended to merge. And even the nationalistic middle class could not pretend to speak for the Indian immigrants who, to some degree, were separate from other sections of the working-class in terms of language, culture and the rigorous labour laws then in vogue.

It was a high property qualification which ensured a narrow franchise and restricted political participation to the plantocracy and most members of the British Guiana middle class. This was largely true even after the 1891 constitutional reform, which was the legal culmination of a growing movement of protest against the domination of the economy and society by the plantocracy. Throughout this domination, it was the planters' political control of the society which was the deciding factor in their retention of their dominant position. This was demonstrated particularly at times when the sugar industry - the planters' economic base - was threatened, as happened during the crises which hit the industry between 1834 and 1905. In such instances, it was their political power which gave the planters the authority to allocate the relatively scarce resources of the society to themselves and away from other sections of the economy. This narrow retention and use of political power was made easier by the connivance of most governors and the officials of the British Colonial Office, who feared the planter oligarchy more than they feared the masses.[74]

After 1884, more and more social groups began to protest against the prevailing conditions. The lower classes found falling wages, bad working conditions and high taxation too great a burden. They found allies in the Georgetown merchants - mainly Portuguese - who saw no benefit in the survival of the dominant sugar industry because it was achieved partly through the reduction of labour costs, and consequently decreased the purchasing power of the rural proletariat. It was upon these that the merchants depended for their prosperity, by virtue of being suppliers to retail shopkeepers in the countryside.[75]

There was growing disaffection with the lack of representation in the legislature, and great distrust of the planters. One newspaper expressed the view that "from the mock representation under which we live it would be madness to expect fair play".[76] Besides the lower class and the Georgetown merchants, the professional class was also against the policies of the Government. Together with Governor Henry Irving, the only Governor before 1900 to stand up to the planters, they advocated economic diversification, changes in the tax structure, complete planter responsibility for immigration costs, rural (village) development, and also what amounted to the constitutional prerequisite of these: the reform of the *Constitution* and the weakening of the plantocracy's power.

The merchants and Coloured lawyers with interests in the gold industry also came out against the planters' policy of resource control which caused the non-sugar sectors of the economy to be left relatively under-developed. Consequently, they advocated better communication with the interior by rail, that the planters bear the complete burden of immigration, and other departures from traditional planter policy. These formed the most radical group in the movement against the planters, which was encouraged by reforms in parts of the British West Indies and Commonwealth at this time.[77] But for all this, it was a movement only in the vague sense that all these groups were in opposition to the planters. There was no unanimity, much less unity.

The many electoral contests during this period, combined with improved educational standards and the growth of the press and reduction in the cost of newspapers, had the effect of politicizing parts of the masses. This was particularly true of the working-class in Georgetown and the surrounding countryside. This task was undoubtedly made easier by the harsh socio-economic conditions which prevailed. They made the people especially receptive to political agitation.

The new *Constitution* of 1891 still left the masses unrepresented. It merely resulted in a slight lowering of the franchise, permitting a rise in the electorate from 2,046 in 1891 to 2,375 in 1892, and 3,067 by 1904. But even though there was a new accessibility of the legislature to merchants, some of whom were elected, the planters strengthened their position in the elections of 1901.[78]

Thus, despite the ministrations of Governor Swettenham and Mr. Ashmore, the Government Secretary who together made some effort to reduce the pressure on the people,[79] the situation was still bleak at the beginning of 1905 when Governor Hodgson opened the legislature.[80] It was clear that British Guiana was in the grip of critical economic problems and of the socio-political troubles which largely resulted from these problems. Observers were unanimous in agreement of the necessity for immediate solutions, and almost so in forecasting impending doom, particularly if palliative measures were not implemented with great expediency. However, they tended to be divided into two schools of thought over the question of a solution. There were those who saw salvation in economic diversification, and usually looked optimistically to gold and/or rice for key roles in this remedy. The others were almost all adherents to the monocrop sugar mentality, which allowed for survival of the Colony economically, politically and socially only if sugar survived and predominated. Among those of the first group was W.A. Ireland who in 1897 felt that British Guiana was "between the devil and the deep sea", and that the Colony's problems could not be solved by halfway measures. To him, the gold industry offered a viable alternative to the unenviable position of national bankruptcy while having to provide for a hungry population.[81] Attention to the gold industry was the only alternative to "seeing a ruined Colony where once King Sugar ruled amidst opulence and prosperity".[82] But if by the 1880s sugar was no longer King, he was certainly no less than Prince Regent, having merely given up the regalia of the office and retained all the powers commensurate with it.

Perhaps, the true measure of the continued overriding dominance and consequent importance of sugar, despite the recurrent crisis in the industry, was indicated by the fact that all H.J. Perkins could claim for gold, the chief pretender to the throne, was that it was "rapidly coming to the front, and will no doubt, if carefully fostered, be, before long, the chief product of the Colony".[83] Among those who placed faith in the ability of the sugar industry to revive itself, even at the expense of other sections of the economy and society, there was an apparent inability to divest themselves of the notion that for British Guiana, sugar was all and all was sugar. Perhaps, it is precisely because they refused to see a prosperous future in any other industry that they showed a marked tendency to anticipate social convulsions ending in chaos attending the decline or demise of the sugar industry.

The Royal Commission of 1897 stood astride these two camps. While recommending the growth of an economically viable peasantry and crop diversification, they considered it hard to overstate the evils which they thought to be consequent upon a collapse of the sugar industry. This position reflected the sober recognition that the ailing industry so dominated the economy and society, that its powerful influence could not be easily abated, but that it was necessary to guard against a future recurrence of the Colony's predicament through economic diversification. The pulse of the sugar industry was still an infallible symptom of the condition of the entire Colony.

There were other observers who saw only social and economic tragedy in the decline of sugar and so sought by all means to prevent both. It is not difficult to find governors, who theoretically were supposed to be guardians of the interests of each section of the population, among the adherents to this view, which was synonymous with the thinking of the plantocracy. Governor Hemming was a classic example. Like Ireland and the Royal Commissioners, he rejected the view that the decline in the sugar industry would affect only a small section of the population. But unlike them, he felt that the interests of the entire Colony and its inhabitants were inextricably bound up with those of sugar. Hodgson in 1905 attached the same great importance to sugar as Hemming did in 1897.[84] Underlying his insistence on retaining the sugar industry's position in the Colony, and thus the existing property relations, were the expectations which Hemming held for the masses, and his apparent refusal to see the entire economic burden under which they laboured. But for all this, he could not help feeling that there was something tragically wrong. He wrote in 1897:

> Even now it is almost impossible to avoid feeling that we are, as it were, sitting on a powder magazine. Orderly and peaceful as the population of the Colony generally is, it cannot be forgotten that it is composed of very inflammable materials, and a spark of disaffection, bred by distress or discontent may easily be fanned into a flame, which could only be extinguished at the cost of much money and bloodshed.[85]

The inflammable materials were all around him. They had existed in the society before the advent of Hemming to the Colony. The high taxation, low wages, lack of political participation and adequate representation, the intransigence of the ruling plantocracy, the privileges of the bureaucracy - all these bred distress, discontent and finally disaffection. By 1905, these conditions had generated latent tensions in the society. They erupted into events that engulfed Georgetown, the East Bank and the West Bank of the Demerara and compelled the indulgence of the masses, the middle classes, the Administration and the Colonial Office until well into the following year. And indeed, this agitated state of the society was only extinguished at the cost of much money and much bloodshed.

Notes

1. Dr. Morris reported that the 1891 census showed that 90,490 people, or about one-third of the Colony's population, were involved in the sugar industry. See *Report of the West India Royal Commission* with subsidiary Report by Dr. Morris and Statistical Tables and Diagrams and a map. (London: HMSO, 1897), p. 84.
2. A.H. Adamson, *Sugar Without Slaves: The Political Economy of British Guiana. 1838-1904.* (New Haven: Yale University Press, 1972), p. 212, "Table 25, Ownership and Control of Sugar Estates, 1904".
3. *Report*, p. 3.
4. *Ibid.*, p. 1.
5. *Ibid.*, p. 25.
6. *Ibid.*
7. W. Alleyne Ireland, *Demerariana. Essays Historical, Critical and Descriptive.* (Georgetown: Baldwin and Co., 1897), p. 62.
8. *Ibid.*
9. *Ibid.*
10. *Report*, p. 5.
11. *Ibid.*
12. *Ibid.*, p. 25.
13. *Ibid.*, p. 26. See also Appendix C, Vol. II, Statistic 151, p. 124.
14. *Ibid.*
15. Adamson, Table 26. "Exports, 1838-1904, Total Value and Major Commodities as Percentage of total value, Triennial Averages." p. 215.
16. *Ibid.*, Table 20. "Sugar Estates Revenues, Cost and Profits, 1882-1901", p. 190. Dr. Morris also noted this decreasing profit margin. *Report*, p. 84. The decrease in production cost may be accounted for by way of reference to increased efficiency within the industry due to pronounced

mechanization. (See *The Colonist*, Saturday, 29 Dec. 1888; C.O. Report on the Blue Book 1884, 1885. Also N.A.G.). The slash in the wages of workers is shown in the great decrease in the wage bill of sugar estates. Adamson, p. 195.

17. Report on Blue Book. No. 477 B.G. 1904/5, p. 19.
18. Sir Augustus Hemming, Gov. of B.G. to the Chairman W.I. Royal Commission. 20 Apr. 1897. See Report, pp. 145-146.
19. For examples, see Adamson, p. 256. The adherents to this view - and they were many and powerful - tended to see the sugar industry as the ultimate guarantor of production, progress and 'civilization' in the Colony. These views were extant among members of the Colonial Office and the plantocracy during the middle of the nineteenth century. For example, see *The Rose Report*, 1850, and Earl Grey, *The Colonial Policy of Lord John Russell's Administration. 2 Vols.* (London: Richard Bent, 1853).
20. Governor Hemming to Chairman of W.I. Royal Commission. 20 Apr. 1897.
21. During this period, there was an ongoing debate over this question of economic diversification. Many prominent individuals and newspapers issued calls for the development of other industries, and often complained of neglect of these so-called "minor industries". For example. *The Nugget*, mouth-piece of the gold interests, naturally carried several leading articles on the subject. See *Nugget*, 18 Aug. 1888; 1 Aug. 1888; 26 Jan. 1889; 23 Feb. 1889; etc. N.A.G. See also Dr. Morris' Report in *Report of the W.I. Royal Commissioners* (1887).
22. Although the rice industry theoretically competed with the sugar industry for labour and afterwards for other resources, it was not viewed with antagonism by the plantocracy. Unlike the gold industry, rice farming did not necessarily take the labourers away from the coastlands and the sugar estates. It was encouraged because the planters recognized that the issue of rice lands was a powerful inducement for immigrants to re-indenture, and also to keep ex-indentured immigrants within close proximity to sugar estates, to which they gave their labour while working on their rice lands during the off-season.
23. The strategies and practices of the planter oligarchy are well documented. See, for example, Adamson's book; also, Brian L. Moore "The Social Impact of Portuguese Immigration into British Guiana after Emancipation," *Journal of Latin American and Caribbean Studies, No. 19, Dec. 1975*, and Michael J. Wagner, "*Structural Pluralism and the Portuguese in Nineteenth Century British Guiana: A Study in Historical Geography.*" (Unpublished Ph.D. Thesis, McGill University, 1975).
24. Ireland, p. 34.

25. *Ibid.*, p. 63.
26. Colonial Office. Report on Blue Book, 1884, p. 15. Also Report on Blue Book 1885, p. 36.
27. Adamson. Table 22 "Total Sugar Estate Wage Bill, 1882-1904", p. 195.
28. Ireland, p. 66. Adamson, p. 93 notes that employers in the gold industry gained large profits by selling articles at prices often 200 per cent above the normal.
29. For all this, see interview with cane cutters in The *Daily Chronicle* Tuesday, 5 Dec. 1905. Reprinted in, *The Riots in Georgetown 1905.* (Georgetown: Estate of C.K. Jardine, 1905).
30. H.J. Perkins, *Notes on British Guiana and its Gold Industry with Maps.* 2nd ed. (London: Sampson Low, Marston and Company Ltd., N.D.C. 1896-97) p. 66.
31. Almost every study of the African peasantry in the Caribbean has some information on this matter. For direct references see especially Rawle Farley, "The Rise of Village Settlement in British Guiana", *Caribbean Quarterly,* Vol. 10, 1. Mar. 1964, and Hugh Paget "The Free Village System in Jamaica" in *Ibid.* But perhaps Mintz's description of this motivation is hard to beat: "They represented a reaction to the plantation economy, a negative reflex to enslavement, mass production, monocrop dependence, and metropolitan control ... their orientation was in fact antagonistic to the plantation rationale." See Foreword in R. Guerra y Sanchez, *Sugar and Society in the Caribbean* (New Haven: 1964), pp. XX-XXI.
32. Adamson., p. 93.
33. The *Nugget* , 1 Dec. 1888.
34. Ireland, pp. 24-36, *passim.*
35. *Ibid.*, p. 65.
36. The *Mining Gazette*, 20 Feb. 1896. Quoted in Ireland, p. 36.
37. *Ibid.*
38. *Ibid.*
39. N.A.G., G.S.O. No. 325. 14 Jan. 1891. T.J. Wakefield and others to Governor - "Complaint of Present System of Registration of gold-labourers", Petition of 12 Jan. 1891.
40. G.S.O. No. 1536. 4 Mar. 1891. Petition of C.F. Hopkinson and others.
41. Adamson, pp. 239 - 40. The tendency for the official members of the legislature to support the planter oligarchy made passage of the relevant legislation far easier.
42. *Ibid.*, pp. 239-41.
43. See also Wagner, pp. 61, 116-118, etc. For exemption of estate supplies and luxuries, see W.A. Will, *Constitutional Change in the B.W.I. 1880-*

1903 with special reference to Jamaica, British Guiana and Trinidad (Oxford: Clarendon Press, 1970), p. 96.

44. Adamson, p. 242.
45. The *Nugget*, 23 Feb. 1889. The British Guiana population was also taxed to pay officials who administered the political decisions of the plantocracy. By 1899, a population of 277,000 was taxed to pay $684,000.00 per year in salaries of officials.
46. Ireland, p. 37.
47. *Ibid.*
48. *Ibid.*
49. *Ibid.*, p. 36.
50. The *Nugget*, Editorial of 26 Jan. 1889. The depression in the sugar industry must have contributed to this situation, although this was left out of the editor's analysis.
51. Adamson, p. 246. See also Table 7, p. 92 for reduction in the Government's share in village revenue from 63.30 per cent in 1883/87 to 1.60 per cent between 1893 and 1904.
52. *Ibid.*, p. 93.
53. J.M. Rohlehr, M.D., C.H.M. Letter to the Editor, *Daily Chronicle*, 8 Dec. 1905, in reply to letter of S.A. Harvey Culpeper, Manager of Ruimveldt Estate, in which the latter said that management and 'free' labour i.e., African workers, fixed wages by 'mutual arrangement' and if the latter did not like the rates they left. Letter of S.A. Harvey Culpeper to Editor, *Daily Chronicle*, 7 Dec. 1905.
54. *Daily Chronicle*. 7 Jan. 1906.
55. Hemming to Chairman of W.I. Royal Commission, 20 Apr. 1897, in *Report* Vol. II, pp. 145-146.
56. PRO. S.A. Robertson, President and H. Aron Britton, Sec., "The People's Association of British Guiana." (*Pro Salute Populi*) Enclosure in Hodgson to Elgin No. 400 of 7 Dec. 1906.
57. Herbert Barclay to the Editor, The *Daily Chronicle*, 13 Dec. 1905.
58. *Report*, p. 27.
59. For all this, see *Chronicle*, Tuesday, 5 Dec. 1905. Note that the probable average of sixty-four cents per day earned by these conductors was equal to what the gold industry paid labourers in 1897.
60. H.N. Critchlow, quoted in Hugh Payne, *Cooperativism Revisited* (unpub. work), p. 314.
61. *Chronicle*, Wednesday, 29 Nov. 1905. See also Ashton Chase, *A History of Trade Unionism in Guyana: 1900 to 1961*. (Georgetown: New Guyana Publishing Co. Ltd., 1964), p. 21.
62. Critchlow, quoted in Payne, p. 314.

63. *Chronicle*, 1 Dec. 1905.
64. *Ibid.*, 3 Dec. 1905.
65. The *Nugget*, 22 Sep. 1888.
66. Report on Blue Book, 1904/05.
67. The *Nugget*, Saturday, 19 Jan. 1889. Comments on remarks of Mr. Hill, City Police Magistrate, on sentencing four females who were charged under the *Vagrancy Ordinance* with being "incorrigible rogues" and conducting themselves in a disorderly manner.
68. N.A.G. Hodgson to Lyttleton, 45, 14 Feb. 1906. Manuscript. N.A.G.
69. Report on Blue Book, 1885.
70. Report on Blue Book, 1904.
71. *Ibid.*, 1885.
72. Adamson, pp. 264-65.
73. *Ibid.* By 1905, there was at least one organization which claimed to represent the African section of the lower class - the People's Association - which sought "to give definite shape and expression to the hitherto inarticulate cry of a landless and disheartened populace". Hodgson to Elgin, No. 400. 7 Dec. 1906.
74. Gordon K. Lewis, *The Growth of the Modern West Indies* (London: MacGibbon and Kee Ltd. 1968), pp. 106 - 107. See also Adamson, p. 256.
75. Will, pp. 96-122. Most of the description of the events leading up to the 1891 *Constitution* are taken, *passim*, from this section of Will's work.
76. The *Nugget*, 23 Feb. 1889.
77. Will, p. 122.
78. Adamson, pp. 251 - 253, *passim*.
79. N.A.G. A.A. Thorne and Philip N. Browne. "Memo to the Secretary of State with regard to the Administration of the Colony." Govt. Secretary's Office. No. 2425. 19 Apr. 1906.
80. N.A.G. "Speech of His Excellency the Governor at the Opening of the Combined Court Annual Session, 1905", Court of Policy Hall, 10 Feb. 1905.
81. Ireland, p. 35.
82. *Ibid.*, p. 63.
83. Perkins, p. 10.
84. Letter of Gov. Hemming to Royal Commissioners, 28 Apr. 1897. Report, 145-146.
85. *Ibid.*

11: The Origins of the Labour Movement

by
Hazel M. Woolford

One of the major contributions of African-Guyanese to the history of twentieth-century Guyana was the birth and growth, especially in its early stages, of labour organisation. This development was crucial to the alleviation of many of the conditions which adversely affected the life of the Guyanese working class. It was due, above all, to the daring and determination of one man, namely, Hubert Nathaniel Critchlow, and the dedication of his lieutenants in their struggle for the Colony's working class.

In 1900, the lot of urban and rural workers was unenviable. The cost of living was high, while wages were low and stationary. The working day was long and there was a high level of unemployment and underemployment. There were no trade unions or any other organisations to represent the workers in their struggle against oppressive, arrogant, and often intransigent employers. To make matters worse, the workers lacked political representation, for the income and property qualifications which made citizens eligible to vote or sit in the local legislature were far beyond the reach of the poorly paid workers[1]

Furthermore, the Government was largely indifferent to the plight of the workers. Thus, it failed to introduce any legislation to regulate wages and hours of work. Rather, it supported the plantocracy and the mercantile community in their exploitation of the workers and used the military power at its disposal to suppress workers' protests. Its attitude was very evident in its reaction to a strike for increased wages by waterfront workers, led by Critchlow, in Georgetown in November and December 1905.[2] On that occasion Governor Hodgson told a meeting of strikers:

> If you break the law in connection with your grievances, it is my duty as governor of the colony, and as

Hubert Critchlow, c 1923

> the person who has to protect the property and interests of the mercantile community to protect them.[3]

The support which he gave to the employers was a major cause of the failure of the strike.

According to Critchlow, in an address which he delivered to the World Trade Union Conference of 1945, the genesis of the trade union movement in British Guiana can be traced back to this abortive protest in 1905. In this address, which he entitled "History of the Trade Union Movement in British Guiana", he declared:

> Our working hours were 10½. The system of a quarter day existed. There was no overtime for night work. We asked the employers to change these conditions. The reply was that we must take them or go. I organised a strike on the waterfront in December 1905. Our claims were for an increase of pay, which was very low. Truckers (called boys although adult men) made two shillings a day. They could scarcely get a whole day's work, taking cargo to the barn.
>
> There was no trade union, and the employers refused. So I got the working men, boys together, and they agreed that when there were six boats in the harbour they must strike. A great thing and at that time I did not know that all the estates in the country followed us and struck on account of low wages.[4]

It was this protest which brought Critchlow into the limelight. It also made him realise the need for a trade union, for its failure was due partly to the organisational weakness of the workers. In January 1906, shortly after the suppression of the strike, Dr. Rohlehr, a middle-class spokesman for the strikers, at a meeting at the Town Hall in Georgetown called upon workers to form a trade union. Later in the year, a meeting was held at the Industrial Institute in Georgetown for this purpose, but did not result in the formation of a labour union.[5] In fact, thirteen more years were to elapse before the establishment of a trade union became a reality in British Guiana.

One major obstacle to the establishment of trade unions was the fact that, as yet they, as elsewhere in the British West Indies, did not enjoy legal recognition in the Colony. The need for a union was accentuated with the outbreak in 1914 of World War I which resulted in a significant increase in the cost of living and other hardships for the working class whose already poor economic conditions deteriorated. There were numerous strikes and other work stoppages during the War. Most of these protests were ineffective, but a few of them were successful. Particularly fruitful was the 13-day strike of waterfront workers in Georgetown in January 1917 which forced employers to grant a wage increase of 10 per cent and a reduction of the working day from 10½ to 9 hours. In December of the same year, some workers in Georgetown secured another wage increase of 10 per cent.[6]

These successes were due largely to the initiative and enterprise of Critchlow who continued to enhance his reputation as the undisputed leader of the waterfront workers. Critchlow continued to lead them in pressing their employers to grant further concessions, for the modest wage increases were soon neutralised by the continuous rise in the cost of living. In March 1918, Critchlow was dismissed by his employers after he refused to withdraw a petition to the Georgetown Chamber of Commerce requesting an 8-hour working day.[7] After his dismissal, Critchlow was unable to secure employment anywhere in Georgetown and eventually he decided to devote his time and energies to organising workers. An early consequence of this decision was his founding in January 1919 of the British Guiana Labour Union (BGLU), the first trade union to be established in the Colony.

Critchlow's success in forming the Union was due to several factors. Firstly, he profited from the growing solidarity among workers in Georgetown, particularly waterfront workers, especially after the strike of January 1917. Furthermore, he was able to take advantage of his growing reputation among these workers.

He was also encouraged by support which he received from Sir Wilfred Collet who had assumed the governorship of British Guiana in April 1917.

Critchlow had a significant meeting with Collet in December 1918 when he led a workers' demonstration to Government House, as a result of which the Governor agreed to meet a small delegation of the demonstrators. Collet, recognising the difficulties which the workers faced and the obvious limitations of their system of representation, advised Critchlow to establish a genuine trade union and to seek the assistance of unions in England. At a public meeting where this suggestion was disclosed to the disaffected workers, many paid the entrance fee on the spot and the BGLU was born with Critchlow as its secretary-treasurer.[8] In June 1919, Critchlow became the Union's full-time organiser with a salary of $20 a month. Later, in 1920, this was raised to $120 a month so as to enable him to meet the eligibility requirements for a seat in the Combined Court.

The formation of the BGLU was clearly a result of the harsh socio-economic conditions faced by the working class who therefore wished to identify with a body which would represent its cause effectively. Had it not been for the severe, depressed conditions in the Colony, there might not have been the need for the establishment of a trade union to seek improved conditions for the workers. Thus, in 1922, Critchlow stressed to a deputation from India which was investigating the possibility of Indians settling in British Guiana, that he wanted the conditions "regarding drinking water, sanitation, etc., improved for those at home" before the local government embarked on any colonisation scheme.[9]

From the inception, the BGLU, although deriving its strongest support from waterfront workers in Georgetown, was a general union, representing all workers irrespective of occupation, location, or race. In addition to waterfront workers, its members included porters, labourers, tradesmen, sea defence and road workers, railway employees, and some estate workers. This general membership would prove to be a serious administrative problem for Critchlow.

In its early years, the BGLU sought to extend its influence. It held frequent public meetings and concerts, especially at Bourda Green and at street corners in Georgetown. The popular venues were James and Albert Streets in Albouystown and Louisa Row and Bent Streets in Wortmanville.

Because Critchlow was under the constant surveillance of police and spies from the employer class, statistical data on the size of the crowds which attended these meetings are available. It was not unusual for these meetings to attract as many as 400 persons and for the Union to hold public meetings twice in a single day. These meetings also reflected the creativity of Critchlow and his organisers as, on some occasions, entertainers with brass bands were in attendance and recitations were said.

The Union also extended its activities to the rural areas of the Colony. According to Critchlow, between 1919 and 1920 he "roped in nearly the whole country. Every estate. I had to travel night and day to keep in touch."[10] He also endeavoured with some success to establish branches of the Union in various areas of the countryside. In 1921, for example, he attempted to establish a branch on the island of Wakenaam in Essequibo. As late as 1926, he continued to travel around the country to open new branches. In March 1926, he opened a branch in New Amsterdam in Berbice. While he was in New Amsterdam, he was invited by other villages in Berbice, including Smithfield and Cumberland, to establish branches there. He was commended for this expansion by the editor of the *New Daily Chronicle* who observed:

> In this respect Mr Critchlow has done his bit in the work of trying to get at the people, teaching them to use their own brains to think for themselves and guiding them in the performance of acting to secure the measure which should be meted to them. This is as it should be, and, with the exercise of prudence as well as of average intelligence, there is no reason why the Union should not achieve its lofty destiny of uplifting the masses and cementing a practicable

> and genuine appreciation between employer and employed.[11]

The initial efforts of expansion were designed particularly to ensure that the Union did not collapse. They were so successful that by the beginning of Jan. 1920 the BGLU had 13,000 members and respectable savings of $9,700 in the bank. The survival and success of the Union were a source of satisfaction to Critchlow who was conscious of the view of critics that: "no Blackman could carry on anything for more than six months."[12] Not surprisingly, the first anniversary of the formation of the Union was an occasion for special celebration at the Parade Ground in Georgetown. Rev. Chase delivered a sermon based on the eighth verse of the third chapter of the Book of Revelation: "Behold I have given you an open door which no man can shut." Among those who paid tribute to the Union were Rev. H.W. Grant, President of the Beterverwagting branch, Francis Dias, the leading Portuguese politician; and Edmund Fredericks, an African-Guyanese barrister-at-law who two years later founded the Negro Progress Convention (NPC).

By the time of these first anniversary celebrations, it was evident that the fledgling Union and its leaders were beginning to make an impact. One of its earliest achievements for workers was in June 1919 when it succeeded in securing the abolition of night and Sunday work in bakeries. Increasing success bred greater militancy and more fearless action. In September 1920, for example, Critchlow led a demonstration to protest against the *Seditious Publications Bill*. This was bold and emphatic action and it became increasingly clear to the colonial administration, the plantocracy and the mercantile class that the BGLU could not be diverted or dissuaded from its aggressive militancy on behalf of the working class. Later in the year 1920, the Union gained a number of concessions, including a further increase of wages for some workers and the appointment of a commission to investigate the cost of living, wages and other conditions affecting stevedores. The commission agreed that it was necessary to improve these conditions by increasing wages.

The Union's next major success was in its struggle for legal status. Although it was active, it was not, and could not be, registered because of the absence of legislation granting legal recognition to labour organisations. In June 1921, however, owing largely to pressure from the BGLU and the Colonial Office in London, harassed by the British Labour Party, the Colony's legislature passed a *Trade Union Ordinance* legalising the existence of trade unions in British Guiana. The intervention of the Labour Party and the Colonial Office was a direct result of an appeal for help from Critchlow, prompted by his consciousness of the fierce hostility on the part of members of the Combined Court to the registration of unions.

One important distinctive feature of the *Ordinance*, which provided for the regulation and registration of trade unions, was that it protected the trade union movement in British Guiana from the attack of employers and damages as a result of strikes, in striking contrast to the 1917 Jamaican ordinance which did not confer such privileges to unions in Jamaica.[13] Under the provisions of this June 1921 *Ordinance*, in July 1922 the BGLU was registered, thus becoming a legal entity. It was the first registered trade union in the dependent British Empire.

On 3 July 1922, shortly before the registration of the BGLU, the Union was able to persuade the legislature to introduce a *Rent Restriction Bill*. This measure was designed to check the behaviour of rapacious landlords who, from at least 1914, had been exploiting the situation of inadequate housing, especially in Georgetown, to impose increasingly high rents on tenants. Such rents were a major contributor to the high cost of living which workers experienced. Not surprisingly, many tenants profited from the new legislation and applied to the Courts to fix their maximum rents. The relief was so substantial that a committee of tenants named 3 July 1922 'Critchlow Day' in recognition of his success in securing the enactment of the *Rent Restriction Ordinance*. This concession, however, was only granted in return for consent by the BGLU to the employers' proposal to reduce wages for a second time within a year. Wages had been reduced arbitrarily by employers in June 1921 without consulting the Union as a reaction to an international recession which resulted in a fall in prices of the Colony's exports and the stagnation of overseas markets.[14] It was with great reluctance that Critchlow agreed to the scheme to cut wages, but he viewed wage reduction as a means of checking retrenchment, to which employers had begun to resort extensively as a response to the recession. In 1923 and 1924, there were further drops in wages.[15]

The *Rent Restriction Ordinance* was only applicable for a year, but the BGLU campaigned successfully for its extension. Admittedly, some landlords eventually began to breach the *Ordinance* and Critchlow found it necessary on at least one occasion, namely in 1929, to send a petition to the Governor about the enforcement of the *Ordinance*.[16]

Apart from rents and wages, the most major issue addressed by the BGLU in the 1920s was that of unemployment and underemployment. In Aug. 1922 the Union staged several well-attended unemployment demonstrations to sensitise the Government and employers to the seriousness of the problem. It also passed resolutions about employment and requested the Government to grant relief by initiating public works, such as road repairs and construction, to provide work. In 1923, Critchlow petitioned the Government against the escalating levels of unemployment and underemployment but without any immediate result. Eventually, some relief was secured when labour was made available with the construction of a sewerage scheme in 1924. The Union, however, had to insist that the jobs be given to local workers in preference to those who arrived from the West Indian islands.[17]

The Union continued to take action to alleviate the plight of the poor, especially the unemployed and underemployed. It offered social services such as a soup kitchen to feed the poor every Saturday morning. Furthermore, in 1930 Critchlow succeeded in getting the British Government to donate 52,000 agricultural tools to the Colony to enable the residents to supplement their living through agriculture. In May of that same year, the Union, in an effort to publicise the needs and problems of workers, initiated the first of what became annual 'Labour Day' marches. It assumed the responsibility for organising these marches until 1942 when the British Guiana Trade Union Council (BGTUC) took over the task.

In spite of its activities, the BGLU did not secure many significant benefits for workers in British Guiana in the latter part of the 1920s. In that period, however, it enhanced its reputation in the Caribbean and further afield. It was able to initiate the establishment of a regional labour congress. Thus, in January 1926, it hosted the first British Guiana and West Indian Labour Congress at the Public Buildings in Georgetown. The delegates included Arthur Cipriani, President of the Trinidad Workingmen's Association; W.J. Lesperan and W.H. Bastick of Suriname; and Grantley Adams of Barbados. Thereafter the BGLU became actively involved in the Caribbean trade union movement.[18]

Critchlow also believed that his efforts to promote the welfare of workers in British Guiana would be enhanced by support from the international trade union community. He was therefore very visible in that community. In 1924, he went to London where he met members of the British Labour Party, the Trade Union Congress and other associations interested in the colonies and obtained promises of assistance from them. In 1925 and 1930, he attended the British Commonwealth Labour Conference, where he presented the demands of the Guyanese working class. At the 1930 Conference, for example, he demanded a reduction in working hours, modification of the franchise to adult suffrage, labour representation in the Legislative Council and social insurance, including old-age pensions and national health insurance. Along with Cipriani, he also called for free meals and books for school children, kindergardens, prison reforms, promotion for policemen to commissioned-officer rank and the establishment of teacher-training colleges.[19]

The BGLU also gained the recognition of the international socialist movement which was soliciting the support of trade unions all over the world.[20] This recognition was strengthened in 1931 when Critchlow attended "The International Trade Union Committee of Negro Workers" in Germany and "The International Red

Aid" in Russia. Such contacts caused Critchlow to be branded a Communist and to be regarded as dangerous by some of his critics. The Union also profited from the support of the British Labour Party in the United Kingdom with which Critchlow maintained regular communication and from which he received encouragement and guidance. F.O. Roberts, an official of the Party and of the British Trade Union Congress, was among the foreign delegates who were present at the BGLU's annual conference in Georgetown in 1926.

By 1930, the BGLU could be credited with a number of significant achievements. This success was largely the result of several key factors. One of them was some of Critchlow's virtues, such as his determination, aggression and energetic pursuit of the welfare of the working class. The Union also benefited during the vulnerable formative phase of its existence from the sympathetic attitude of Governor Collet who had some appreciation especially for Critchlow. This was very obvious in April 1919 when Critchlow was in trouble in the wake of a mass-meeting which he held in support of his demand for an 8-hour working day. He was arrested and charged with sedition[21] because he printed and circulated a handbill with the following militant verse:

> To arms to arms, ye brave
> The avenging sword and shield
> March on, March on
> All hearts, resolve to liberty and death.

Collet intervened and the charge was dropped. Collet's favourable opinion of, and disposition towards, Critchlow were also evident in a dispatch to the Colonial Office in July 1920 in which he observed:

> Critchlow himself seems to be not an unreasonable man, but the members of the union are not always willing to take his advice, and in order to retain his position he is occasionally compelled to do what I think his better judgement would disapprove.[22]

It was indeed a fact that on numerous occasions when Critchlow faced crises in the Labour Union, he was forced to adopt a position which was in contradiction to his ideals.

The Union's success was also due partly to the nature of *the British Guiana Trade Union Ordinance*, which protected it from victimisation and legal responsibility for damages that employers suffered as a result of strike action. This protection enabled the BGLU not only to survive, but also to be more militant than it otherwise might have been.

The Union's experience was in striking contrast to that of many other unions in the Caribbean. For example, while the BGLU progressed, the Longshoremen's Union, which was founded in Jamaica in 1908, ceased to exist by the end of World War I largely because the trade union ordinance that had been introduced in Jamaica did not protect the union against damages which occurred as a consequence of strike action. In fact, as late as 1930, British Guiana was the only Colony in the Caribbean where *the Trade Union Ordinance* provided such protection.

Finally, the cause of the BGLU was assisted significantly, especially initially, by the usefulness of its newspaper, the *Labour Magazine*. The introduction of this medium of communication was considered necessary both for organisational purposes as well as to sensitise its members and the general public concerning the work of the Union. In fact, it is believed that the militancy of the Union and the forthrightness of the *Labour Magazine* were largely responsible for the enactment of *Ordinance* No. 17 of 1921 which legalised the existence of trade unions in British Guiana.

Even though these factors were crucial to the effectiveness of the BGLU, the Union achieved only limited success in the 1920s. The limited nature of its gains was particularly evident in its efforts to improve conditions for workers in the two vital areas of wages and unemployment and underemployment. It was also obvious in the Union's inability to secure an 8-hour working day for all categories of workers and in the failure of its youth arm, which was established in 1924 but had become defunct by 1929 owing to lack of support. Another failure which the BGLU experienced was in its attempt to raise funds through cooperative business ventures. Its first such experience was in 1920 and 1921. About January 1920 the Union decided to raise $3,000 to start a cooperative enterprise called the Industrial Trading Company. Before all the shares were allotted, the members insisted that a start should be made. Credit was taken and the Company purchased 500 bags of rice at $8 a bag with the hope of retailing them at about $13 a bag within three weeks. Shortly after the purchase, however, the price of rice fell on the open market and the Company was forced to resell the rice at $7 a bag, thus incurring a loss. Not surprisingly, the Company declared itself insolvent soon after. In short, by June 1921 it had collapsed mainly because of mismanagement by its employees and its inability to compete with the prices offered by the merchants in Water Street in Georgetown. According to Critchlow, this failure left him with the idea that "in the interest of the workers we must get control."[23]

Even more disappointing to the Union than this unsuccessful business venture was the failure of its main protest in the 1920s. This occurred in 1924 when, on 31 March, dock workers in Georgetown, in response to a call by the Union, went on strike to force their employers to meet their demand for higher wages. The strike was followed by a demonstration through the streets of Georgetown. On 3 April, a large group of workers from sugar plantations on the East Bank of Demerara, whose cause was also supported by the Union, set out on a march to the city to demonstrate solidarity with the striking dock workers. The group was stopped at Ruimveldt and eventually dispersed after a combined force of the Police and Militia fired upon the crowd, killing 13 and wounding 24 workers. Ultimately, this use of force and other forms of opposition from the Government and lack of compliance by employers served to ensure the failure of the protest.[24]

In the 1920s, the most conspicuous failure the BGLU experienced was probably the sphere of political demands. It focused on political questions especially in the late 1920s when the Colony was faced with the prospect, and then the reality, of the introduction of Crown Colony rule. Apart from its opposition to Crown Colony government, the Union's major political demands in the 1920s were the extension of the franchise to women, universal adult suffrage, the representation of labour in the Legislative Council and self-government. Apart from the grant of the franchise to some women, none of these demands was met until at least the 1940s.[25] The limited success which the BGLU achieved in the 1920s was due partly to its weaknesses and a variety of obstacles which it encountered. The most persistent and most formidable obstacle was the hostile environment in which the Union was established and for many years grew. The Union often faced hostility from the ruling class and employers, especially planters and merchants, many of whom regarded the representatives of labour as dangerous elements in the society. The Union was accused of fomenting strikes and other disturbances irrespective of their location. Critchlow and other Union officials and their public meetings were usually subject to police surveillance.[26] Critchlow was conscious of such opposition and harassment. As he is reported to have observed during a public meeting in May 1928:

> He don't want no man to get themselves in no trouble for the Government don't like him and they will do anything to put him in prison but he is a free English subject and can speak as he likes. He don't mind how many spies is sent out to listen to him and to report him.[27]

At that same meeting, he is also said to have remarked:

> There was a Colonel by the name of Mekinniss, he send a Policeman to stop a dog from barking because he can't get to sleep and the police was unable to stop the dog from barking he charge the PC and fine him. Those are the same men against him although it is he who made them get more money on their salaries.[28]

The BGLU also suffered from opposition from the press. There were some newspapers, especially those owned or controlled by the mercantile community, which were particularly hostile to the Union. They seized any opportunity to spread dissension among the working class and to undermine the leadership and militancy of the Union.[29]

In its early years, the BGLU was severely affected by internal strife. Basic to this problem was the fact that some middle-class Black and Coloured professionals who were supporters of the union felt that their education and experience made them better qualified to lead the workers than Critchlow who had been forced to leave school at an early age because of the death of his father. Rumours began to circulate in 1919 that Critchlow was an uneducated man and that the Union's funds were too much for him to handle.

At a meeting of the Union on 19 January 1920, it was proposed that he should hand over all the funds of the Union by 10:00 a.m. on the following day to Dr. T.T. Nichols, J.S. Johnson and A. Mc Lean Ogle, who were lawyers. The motion was rejected and a vote of confidence in Critchlow was passed. The fact was that, at that time, the Union was not registered and all the banks had refused to take deposits in its name. The funds were therefore deposited in Critchlow's name, but he had honestly held his trust.[30] Serious attempts to oust Critchlow from his position in the Union continued for at least another year, but without success. The dissatisfaction engendered caused many members to lose confidence in the Union and to cease to associate with it.

The declining membership, after the initial two years of growth, severely hampered the Union, as shown in the following statistics:

Year	1921	1924	1925	1926	1927	1928	1929	1930
Membership	7,000	418	516	387	200	75	171	93

This decline was due to other factors besides the internal strife, mainly the economic depression in the Colony and its impact on wages. Members of the Union complained that they were financially incapable of paying the dues. Some of them discontinued their membership because they felt that the Union had become impotent in its efforts to bargain for higher wages. What they did not realise was that employers, especially the owners of the sugar industry, were reluctant to pay higher wages because, as they insisted, they were not in a sound financial position. Perhaps the Union could have done more to sensitise its membership to the true dimensions of the economic crisis. Eventually, by 1930, it was forced to suspend its membership dues because of the falling off in membership.[31]

The numerical decline had a severe impact on the Union, plunging it into serious financial straits. The financial statement for 1929, for example, showed the income as only $1,030.69 and the expenditure as $1,022.74. Debts included unpaid salaries and rent. In these circumstances the Union had to curtail its activities and had no hope of accumulating a strike fund, which Critchlow had started in 1924.[32] Lack of financial and human resources meant that it was impossible for the Union to provide adequate representation for all workers in a territory as extensive as British Guiana.

The Union's effectiveness was also hampered by its lack of political influence. Critchlow was very conscious of this weakness. It was his opinion that the Government should be composed of representatives of the people. He was, of course, particularly concerned that labour should be represented. In 1939, when he appeared before the Moyne Commission, he expressed his view forcefully when he said:

> At the present time the majority of us have no vote and therefore no member of the Legislative Council is going to do anything for the people. I have been asking the government for certain legislation since 1922. The interests impeding this legislation are strongly represented but the interests desiring it are scarcely represented at all.[33]

In spite of these major obstacles and weaknesses, the BGLU not only survived but also, by 1930, managed to secure significant benefits for workers. Although its leaders were mainly African-Guyanese and its strongest supporters were African-Guyanese waterfront workers, the Union sought to represent all workers, irrespective of race, occupation or location. It championed the cause of East Indian sugar estate workers especially on the East Coast and East Bank of Demerara, particularly from 1924. It collaborated with the British Guiana East Indian Association (BGEIA) in seeking better wages for these workers and in providing leadership and direction to them.[34] In short, the BGLU did not deviate from its original purpose of being a general union which would represent all workers. This was recognised by many East Indian workers and spokesmen. For example, in 1933, A.R. Khan, an East Indian member of the defunct Canadian Seamen Union, observed:

> We hope everybody here will join and become a member of the BGLU. It is formed for every nation in the Colony and not for the Negroes only as some say. Without pressure Ladies and Gentlemen we will not get what we want. We have four enemies against us, the Lawyers, Ministers, Landlords, and the Capitalists. Comrades you should consider your leader Mr Hubert Critchlow, it is through his instrumentality that the Government has regard for the working class man.[35]

Critchlow, however, was conscious of the limitations of the BGLU. He encouraged workers to establish their own unions, if they were dissatisfied with the BGLU. His principal concern was that all workers should become organised and properly represented.

Through his influence many unions were established in the 1930s and 1940s, ushering in a new phase in the history of the trade union movement in British Guiana. The first such unions were the British Guiana Workers League, founded in 1931 by A.A. Thorne, and the Manpower Citizens' Association, which was formed in 1937 and led by Ayube Edun.[36]

Notes

1. Hubert N. Critchlow, "History of the Trade Union Movement in British Guiana," the text of an address given at the World Trade Union Conference of 1945.
2. The most informative account of the 1905 protest is Francis Drakes (now Kimani Nehusi), "The 1905 Protest in British Guiana: Causes, Course and Consequences" (Unpublished M.A. Thesis, University of Guyana, 1982).
3. The *Daily Chronicle*, 2 Dec. 1905.
4. Critchlow, "History."
5. Hazel M. Woolford, "History of the Guyana Labour Union ,1919-1986" (Unpublished typescript), p. viii.
6. Ashton Chase, *A History of Trade Unionism in Guyana 1900 to 1961* (Georgetown: New Guyana Company Ltd., 1966), pp. 42-49.
7. Critchlow, "History"; Chase, pp. 49-50.
8. Critchlow, "History."
9. Report by Dewan Bahadur Pillai and U.N. Tiwary on the Scheme for Indian Immigration to British Guiana (Simla, Superintendent Government, 1924), Part I, p. 95.
10. Critchlow, "History."
11. *Daily Chronicle*, 6 Mar. 1926.
12. Critchlow, "History."
13. See Ordinance No. XVII of 1921 entitled "An Ordinance to provide for the Regulation and Registration of Trade Unions."
14. Chase, pp. 62-3
15. *Ibid.*, p. 62.
16. Inspector General of Police to Colonial Secretary, 2 May 1929, GNA.
17. Chase, pp. 65-6.
18. *Ibid.*, pp. 73-5.
19. *Ibid.*, pp. 72-3, 76.
20. Winslow Carrington, *The Trade Union Movement: Its History and its Growth* (Georgetown: TUC, n.d.), p. 3.
21. Critchlow, "History."
22. *Ibid.*
23. *Ibid.*
24. The most informative accounts of the 1924 protest are: Ann Spackman, "Official Attitudes and Official Violence: The Ruimveldt Masscre, Guiana 1924", *Social and Economic Studies*, Vol. XXII, No. 3 (Sep., 1973); Silvius Wilson, "The Background to the Ruimveldt Incident of 1924", *History*

Gazette, No. 67 (Apr. 1994); Silvius Wilson, "The Causes of the Ruimveldt Incident of 1924," *History Gazette*, No. 68 (May, 1994).

25. Hazel M. Woolford, 'Hubert Nathaniel Critchlow: The Crusader", *History Gazette*, No. 43 (Apr. 1992), pp. 7-8.
26. Woolford, "History", p. xi.
27. Inspector General of Police to Colonial Secretary, 2 May 1928.
28. *Ibid.*
29. Woolford, "History", p. xiii.
30. Chase, pp. 51-2.
31. Woolford, "History", pp. 37-8, 48-9.
32. *Ibid.*, p. 38.
33. Report of the West India Commission, 1939.
34. Wilson, "The Causes", pp. 5-12.
35. Reports of the activities of the British Guiana Labour Union, No. 173/32, 4 Jan. 1933, cited in Woolford, "History", p. xiii.
36. Woolford, "Hubert Nathaniel Critchlow", pp. 6-7.

12: The Coming of Crown Colony Government in 1928

by
James G. Rose

The nineteenth century constitutional arrangement in British Guiana was a unique system of administration. The Court of Policy, introduced in the 1690s,[1] was made up of the *Commandeur*, his secretary and two or three managers of the plantations belonging to the Dutch West India Company (WIC). This body met periodically to discuss the affairs of the Company and, on occasions, addressed attention to matters of judicial significance. In the beginning, this was a very informal arrangement but, some years later on 28 September 1718, it was institutionalised as the *Raad van Politie en Justitie* - The Council of Policy and Justice.[2] At the same time, the clerk of the Company was invited to become a member, while the secretary of the Company was identified as the functionary next in authority to the *Commandeur*.[3]

In 1739, after much agitation, private planters grudgingly were permitted to sit with the Company's managers in the Council.[4] In 1746, six officers of the burgher militia were constituted into a College of *Kiezers* (Electors) with the express purpose of nominating the representatives from the free planter community to the Council of Policy and Justice.[5] Over a period, the Council of Policy was separated from the Council of Justice (1750), was enlarged and gathered to itself diverse other functions.[6]

The evidence suggests that almost from the beginning there were divisions within the Council over issues, a few of which were critical to the ultimate structure and function of the organisation.[7] One of the really contentious issues was the jurisdiction of the Council over matters pertaining to the finance of Colony. There was a Company (King's) Chest derived from customs duty and a head tax on slaves. This revenue was used to defray all colonial expenses. There was, as well, the Colony Chest, over which the colonists exercised some measure of control by virtue of the fact that all contributory taxes necessitated their consent.[8] The problem here was the tendency on the part of the *Commandeur* to charge expenses perceived as belonging under the jurisdiction of the Company Chest to this fund.

The other thorny issue concerned the role and function of the *Kiezers*. Did they have rights so far as Company issues were concerned, or were they restricted to Colony affairs only? Since they were derived from the burgher militia, their jurisdiction over things colonial was understood. But the burghers preferred to be seen as having a jurisdiction extending across Company affairs as well, and this produced early conflicts which had to be speedily resolved.[9]

In 1784, a crisis arose when the States-General attempted to reduce the representation of the free planter community and, more importantly, the right of nomination, perceived as the elective principle, from the burgher community, the College of *Kiezers*.[10] Protest and agitation produced an investigation in 1786 resulting in the Concept Plan of Redress of 1787.[11]

The Plan was something of a mixed blessing for, while it offered the free planter community equal representation with the Company officials, it seemed to be denying the right to discuss the finances of the Colony. It should be noted that equal representation in itself was coming much later than it had been earned, for the free planters were by far the dominant economic group in the society. This fact was recognised in the enlargement of the membership of a separate College for Demerara. The free planter community, however, was disturbed by the implied right of the Governor, in agreement with the *Commandeur* of Essequibo and Demerara and sitting with the Fiscal, to control the revenue. This reversal created much distress and, as a consequence, on 12 January 1795, new instructions suggested that the Government and College of *Kiezers* should watch over the colonial fund. This joint meeting took place on 22 June 1795, when the Court of Policy and the College of *Kiezers* met to discuss matters of a financial nature and decided that this combined council would henceforth supervise the raising of funds and regulate its expenditure.[12] In this way, the College of *Kiezers* was, for this peculiar purpose, transposed into a College of Financial Representatives.

The true implications of the combination of a single interest were soon realised, and the concession was withdrawn on 11 June 1796. This brought to an end the functioning of what had come to be known as the Financial Department.[13] These developments coincided with the capture of the colonies by the British, who retained possession pending the return to peace. It was argued convincingly by the plantocracy that the new arrangement, in which the Governor would put an estimate of annual expenditure to the Court of Policy, and allow the Combined Court to determine the ways and means of funding the estimate, was the practice at the time of capitulation. The *Articles of Capitulation* made sacred and inviolable those institutions, practices and customs which were in existence at this time. The planter community argued that its control over the revenue was a recognised practice at the time of the capitulation and therefore was to be continued by the British in keeping with the *Articles of Capitulation*.[14]

In 1803, the British took over the administration of the Guiana colonies for the third time.[15] The *Articles of Capitulation* undertook to uphold the existing institutions and practices, presumably confirming the Combined Court in its participation in the consideration of financial matters. The British were confirmed in their control of the colonies in 1814 and the colonies were unified in 1831. With the abolition of slavery, the old system of raising revenue by a tax on slaves could no longer work, so a new system had to be devised. The Colonial Office directed the Government to induce the Combined Court to grant the King's Chest a fixed sum of £17,500, in return for which it conceded to the Court that the Civil List, "... though continuing to be prepared as at present by the Court of Policy, shall be discussed in detail, freely, without reserve by the Combined Court..."[16] In this way, the oligarchy gained British acceptance of its control of the revenues of the Colony.

Emancipation threatened the existence of the sugar economy. Labour problems created the need for immigration, and immigration generated a need for funding. This forced the planter oligarchy increasingly to strengthen its stranglehold on the administrative machinery, to the exclusion of all other interests and, more often than not, at the expense of the Colonial Office.[17] This was vital to the interests of the planters since they needed to control finance to be able to assist themselves through state funding. As interests other than sugar emerged, they demanded access to the political process, but this could not be granted at such a critical juncture. The franchise was restricted. It was based on ownership of property and on the extent to which that property was cultivated. Agitation persisted against this form of discrimination but, essentially, what was sought was not so much a change in structure and function as in eligibility. Limited gains were achieved in 1849, 1852 and again in 1855[18] during periods of particularly intense agitation.

The second half, and particularly the final quarter, of the nineteenth century, saw the sugar economy in deep and almost chronic recession. The peasantry was also in decline. The independent Creole community was systematically dislodged from its huckstering activities. The labour force was being contracted and the wage rate considerably reduced. The independent embryonic Portuguese commercial sector was also ailing in the wake of the recession in the dominant sugar economy.[19] All sectors clamoured for relief and sought amelioration through political action. By the 1880s, the need for constitutional reform of a profound nature was admitted by the Colonial Office, its local chief servant, Governor Henry T. Irving, and the planter oligarchy.[20]

In the attempts to deal with this situation, however, the Colonial Office was restrained by countervailing issues, especially the colour question. Liberalisation of the franchise would lead to increasing access of Africans to the legislature and, since they enjoyed a numerical preponderance in the population, it was not difficult to foresee their taking complete control of this body eventually. But the Africans were considered unsuited for the exercise of power, particularly in so far as this power could be used against White economic interests. This was of critical importance because, as the Whites perceived it, Africans, "... knowledge of economics, finance and commerce has oft times not a very deep foundation..."[21]

It was also no secret that the disaffected African peasantry and Creole groups were still at war with the White oligarchy. Their repeated calls for state-funded drainage and irrigation and a relaxation of the prohibitive and punitive tax system, and the consistent rebuffs which they suffered from the White power structure, were compelling reminders of this contest.[22] The anti-Portuguese riot of 1889 was essentially displaced anger by the urban Creole sector.[23]

Once again, the survival of the sugar economy depended on the control of the political process. The 1891 reforms abolished the College of *Kiezers* and introduced direct elections for the elected section of the Court of Policy by those already qualified to vote for the Financial Representatives. The Court of Policy was enlarged from 10 to 16 by the addition of three official and three elected members. The electorate was also enlarged by a property qualification of the ownership of immovable property to the value of not less than $7,500, and the reduction of the income qualification from $600 to $480 per *annum* for access to the franchise.[24]

These gains were carefully counterbalanced by the exclusion of aliens, a measure aimed at immigrant Portuguese, and the retention of the iniquitous system of open voting. The establishment of an Executive Council, to which was transferred the executive and legislative functions of the Court of Policy,[25] was exceedingly significant. This transfer of functions effectively emasculated the Court of Policy. Finally, the Governor was invested with the power to dissolve the Court of Policy and unseat the Financial Representatives. These measures were all designed to strengthen the hand of the Governor and the Government section of the legislature.[26] But at the same time, they were intended to secure the special interest of sugar from the aggressive competition of other economic interests.[27]

Since Africans were totally unacceptable and the Coloured class was not wholly accredited,[28] the White section was expected to continue its dominance over the system. Yet, the conceded reforms reduced the alienation of the commercial class and gave it access to the political system.[29] This was significant since it split and isolated the African and Coloured sections.[30] Indeed, the earliest post-1891 evidence indicated quite clearly that the Coloured had lost ground to the White commercial sector. In the pre-reform representative roll, there were thirteen Europeans, four Coloureds and one African. These were made up of four plantation proprietors, three attorneys, one planter, two bank managers, the manager of one of the local railway companies, three merchants and three barristers. Under the new *Constitution*, the election results revealed that out of fourteen persons elected, two were proprietors of sugar estates, two attorneys, three planters, five merchants and two lawyers. The planter class, like the Coloured group, had lost ground to the commercial class.[31]

In fact, even though they were to some extent responsible, the reforms to the *Constitution* do not alone account for this slight shift. The reforms in the franchise indicated a widening of the electorate; yet, while the 1891 electoral roll numbered 2,210, the immediate post-reform electoral roll stood at the reduced number of 2,046.[32] The very belief that the reforms were not only moderate, but, in a real sense, a betrayal of the Coloured class may have influenced some of the former voters against registration. On the other hand, many aliens previously enfranchised were now disenfranchised. There was also the problem of military service. It would seem that "...after 1891, all those registering for the franchise would also in effect have declared themselves available for military service," which seems to have been unpopular among some sections of the community.[33]

The machinery did not function in a manner encouraging to the newly enfranchised. There were complaints about a shortage of registration forms[34] and, in addition, Africans and Coloureds were deliberately obstructed in their efforts to become registered.[35] It seems that every opportunity was taken to deem them illiterates or, in other ways, ineligible.[36] Furthermore, the time available was much too short and many of the newly qualified seemed unaware of the procedure as well as the import. Then too, miners and those in the timber industry located in the interior were totally excluded.[38] Finally, the iniquitous practice of the open ballot discouraged many from participating for fear of victimisation in one form or another.[39]

On the one hand, it was not difficult to explain the moderation of the reforms. The Colonial Office was not prepared to be liberal at the expense of the planter class, already burdened with serious economic problems.[40] It was reluctant to encounter the criticisms anticipated in the British Parliament from the strong lobby which supported colonial economic activity.[41] Also, the grave importance which it attached to the procurement of an enlarged Civil List discouraged any attempt at radicalism.[42] On the other hand, Governor Sir Henry Irving was resolute about meaningful changes. He was strongly against a *Constitution* in which "...one interest only is represented and in which that interest can, when it may deem proper to do so, bring about a deadlock in public affairs".[43] Irving was enterprising. He persuaded the planters that changes were necessary. However, he was abrasive and, in the circumstances, the Colonial Office deliberately withheld changes until he was replaced.[44] Governor Viscount Gormanston actually encouraged the planter oligarchy to oppose any attempt to change the *Constitution*.[45]

The Colonial Office, the Governor, and the planter body were able to get away with this *volte face* because, in reality, there was an absence of a really radical pressure group bent on achieving meaningful changes. The middle class was composed of two conservative elements: firstly, the domestic capitalist who wanted to be granted privileges similar to those enjoyed by foreign capital, and secondly, a Coloured and African intelligentsia/professional group who wanted recognition, but who, at the same time, was suspicious of similar ambitions of the African working-class. Neither element craved profound structural changes. It was easy therefore for the Colonial Office to satisfy such demands by offering limited concessions. There was, as always, the commitment given in 1803 to honour the *Articles of Capitulation*. All the same, it is significant to note that the Colonial Office never perceived itself as duly hampered. Thus, the Secretary of State told Governor Gormanston:

> In... your request for instructions as to how far any reform of the *Constitution* of the Colony can be effected without Imperial Legislation, I have to acquaint you that as the Colony was added to the British dominion by conquest confirmed by the concession contained in the Treaty of 1814, the power of making laws was from the first, exercisable by the King in Council.[47]

In short, it was not that the British Government could not but, rather, that it chose not to, legislate for the Colony. Yet, what was not manifest was latent. In 1896, secret balloting was introduced. The Colonial Office for some time was bothered by the abuses of open balloting and in 1891 had reluctantly conceded this clause. The timely withdrawal of this device one year before the general elections of 1897 helped other interests to exploit the latent flaws in the 1891 *Constitution*.[48]

Furthermore, it does seem that the reverses of the 1892 elections inspired the Coloured and African elements to improve their performance at subsequent elections. Their politics became more radical, more flamboyant and better organised. The report of the Royal Commission of 1897 gave added impetus to those opposed to the sugar interest, when it virtually certified the death of the sugar industry and demanded recognition of other forms of economic activity.[49] Moreover, the issue of race, never far below the surface, emerged as a critical factor in all subsequent election campaigns.[50] Finally, there definitely was a new consciousness, manifested in intense working-class militancy and protests.[51]

While working-class organisations, still few in number, were not directly associated with any particular political organisation, and although no really mass-based political party was in existence, it appears that a direct correlation existed between working-class restiveness and heightened consciousness among the masses. This was recognised by the middle-class politicians who chose to exploit the African platform. This encouraged those Africans and Coloureds recently admitted to the franchise to stand more solidly with the African and Coloured caucus. The result was the increasing gains of these politicians and the corresponding marginalisation of European representation in the legislature.

This ouster of the White element is critical to an understanding of what was to take place in the 1920s. In the immediate post-reform elections this consequence was not obvious, but it became increasingly evident, particularly when further liberalisation took place in 1909.[52] Such a development was important because the bulk of the newly enfranchised came from the lower classes, particularly African and Coloured, and some second-generation Indians. This class of voter had its own concerns, grievances and ambitions, and it was apparent that these did not coincide with those of the White oligarchy.[53]

This divergence produced a shift in electoral issues which tended to radicalise the political process.[54] The oligarchy complained that the process had been vulgarised,[55] a factor which may partially account for its withdrawal. Its inability to carry the new issues convincingly to the recently enfranchsied seems to have been another motivating factor. Further, the fact that the distorted socio-economic formation produced recurrent racial issues kept the Whites on the defensive, making some of them extremely unpopular, particularly at election time. This prompted some of them to withdraw from politics even when an electoral contest was unnecessary.[56] The fact that their concerns and ambitions were still given priority consideration in the Executive Council would have considerably helped to ease their withdrawal from public contest.[57]

In addition, the introduction of secret balloting reduced the possibility of victimisation and ensured a greater measure of confidentiality.[58] The planters' control of the electorate through coercion and mystification was thus undermined, thereby helping to reduce their efficacy at the polls.

As early as 1897, Edward Davson, an Englishman, planter and bigot, proposed the abolition of the 1891 *Constitution* on the ground that too many Africans had been enfranchised. He lamented the fact that African representatives with no stake in the economic well-being of the Colony had begun to take over the legislature.[59] In a lecture to the Royal Colonial Institute, Davson declared: "I do not believe that in any Colony of the Empire the White element should be subject to the coloured whether it be African, brown or yellow..."[60] In 1889, Rev. J.G. Pearson was even more explicit. He lamented "the futility of speaking of legislating for, and treating, the Africans as upon all fours with ourselves."[61] He had earlier noted:

> We govern him by the same laws as we govern ourselves and that in the abstract is right, but probably in practice laws apparently equitable would prove tenfold more beneficient... we owe it to the Negro to think for him, to help him by placing over him trustworthy men armed with almost feudal authority to enforce such social duties as devolve upon him and so save him from himself... We legislate as men for men; and so far as men are concerned all is well, but the Negro is a child.[62]

This attitude was significant since it aggravated already existing tensions between the Africans and Whites as the economy continued to founder and black faces increasingly appeared in the legislature. The appearance of African representatives in the Combined Court was particularly frightening to the planter class and the commercial interests. This development would have been a spectacle of more than passing concern to these economic interest groups at any time in colonial history but was even more a concern since the collapse of the local economy in the 1880s. Control of the Combined Court once again became increasingly important as the crisis prolonged and deepened. Working-class protests began in a disorganised fashion in the first decade of the twentieth century but became more organised and broad-based in the second decade.[63] World War I brought temporary relief to the employer class, but none to the disaffected working-class. Control of the political process was necessary to influence the concessions dispensed to workers in an effort to defuse their militancy. Yet, because of the political gains of the Coloureds and the Africans, it was difficult to exercise this control. In 1922, the Chief Secretary, and on occasions Officer Administering the Government, made this telling point:

> So far the effect of the (1891) reform has mainly been to transfer to the African and Coloured element much of the power formerly possessed by the planters while leaving the Government of the Colony still in a permanent minority... in the Combined Court... For when sugar was King, the Combined Court did at least continuously pursue a policy which would benefit the sugar industry. But since the reforms of 1891 it is questionable whether any definite policy whatever has been consistently pursued by the Combined Court.[64]

There were, of course, two sides of this perceived inconsistency. In the first place, it was no secret that the incumbents were not revolutionaries bent on the destruction of sugar.[65] This was manifest in the joint appeal made to the Commission led by E.F.L. Wood for the amelioration of conditions adversely affecting the sugar industry.[66] That the Combined Court was not *ipso facto* anti-plantation or anti-White was always an accepted fact, sometimes worrying to African lower-class leadership. But whereas in the past sugar, as King in the Combined Court, could use its command of this forum to exclude itself from its obligations to colonial welfare, it could no longer do so as a consequence of the marginalisation of its influence in the Combined Court. Equally crucial was the fact that the incumbents were not reluctant to apportion sugar its fair share of taxation.[67]

Since the beginning of Constitutional Government, and particularly since 1798, the planter's control of the Combined Court had always been a critical factor in his survival of one crisis after another. On three occasions, in 1835, 1840 and 1847-8, planter-controlled Combined Courts had refused to vote the supplies, and the Government had been forced to grant concessions.[68] In 1887, Governor Irving was moved to complain about this stranglehold, noting that:

> ...a *Constitution* in which one interest only is represented and in which that interest can, when it may deem proper to do so bring about a deadlock, in public affairs... is politically indefensible, and necessarily breaks down the moment the elective members come into collision with the Government acting on behalf of the unrepresented classes.[69]

When the planter oligarchy was displaced in the Combined Court, this monopoly was transferred to the new incumbents. The mere fact that the new controllers were Africans and Coloureds frightened the plantocracy, the commercial class and the Colonial Office. All were still convinced that sugar should be treated as special and became perturbed on those occasions when the Combined Court failed to do so. This is not to suggest that the Combined Court was unaware of the importance of sugar to the economic welfare of the Colony. Nor was the Combined Court, as a group, uniformly opposed to protection for sugar. The crux was that it was not prepared to offer uncritical support and protection to sugar exclusive of all other economic interests. In a real sense, while sugar remained important, it was no longer perceived as the only important economic activity in the Colony. Henceforth, it would have to share its importance with other sectors of the colonial economy.

This was but one consequence of the post-1891 shift in power in the Court. There were two other effects of similar significance. One was the lukewarm support given to the Government's development programme in the Court. The other concerned the general implications of the Court, with its new composition and its control of taxation, for attracting overseas funding and investments, both of which were accepted as critical to economic recovery.[70] While the withdrawal of uncritical support for the sugar economy was considered grave, what was interpreted as the Court's lack of sympathy for the problems faced by the Government was an even more serious cause of concern. The Colony hovered on the brink of economic collapse and an 'unpatriotic' and 'irresponsible' group of politicians was seen to be bent on facilitating economic disaster.

The situation was not quite as simple as official critics often contended. The Government made up the annual budget and presented it to the Combined Court. This body was charged with raising the revenue to fund the estimates. The Court could delete items or reduce the cost of items in the estimates, but it could not add items thereto. In its deliberations, the Court decided who, and what, were to be taxed for the current year. Herein lay the first crisis. When the planter oligarchy was in charge, the burden of taxation fell heavily on the unrepresented classes and, to a lesser extent, the commercial sector. When other interests took control of the Court, they sought to correct this disequilibrium by redistributing the taxes and by bringing some measure of relief to other sectors and to the poor, by attempting to curb Government spending.[71] These initiatives gradually produced deficits and these induced the Court to levy taxes on the dominant sectors of the economy, namely sugar and bauxite.[72]

In the post-1916 period, considerable controversy raged over the increasing magnitude of government spending, particularly since this coincided with a severe economic crisis, underemployment, unemployment, wage cuts and high taxation.[73] The Court charged the Government with reckless spending, while the Government accused the Court of indifference, tardiness and sabotage. It is important to note, however, that towards the 1920s, in direct response to chronic economic recession, the Government had initiated serious measures to expand and diversify the colonial economy.[74] These efforts necessitated an ever-expanding budget. Simultaneously, the recession forced the Government to seek to have more and more members of the establishment on the permanent Civil List.[75] Both trends tended to inflate the annual estimates and this raised the ire of the Court. When some names were struck off the List or their salaries questioned or reduced, both the Government and the Colonial Office accused the Court of scaring away public servants, thereby impeding economic development and aiding a prolongation and a deepening of the economic crisis.

Furthermore, it was believed that the reluctance of the Court to support uncritically everything put before it, its taxing of the dominant economic sector and its general attitude of hostility to the Government jeopardised the Colony's chances of benefiting from the best overseas funding available.[77] The best loans, particularly those contracted through the Crown Agents and guaranteed by the British Government, were to be had at much lower interest rates than those obtained through other agencies.[78] The exclusion from Crown Agents' assistance automatically deprived the Government of much needed capital for development projects. Similarly, the inability of the Government to be assured of internal funding through the Court rendered the Colony's ability to repay or service any debt contracted internally or externally exceedingly unpredictable.[79] This weakness placed the Colony in an unfavourable light to donors and lenders in general. At the same time, taxes such as those levied on sugar, an ailing industry, and bauxite, a new economic venture, tended to frighten away prospective investors to the detriment of the Colony.[80]

In these circumstances, the Colonial Office chose to blame the Court for the Colony's indebtedness. Essentially, what ought to have been argued was that, by not granting enough financial coverage to the colonial budget, the Court may have contributed to a deficit in the budget. Furthermore, by this same reluctance, the Court may have reduced the avenues for external assistance and thereby inhibited economic recovery. In either case, the Court might have justifiably responded that by not supporting the Government's liberal fiscal policy, it was attempting to put a brake on government's spending at a time when prudence was necessary, bearing in mind the problems in the economy.[81] The accusations were presented in a form suggesting that the Court was in some way responsible for the excessive spending. This was wholly unfounded, since it was the Government which made up the estimates and, while the Court could delete, it could not add to the estimates. The crisis stemmed from the reluctance of the Court to support the Government's programmes.[82]

The Colonial Office chose to see and interpret this conflict in terms of a group of elected representatives possessed of power but at the same time devoid of a proper sense of responsibility. The Government, on the other hand, was deprived of power in the Court. It was also subject to strict accountability to the British Government and the general public for its inability to bring economic relief to the Colony.[83] This "wholly untenable" situation, it was argued, had to be speedily corrected. Yet this was not a novel situation.

Perhaps the most important innovation of the 1891 reform was the Executive Council. While in a formal sense such a council did not exist prior to 1891, an informal arrangement permitted the Court of Policy the exercise of some of the duties of an Executive Council.[84] This relationship did not of course apply in matters of 'overriding imperial concern' for, on such occasions, the Governor could, and nearly always did, act on his own.[85] Further, since the Court of Policy had not been appointed an Executive Council, the Governor was never duty-bound to consult with it or to be guided by such advice as was given when consultation did take place. Finally, while the records tended to suggest that such consultations took place with the Court of Policy, the practice was to consult only with the official section, and not so much with the elected representatives.[86]

Some particularly influential and amenable members of the planting community, who happened to be among those elected to the Court of Policy, also may have had access to the consultative process. This nexus between important economic interests and extra-legal consultation was critical, since at all times, economic interests, and therefore access to the consultative process, coincided with whiteness, and may in fact explain the functioning of this body. It appears that this pseudo-executive arrangement, notwithstanding occasional minor controversies, continued satisfactorily until the advent of the Coloured and, in some respects, commercial interests. It was at this juncture that the Executive Council became a 'fall-back' position of safety from pressure politics, intended to strengthen the hand of the Government, to preserve planter prestige, and to protect his vested interests.

After 1916, the Executive Council became the locus of controversy, not so much because it relieved the Court of Policy of the administrative functions which this latter body had been accustomed to performing and which it had come to see as its right, but rather because subsequent Governors chose to violate the spirit in which the Executive Council was expected to function.[87] From the beginning, there were complaints that the Executive Council had increased the strength of the Governor at the expense of the legislature. It was also noted that it disrupted the calm and goodwill which had characterised the consultative process. Now that the Governor was authorised to nominate members of the Court of Policy to the Council, he had created a serious division among the ranks by choosing only from among the nominated representatives. Further, since the proceedings of the Council were secret, the rest of the Court of Policy in effect was excluded from participation in the Executive Council.

In the beginning, however, successive Governors did in fact appoint elected representatives to the Executive Council, but controversy arose over the tendency to appoint either planters or their White sympathisers. In fact, the Governors placed considerable store on the advice which they could, and did, receive from those colonial notables. Consultation with such worthies was preferred over that with any other sector of the society. This was illustrated in the treatment meted out to the elected representatives. They were considered unofficials and as such were eligible for appointments to the Executive Council. But since the *Constitution* did not stipulate elected representatives, this was not necessarily a right, even though, as elected representatives in the Court of Policy, they had every expectation of such nomination and indeed some of them were so appointed. Subsequently, as the White sector became smaller in the Court of Policy, and its places were taken by Africans, Coloureds, Portuguese and, after 1912, Indians, it was more difficult for Governors to recruit White nominees to the Council. As a consequence, in 1916, Governor Wilfred Collet discontinued the practice of nominating from within the Court of Policy.[88]

Collet stated that he found the elected representatives cantankerous and hostile.[89] Subsequent governors found support for his policy in the Colonial Office, where the thinking was that the inclusion of the elected representatives was essential only as a preparation for responsible Government.[90] Since British Guiana was not considered as being set on this course, it was not considered necessary to nominate the elected representatives to the Council. The varying of the old practice created unnecessary but fertile ground for animosity between the elected representatives and the Government, producing in a very real sense an almost unified opposition within the Court of Policy[91] which was transferred to, and was bitterly fought out in, the Combined Court. This contest resulted in interminable financial disputes, always with racial overtones, that would help to bring about the final withdrawal of the *Constitution*.

There could be no doubt that Governors such as Collet in no way actually violated the *Constitution* when they chose to exclude the elected elements from the Council. Their action received the open support of the Colonial Office. The problem was that the period was one of severe economic recession when unity among all the sectors was important. The conditions for this unity were created when elected representatives served in the Executive Council and came to see themselves as part of the Government. On the other hand, these conditions were subverted when elected representatives were excluded. No doubt, this explains why the Governor frequently found it difficult to win the support of any member of the elected representatives in time of dire need.[92] After 1916, no representative felt responsible or obligated enough, by virtue of his inclusion in the Executive Council, or camaraderie, to support the Government's position. Any such sympathy was alienated; all opportunities for establishing a coalition were passed over and militant opposition was the result.

In the midst of all of this, the Commission led by E.F.L. Wood visited the Colony. Its report pronounced optimistically on the future prospects of the Colony, expressed satisfaction with the workings of the *Constitution* and seemed oblivious of the problems and seething anger of the dispossessed. The brief post-war boom ended in the-mid 1920s, and the Colony was immediately afflicted with a new recession in the economy. Unemployment and underemployment increased.[93] Prices went up and wages were cut twice, once in 1921 and again in 1922.[94] Rents, which were normally high, rose and tenants, particularly those drawn from the working-class who could not normally pay their rents, now found such obligations impossible.[95]

The people took to the streets demanding employment, living wages and rent restrictions. This restiveness was not confined to the urban areas; estate workers took strike action and threatened to join with the urban dispossessed to force concessions from the employer class. The colonial authorities panicked, the police opened fire and 12 workers were killed at Pln. Ruimveldt in 1924.[6] Middle-class politicians, Portuguese, Coloured, African and Indian, made capital of the crisis. They appeared prominently among the dispossessed, agitating and articulating but doing little else since, in a real sense, they were themselves unaware of the wider crisis in international capitalism, and perhaps even more so because they were themselves afraid of a militant working-class.[97]

On the political front, the situation was complex. The process of middle-class displacement of the planting interest in the legislature was accelerated as a consequence of the ongoing struggle, party organisation and increasing enhancement of the recently enfranchised. A bitter contest produced a stalemate in the mayoral elections of 1922, resulting in an acrimonious libel suit. One daily newspaper was forced to close its doors as a result of the court judgement.[98] The Popular Party emerged as a significant political force, appearing to be more than a mere election campaign organisation. It capitalised on the various issues abroad and joined in the general agitation of the British Guiana Labour Union (BGLU). The election campaign of 1926 was bitterly contested. Economic development and political reforms, not unexpectedly, were the major issues. The Popular Party won the elections, but the results were immediately challenged[99] and, as a consequence, five of eight candidates were unseated by the Court. Against this background, the financial situation reached a critical level and was exploited by the plantocracy to reverse the electoral results by bringing about the eventual overthrow of the *Constitution*.

The Court controlled the fiscal system, devising ways and means of raising the taxes to fund the annual estimates. Increasingly, however, conflict emerged over what the Court perceived as extravagance on the part of the Executive and what the Executive convinced itself was sabotage on the part of the Court. The root of the conflict lay in the depressed economy. In the post-war years, prices fell for sugar, and Guiana lost the Caribbean rice market to suppliers from the Indian sub-continent.[100] Efforts to improve the situation proved futile. From 1920, with the singular exception of 1923, budgets of the Colony showed substantial deficits. In 1926, the year of election, the deficit was £119,364 and, in 1927, it was £97,163. In 1927, the total assets and liabilities stood at £1,728,194 and £1,910,904 respectively. The accumulated deficit at this time stood at £182,710.[101]

In any British Colony this would have been considered a serious situation. What was cause of even graver concern in Guiana, however, was the fact that the Colony's funded debt stood at £3,000,000, and its short-term debt to the Crown Agents was in the vicinity of £1,300,000, producing a disturbing foreign debt of £4,300,000.[102] Critics were quick to point out that a debt of this magnitude worked out to about £14 per person in the overall population: nearly the highest in the British Empire.[103] Another frightening aspect of this debt was the fact that 80 per cent of the Colony's revenue was derived from customs duties.[104] This was a factor of critical concern since the annual Tax Ordinance was jealously controlled by the Court.

The Colonial Office was moved to appoint a Royal Commission in 1927 to examine and make recommendations on the Guiana *Constitution*. The conduct of the Commission was sufficient to raise eyebrows, even without its reactionary conclusion. It pronounced that "the Government in British Guiana have never been able to govern". It argued that the Combined Court was "in the position of a minor who can overrule his own trustees". The report was contentious, but it was obvious to all that changes in the *Constitution* were necessary. The controversy sprang from the nature of the changes. As early as 1914, the Colony in a 'referendum' gave an undertaking to support changes in the *Constitution* in exchange for economic development. World War I (1914-1918) intervened,[106] but the post-war recession created an even greater need for development. The 1927 Commission reasoned that:

> The situation was possible as long as the function of the administration was confined to attempting to prevent misgovernment. It is not possible when the Government are expected to take a direct and active part in the development of the country and the improvement of the condition of the people.[107]

This the elected representatives could not accept. Development was impeded by the Colony's parlous financial situation. Budgets were not balanced because the Government did not have effective control over taxation and, as a consequence, Guiana could not raise loans on the better markets of Britain. This the elected representatives rejected. In 1914, Sir Walter Egerton observed that a loan from the British money market without imperial control was unthinkable.[108] Secretary of State Harcourt supported him:

> You have rightly assumed that without full Imperial Control over the finances of the Colony there could be no question of advances being made from the Imperial Treasury.[109]

In a very real sense, this was political blackmail. The Colonial Office was demanding full control in return for economic assistance. In 1914, the local representatives were willing to surrender their jealously guarded rights and privileges in exchange for economic development but in 1927 they were not prepared to do so, and they would not be coerced. However, they were prepared to fight for other changes.[110] They demanded an extension of their powers; they wanted the executive to be selected from those elected by the people. The old guard had been swept aside and should not be reconstituted more powerful than ever in the Executive Council. They condemned the Colonial Office for attempting to thwart the will of the people as expressed in the 1926 elections.[111] "Give power to the people" was the basic demand of the elected representatives.

Against this background, two developments conspired to decide not just the nature of the constitutional change but the timing of such changes as well. In 1927, the Court rejected *en bloc* the Government's proposal to raise revenue by means of "an emergency surtax of 10 per cent on every duty and on every surtax except that payable on machinery... as well as on every tax, duty, licence and other charges".[112] Instead, it imposed a one-year tax on sugar and bauxite. This step was immediately criticised by the planting interest, the Government and the Colonial Office.[113]

This situation was aggravated by two scandals which rocked the capital. The more serious of these affected the City Improvement Scheme when the consulting engineers walked off the job and left the country, claiming they would not subject themselves to the demeaning treatment meted out to them by the Court.[114] The entire project had been causing considerable concern. For one thing, its budget had been exceeded by more than 150 per cent. Secondly, doubts had been created in the minds of the public about the competence of the consulting engineers particularly after the senior consultant became ill, left the country in search of expert medical attention and was replaced. Finally, the consultants were hypersensitive to any criticism emanating from colonial politicians who, apart from being African, were considered irresponsible and irrelevant.[115] Their abrupt departure, coming so soon after that of Mr. Wood, the Conservator of Forests, who also had left the Colony suddenly,[116] seemed to confirm the worst predictions of the Colonial Office. The officials there felt that the Court's control of the Colony's finances and its reluctance to adopt a more liberal and conciliatory attitude would scare away expatriate public servants, block external financial assistance and impede economic recovery.[117]

Reactionary elements in the country, and their allies abroad grasped the opportunity this situation presented and accelerated the drift towards Crown Colony Government. A local Constitutional Commission, drawn mainly from this same group of ultra-conservatives, capitalised on the advantages this atmosphere presented. It criticised the existing constitutional arrangement and suggested sweeping changes.[118] In the situation and atmosphere of the time, no one was surprised that it succeeded. Both the Court of Policy and Combined Court were replaced by a single Legislative Council comprising fourteen elected representatives and fifteen nominated members. This latter category was made up of two *ex-officio* members, namely the Colonial Secretary and Attorney General, eight nominated officials and five nominated unofficial members sitting with the Governor. Ten members sitting with the Governor constituted a quorum.

In addition to the numerical advantage which the Government enjoyed in the Legislative Council, the Governor was equipped with a casting vote and special powers of reservation through which he could overturn an adverse vote in the Legislative Council. The Executive was retained; it now consisted of eleven members to be drawn exclusively from the Legislative Council, including the Colonial Secretary, the Attorney General, four nominated officials, three nominated unofficials and two elected members nominated by the Governor. Five of these members comprised a quorum. The Commissioners were particularly concerned with protecting the main economic interests and recommended that they be given special consideration when selecting nominated officials. The franchise was extended to women on the same basis as enjoyed by men. These recommendations were accepted by the Colonial Office, enacted by the British Parliament on 28 March 1928, and introduced into British Guiana in July 1928. Thus, the elected representatives were transported from a position of power and influence to one of impotence.

Recognising this reversal, Governor Sir Cecil Rodwell pointed out that the old *Constitution* was never intended to be a short cut to self-government even though it had been erroneously perceived in this light by the elected representatives. Essentially, it had always been a *cul-de-sac*. Crown Colony Government therefore was an attempt by the British to reverse the Colony out of the *cul-de-sac* and put it on the road to real constitutional advance.[119] Cecil Clementi supported the Governor. Crown Colony Government, he claimed, had rescued British Guiana from the quagmire in which it had floundered for more than a century.[120]

The local population was not convinced and protested vehemently. Lord Snell, leader of the 1926 Royal Commission, also dissented. He considered the reverses "an enormously serious thing" and observed that Guiana had fared much more harshly under its own hand than it would have under his.[121] In truth, the explanation was to be found in both the mandate and composition of the *Constitution* Commission. The Colonial Office very pointedly instructed the Commission to change the existing constitutional arrangement. The Commission had been given a choice of altering the powers of the Court of Policy and Combined Court to strengthen the Government or of replacing them completely with a Crown Colony *Constitution*.[122]

The conservative nature, economic interest, ethnicity and class affiliation of the Commission clearly indicated the direction in which the reforms would be fashioned. Of the seven members, four were officials and three unofficials and only one, Mr. E.G. Woolford was not White.[123] Two of them were ex-officio members of the Court of Policy and two were planters. The European orientation of the Executive Council was represented by the overwhelming majority in the Commission. It is also significant to note that the only non-European expressed strong reservations about the findings of the Commission in a minority declaration. In the Combined Court, the terms of reference of the Commission were deemed destructive of the rights of the people of Guiana. They were condemned as prejudging the essential issue as to whether change was indeed necessary at all. In terms of the nature of the changes to be brought about, if they were necessary, the terms of reference deprived the Commissioners of the need to exercise any initiative. They were afforded no opportunity to do but as the Secretary of State had instructed them. The Commissioners were criticised as being too pro-European and pro-Executive to permit a balanced judgement.[125] The majority of them were drawn from that very sector which had been demanding a derailment of the type of arrangement. Similarly, the Commission was composed of that group which had been expressing alarm at the non-European access to political power. Finally, it was made up of those very persons who had felt threatened by the Combined Court over the past decade. Cecil Clementi, a militant advocate of these sentiments, reasoned:

> ...that unless the *Constitution* is revised, the position of the inhabitants of the British race in this Colony will become intolerable and that inadequate protection will be afforded to the interests of the planters and the large mercantile firms which are the mainstay of the revenue...[125]

The process of emasculating the elected representatives, which had begun with the appointment of the Executive Council, was now completed. First, in 1891, the Court of Policy was shorn of its power then, with the abolition of the Combined Court, the elected representatives were divorced from their former financial privileges. Within the Legislative Council, the fourteen elected representatives were outnumbered by the nominated section. Furthermore, the situation was such that even if by persuasion, or the compelling nature of the issue, the elected representatives succeeded in having their way against the Government, the Governor was equipped with reserve powers to reverse such a gain. In all ways possible, the position of the elected representatives had been severely circumscribed by the new *Constitution*.

While the *Constitution* stipulated that two elected representatives sit on the Executive Council, the 'oath of secrecy' prevented effective communication with other representatives. This reduced those nominated to the Council to the role of 'dummies', a very unhappy situation against which they protested vehemently but with little avail.[126] There were also two major criticisms against the Executive Council. In the first place, the elected members were under-represented on the Executive Council; and secondly, the secrecy oath reduced the effectiveness of the limited exposure provided the elected representatives in the Council.

Of considerable significance was the fact that the Colonial Office had always promised economic development in exchange for effective control over the Government. Crown Colony Government epitomised this control and was supposed to have swept aside all obstacles to economic development. But two decades after the change, no discernible benefits had accrued to the Colony. Elected representative E.G. Woolford had warned against this possibility, when he confessed that he would have been willing to cooperate in the handing over of power to the Governor had he been assured that any "material benefit would be gained thereby... No such prospect, however is being held out to the Colony".[127]

The recognition that the *Constitution* was "a delusion and a failure" no doubt helped to fuel the widespread working-class revolt that occurred in the 1930s.[128] Not only had economic assistance not materialised from the British as had been promised, but the deepened crisis in the 1930s gave the lie to the much vaunted 'British Imperial trusteeship' and 'Government in the interest of the unrepresented'. The working-class was never convinced that the British, or the Colonial Government was on its side. It was convinced that the old conspiracy to shift the burden of the crisis from the economic sector to its back was continuing unabated. In the circumstances, no one was really surprised that the 1939 Royal Commission concluded that any attempt at socio-economic change must be premised "upon greater participation of the people in the business of Government". Furthermore, the Commission suggested that, in order to be meaningful, such changes should be as liberal as possible.

Thus had the people enjoyed power and influence, and thus had these been taken away from them. But their level of political consciousness had been stirred and forces, both local and international, would help that consciousness to grow and increasingly to reject the withdrawal of power and demand that those powers be returned to them.

Notes

1. Cecil Clementi, *A Constitutional History of British Guiana* (London: Macmillan, 1937), p. 24.
2. P.M. Netscher, *History of the Colonies : Essequibo, Demerara and Berbice. From the Dutch Establishment to the Present Day* (S. Gravenhage: Martinus Nijhoff, 1888), trans. by W.E. Roth (Georgetown: 1929), p. 42.
3. *Ibid.*
4. James Rodway, *History of British Guiana*, Vol. 1 (Georgetown, 1891), 102.
5. Clementi, pp. 28-29.
6. Rodway, Vol. 1, 76-77.
7. D. Davis, "The Records of British Guiana", *Timehri*, Vol. 11 (1888), 239. See also British Guiana/Venezuela Arbitration 1899, No. 1V of Appendix to British Guiana Case, 185-6.
8. *Ibid.*
9. *1832 Local Guide of British Guiana*, p. 11.
10. James Rodway, *History of British Guiana*, Vol. 11 (Georgetown, 1891), 24-40.
11. *Demerara and Essequibo Vade Mecum* 1825, 54-7.
12. Clementi, p. 409.
13. Mohammed Shahabuddeen, *Constitutional Development in Guyana 1621-1978* (Georgetown: Guyana Printers Ltd., 1978), p. 43.
14. *Minutes of the Council of Policy*, National Archives of Guyana (N.A.G.).
15. The British captured the Guiana colonies in 1781, 1796 and finally in 1803. The colonies were ceded to the British in 1814.
16. Clementi, pp. 106 - 109.
17. The local oligarchy refused to vote the supplies in 1835, 1840 and again in 1848. In each instance, it extracted legislative concessions from the British.
18. See N.A.G., Minutes of the Court of Policy (M.C.P.), 19 May 1852, 16 Aug. 1855; 18 Sep. 1855; 25 Aug. 1857.
19. For an elaborate discussion of these issues, see Walter Rodney, *A History of the Guyanese Working People, 1881-1905* (Baltimore: Johns Hopkins University Press, 1981); Francis M. Drakes, "The 1905 Protest in Guyana: Causes, Course and Consequences", (Unpub. M.A Thesis, University of Guyana, 1981).
20. H.A. Will, *Constitutional Change in the British West Indies 1880-1903* (Oxford: Clarendon Press, 1970), pp. 95-122.
21. Edward R. Davson, "British Guiana and Its Development," A Paper read

before the Colonial Institute, 24 Apr. 1908, 16.

22. Tota Mangar, "The Administration of Sir Henry Turner Irving as Governor of British Guiana 1882-1887; A Study in Astuteness and Resoluteness", (Unpub. M.A. Thesis, University of Guyana, 1987).
23. Brian L. Moore, "The Social Impact of Portuguese immigration into British Guiana after Emancipation," *Boletin de Estudios Latinoamericanos y del Caribe*, Vol. X1X, (1975).
24. N.A.G., Governor Gormanston to Secretary of State Knutsford, No. 209, 20 Jun. 1890. See also the reply, Secretary of State Knutsford to Governor Gormanston, No. 261, 14 Oct. 1890.
25. N.A.G., Letter Patent, 5 Mar. 1891, in *Official Gazette*, 2 Jan. 1892.
26. N.A.G., Governor Gormanston to Knutsford, No. 4, 3 Jan. 1980.
27. Harold Lutchman, *Planter Power in the Politics of Former British Guiana* (Turkeyen: University of Guyana, 1968).
28. See Davson,. 14-16.
29. Will, p. 148. See also V.T. Daly, *A Short History of the Guyanese People* (London: Macmillan, 1975), p. 269.
30. Clementi, pp. 313 - 14.
31. *Ibid.*
32. Will, p. 147.
33. *Ibid.*
34. *The New Daily Chronicle*, 19 Jun. 1927.
35. *Ibid.*
36. *Ibid.*
37. *Ibid.*
38. *Ibid.*, 28 Jun. 1927.
39. T.W. Bracey as reported in the *Demerara Daily Chronicle*, 9 May 1882. See also speeches by Woolford, Phillips, Cunningham in The *Daily Chronicle*, 30 Jan. 1886; 27 Aug. 1889.
40. Lutchman, *Planter Power*, p. 7.
41. *Ibid.*
42. N.A.G., Knutsford to Governor Gormanston, Confidential, 30 Apr. 1890.
43. N.A.G., Governor H.T. Irving to Secretary of State Holland, 407, 22 Oct., 1887.
44. Will, pp. 111 - 17.
45. N.A.G., Governor Gormanston to Secretary of State Knutsford, 176, 20 May 1888.
46. Clementi, p. 305-7.
47. N.A.G., Knutsford to Governor Gormanston, 300, 18 Nov. 1889.
48. N.A.G., Gormanston to Knutsford, 4, 3 Jan. 1890.
49. Great Britain, *Report of the West Indian Royal Commission 1897*, (Lon-

don: HMSO, 1897).

50. *The Echo*, 20 Jan. 1892, 16, 22 Jan. 1897.
51. Drakes, "The 1905 Protest..."; Ashton Chase, *A History of Trade Unionism in Guyana 1900-1961* (Georgetown: New Guyana ,1964).
52. Clementi, p. 318. The franchise was reduced from $480 to $300 a year.
53. N.A.G., Attorney General Joseph Nunan to Egerton, Confidential, 25 Jul. 1925.
54. The *Daily Argosy*, 11 Jan. 1928.
55. Letter to the Editor, *Ibid.*, 24 Aug. 1916.
56. Note the case of Cecil Farrar (1921). Even though he was returned unopposed, Farrar resigned. See Harold Lutchman, *The 1891 Constitutional Change and Representation in the Former British Guiana* (Georgetown: CLC Political Science Series, 1970).
57. Harold Lutchman, *Some Aspects of the Crown Colony System of Government* (Turkeyen: University of Guyana, 1968),. 20-24.
58. See Note 39.
59. Cited in Shahabuddeen, *Constitutional Development*, p. 416.
60. Davson, 16.
61. J.G. Pearson, "The Negro in the West Indies," *Timehri*, Vol. VIII (1889), 224.
62. J.G. Pearson, "The Negro's Grievance," *West Indian Quarterly* (1885-6), 141-2.
63. Drakes.
64. Sir Cecil Clementi, "Colonisation in British Guiana 1922," *United Empire*, XIII, 449- 0.
65. Lutchman, *Planter Power*, p. 6.
66. *Ibid.*
67. Great Britain, *Memorandum of the Elected Members of the Combined Court 1928* (London: HMSO, 1928), pp. 47-50.
68. David Chanderbali, "Sir Henry Light: A Study of Protection and Paternalism," (Unpub. M.A. Thesis, University of Guyana, 1977).
69. N.A.G., Irving to Holland, 407, 22 Oct. 1887.
70. Great Britain, *Memorandum of the Elected Members*, p. 47.
71. *Ibid.*, p. 48.
72. *Ibid.*, p. 49.
73. N.A.G., Vote of Censure by Mr P.A. Fernandes, *Minutes of Combined Court*, (M.C.C.), Thursday, 29 Dec. 1927.
74. Great Britain, *British Guiana Commission* 1927, 52-53.
75. N.A.G., M.C.C., 29 Dec. 1927.
76. Great Britain, *British Guiana Commission 1927* (London: HMSO, 1927) Cmd., 2841, pp. 52-53.

77. N.A.G., M.C.P., 14 Dec. 1927. See also Great Britain. *Memorandum of the Elected Members* (London : HMSO, 1928) Cmd. 3047, pp. 70- 2.
78. J.W. Harper-Smith, "The Colonial Stock Acts and the 1891 British Guiana *Constitution, Social and Economic Studies*, Vol. XXV, 3 (Sep., 1965), 252 - 63.
79. J. Van Sertima, "The Colony's Financial Position," *Timehri*, Vol. III, 1 (1912). See also N.A.G., Letter from Agents for the Colonies to the Under Secretary of State for the Colonies, 1 Jan. 1928.
80. The *New Daily Chronicle*, 6 Mar. 1925, 10 Feb. 1927; N.A.G., M.C.P., 9 Feb. 1927.
81. N.A.G., Memorandum from P.A. Fernandes, M.C.P., 29 Dec. 1927.
82. Great Britain, *Memorandum of the Elected Members*, pp. 84-86.
83. Great Britain, *British Guiana Commission 1927* (London: HMSO, 1927), pp.51-55.
84. N.A.G., Governor Gormanston to Knutsford, 3 Jan. 1890. See also Irving to Derby, 14 Oct. 1883.
85. N.A.G., Governor Wodehouse to Secretary of State for the Colonies Herbert, No. 35, 23 Mar. 1855.
86. N.A.G., Irving to Derby, Confidential, 14 Oct. 1883.
87. Great Britain, *Memorandum of the Elected Members*, pp. 38-2.
88. Please see speeches by Governor Thompson. M.C.P. 14 Dec. 1923 and 17 Jun. 1924.
89. *Ibid.*
90. E.F.L. Wood, *Report of his visit to the West Indies and British Guiana, Dec. 1921 - Feb. 1922* (London: HMSO, 1922), Cmd. 1679, pp. 9-10.
91. Great Britain, *Memorandum of the Elected Members*, pp. 39-40.
92. *Ibid.*, pp. 39-40.
93. R.F. Webber, *Centenary History and Handbook of British Guiana* (Georgetown: Argosy Company Ltd., 1931), pp. 43-48. See also The *New Daily Chronicle*, 6, 8 Feb. 1927.
94. Chase, p.62.
95. *Ibid.*, p. 64.
96. Francis X. Mark, *Organised Labour in British Guiana* (Puerto Rico, n.d.).
97. Francis M. Drakes, "The Middle Class in the Political Economy of British Guiana 1870-1928," (Paper presented at Post-Graduate Seminar, Caribbean Societies, Institute of Commonwealth Studies, University of London, 3 Mar. 1987).
98. Webber, p. 344.
99. The Popular Party won 14 seats.
100. Great Britain, *Memorandum of the Elected Members*, p. 51; Webber, pp. 343-4.

101. Clementi, p. 392.
102. *Ibid.*
103. *Ibid.*
104. *Ibid.*
105. Great Britain, *British Guiana Commission*, 52.
106. British Guiana, *Combined Court Sessional Papers, No. 779* of 1914, pp. 9-11.
107. Great Britain, *British Guiana Commission*, p. 51.
108. N.A.G., Governor Sir Walter Egerton to Mc L. Harcourt, Secretary of State for the Colonies, 5 Jan., 1914.
109. N.A.G., Mc L. Harcourt to Governor Sir Walter Egerton, 21 Apr. 1914.
110. Great Britain, *Memorandum of the Elected Members*, pp. 76-7.
111. *Ibid.*, pp. 38-62. See also "First Shots Fired in the *Constitution*al Struggle," The *Daily Chronicle*, 1 Jul. 1927.
112. *Ibid.*, pp. 47-48.
113. Great Britain, *Report of the British Guiana Commission*, pp. 60-61. See also Roy Wilson and H. Snell, "The Future of British Guiana," *West Indian Committee Circular*, Vol. XLII, 14 Jul. 1927.
114. Great Britain, *Memorandum of the Elected Members*, pp. 60-61. See also N.A.G., Letter from Messrs. Howard Humphreys and Sons to the Crown Agents for the Colonies, pp. 72-78.
115. Great Britain, *Memorandum of the Elected Members*, pp. 72-78.
116. N.A.G., M.C.C., 13 Jul. 1927.
117. Great Britain, *Report of the British Guiana Commission*, pp. 52-53.
118. See recommendations contained in Great Britain, *Report of the British Constitution Commission* (London: HMSO, 1927).
119. Governor Sir Cecil Rodwell, "The Problems of British Guiana," *United Empire*, Vol. XVII, 3rd Series (1927), p. 680 quoted in Shahabuddeen p. 448.
120. Clementi, p. 402.
121. Quoted in Shahabuddeen, p. 455.
122. N.A.G., Mr L.S. Amery, Secretary of State for the Colonies, to Governor Sir C. Rodwell, 144, 25 May 1927 and criticised by A.R.F. Webber, P.A. Fernandes, R.Y. Evan Wong in the Combined Court. See M.C.C., 13 Jul. 1927.
123. There is a distinct possibility that Mr Hector Joseph, Immigration Agent General, a member of the Commission, was both a Jamaican and a Coloured gentleman as well.
124. N.A.G., M.C.C., 14 Jul. 1927.
125. N.A.G., Mr Cecil Clementi, O.A.G., to Bonar Law, Secretary of State for the Colonies, 31 Jun. 1916.

126. N.A.G., Governor Denham to Lord Passfield, Confidential, 28 Jul. 1930. See also Douglas Jones, Attorney General to Lord Passfield, 71, 30 Jan. 1930.
127. Great Britain, *Report of the British Guiana Commission*, p. 13.
128. N.A.G., Governor Lethem to Lord Stanley, 8 Oct. 1943. (Confidential).
129. Great Britain, *West India Royal Commission Report*, (London: HMSO, 1938), Cmd. 6607, p. 373.

13 : Women in Guyanese Politics, 1812-1964

by
Hazel M. Woolford

This chapter seeks to trace the development of women, especially African-Guyanese women, in the politics of British Guiana. Politics has been defined as the art and science of directing and administering states and other political units. Women in British Guiana, however, did not begin to assume such a role until the 1950s.

This essay focusses on the legislation and institutions which initially excluded women from the franchise and political office. It then examines women's supportive role in Guyanese politics and their active involvement eventually as politicians. Finally, it speculates about the reasons for the low percentage of female candidates at national elections. It should be noted that, because of the limited participation of women in the pre-1940 era, major emphasis has been placed on their involvement in the subsequent period from 1940 to 1964.

Colonial Guyanese society was patriarchal. Women of every race and colour were debarred from taking up positions in the political administration up to the early twentieth century because of the posture of the members of the Courts and the high property qualifications.

Females were never eligible for membership of the Court of Policy, the College of Electors and the College of Financial Representatives. The College of *Kiezers* also disallowed women from becoming members. In a proclamation of 1812, Governor Carmichael conceded the vote to women, but this privilege was withdrawn by section 8 of the *Franchise Ordinance* of 1849.[1]

By section 1 of *Ordinance No. 1* of 1864, women were formally refused membership of the Court of Policy. Exclusion from the

Court as well as from the College of Financial Representatives was continued by sections 12 (1), 33 and 53 of the *British Guiana Constitution Ordinance No. 1* of 1891. Section 12(1) stated: [A woman]...is not entitled to vote at the election of a member of the said Court for any Electoral District or Division". Section 33, which dealt with Financial Representatives, stipulated:

> The qualifications for election as a Financial Representative shall be the qualifications herein before prescribed for election as an elected member of the Court of Policy. Provided that either of the following property qualifications in lieu of those specified in sub-section five of section twelve of this Ordinance:-
>
> (a) Receipt of a clear annual income of not less than one thousand, four hundred and forty dollars arising from any kind of property in the Colony not mentioned in the other property qualification over and above any interest payable under any mortgage thereon, or
>
> (b) Receipt of a clear annual income of not less than one thousand, four hundred and forty dollars from any profession, business or trade carried on in the Colony.

These qualifications were prohibitive and were reinforced by section 53 which emphasised that:

> Subject to the provisions hereinafter contained, every male person shall be entitled to be registered in any year as a voter, and when registered to vote at the election of a member of the Court of Policy or of a Financial Representative for an Electoral District or Division as the case may be, who is qualified as follows, that is to say:

(1) Has attained the age of twenty-one years.
(2) Is under no legal incapacity.
(3) Is a British subject by birth or naturalisation; and
(4) Possesses within the District or Division some one of the following property qualifications hereinafter mentioned.

Constitutionally therefore, women were not qualified for the vote and were automatically disallowed from membership of any branch of the legislature.

In 1923, Mr Robert Edward Brassington argued unsuccessfully in the Combined Court for the vote to be given to certain categories of women.[2] He was replaying a role which had been enacted in the English Parliament in 1867 by John Stuart Mill who lost in his bid to have the franchise extended to women.[3] Later in 1927, Hubert Nathaniel Critchlow also addressed the question of extending the franchise to women. At a public meeting, it was reported that he said that "every man and every woman has the right to exercise their franchise as long as they are above the age of twenty-one like Mrs. Pankhurst in England, and that's what he wants the women to do out here".[4]

On the recommendation of the British Guiana Constitution Commission of 1927, the vote was restored to women in 1928. However, section 21(1) of the *British Guiana Order-in-Council* made women ineligible for membership of the Legislative Council.[5] The West Indian Royal Commission of 1938-39 recommended that women should be appointed to all boards and local authorities and that they should be nominated to the legislature if no representation of women's interests was secured by election. In April 1940, representatives of fourteen trade unions agreed with the motion that the franchise be extended for central and local Government elections.[6] The motion was forwarded to the Governor.

During 1941 when Hubert Critchlow appeared before the Franchise Commission, he opined that female members of the British Guiana Labour Union were not eligible to vote because they were mainly employed in low-paying jobs. He insisted that women were just as intelligent as men. His efforts were successful. The Commission recommended that women be permitted to become members of the legislature. Consequently in 1945, the *British Guiana (Constitution) Amendment Order-in-Council* authorised women to become members of the legislature. The franchise income was later reduced from $40 to $10 per month and in 1947 this requirement was within the reach of every adult except housewives who had no visible income or property.

Thus, by 1947 some of the major obstacles to the active participation of women in politics had been removed. Significant progress had been made since the late 1880s when women first began to display more visible interest in local politics. This was during the struggle undertaken especially by African and Coloured middle-class males for constitutional reform to break the virtual monopoly of political power enjoyed by Whites. African women welcomed the resultant change of the British Guiana *Constitution* in 1891. They attended political meetings and although they neither had votes nor were eligible for political office, they guided and directed many of the enfranchised male citizens how to use their votes. Partly because of their role at the elections of 1897, some representatives of the African masses were elected to the legislature. Women also played a very influential role especially in the elections of 1916, 1921 and 1926.

Some women supported their husbands who were politicians and also tried to develop and maintain contact with the masses by their involvement in social work. Notable among them was Violet Thorne, the wife of A.A. Thorne, a scholar, journalist and politician. Their example was followed by women of other racial groups, such as Alice Singh, whose husband, Jung Bahadur Singh, was a medical practitioner, trade unionist and politician, and Amelia Lee, the wife of Theophilus Lee, a politician and trade unionist.

Very prominent among the African-Guyanese women who later supported male politicians was Gertrude Collins. In 1947, she campaigned for the election of both John Carter and Hubert

Critchlow. This experience by African women in supporting their male colleagues gave them self-confidence and emboldened some of them eventually to run for seats in the Legislative Council. Esther Dey, for example, later observed that "it was through reading speeches prepared by the late A.A. Thorne that I became imbued with the desire to became a politician".[7]

Women's growing involvement in politics received a major impetus in 1946 when, on 9 July, the first women's political organisation, the Women's Political and Economic Organisation (WPEO), was formed at the Library in Georgetown. It has been suggested that the stimulus for its formation came from the announcement that Audrey Jeffers, a social worker in Trinidad, had run for a seat in the Trinidadian Legislative Council.[8]

The main objectives of the WPEO were to develop the political consciousness of the women of British Guiana, to encourage their political education and to formulate a platform in connection with the 1947 elections. The leaders of the movement, who included several African-Guyanese, were Janet Jagan, President, Winifred Gaskin, Secretary, Frances Stafford and Muriel Belgrave, Vice Presidents, and I. Friday, Treasurer. The committee members were Mildred Mansfield, Irene Campbell, Una Matthews and I. Fowler.[9] These were all middle-class women. A few weeks before the formation of the Organisation Winifred Gaskin had urged women to come out of the kitchen and be registered in the elections. She told them: "We could use our power to bring about legislation for better houses". [10]

The WPEO appealed to women of all classes, races, creeds and occupations, housewives and social workers, domestics and civil servants. In an article in the *Daily Chronicle* headlined 'Would you vote for a woman?', the journalist opined that women had the power to mould the nation.[11] He suggested that Winifred Gaskin, Janet Jagan, Radhika Kawal, Marie Bayley and Amelia Lee were potential leaders. Of these Gaskin and Jagan later became prominent politicians.

The first political meeting for women was held in the Town Hall,

Georgetown, on 12 July, 1946. Long before the hour set for its commencement, 120 women had registered as voters. When the meeting actually started, the Hall was crowded. The women who were on the platform were Janet Jagan, Winifred Gaskin, Frances Stafford, Amelia Lee, Betty Persaud, Muriel Belgrave, Mildred Mansfield, Evilina Davis and Johanna Harris. Prominent men in the society also attended the meeting and a few assisted in registering the women. These included Sir Eustace Woolford, KC, OBE, Deputy President of the Legislative Council, and Mr Arthur Seymour. The meeting was successful. Eric Roberts expressed the following sentiments in an article entitled "Enter women in the Political Arena":

> July 12, 1946 will be inscribed as a memorable night in the political history of this country. For more than five hundred women from all classes and walks of life banded together for the sole purpose of forming this Association... What they demand are legitimate, human and essential suitable for their requirement in the domestic field.[12]

The WPEO Executive Council held its first meeting on 30 July, 1946. It proposed to publish a monthly newsletter to be called *The Guianese Woman*. One member, Mrs. Fowler, suggested that the Organisation should nominate a woman to run for a seat in the forthcoming Legislative Council elections. Frances Stafford, however, opined that women were not ready for political office. Other Council members disagreed with her, suggesting that once the public was sensitised, women could venture out as candidates for general elections. The Organisation aimed to achieve better housing conditions, continuation of price control with an increase in Government's subsidy on essential foodstuffs, improved travelling facilities and medical services, free and compulsory education, the abolition of the age limit of 11 years for a boy to enter Queen's College and the elimination of blackmarketing. These were very ambitious objectives.

In order to encourage women to be sensitised to political issues, Frances Stafford addressed members of the Women's Institute in the Welfare Hall, Barr Street, Kitty. She insisted that if women registered and voted for women, day-care centres would be opened to care for the children whose mothers had to work, especially the domestics who worked long hours. The Organisation strove to organise the women in Georgetown. By the end of 1947, there were 143 women on the membership roll. Branches were established in Lacytown, Kingston and Queenstown.

The first social problem which the WPEO addressed was housing. A housing committee, made up of Frances Stafford, Irene Campbell and Mildred Mansfield, was very critical of the Wortmanville Housing Project which was described as a cowshed and a concentration camp. The women observed that:

> It would seem that since these houses are being built for the benefit of the poorer classes absolutely no interest has been taken to make the houses look attractive or even to make the arrangements of the rooms in accordance with improved methods.[13]

They forwarded their protest to the Secretary of State, the British Labour Party, the Fabian Colonial Bureau and the British Board of Trade.[14] The Wortmanville issue was also discussed in the British Parliament.[15] The WPEO held a public meeting to highlight its many deficiencies and to express their strong opposition. Winifred Gaskin concluded that 48 families had been committed to 'a living death above the graves in an abandoned graveyard'.[16]

A memorandum was prepared for submission to the Officer Administering the Government, the Hon. W.L. Heape. Johanna Harris, the first and only female president of the British Guiana Labour Union, moved that it be adopted. The men who attended the meeting were invited to support the female politicians in the forthcoming elections for the Legislative Council. Hubert Nathaniel Critchlow advised the WPEO to send a copy of the memorandum to the Housing Committee of the Legislative Council as well as to the Government. An anonymous gentleman urged that two members of the Organisation should be appointed members of the Housing Committee and that one of these women should supervise the Wortmanville Housing Project. The meeting endorsed the memorandum and adopted the resolutions of the two gentlemen. The Organisation made several recommendations to the Government. These included the following:

(1) The steps of each building be made wider and risers added and that the stairs and landing be enclosed.
(2) A roof or shed be built to cover the second floor platform.
(3) The floor level vent be closed.
(4) At least 2 shelves and one dresser and a small cupboard be added to each kitchen.
(5) An extra prop be put beneath the kitchen sink.
(6) Precautions be taken against fire by addition of galvanised sheeting or other fire-proof material to kitchen.
(7) Kitchens in buildings not yet completed carry an open hearth or depth in cement slab to accommodate coalpots.
(8) A connecting door be cut between bedrooms.
(9) The passages along the bath and toilet be utilised to enlarge both by including them within one room.
(10) In buildings now being put up, plans be altered, if possible to allow the toilets to be placed in line with bedrooms so as to save crossing the living room to reach them.
(11) Windows be added to the north and south of each building.[17]

On the 21 August 1946, the WPEO, led by Janet Jagan and Juliet Benthan, joined a demonstration of more than 3,000 workers to support the Trade Union Council's (TUC's) demand for improved housing and better wages. The women demanded that the Government give working-class tenants the right to vote, to be elected to the Town Council and to remove members of the Legislative Council if they were not functioning effectively. One placard declared: "Remove the Perpetrators of the Wortmanville Housing Scheme".[18] It was evident that these women saw themselves as defenders of the workers' rights. The efforts of the WPEO to improve the Wortmanville Housing Scheme attained the desired objective. The editor of the *Daily Chronicle*, in commending the Organisation for the improvements, noted:

> ...and while the Women's Political and Economic Organisation do not want to crow, the feeling is general that the Courageous Ladies of this new movement are responsible for them.[19]

The Organisation was also concerned about the plight of domestics. Frances Stafford called for the establishment of a strong Domestic Servants' Union. She suggested that domestics should work for ten hours, from 07:00 a.m. to 7:00 p.m. with two hours off during the day. She also advocated that establishments which demanded long hours institute a shift system. Furthermore, she recommended that a system of Colonial Insurance be established which would provide for the aging domestic servant. In her opinion, the Domestic Servants' Union, when established, could open a technical school in collaboration with the employment agency. Workers would then be trained and the graduates could be graded with a higher salary for the upper levels. Thus, grade 'A' workers would comprise butlers, cooks and children's nurses; grade 'B' would consist of those who did less highly-skilled work and younger girls who were trying to qualify for grade 'A.'

Hubert Critchlow agreed that domestic servants should work from 07:00 a.m. to 7:00 p.m., but suggested that they should have a three-hour break. He also recommended a half-day off each week, no work every other Sunday and that employers should provide the uniforms. Neither person considered that the domestic was abandoning her family for ten hours. However, while Stafford sought to enfranchise these women, there appeared to be disagreement within the WPEO.

During August 1946, the first indication that there was conflict in the WPEO appeared. The editor of the *Daily Chronicle* claimed that Janet Jagan was using the Organisation for her own personal gains; Frances Stafford was accused of being too conspicuous, and race, suspicion and envy were identified as the causes for the discontent.[20] The WPEO responded immediately to the article, accusing the editor of the *Chronicle* of making strife in the Organisation by his allegations. In their letter to the editor, the women commented:

> We wish to state clearly that there is no semblance of disunity within the WPEO and there is absolutely no truth in the irresponsible statement that the Organisation is in a dying condition.

It should be clearly understood that, however great the calumniations, the members of the WPEO would not be disconcerted. "We can stand anything. We can take it"[21] However, in spite of the ladies' protestations, there was ennui among members. In an open letter to the Executive Council of the WPEO in 1947, Stafford complained that although she was a member of the body, meetings were held when it was known that she had other engagements. She concluded that "it would be a thousand pities if this Organisation of ours peters out through lack of cooperation and good fellowship".[22] Stafford, like the Council, was committed to the survival of the Organisation, but she refused to be disregarded.

Moreover, there must have been other members who were disaffected. In 1948, the Queenstown Branch withdrew and 1950 witnessed the demise of the Organisation. Moreover, while initially Stafford had reservations about women being nominated as candidates for the national elections, she subsequently altered her opinion and stood as a candidate for the 1947 elections.

Frances Stafford and Janet Jagan were the first women to compete for seats in the legislature. This development occurred at a time when female politicians were in the minority even in the most developed countries. Stafford contested the Georgetown South seat nominated by Ada Archer and seconded by

Ramdanhie. Her rivals were Joseph Gonsalves, a solicitor, Joseph Prayag Lachmansingh, a medical practitioner, Hubert Critchlow, the General Secretary of the British Guiana Labour Union (BGLU) and Oscar Wesley Bishop, a journalist and author. Janet Jagan contested the Georgetown Central seat. Her opponents were Percy Claude Wight, a broker, and Leon Schuler, the Managing Director of the British Guiana Lithographic Company, Ferdinand Christopher Archer, a tailor, and John Fernandes, a merchant.

John Carter recognised the importance of the role of women in the 1947 elections when he had predicted that the women would be the deciding factor.[23] P.H. Daly accused the WPEO of fence-sitting because they had indicated that they were not sponsoring Jagan and Stafford.[24] In response to Daly's criticism, Hilda Devonish, a former member of the WPEO, wrote:

> Is Mr Daly suggesting that the WPEO should follow the lead of those same criticised generations who voted out of sentiment and not reason? Does he suggest a repetition of the pattern by voting for any woman who came forward solely because she is a woman? Does his feminism mean setting aside the hierarchy of men and substituting one of women or should it not mean cooperation with men for a change from blind and one-sided to enlightened and sane politics? We prefer our interpretation; we have given no advantage to the women candidates of our choice.[25]

It cannot be denied, however, that the WPEO had changed its position as regards actively participating in national politics. The Organisation was almost inactive. Despite this ambivalence, the two women vigorously campaigned in their constituencies. During her political campaign, Stafford denounced the Government for reducing the subsidy on milk, cooking butter and salt-fish rather than increasing the tax on lip-stick, rum, whisky and tobacco. She described herself as an independent socialist. Her manifesto called for the following:

(1) Better housing and better living conditions;
(2) Need for a creche;
(3) A better economy; and,
(4) Technical education.

Among the persons who campaigned for Stafford were Alice Singh, Betty Kallo and Mildred Mansfield. The *Daily Chronicle* and the *Daily Argosy* agreed that the tussle was between Critchlow and Stafford. However, she lost to Critchlow. He polled 1,682 votes in comparison to her 1,211. The Albouystown electorate gave her the only majority at the polls. Although she congratulated Critchlow for winning the seat, she stated that she could not compliment him on the methods which he had employed in securing votes.[26]

It was claimed that Janet Jagan was persuaded by her husband and Jocelyn Hubbard to stand for the seat.[27] In her election campaign she called for:

(1) Elimination of all the nominated seats in the Legislature - the majority of the nominated seats were occupied by capitalists;
(2) Adult suffrage - any intelligent person who worked should be allowed to take part in the Government of the country;
(3) The lowering of the qualification of candidates for seats in the Legislative Council in order to give young people a chance of getting into the Council;
(4) The introduction of a system of recall in order to check on the faithfulness and honesty of purpose of representatives;
(5) The reduction of the term of office from 5 years to 3 or 4;
(6) A 40-hour week without reduction in pay;
(7) More technical and vocational training;
(8) Slum clearance;
(9) A School of Nursing and a Health Insurance Scheme;

(10) Increased taxes on exports of raw products;
(11) Subsidisation of essential foodstuffs;
(12) More efficient and economical drainage and irrigation; and,
(13) Guaranteed prices for agricultural produce.

Janet Jagan lost to John Fernandes, who obtained 1,193 votes, while she gained 742. It was small consolation that she and Frances Stafford had come second in their constituencies.

In January 1948, Eustace Williams filed a petition against Critchlow and his agents, accusing him of illegal practices at the 1947 elections. Williams alleged that Critchlow had allowed false statements to be published to defame the character of Mrs. Stafford, contrary to the provisions of the *Legislative Council (Election) Ordinance of 1945*. It was claimed that one of Critchlow's campaign managers, R.B.O. Hart, had told the constituency, that Mrs. Stafford had kicked an African servant's child down the steps and was convicted and fined $5.00 by the magistrate. Critchlow was unseated. However, Stafford lost to John Carter in the by-election. In spite of her daring, Stafford never attempted to stand for election again.

The involvement of African-Guyanese and other women in local politics entered a new phase after January 1950 when the People's Progressive Party (PPP) was formed. This Party had evolved from the Political Affairs Committee which had been established in 1946 by Dr. Cheddi Jagan, Janet Jagan, Jocelyn Hubbard and Ashton Chase. The leadership of the Party comprised Cheddi Jagan, Leader; Forbes Burnham, Chairman; and Janet Jagan General Secretary. Janet Jagan also became the editor of its new organ, the *Thunder*.[28]

The PPP was the first mass-based Party to be established in British Guiana. In 1951, the Waddington Commission recommended universal adult suffrage and, by *Ordinance No. 2 of 1952*, it was introduced. At the 1953 General Elections, the PPP fielded three female candidates, namely, Janet Jagan, Jane Phillips-Gay and Jessica (Jessie) Burnham. The other females to stand for seats were Gertrude Collins (of the National Democratic Party), Hermina Lepse-Brown (an Independent) and Esther Dey. Among the women who campaigned for the PPP in this election were Winifred Gaskin and Margaret Ackman. In short, almost all the female candidates at this election were African-Guyanese.

The PPP won 18 of the 24 seats at the elections held in April. The three women were successful, but they were not appointed Ministers. Percy Armstrong, editor of the *Guiana Times*, suggested that Janet Jagan had wanted to be Minister of Social Welfare and Local Government, but stepped down.[29] She was appointed Deputy Speaker. In her maiden speech in the Legislative Council, Jessica Burnham, in recognising the critical role of women in politics, opined:

> Your Honour, I do feel proud to be here, and when I say 'proud' I mean it in every sense for I stand here as one of the representatives of the people and as a woman. In the past, British Guiana was looked upon as being static politically. However, it has now made history in the Caribbean in that at the recent General Elections the electorate placed at the head of the polls three women. May I here say that the development of a country depends on the progress of the women of that country. The fact cannot be overlooked that it always requires a feminine touch to complete any project.[30]

During their stay in office, the female members of the PPP championed the rights of the disadvantaged. Jessie Burnham called for the establishment of nursery schools and trained nursery school teachers. Jane Phillips-Gay was closely associated with the sugar workers and supported the amendments to the *Workmen's Compensation (Consolidation) Ordinance, 1952*, on the grounds that it was not only an ordinance that would benefit the relatives of an injured worker when he died but also if he was otherwise incapacitated.[31] She called for the introduction of women drivers on the sugar estates, informing the members of the Legislative Council:

> I am a woman, and I tell the women workers I am in sympathy with them when they have to report to the driver concerning all their whereabouts if not, they are charged with being lazy. It is certainly high time that women drivers should be in the field.[32]

She also supported strongly the introduction of the *Labour Relations Bill* because, in her opinion, it would benefit the sugar workers. Janet Jagan represented the plight of the domestic servants and rice farmers and called for the removal of the *Undesirable Literature Ordinance*. There is no doubt that in the legislature these women articulated the grievances of the people.

After the PPP had spent 133 days in office, the *Constitution* was suspended and the Party was removed from power by the British Government. Women were very prominent in the events which followed. Janet Jagan was periodically subjected to raids. On 3 April, 1954, Cheddi Jagan was arrested for breaching the emergency regulations. In response to this, on 4 April Janet Jagan led a procession of protesters, composed mainly of female members of the PPP. Janet Jagan, Martin Carter, Rory Westmaas and thirty others were arrested. The female members who were outside Brickdam Police Station begged to be arrested and shouted: "We want Cheddi Jagan".[33]

In Port Mourant, women and teenagers protested the imprisonment of Janet Jagan. She and the others were charged, firstly for holding a procession, deemed likely to cause disturbance of public order, without permission in writing from the police and, secondly, for being in a meeting together with more than five persons which could have led to a disturbance of public order. They were released on bail. It was alleged that while the PPP supporters were on their way to Party headquarters, they attacked the policemen on Regent Street. Most of the rioters who were arrested were women.

When Cheddi Jagan was re-arrested for flouting the regulations, there was a demonstration mainly by women outside Government House, the Governor's residence. Some of them were later arrested. There was also another group of women marching outside the Promenade Gardens. When the policemen arrived on the scene, some hid between the ferns and flower beds or pretended to be nurse maids. The story was recounted of one activist who, on seeing a policeman approaching, wagged her finger in the face of a youngster and said, "I'll tell mummy you're a naughty boy". The policeman tapped her arm and said, "You're a naughty girl too. Come on, you playing smart, nuh?". She was taken to the police station. However, this incident did not prevent Mrs. Jagan and her supporters from demonstrating against the arrest of Dr. Jagan.

The statue of Queen Victoria was bombed as a form of protest by unknown persons on 25 May 1954. After the statue was bombed, the homes of the leaders of the PPP were searched and Mrs. Jagan was charged for "unlawful possession" of a copy of the Police manual instructions on riot, drill and illegal assembly. She appealed. Her husband was jailed. She pursued the civil disobedience campaign and attempted to set aside the Queen's birthday to be a day of mourning for the imprisonment of her husband. She also lost her illegal procession's appeal and was fined $250 or a prison term. On 6 September a warrant was issued for her arrest. Friends hid her and in the wee hours of the morning she returned home. Before dawn, the Police Security Inspector, Mervyn Barrow, went to the Jagans' home where she informed him that she would not pay the fine. She was later sentenced to six months' imprisonment with hard labour and served the term.

After the suspension of the *Constitution* and the ousting of the PPP, an Interim Government was installed on 4 January, 1954. *The British Guiana (Constitution) (Temporary Provisions) Order-in-Council of 1953* provided for a nominated Legislative Council consisting of 27 members, including three *ex officio* members. Two African-Guyanese women, Gertrude Hyacinth Collins and Esther Dey, were nominated unofficials of the Legislative Council. They were very vocal in the Council's deliberations.

During her term in office, Gertrude Collins supported the Demerara Bauxite Company's decision to process bauxite into aluminium because she foresaw that it would provide additional jobs. She also demonstrated concern for the number of underprivileged children who were accommodated at the Palms geriatric home. For nine years she agitated for the Government to find more suitable lodging for the children. Furthermore, she was concerned about the high unemployment rate which, in her opinion, seriously affected the economic development of the Colony. Consequently, she supported attempts to develop the Colony industrially. Understandably, Collins approved the *Hydro-Electic Power Bill* and rightly stated that cheap electric power would play an important part in the industrialisation of the Colony. As a trade unionist she also fought for improved conditions for the workers, once declaring in the Legislature:

> I would consider that I wasted my time in this Interim Legislature if I had not brought the grievances of those public servants to the attention of the Government.[34]

One of her main expectations was to see the Guyanisation of the Public Service, where qualified Guyanese would be appointed to senior positions held by expatriates. Collins also wanted British Guiana to federate with the West Indies because, in her view, the region would be stronger economically. It cannot be denied that Collins was a stalwart and an example to female politicians.

The other female member of the Interim Government who articulated the grievances of women and workers was Esther Dey. As a nominated unofficial of the legislature, Esther Dey described herself as a 'floor member'.[35] She was the only female member of the Finance Committee of the Interim Government. In supporting West Indian Federation, she perceived that economic development would benefit women because their menfolk would obtain employment. It was her view that technical education should be taught in order to reduce dependency on skilled personnel from abroad. She also wanted the children housed in the Palms to be removed to a "cottage home" where they would be nurtured.[36] She was interested in the welfare of women and urged the Government to assist those who were involved in cottage industries. She recommended that post-natal education be taught in schools. She also expressed concern over the fate of boys after they left the Essequibo Boys' School and suggested that they be taught a trade and be encouraged to pursue useful forms of employment.

She supported the *Marriage Amendment Bill* which was an "Ordinance further to amend the Marriage Ordinance", but objected to girls marrying at twelve years of age. In supporting the Bill, she pointed out that East Indian women would receive 'proper matrimonial prestige'. She argued that the Bill would not interfere with the customs of any ethnic group and said that she had no objections to East Indian girls marrying according to Hindu and Muslim rites, if the marriage was legalised. Her attitude to marriage was further expressed when she asserted:

> I am a woman and will not oppose a Bill which improves the prestige of the women of British Guiana and moreso the Indian women.[37]

Dey and Collins continued to represent the Guyanese people in the legislature until the life of the Interim Government terminated on 29 June, 1957, thus providing for the national elections.

In the elections, Cheddi Jagan and Forbes Burnham led separate parties because in 1955 the PPP had split into two factions, namely, the Jaganite PPP and the Burnhamite PPP. Some historians have suggested that one of the effects of the suspension of the *Constitution* had been the break-up of the People's Progressive Party. Others have attributed the bifurcation to a power struggle within the Party. This paper will not attempt to discuss the issue, but notes that Jane Phillips-Gay and Jessie Burnham became affiliated with the Burnhamite PPP which was subsequently renamed the People's National Congress (PNC) and had always been supported by women. They were attracted either by the charismatic leadership or the commitment and zeal of the female members.

In 1955, Governor Patrick Renison succeeded Governor Alfred Savage. Forbes Burnham expressed his disapproval of the new Governor's appointment by leading a demonstration consisting mainly of women. The editor of the *Guiana Times* described these women as a 'Kangalang' Party - consisting of domestics and market hucksters. Undoubtedly, the editor of this journal held the position that the Party's base was the working-class women, who in his opinion were not suitably qualified to assume leadership roles in the Government.

Although women played a meaningful role in political parties, there was an insignificant number of female candidates in the elections of 1957. There were five females among the fifty-five candidates. These were Jessica Huntley (PPP) who contested in electoral district No. 2 - New Amsterdam; Jessie Burnham (PNC), candidate in electoral district No. 4 - Western Berbice; Jane Phillips-Gay (PNC), candidate in electoral district No. 5 - Eastern Demerara; Muriel Nurse (PNC) in electoral district No. 18 - Georgetown Central; and Janet Jagan (PPP) in electoral district No. 13 - Western Essequibo.[38] The PPP won the elections. Janet Jagan polled 3,802 votes as against her nearest rival who gained 1,719. The other women lost in their bid to obtain seats in the legislature. After the elections, Jessie Burnham left the PNC and returned to the PPP because of a dispute with her brother, later authoring the pamphlet, *Beware My Brother Forbes*, in which she said that her brother was never keen on her entering politics.

Janet Jagan was appointed Minister of Labour, Health and Housing in the new PPP Administration. The Labour and Medical departments came under her jurisdiction as well as the Registrar General and the Government Analyst. Among the issues which occupied her attention during her term in office were the debate for domestic servants to be protected by the *Workmen's Compensation Ordinance*, recognition of the BGLU at Atkinson Field and houses for the working-class.

In spite of the defeat, the PNC strove to regain ground and attempted to mobilise women. On 5 October, 1957 the Women's

Auxiliary of the PNC was formed with Jane Phillips-Gay as chairperson. P.H. Daly criticised the composition of the executive, claiming that the PNC was guilty of "allowing the non-militant middle-class women to take over control".[39] The *Thunder*, in supporting Daly, claimed that the Women's Auxiliary of the PPP had 99 per cent of working-class women and was led by working-class women, while those who formed the executive of the Women's Auxiliary of the PNC were 'mild-toned ladies'.[40] This observation conveyed the idea that the leaders of the Women's Auxiliary of the PPP perceived their role as political activists was to represent working-class women. It was their contention that this was not the position of the Women's Auxiliary of the PNC. However, the PNC undertook to engage the attention of women and prepared to contest the elections held in 1961. This election witnessed the largest number of women to exercise their franchise since 1953. The *Guiana Graphic*, in commenting on the large turn out of women, noted:

> Never before in the history of local elections had so many women turned up to vote. They were there before the light of dawn and remained with dogged patience - the symbol of feminine determination. The colourful spectacle of these women in gay costumes, some clutching children, some according to custom were barefooted - all serious and determined women, was a memorable one.[41]

The women who contested this election were all African-Guyanese, namely, Jane Phillips-Gay, Winifred Gaskin and Caroline John. One hundred and four men were nominated. Jane Phillips-Gay lost to Balram Singh Rai of the PPP in the Demerara Coast - East district; Winifred Gaskin was defeated by Peter D'Aguiar in Georgetown Central; and Caroline John lost to John Carter in the Werk-en-Rust district.

In 1961, the *Constitution* provided for a nominated Senate. It consisted of thirteen members, among whom were Christina Allicock and Anne Jardim. Janet Jagan had not contested a seat and was only appointed Minister of Home Affairs after the incumbent, Claude Christian, died of a heart attack. In 1964, she resigned her seat allegedly because of the lack of confidence by the community in the Police Force, who, in her opinion, had not been impartial in the disturbances. She claimed that they searched homes of Indians because they were members of the PPP. In response to Mrs Jagan's assertion, Senator Anne Jardim insinuated that "Mrs Janet Jagan was capable of not only crocodile tears but also crocodile blood must be going through her veins for her attempt to blame the Police Force for what happened".[42] Evidently, she did not believe that the Police should take sole responsibility for the crisis.

In the 1964 General Elections the political parties involved more women than they had done in previous elections. There were 200 candidates, of whom 15 were women.[43] It is a fact that from this period one witnessed the participation of a greater number of women as candidates in the general elections and as Government ministers. The years under examination have shown that female candidates were always in the minority, even in 1964 when they appeared to be a higher percentage than in the past. The causes for this were complex. It was claimed that women preferred to be involved in social work than in politics. But Muriel Belgrave considered this explanation too simplistic. In 1946, she said: "As long as women are barred, or bar themselves, from participating in the legislative work of the Colony laws will never be wholly sound or complete, because in making them half the brains of the Colony are not exercised."[44] It was also contended that influential men were largely responsible for the disproportion of the sexes in politics.

Although this might have been confirmed in some instances, it was not always accurate. Men did support female politicians. This was illustrated in the Georgetown Town Council in 1946 when Marie Bayley, the only female town councillor, complained about her motion not being put on the agenda. Mayor Vibart Wight claimed that he had instructed the Town Clerk to delete it from the agenda because it was not worded correctly. She was supported by A.A. Thorne and Joseph Gonsalves and only withdrew the motion after she learnt that the Town Council had taken steps to correct the problem which she had brought to the attention of the Councillors. In this incident, the councillors had called on the Mayor to explain his behaviour and had been dissatisfied with his initial interpretation of the motion.

In 1961, the *Guiana Graphic* queried: 'Is this the woman's world that everyday we hear so much of?'. Is it that our women's convictions are not strong enough to persuade them to take more positive action in handling the affairs of the country?'[45] However, there was a stigma attached to women's involvement in politics. Gertrude Collins, among others, was a victim of this attitude. The few women who participated actively in politics were considered unfeminine. They did not conform to the general concept of the role of women. But in breaking away from the pack, they were able to bring into sharp focus the true condition of the dispossessed, particularly the down-trodden women.

In conclusion, it must be emphasised that women were initially disqualified from entry into politics partly by the stringent property qualifications. Later, although the opportunity arose, some preferred social work to active participation in politics. However, by the 1940s, the minority who aggressively fought for the improvement of their people had begun to make a significant impact on Guyanese society, despite the hostility of the press and some of their womenfolk. They realised their full potential and understood that they had an important role to play in the decision-making process in Guyana. Their example encouraged women at all levels to join in the fight for Guyanisation and self-government.

It is a fact that some women, because of their high profiles, would not escape the notice of the historians, but the nameless ones also contributed to the evolution of the role of women in politics.

Notes

1. M. Shahabuddeen, *Constitutional Development in Guyana, 1621-1978* (Georgetown, 1978), p. 273.
2. Brassington was labelled the "Doughty Champioin of the People's Cause" and "Tribune of the People", *Daily Chronicle*, 12 Oct. 1921.
3. Sheila Rowbothan, *Hidden from History: Rediscovering Women in History from the 17th Century to the Present* (New York, 1976), p. 50.
4. Constable Bobb to Inspector of Police, No. 2177/28, 2 May, 1928.
5. Shahabudeen, p. 285.
6. *Guiana Review*, 7 Apr. 1940.
7. Hansard, 3 May, 1956.
8. *Daily Chronicle*, 13 Jul. 1946.
9. *Ibid.*
10. *Guiana Graphic*, 10 Jul. 1946.
11. *Daily Chronicle*, 12 Jul. 1946.
12. *Ibid.*, 28 Jul., 1946.
13. *Ibid.*, 9 Aug., 1946.
14. *Ibid.*, 10 Nov., 1946.
15. Roberta Kilkenny, "Women in Social and Political Struggle: British Guiana, 1946-1953", Paper presented at the Association of Caribbean Historians' Conference, 1984, p. 12.
16. *Daily Chronicle*, 15 Aug. 1946.
17. *Ibid.*, 18 Aug. 1946.
18. *Ibid.*, 22 Aug. 1946.
19. *Ibid.*, 7 Nov. 1946.
20. *Ibid.*, 29 Aug. 1946.
21. *Ibid.*, 30 Aug. 1946.
22. Frances B. Stafford to the Executive Council of the Women's Political and Economic Organisation, 23 Mar. 1947.
23. *Daily Chronicle*, 27 Oct. 1947.
24. *Ibid.*, 16 Nov. 1947.
25. *Ibid.*, 23 Nov. 1947.
26. *Daily Argosy*, 27 Nov. 1947.
27. *Ibid.*, 15 Nov. 1947.
28. Gail Teixeira, "Janet Jagan Honoured" (1989).
29. *Guiana Times*, Aug. - Sep. 1954, p. 30.
30. Hansard, 18 Jun., 1953.
31. Hansard, Session 1953 (18 May - 8 Oct., 1953), 534-535.
32. *Ibid.*.

33. *Guiana Times*, Aug.-Sep. 1954, p. 18.
34. Hansard, 1 Mar. 1957.
35. *Ibid.*
36. *Ibid.*, 21 Dec. 1956.
37. *Ibid.*, 25 Jun. 1957.
38. *Report on the General Election,* 1957. Appendix 1, Table 1.
39. Reported in the *Thunder*, 9 Nov. 1957.
40. *Ibid.*
41. *Guiana Graphic,* 21 Aug. 1961.
42. *Daily Chronicle*, 2 Jun. 1964.
43. The women represented the political parties as follows: PPP - Janet Jagan; PNC - Winifred Gaskin, Gwendoline Welshman, Norma Jackman, Sylvia Mc Garrel, Hyacinth Goddett, Margaret Ackman; UF - Clementina Da Silva, Teka Leung, Cleo Rich, P.N. Faria; JP - Juanita Thijs; NLF - Elsie Latchman, Eudora Theresa Forde
44. *Daily Chronicle*, 17 Nov, 1946.
45. *Guiana Graphic*, 30 Jul. 1961.

14: The Development of Political Organisation up to 1953

by
Kimani S. Nehusi

The original People's Progressive Party[1] was the first mass-based, multi-racial, political organisation in the history of Guyana[2], a multi-racial society in which the masses had traditionally suffered at the hands of exploiters. It was also the first genuine political party in the country.

For these very reasons, the original PPP was the first political organisation to recognize clearly that the fundamental contradiction in the society then, as it is now, was that between labour and capital. It was also the first political party consciously to set out to resolve this major contradiction, as well as the other secondary ones, for the benefit of the working people of the land.

It was too, the first political group with a permanent central organisation, a bureaucracy, and a guiding ideology which, together with a well-thought-out programme, united the Guyanese working people and their allies into a force. This force dominated its political environment beyond all expectations, winning 75 per cent of the seats contested in the 1953 General Elections, merely three years after its formal launching in January 1950. It was a stunning success. In essence, the original PPP was the first political organisation to satisfy the perceived political needs of the overwhelming majority of the Guyanese people. It represented a qualitative transformation in the political organisation extant in Guyana before 1950, and in the kind of politics practised before its advent.

But the original PPP did not appear on the Guyanese political scene out of nowhere. It had its genesis in the increasing *conscientizacao* of the Guyanese people, the liberalization of the franchise, and the application of Marxist political theory to the Guyanese society by radical young intellectuals.

Long before the era of the original PPP and the leaders of this Party, many organisations and leaders had fought for progress in the country. Some organisations were limited because they were based only in some sections of the working people. Others were restricted because they sought to advance only the cause of the so-called middle class. Some leaders were unsuccessful because they failed to comprehend the fundamental conflict between labour and capital in the society. Others did not succeed because they did not understand the necessity for unity against a common enemy. But it remains the truth that the lessons and the fluctuating material gains of this struggle were handed down from generation to generation in the Guyanese political culture.

In January 1950, the material, political, ideological and organisational results of this struggle were meagre in terms of what was to be achieved in the next three years. British Guiana was still very much in the grip of British colonialism. The country was a Crown Colony. The great majority of the Guyanese people were excluded from the franchise and from the formal political process.[3] On the other hand, the British Governor stood at the head of both the wholly-nominated Executive Council and the partly-elected Legislative Council. The economic life of the Colony was dominated by sugar and bauxite multi-national companies (MNCs), while the workers were still disunited, poor in material things, poor in health, in education, and in ideology.

The Guyanese political culture was still dominated by divisive sectional interests. Organisations such as the Guiana Industrial Workers Union (GIWU), British Guiana Labour Union (BGLU) and Man Power Citizens' Association (MPCA) were based on industrial sections of the working people and so could not speak for them all. Again, The League of Coloured People (LCP), British Guiana East Indian Association (BGEIA) and Portuguese Club were based on social sections of the Guyanese people and could not represent them all. The established church was a part of the colonial system, obfuscating its role in helping to keep the poor,

poor and the rich, rich. None of these organisations confronted the problems of the society on a national level.

This was first attempted by the Political Affairs Committee (PAC). Although it was not a political party, the PAC was the embryo and forerunner of the original People's Progressive Party.[4] It was deliberately conceived as such, aiming from its inception "to assist the growth and development of the Labour and Progressive Movements of British Guiana, to the end of establishing a strong, disciplined and enlightened Party, equipped with the theory of scientific socialism".[5] The Committee also aimed to provide the Guianese masses with information and scientific political analyses of both local and international current affairs, and to develop discussion groups by circulating relevant printed matter.[6]

The PAC was a small discussion group formed in 1946 by Cheddi Jagan, Janet Jagan, Jocelyn Hubbard and Ashton Chase. At first, the major influence on the public was the increasingly popular *PAC Bulletin*, the first issue of which appeared on 6 Nov. 1946. Later, PAC discussion circles helped to develop and clarify ideas and thus indirectly influenced the developing consciousness of the Guyanese people. Later still, public meetings helped PAC leaders to communicate with the people.

However, the *PAC Bulletin* remained the major educational instrument. In simple language it applied Marxist-Leninist theory to the Guyanese socio-economic formation to explain this Guianese reality to the people. The PAC leaders saw clearly that if they were to achieve their aims, one of their chief tasks had to be the education of the masses about basic political and economic questions in colonial Guyana.

They also realised that, while the increasing participation of the masses in the struggle for change had increased their consciousness, the latter's understanding of the economic and political bases of colonialism was generally either non-existent or faulty. These leaders realized, too, that their own ideas were too novel to provoke widespread reaction and understanding among the Guyanese people. This was particularly true of race and other divisive issues, for the people were accustomed to the then political fare of narrow sectoral loyalties.

From the pages of the *Bulletin* the structure of the society was unveiled. Poverty and class relations were discussed and (eventually and inevitably) capitalist exploitation was unmasked "as the foundation from which the depredations and evils of colonialism flowed".[7] Thus, the PAC isolated British colonialism as the enemy of the people and used its oppression as a *cause célèbre* around which it tried to unite the Guyanese people. The local foci of British capitalist control and exploitation - the Governor, the colonial legislature and the sugar and bauxite companies - were all attacked for their roles in keeping the working people poor and exploited.

The PAC also fought against such obstacles to the people's struggle for a just society as the *ad hoc* political 'parties' with limiting sectoral programmes and appeal, a consequent absence of permanent, professional bureaucratic party machinery, the domination of the middle-class intellectuals and businessmen in positions of leadership, the absence of a coherent plan for the development of the country for the workers, and the absence of a common ideology to weld the fractious working-class together into a common, centrally directed force against its enemies. The PAC geared itself to establish a party which would change this system, erect a radically restructured economy, establish an independent Guyanese state, and lead it to socialism.[8] It was courageous even in announcing such aims.

The PAC existed for three years, from Nov. 1946 to December 1949. In this time it "...worked with the trade union movement, spreading new and progressive ideas, giving solidarity, both local and foreign ... teaching and holding classes in Marxism-Leninism, preaching and practising internationalism, guiding working people into struggle and laying the foundations for a political Party to be equipped with the theory of socialism".[9] By 1949, its leaders had already gained valuable political experience, raised the consciousness of the masses and established an important working relationship with them. Since 1947, PAC had recognized the necessity for a qualitative change in the people's struggle against capitalism, and had decided on a concomitant new kind of workers' rganisation. By 1950, the work of the PAC had prepared both its members and the people. The vision of a workers' party leading an independent Guyana to socialism remained strong. But in 1949, the next task of the PAC was to transform vision into reality.

Thus, even though there was no party organisation before 1950,[10] the ground had been well prepared for the forthcoming People's Progressive Party (PPP). Indeed, the party organisation and officers had been identified since the second half of 1949. However, it was not until early in 1950 that the party was officially launched at a meeting called for that purpose at the Progressive High School in Georgetown.[11] This party was qualitatively and quantitatively superior to all preceding local organisations which had sought to exert influence upon the politics of the land, including the Sugar Producers' Association (SPA), which was the political organ of the sugar planters.

Besides the careful and valuable preparation of the PAC, the original PPP benefited from having leaders who had significant previous political, trade union and organisational experience, the articulation of a relevant, attractive, nationalistic programme in catchy Marxist terms which the masses and other socio-economic groups found lovable, and the initiation and mastery of a powerful party organisation which eventually proliferated throughout the country.

In 1950, Dr. Cheddi B. Jagan was undoubtedly the most experienced and most popular of the leaders of the original PPP. From the time of his return to Guyana on 5 October, 1943, he had made it his policy to work with progressive people wherever they were to be found;[12] but among existing organisations, a lack of enthusiasm for the needs of the ordinary people caused him to move from one to the other, and eventually join with similar-minded people to found their own. Thus, he worked with the British Guiana East Indian Association (BGEIA), but left it because, like the League of Coloured People (LCP), its counterpart among the Africans, it was dominated by middle-class interests and had no emphasis upon programmes for the masses.[13] Dr. Jagan then became an official of the Man Power Citizen's Association (MPCA), but was relieved of his office because of difficulties with the union's leadership, which was becoming unprogressive. It soon after became a 'Company' union.[14] Dr. Jagan then became closely associated with the newly formed Guiana Industrial Workers' Union (GIWU) and later, accepted the position of President of the Sawmill Workers Union. By this time, Dr. Jagan had already helped form the PAC and had been a member of the Legislative Council since 1947.

Other leaders of the original PPP would bring experiences gained from similar involvement of lesser magnitude in existing organisations. Thus Ayube Edun, Jai Naraine Singh and Dr. Joseph Prayag Latchmansingh would also have experience in the BGEIA, Dr. Claude Denbow in the LCP, and Edun in the MPCA. Sidney King and George Younge of Buxton were experienced Local Authority men. Janet Jagan and Winifred Gaskin had gained considerable expertise from their organisation of the Women's Political and Economic Organisation (WPEO). Later on, young intellectuals such as Rory Westmaas, Martin Carter, Keith Carter, Lionel Jeffrey and Rodwell Atherly joined the original PPP. Besides being better educated academically, these young men offered the distinct advantage of having steeped themselves in Marxism-Leninism prior to their involvement in the PPP.

The Party held its first congress on 1 April 1951 when its first *Constitution* was adopted. In this document was enshrined the pursuance of the goal of national self-determination and independence.[15] Later, when a preamble was introduced, it enunciated this goal more grandly:

> In the firm belief that the people of British Guiana, like peoples everywhere, are entitled to the full enjoyment of all the human rights and fundamental freedoms often proclaimed as the common standard of achievement for all peoples and nations, we ... have resolved to combine our efforts to achieve the

> National Independence of British Guiana, and to secure for all Guianese social progress and increasingly better standards of life.[16]

At this first congress too, L.F.S. Burnham was elected Party Chairman; Dr. C.B. Jagan, Leader of the Legislative Group; H.A. Fraser, First Vice-Chairman; C. Wong, Second Vice-Chairman; J. Jagan, General Secretary; S. King, Assistant General Secretary and Ram Karran, Treasurer. Members of the General Council were A. Chase, R. Luck, F.O. van Sertima, I. Cendrecourt, M. Thompson, H. Critchlow, E. Kennard, T. Lee, V. Fingall, Jai Naraine Singh, S. La Taste, J. Latchmansingh, C. Cambridge, F. Bowman and Pandit S. Misir.[17]

The *Constitution* also made provision for an annual Party congress, which was charged with the responsibility to "adopt platforms, elect officers, and generally determine Party organisation and policy".[18] Party groups were organised in communities throughout the country. It was these groups which elected delegates to the Party congress which in turn elected the General Council. A smaller Executive Committee was elected from this General Council to run Party business on a daily basis. This mode of organisation ensured that every Party member had a chance of electing officials and determining policy. Indeed, "this democratic structure may have been the Party's most important contribution to West Indian political life".[19]

This mass participation in the Party was facilitated by a highly centralized and extremely efficient network of officials and communication which reached from the first rung among the grassroots to the General Secretary - in these early years, Janet Jagan - at head office in 199 Charlotte Street, Georgetown, and back again to the grassroots.

The local group was the basic unit of the Party, both in theory[20] and in practice.[21] Each group would have a Chairman, Secretary, Vice-Chairman, Treasurer, Committee members and ordinary members. Each group decided when it would meet. Most met weekly. In farming areas, this was not possible throughout the year, and few meetings were held during crop time. However, there was intense Party activity after the crop.

Above the Party group was the constituency group. This was a grouping of Party groups in each electoral constituency. Based upon one delegate to each five financial members in a group, it had power to elect Party representatives in open elections on any level; but its nominations were subject to the approval of the Central Executive.[22] From its inception, the original People's Progressive Party aimed at being a mass Party. "Everyone who wanted to join had a good chance of being admitted,"[23] though persons of very bad reputation in their districts were excluded. It was not a cadre party. Members were not required to be politically active, but each group had mobilizers in its area. The Party worked towards some measure of discipline among its members, each of whom could be faulted for missing a certain number of meetings and/or falling behind in payment of dues. There were also sanctions for acting in a manner prejudicial to the best interests of the Party.

The mobilisation of the Guianese masses was an essential, perhaps the most essential aspect of the concept of the PPP as a mass-based political organisation to fight colonialism, represent the masses and lead the country to independence and socialism. Since the days of the PAC, most of those who eventually became members of the leadership of the PPP had consciously developed a pro-people posture and worked primarily to develop a relationship with the masses which supported the aims of the committee. After the formation of the PPP, this process was accentuated.

Their previous experiences and political record equipped the PPP leaders with a repertoire of advantages which they deployed effectively over existing rivals. Besides, their introduction of a new kind of politics, in which there was mass participation, aided the process which took the original People's Progressive Party to a majority victory in the 1953 elections. This eventually frightened the British into the orchestration of the savage overthrow of a legally-elected and democratic Administration and the derailment of the nationalist movement in Guyana. Hence, the use of personal influence, links with existing organisations and the formation of new ones, regular public meetings throughout the country, pickets, demonstrations, petitions and other forms of demonstrations around public issues became devices increasingly used by the leadership of the Party; they count among the Party's contributions to Guyanese political culture.

The task of mobilising the people was tackled in a number of ways, but the most important remained the formation of Party groups throughout the land. About two or three leaders of the Party went into an area - usually at the invitation of people there but sometimes because they considered it a good place to organise the people. Police permission was obtained and three or four speakers arranged for a public meeting to which all were invited. The Party always tried to have as chairperson someone from the district who knew its problems. One of the speakers would talk about how to join the Party, and interested persons were asked to gather after the meeting. The latter were then asked to identify someone to represent the Party in the district. The Party's official receipt book for registering members would be left with that person. It was usually filled quickly. The person in charge would then post or take the subscriptions and book to Party Headquarters in Georgetown. Sometimes, another receipt book was needed. In any event, a date would be fixed at which a Party organiser would visit the district to meet members, give them their membership cards, introduce them to the rules and principles of the Party, ask them to continue making new members if they were not ready to form a group, and otherwise fix a date for the election of office-bearers.[24]

If the local dignitary who chaired the initial public meeting became involved in this process, his influence alone was enough to assure him a post, usually chairman. Hence, Ayearst's observation that the Chairman of the group was normally a local bigwig, but the real work was usually done by the secretary, who attained this post by reputation for ability and dedication.[25] It was the secretary who kept the local group in touch with the Party headquarters through the General Secretary - Janet Jagan - and through whom in turn the Party Executive communicated with the constituency committees and grassroots.

The personal contacts and influence of Party leaders were used to stimulate interest in the original PPP. Dr. Cheddi Jagan's dental surgery was very instrumental in this process. There, literature was distributed and discussions held. The same activities took place in Forbes Burnham's lawyer's office, but on a lesser scale.[26] Sidney King was well known on the East Coast, where he was a teacher. He also had teacher contacts through the British Guiana Teachers' Association (BGTA). Ashton Chase exerted great influence as a trade unionist.

In the early days, Chase and Burnham had mainly urban contact with the people, while Jagan's influence and contact were country-wide. He had held many public meetings before the Party was formed, often with King. The social convulsion at Plantation Enmore in 1948 had given these two, along with Janet Jagan, Ram Karran and others, a lot of publicity and popularity with the working people.[27] Besides, Dr. Jagan's role in the Legislative Council in proposing motions for social reform and consistently opposing 'unpopular Government measures' won for him many working-class admirers and sympathisers.[28] Thus, the Party leadership had contact with politically active people in most areas of the country.[29]

In these early days, groups were formed over most of the coastland, but many parts of the hinterland were excluded because of restrictions from visiting Amerindian reservations and the concessions of foreign companies at places such as Winiperu and Mackenzie. However, Dr. Jagan had greater access than the other leaders because of his privilege of being a member of the Legislative Council.[30]

By the end of 1952, the first phase in the formation of Party groups had been completed. The North West District, Bartica, Mackenzie, East Coast and East Bank Demerara, New Amsterdam, Corentyne, Kwakwani, Ituni, the Essequibo coast and Islands, Pomeroon and Mazaruni-Potaro districts all had groups by then. There were few areas which were not organised. All groups were regarded as lawful arms of the Party, and each could carry on activities in the Party's name. Often, a signboard showed the meeting place of the PPP group.

The groups raised money for the Party through dances, raffles, and other activities of this nature. Often, a group would put on a programme which included a public lecture. Members at the grassroot level expressed opinions on matters of importance generally carried in the press, which was sometimes biased against them. Party groups also passed resolutions on Party policies on specific issues. In this way, they helped to increase the consciousness of the people and strengthen the democratic structure of the organisation, for it was widely recognized that ideas did not originate only at the centre of the Party.[31]

The leadership core of the PAC and PPP had steadily expanded its influence and support until it represented a wide cross-section of the Guyanese people. By 1951, even one of Dr. Jagan's staunch detractors had recognized that the PPP parliamentary leader's activities in the House had "... won him wide popularity as the champion of the working-classes and (remained) the foundation of the solid support which he (then enjoyed) from a very wide section of the working-classes of the Colony".[32] By then, the multi-racial aspect of the Party's nature was clear to this anti-PPP observer, who recorded that the Party membership - which he numbered at 3,060 - was "fairly evenly distributed among the Africans, East Indians and mixed races".[33]

From the inception even of the PAC, the multi-racial nature of the nationalist movement in the country was proclaimed and practised. However, the 1947 General Elections experience sensitised the leaders to the reality that charisma and race were important determinants of election results.[34] This was analysed to mean that the movement had to acquire a multi-racial image to attract in large numbers, both East Indians and Africans who together amounted to over 80 per cent of the country's population. Besides a multi-racial group of leaders, an important concomitant of this image was found to be the recruitment of "an

African leader who had the same magnetic appeal among Africans that Cheddi Jagan had among Indians".[35] Forbes Burnham, a Guyanese lawyer educated in London and an outstanding orator, was chosen at the time the group transformed itself into the PPP. Thus dual charisma and dual race came to be installed in the leadership of the original People's Progressive Party.

It is misleading to conclude that ideology took a back seat in this process. It would also be erroneous to assume that this question dominated the Party. The truth is that the original People's Progressive Party was no Marxist-Leninist Party but a grouping of a wide cross-section of Guyanese nationalists which included among its leadership a strong group of Marxists and others whose strident nationalism found facile expression in Marxist rhetoric. Unlike the other territories in the English-speaking Caribbean, it was the radical Marxist left wing which dominated the original PPP and the nationalist movement from its inception.[36]

Much of the Party machinery, the secretariat, the publications and organisational work, were under the control of Marxists and people with interests in Marxism. Indeed, Marxists could usually carry the vote in the Central Executive. It was this Marxist faction within the PPP leadership which organised youth groups such as the Pioneer Youth League (PYL) in Georgetown and the Demerara Youth Rally (DYR) on the East Coast of Demerara.[37] These young, lower middle-class radicals also formed the Peace Committee. Forbes Burnham, in middle-class background and university training not unlike most of them, became one of their chief opponents within the Party.[38]

In these years before 1953, no one openly rejected Marxism, though Dr. Joseph Latchmansingh, Jai Narine Singh and Aubrey Fraser would later do so. Dr. Hanoman, a one-time executive member like those others, was neither Marxist nor socialist. There were also Fabian socialists among other, older members of the Party hierarchy. But there were no open conflicts over the programme because the overpowering presence of capitalism, especially in the form of Booker Bros. McConnell & Co. and the bauxite companies, dominated the consciousness of the hierarchy.[39] While most of the leaders were familiar with the tenets of Marxism, the situation was different among the rank and file. No serious drive was ever made to inculcate Marxism in them. However, the more ardent and discerning followers were undoubtedly familarised with at least Marxist phraseology gleaned from speeches and Party literature, especially *Thunder*, the Party newspaper,[40] and also from classes organised by the Party.

Thunder was one of the key means by which the PPP bureaucracy maintained contact with its members, especially the masses, at whom many of its articles were aimed. It was "basically an educational paper, carrying well prepared articles on the class struggle, studies on imperialism, exposés of the wrongs of our society."[41] Essentially a grander version of its ideological predecessor, the *PAC Bulletin*, *Thunder* put forth a constant stream of articles on various issues which exposed how the society worked, who benefited from the exploited workers' labour, what had to be done to correct the situation, outlined the ideas upon which a new society was to be built, and adopted a vigorous progressive posture on the side of other exploited people fighting for their rights in the world. In essence, it attempted to provide its members with a wide education in local and international politics.[42]

In many ways besides ideological continuity, *Thunder* cannot be divorced from the *PAC Bulletin*. Before the advent of the *Bulletin*, the newspaper was an important source of information for a growing number of Guyanese people. However, no newspaper presented them with the analyses and ideological tools that these featured. The language was new. It was the language of Marxism-Leninism. Already awakened by the PAC, interest in this new kind of politics quickened with the advent of *Thunder*. Many people joined the PPP because of what they read in the Party's newspaper.[43] Both were relatively easy to acquire. The *Bulletin*, in limited numbers, was distributed free,[44] while the *Thunder* cost a penny.[45]

The activities and methods of the Party won it more and more attention and more members. The representation of the people's cause on issues in various localities in the country, pickets, demonstrations, public meetings, petitions, distribution of literature - in a word, the politics of exposure and protest - were used to get its message across to Guianese. These methods were new to Guiana. They ushered in a qualitative transformation of the kind of politics practised in the country. Systematic public meetings were held all over the country, not just at election time and not only in heavily-populated areas. While their political opponents were idle, the PPP used these occasions to meet with the people of the country, explain its policy and programme, show them why they needed to be organised into a political party, the nature of the party they needed, and preached the new creed of racial unity.

By October 1953, a wide cross-section of the Guyanese nation supported the Party. These included the majority of workers and farmers of all ages, parts of the middle-class civil servants, professionals, teachers, many Indians in the local manufacturing class, and many of the local African petite bourgeoisie and others.[46] In this process of the political education of the masses, discussions and seminars were regularly held to provide intensive experiences for Party members. This was especially true of the early years.[47] Classes on ideology were sometimes held in given areas. Labour and the role of the working people, Guianese history, and constitutional change were all topics discussed.[48] Besides attacking such basic issues as the living and working conditions of the people throughout the country, the PPP also took the side of the people in issues at the local level. Sometimes, when the Party had the means, it attempted to correct some of these situations. The literacy campaign based in the Indian villages is of particular importance in this respect. These activities won for the Party an increasing amount of respect and followers.[49]

Large numbers of people were mobilized and participated in these activities. Sometimes, the Party organised a programme to portray its position upon a specific issue. This occurred in response to the advent of the Waddington Commission. The PPP organised a country-wide petition campaign to present its demands to the Commission. When the Commission presented its proposals, the Party organised another petition, this time against some of them. Again, street-corner meetings were held and signatures collected throughout the country. Mobilisation of the people was a cornerstone of the PPP's protest.

The public debate and protest provoked by the Waddington Commission arose primarily because the PPP regarded the Commission as an opportunity to achieve some of the aims of its programme. The Party's first programme, published in April 1950,[60] included most of the demands for constitutional reform made during the sitting of the Commission. These demands added up to the strong case for universal adult suffrage and self-Government made by Cheddi Jagan and Forbes Burnham, the Party's two representatives before the Commission. The Party's programme also called for an end to colonialism, first employment opportunities for Guianese, recognition of unions supported by a majority of workers, housing for the poor, security of tenure for rice farmers and land development.

The PPP leadership had decided that, at that juncture, change could not result from action in the legislature because a majority of legislators did not represent the people. Hence the accent was on protest. Besides, protest was a way of directly involving the people in the formal political process. The PPP had been well-prepared for these radical innovations in Guianese politics from its inception. Despite the history of protest in Guiana, it was the first political group to adopt a systematic analysis of the country's problems to see how they could have been corrected.[51] This was a conscious diachronic investigation in which the PPP's founders tried to identify and avoid the pitfalls of previous political organisations.[52] This process, informed by existing ills in the society, resulted in the Party's mass-based, multi-racial and highly-organised character and a programme which aimed at radical change within, and raised the spectre of change of, the system. This was a direct attack upon the existing structure of Guianese society and those who profited from this structure, chiefly international capitalism as manifested mainly in the sugar and bauxite companies and their local adherents.

These were powerful enemies. But it was the first time the power structure was confronted with such a well-organised challenge. It was a well-planned and well-orchestrated attack. The leaders of the original PPP understood the nature, if not the immense difficulty, of the task they had undertaken. The work they had done among their compatriots had produced what was probably the most enlightened working-class in the Anglophone Caribbean at that juncture. Guyanese nationalism had been aroused. Significant numbers of most sections of the country's population had been won over to their cause. But the Party remained opposed by the propertied interests and the British Government, which was alarmed by the radical posture and Marxist leanings of the PPP's leadership.

Since 1947, Vincent Roth declared in the legislature that PAC meant "Push All Communism",[53] but there was no crusade against Marxism-Leninism, which was then an unpopular creed.[54] However, the onset of the Cold War facilitated the political opponents of the PPP with increasing room to manoeuvre against the Party. All radicals were lumped together in the category of `communist', and communism was equated with everything which was evil. This soon became a full-blown campaign against all progressives. It was spearheaded by the secret machinery of the British Government and was not limited to British Guiana.[55] These forces were greatly distressed by the large volume[56] of progressive literature imported and circulated by the PPP. Although most were on sale in London:

> the British Governor found them dangerous to British Guiana, and banned a long list of them ... at almost the same time when the British Government declared from London that it was extending to all its colonies the *Convention of Human Rights*, which particularly affirms the right to receive and import ideas through any medium.[57]

Several radical West Indian Labour leaders were banned from entering the Colony of British Guiana and many leaders of the PPP were banned from West Indian territories. In British Guiana,

Mr. Lionel Luckhoo, nominated to the Legislative Council by the Governor, gave notice of a motion recommending that the Government enact legislation "... prohibiting the entry into the Colony of literature, publications, propaganda or films which are subversive or contrary to public interest".[58] This quickly became known as the `Dunce Motion' and received wide condemnation as an attack upon democracy.[59] Nevertheless, it was passed on 14 March 1952.[60]

The PPP used the occasion of the Bill to continue its mobilisation of the Guyanese masses with street-corner meetings, pickets and demonstrations.[61] The Bill became a central issue in the 1953 elections, and helped ensure the defeat of Mr. Luckhoo and his Party.[62]

Notes

1. This essay, in its present form, represents the results of a preliminary investigation of the topic. The term "original PPP" is used to differentiate the organisation launched in January 1950 from the "present PPP", and also the People's National Congress (PNC), which for a time was also called PPP. Then there were two PPPs. These two organisations, the present PPP and the PNC, resulted from a split in the 'original PPP' in 1955.
2. See R.R. Premdas, *The Rise of the First Mass-Based, Multi-Racial Party in Guyana* (Georgetown, 1972).
3. The narrow base of the franchise was constructed upon attainment of the age at 21 years; ownership or tenancy of three acres worth at least $150.00 or of property valued at least $45.00 per year. Legislative Council membership was based on an income of $1,200.00 per annum, ownership of real estate valued at $1,000.00 or lease of property to the value of $300.00 per year. In each case, the candidate had to be literate in the English Language. See Morley Ayearst, *The British West Indies: The Search for Self-Government*. (Washington Square, New York University Press, 1960), pp. 112 - 113.
4. Janet Jagan, *Twelve Years of the PPP: An Account of the Party's Long Struggle against Privilege and for the Rights of the People*. (Georgetown: New Guyana Co. Ltd. 1961), p. 3. See also Premdas, p. 2.

5. From "The Aims of the Political Affairs Committee" *PAC Bulletin* (6 Nov. 1946), p. 1. See also PPP: "The Struggles of the PPP for Guyana's Independence" (Ruimveldt: New Guyana Co. Ltd., 1966), p. 9, and Janet Jagan, "The PAC", *Thunder*, Vol. 13, No. 3 (Jul.-Aug. 1981), pp. 5 - 6.
6. "The Aims of the Political Affairs Committee", *PAC Bulletin* (6 Oct. 1946), p. 1.
7. "Wages and Profits", *PAC Bulletin* (7 May 1947), as quoted in Premdas, p. 11.
8. Janet Jagan, "The Political Affairs Committee", *Thunder*, Vol. 13, No. 3 (Jul.-Aug. 1981), p. 5.
9. *Ibid.*, p. 6.
10. This writer has encountered no evidence to validate Ayearst's contention that "The PPP organising drive had started as early as 1948 with the activities of field representatives throughout the Colony", although it is true that "When the PPP was founded officially in 1950, it was far more than a paper Organisation". See Ayearst, *The British West Indies ...*" pp. 116-117.
11. Interview with Eusi Kwayana, 11 Feb. 1984. Kwayana was known as Sidney King in this era.
12. Interview with Dr. C.B. Jagan, 27 Sep. 1983.
13. C.B. Jagan, *The West on Trial. The Fight for Guyana's Freedom..* (Berlin: Seven Seas Publishers, 1966), p. 60. For this neglect of the working people by the BGEIA, see also Andra P. Thakur, "Guyana: The Politics of Race and Class 1953-1964" (Unpub. MA Thesis, Dept. of Anthropology, University of Alberta, Ed., Alberta, 1973), p. 61.
14. Jagan: The *West on Trial*, pp. 60-61. See also Premdas, *The Rise*, ... Note 23, p. 35; J.G. Rose, *The 1948 Enmore Incident* (Georgetown: Curriculum Development Centre - Ministry of Ed. Social Dev. & Culture, 1982), pp. 18, 25, *passim*, and Ashton Chase, *A History of Trade Unionism in Guyana: 1900 to 1961* (Georgetown: New Guyana Co. Ltd., n.d.), pp. 146 - 147.
15. PPP, *Constitution of the People's Progressive Party. Ratified and Adopted by First Congress of PPP on 1 Apr. 1951.* (Georgetown: Arcade Printery, 1951), p. 1.
16. PPP, *Constitution of the People's Progressive Party. Revised and Adopted, 30 Mar. 1958.* (Georgetown: Labour Advocate Job Printing Dept. 1958), p. 19.
17. PPP: *People's Progressive Party: 21 Years. 1950 - 1971* (Georgetown: New Guyana Co. Ltd., 1971), p. 5.
18. Philip Reno, *The Ordeal of British Guiana.* (New York: Monthly Review Press, 1964), p. 14.

19. *Ibid.*
20. PPP, *Constitution of the People's Progressive Party. Ratified & Adopted by First Congress of PPP on 1 Apr. 1951*, p. 3.
21. Interview with Eusi Kwayana 27 Jan. 1984.
22. PPP, *Constitution of the PPP*, pp. 5-6.
23. Interview with Eusi Kwayana. 27 Jan. 1984.
24. *Ibid.*
25. Ayearst, p. 117.
26. Interview with Eusi Kwayana. 27 Jan. 1984.
27. Rose, *The 1948 Enmore Incident* p. 28, Note 35.
28. Memorandum on PPP from W. Orrett, Commissioner of Police and Officer-in-Charge, Special Branch, to All Officers. Secret. n.d. (about 1951). Encl. Minute of W.A. Orrett to Colonial Secretary, 51.05.01, N.A.G.
29. Interview with Eusi Kwayana, 27 Jan. 1984.
30. Memorandum of W.A. Orrett, 1 May 1951.
31. Interview with Eusi Kwayana 27 Jan. 1984.
32. Memorandum of W.A. Orrett, 1 May 1951.
33. *Ibid.*
34. Premdas, p. 20. See also Janet Jagan, *Twelve years* ..., p. 5.
35. Premdas, p. 21.
36. Cheddi Jagan, "Congress Speech Delivered at New Amsterdam, 1956" (University of Puerto Rico, College of the Social Sciences), p. 4.
37. Interview with Eusi Kwayana, 27 Jan. 1984.
38. Interview with Brindley Benn, 29 Sep. 1983. Benn was Deputy Premier in a PPP Administration before he broke with the Party. He later led the Working People's Vanguard Party (WPVP).
39. Interview with Eusi Kwayana, 11 Feb. 1984. There was conflict over the Pro-Moscow stand of the PPP, to which Forbes Burnham objected. There was also conflict between the lawyers and Cheddi Jagan.
40. When the PAC became the PPP its *Bulletin* became *Thunder*, official organ of the PPP. Initially a monthly, *Thunder* was first published in Jan. of 1950 and aimed to give its readers "progressive local and international views and news". *Thunder*. Vol. 1, No. 1. (Jan. 1950), p. 1. *Thunder* later became a weekly.
41. Janet Jagan, "Twelve years ...", p. 8.
42. See *Thunder*, for this period.
43. Interview with Brindley Benn, 29 Sep. 1983.
44. Cheddi Jagan, *The West on Trial*, p. 62.
45. *Thunder*, Vol. 1, No. 1. (Jan. 1950), p. 1.
46. Cheddi Jagan, "Congress Speech Delivered at New Amsterdam, 1956", p. 6: See also *LCP Sentinel*, Sunday, 3 May 1953.

47. Janet Jagan, *Twelve years* ..., pp. 7 - 8.
48. Interview with Eusi Kwayana, 27 Jan. 1984.
49. *Ibid.*
50. PPP, *People's Progressive Party: 21 years 1950 - 1971*, p. 7.
51. Janet Jagan, "Twelve years ...", p. 10.
52. Interview with Eusi Kwayana, 83-12-14.
53. Interview with Dr. Jagan, 83-09-27. See also C. Jagan, *The West on Trial*, p. 104.
54. Cheddi Jagan, *The West on Trial*, pp. 62-63.
55. See for example C.A. Herbert, Security Liaison Officer, Trinidad, (secret), to Commissioners of Police: Trinidad; Barbados; B.G; Leewards Is; Administrators of Grenada, St. Lucia; St. Vincent and Dominica. Oct. 1951. Also Circular of S.S. for Colonies No. 378/52, (secret), 16 Apr. 1952.
56. At least a half million publications were imported and distributed in Guyana by the PAC and PPP between 1946 and 1952. See Reno. p. 15. Also Premdas, p. 13.
57. Reno, p. 15.
58. Lionel Luckhoo, Notice of Motion, 30 Jan. 1952. "Subversive Publications Legislation." 337/3, Vol. II. Encl.
59. Special Branch (British Guiana Police Force), "Report on a Mass Meeting held by the Trade Unions Council, GIWU, LCP, PPP and the FUGE at Bourda Greene (sic) on Sunday 22 Mar. 1952". Confidential, Wittenham to Col. Sect. 24 Mar.. 1952. Encl. See also Brentnol Blackman, Sect. BGTUC. to Col. Sect., 21 Mar. 1952; John La Rose, Provisional Gen. Sect., West Indian Independence Party of Trinidad and Tobago to Governor of B.G., 5 Mar. 1953, and Editorial of the *LCP Sentinel*, Sunday, 1 Mar. 1953.
60. B.G., Fourth Legislative Council. Fourth Session, 1951-52. Resolution No. XVIII.
61. Governor of BG to Secretary of State, 15 Mar. 1952. Telegram.
62. Janet Jagan, *Twelve years* ..., p. 11.

Part IV

Post-Independence Period

15 : State Capitalism in Guyana: An Assessment of Burnham's Co-operative Socialist Republic

by
Clive Y. Thomas

1953 was a watershed year in the political development of Guyana. After centuries of mass struggle, first against colonial slavery and later its modified form, the system of indentured immigrant labour, the twentieth-century national Independence movement had succeeded in forcing the colonial authorities to hold elections under a system of universal adult suffrage and a *Constitution* that offered what was for that time a relatively high degree of 'internal self-government'.

The previous *Constitution* was the classic Crown Colony type, in that it provided for a legislature and executive made up mostly of nominated Colonial Office officials, with the 'elected' element being elected by the 3 per cent of the population which was then entitled to vote, despite an overall literacy rate of 80 per cent in the country. In the 1953 elections, the People's Progressive Party (PPP) won 18 of the 24 elected seats and formed the first Marxist Government to be elected to office, if not power, in the British Empire. However, within 133 days of the election and formation of the Administration, the Colonial Office intervened forcibly, dissolved the Government and suspended the *Constitution*.

The electoral success of the PPP had been based largely on the achievement of a broad unity among the masses of the two dominant ethnic groups: Indians and Africans. But after the suspension of the *Constitution* an active colonial policy of 'divide-and-rule' was pursued and, by 1955, the PPP and the mass movement it embraced were split into two main groupings. One of these was led by Cheddi Jagan, leader of the original PPP, and the other by Forbes Burnham, the Chairman. In the internal struggles that followed, the latter failed in his bid to inherit the leadership of the original PPP and instead, in 1957, formed, from his faction, the People's National Congress (PNC). The split was based on both ideological and ethnic differences.

The suspension of the *Constitution* was followed by four years of Colonial Office interim rule. When elections were held under a modified *Constitution* in 1957, Cheddi Jagan's party won; the same thing occurred again in the 1961 elections. This forced the colonial power to resort to a well-documented manoeuvre in collaboration with the PNC, the US Government and the CIA. The manoeuvre required the provocation of internal unrest and a modification of the electoral basis of the *Constitution* (by replacing the 'first-past-the-post' electoral system with one based on proportional representation) in order to install the PNC to office with the new elections held in 1964. In May 1966, formal constitutional power was handed over to the PNC Administration under the leadership of Forbes Burnham.

Space does not permit any lengthy discussion of this period and the interested reader should consult Jagan (1966) and Thomas (1982) for an extended analysis. For our immediate purpose, however, certain features of the Independence settlement need special emphasis because of their later significance.

First, an examination of the circumstances surrounding the Independence settlement arrived at between Burnham and the colonial authorities reveals that this was based on the exclusion of the masses and, in particular the PPP as the then organised expression of the masses, from any real political power.

Secondly, in order to achieve this, the electoral system was undermined as the colonial power, in collusion with the PNC, resorted to the most cynical manipulation of the *Constitution*. This is an important point, since as Thomas (1982) has stressed, in the political history of Guyana, constitutional struggles, while important in themselves, have usually reflected deeper social considerations connected with the state of the class struggle and the question of which class wielded political power in the country. When to this is added previous recourse to arbitrary interventions against the *Constitution* as occurred in Guyana in 1928, 1953 and in 1978, it is clear that, despite the tradition of Westminister-style parliamentarianism in the English-speaking Caribbean, neither rulers nor ruled in Guyana have functioned in terms of an enduring legal framework within which the exercise of state power occurs.

Thirdly, the events of 1953 and after, particularly as they unfolded in the context of the Cold War hysteria of this period, brought Guyana, although a British colony, more and more within the orbit of American strategic interests. Inkeeping with the hegemonic and hemispheric role of American imperialism at the time, the American Government asserted its influence on Guyana's politics not only through the British Government, but directly through crude interventions in the country's domestic affairs. This incorporation of Guyana into the orbit of American interests was no doubt influenced by the consideration that the PPP, the majority Party of this period, under the leadership of Cheddi Jagan, was clearly supportive of the official pro-Moscow grouping of communist and workers' parties.

Perhaps, above all else, the Independence settlement demonstrated that there was no 'smashing of the colonial state' in Guyana. The absence of a revolutionary break with the colonial state structure, however, should not be allowed to mask the fact that the post-colonial state, almost as it were on the morrow of Independence, began a significant dimensional growth in three areas, namely, bureaucratisation, militarisation and ideologisation. This development was a functional imperative of two considerations. One was that Guyana became a new state in a capitalist world system made up of nation states. The other was that the state of internal class struggle in Guyana required that state power should play a vital role in the consolidation of a hegemonic class in the country.

The underdevelopment of the two dominant classes of our historical age (working-class and bourgeoisie) in Guyana, combined with the country's highly complex and variegated class structure, in which ethnic factors play critical roles, resulted in a certain fluidity of political power and in the particular instrumentalist role that the state is playing in class formation. In the development of capitalism in Europe and America the consolidation of economic power by the bourgeoisie preceded their acquisition of state and political power. In Guyana, as elsewhere in the capitalist periphery, the reverse is generally occurring: that is, political/ state power is being used as an instrument for the consolidation of a developing ruling class.

In 1970, four years after Independence, the ruling Party declared Guyana a Co-operative Socialist Republic. A number of factors prompted this particular development. To begin with, the broad mass of the population had a very militant anti-colonial tradition. This militancy is reflected in the early maturing of relatively highly developed trade union structures in the country. The harsh conditions of plantation labour and enclave mining and the influence of anti-colonial ideas on these were no doubt mainly responsible for the high level of class consciousness among the main sections of the work force in the sugar and bauxite industries, although ethnic differences (the sugar workers are mainly of Indian descent and the bauxite workers mainly of African descent) hindered the growth of cross-industry class solidarity.

Secondly, the tradition of militant anti-colonialism and trade unionism was both product and producer of a situation in which large sections of the work force were influenced by Marxist ideas and functioned within organisations that claimed a Marxist-Leninist leadership. This is seen in the history and development of both the PPP itself and of its associated trade union - the Guyana Agricultural and General Workers' Union (GAWU) - the largest trade union in the country and one which has organised labour on the sugar plantations since the 1940s. The combination of these factors meant that all effective opposition to the PNC state occupied the 'left' of the political spectrum, a development strengthened by the fact that the local 'businessman's party', the small United Force, which had entered a coalition with the PNC in order to remove the PPP from office in 1964, had been all but absorbed into the PNC structure.

Thirdly, the PNC's need to use the state to transform itself into a national bourgeois class meant that it had to adopt a popular socialist rhetoric if this process was to be made acceptable to the masses. It is this situation which forced the state to seek to establish its legitimacy in populist-socialist ideology, hence the Co-operative Socialist Republic.

In concrete terms, the declaration of this republic was promulgated as embracing four fundamental features of the new state. The first of these was the expansion of state property over the 'commanding heights' of the economy through a programme of nationalisation. Historically, the economy of Guyana has been narrowly based on the production and sale in the world market of three primary products: sugar, rice and bauxite-alumina. Sugar and bauxite-alumina together accounted for approximately 90 per cent of export earnings and 33 per cent of GDP and continue to be as they have been during this century, the largest employers of wage labour. But these industries were owned and controlled by foreign capital. About 90 per cent of the sugar plantation assets were owned by Booker Bros. McConnell & Co. Ltd., a world-wide Transnational Corporation (TNC) based in the UK. At the time of nationalisation, the remaining 10 per cent of the plantation's assets were under the control of Jessel's Securities, a speculative financial corporation also based in the UK. Only 10 per cent of the sugar cane plant was cultivated in the peasant economy, while the two TNCs owned all the processing facilities. Bauxite-alumina production was also organised through two TNCs (Alcan of Canada, by far the larger producer, and Reynolds of the USA). Both were operated as enclave mining activities located in interior settlements.

Rice was cultivated as a peasant crop and this industry grew up under the patronage of the colonial state and the estates, both of which saw it as a complement to sugar production, since it produced a basic staple, found outlets for labour in the off-seasons of the sugar crop, and did not compete significantly with sugar for agricultural land. Despite Guyana's large land area (83,000 square miles) relative to population (currently about 800,000 persons), agricultural land is in scarce supply, as a complex system of drainage and irrigation is required before the coastal strip, on which over 90 per cent of the population is settled, can be successfully cultivated.

TNC control of the Guyana economy was not confined to these two major industries. Other activities, for example, retail distribution outlets, drug manufacture, alcohol production, shipping, cable and wireless communications, foundries and small-scale ship yards, were all under strong TNC direction. After the completion of the nationalisation of sugar in 1976, the Government boasted that it now 'owned and controlled 80 per cent of the economy of Guyana'. The pattern of nationalisation was aptly described by Kwayana (1976) as that of the 'mortgage-finance type'.

This meant firstly, that a commercial 'repurchase' of Guyanese assets was negotiated. There is not a single instance of any TNC being dissatisfied with the terms of compensation of these nationalisations. On the contrary, as Thomas (1978) has pointed out, there is strong evidence that, in the cases of nationalisation of the two sugar TNCs, it was the companies that first approached the Government offering their assets for sale. In both instances, this was prompted by the severe financial pressures these companies were facing in the UK.

Secondly, the effect of such a commercial repurchase was to turn national assets into a national foreign debt, denominated in external currency; this meant that a heavy premium was placed on all future foreign exchange earnings.

Thirdly, the stipulation in these agreements that compensation payments would be made out of the 'profits' of the nationalised entities has always been a dead letter. The reason for this is that these companies continued to rely on the world market for capital financing and the implementation of any such policy would certainly have led to a drying up of these sources of finance. Thus, it has been observed that despite heavy losses in some of the nationalised entities, the Government did not enforce the stipulation and ran the risk of becoming a 'defaulter' on these debts.

Fourthly, the nationalisation agreements included the usual array of new contractual obligations into which the state was expected to enter. These covered marketing the product overseas, the purchase of equipment and supplies required to operate the industry, management operations in the enterprises, and licences, fees and other royalties and patent payments for the utilization of technology in the industries.

The second principal feature of co-operative socialism was its incorporation of a declaration by the Government that, henceforth, the strategy of national development would be embraced in a programme of feeding, clothing and housing the nation. This, it was claimed, substituted the 'private profit' motive with the social goal of making 'the small man a real man'. This programme was embodied in the 1972-76 development programme and from the outset was heavily propagandistic. Thus it was that the 1972-76 development programme, which was supposed to have incorporated this basic principle of economic planning, first appeared as a public document in draft form in July 1973, and has never been revised and presented as a document for public scrutiny. Moreover, as we shall see later, the actual course of production bore little relationship to the objective of 'feeding, clothing and housing the nation by 1976', which the draft proclaimed.

The third feature of co-operative socialism was that, given a tri-sectoral national economic structure (private, state and co-operative), the co-operative sector should be the dominant sector. It was through co-operative ownership and control that the socialist foundations of the society were to be laid.

Historically, the co-operative sector in Guyana has been, and remains, a very minuscule part of the national economy. But even among institutions designated as co-operative and founded by the state, e.g., the Guyana National Co-operative Bank, these do not function or operate on co-operative principles. They are usually state-run and operate on ordinary commercial principles, whatever the formal co-operative ownership structure may appear to be.

Many of the economically significant co-operatives formed through private initiative also operate on capitalist principles. Thus, many co-operatives employ wage labour as membership does not mean automatic enfranchisement and the owners of the co-operatives then proceed to accumulate on the bases of exploited wage labour. Because of tax concessions afforded to co-operatives, many enterprises find the co-operative a convenient form for private accumulation. In addition, many co-operatives organised with specific and limited objectives in mind; e.g., a land co-operative may be formed in order to acquire a piece of land, but after the land is acquired it is then sub-divided and exploited on an individual basis.

The fourth feature of co-operative socialism was its claim that, as part of 'socialist doctrine', the ruling Party (the PNC) was 'paramount' over all other parties and over the state itself. As the Administration did not come to power either on the basis of free and fair elections or as the result of a popular social revolution, this was in effect a thinly disguised proclamation of a 'dictatorship'. The policy of paramountcy was enshrined in the creation, in 1973/74, of the Office of the General Secretary of the PNC and Ministry of National Development (OGS PNC & MND). As the name suggests, the PNC Party office was merged into a department of the state and financed through public funds.[1] The state thereafter rapidly proceeded to make it clear that there could be no legal or constitutional change of government. The rigged elections in 1973, the postponement of elections due in 1978 and the rigged elections of 1980, are an indication of how earnestly the process of fascistisation of the state developed. A truly authoritarian state (Thomas, 1982) was entrenched in Guyana.

However, before examining in the next section how this degeneration of the polity occurred, it is essential to make an important observation on these developments outlined here. The features of co-operative socialism outlined above were combined with certain publicly, self-advertised, 'radical' foreign policy initiatives by the state: the recognition of Cuba; support for the *Movimento Popular de Libertaçao de Angola* (MPLA) in Angola; militant anti-apartheid rhetoric; support for the 'Arab cause'; support for a New International Economic Order; visits to, and contacts with, Eastern Europe and China, and so on. When examined closely, however, many of these pronouncements can be seen to have been merely propagandistic. Thus, support for the MPLA came only during the final stages of the war, the Guyana Government having all along given its support to the CIA-backed group: *União Nacional para a Independencia Total de Angola* (UNITA). Recognition of Cuba was also undertaken as part of a broad-based Caribbean initiative embracing regimes of differing outlooks united on the basis of the need to assert an independent and separate identity for the region.

However, despite such evidence of the real worth of Government propagandizing in the area of foreign policy, the acts of nationalisation plus socialist and other progressive rhetoric produced a number of theorists who argued about the 'radicalisation' of the regime (Mars 1978; Mandle 1976, 1978). These were joined by the PPP; the same Party which, after the 1973 elections, had launched a programme of 'passive resistance and civil disobedience', began in 1975 to proclaim a policy of 'critical support' for the PNC Administration because of the 'radical turn' the regime was taking.

The new position held by the PPP reflected its formal adoption of the line of argument contained in the *Havana Declaration* of 1975 which, as Thomas (1977) has pointed out, was the acceptance by communist and workers' parties of the hemisphere of the application of the 'non-capitalist thesis' of revolutionary democracy to the region. A critique of this line of argument has been developed elsewhere, but it is important to note two major points at this stage. One is that the alleged radicalisation of the state in Guyana was accompanied by anti-democratic measures, some of which were indicated above: for example, rigged elections designed to deny the will of the electorate. At the broader democratic level, these developments included the suppression of human rights, trade-union rights, the rule of law, and the traditional 'independence' of the judiciary, in the society. It was clear, therefore, that theorists of the radicalisation of the state did not see radicalisation as being premised on the increased access of the working-class and peasantry to the development of their own forms of democratic organisation through which their power could be exercised. On the contrary, radicalisation was interpreted here as consistent with the reduction of the limited access of the masses of the working people to these rights and in this view therefore, radicalisation and democratic development were in real opposition.

Secondly, the line of argument ignored the internal class struggle and the role the state must necessarily play in the consolidation of a hegemonic class in the capitalist periphery. In the periphery, the state is not only an object of class conquest, thereby constellating in its structure a dominant class, but in the complex circumstances of an underdeveloped bourgeoisie and working-class it is the principal instrument for the long-run consolidation of one or other class as the dominant class. In this sense, therefore, radicalisation can be measured only in terms of the possibilities opened up for working-class advance in the new state structures and a broadening of the democratic base of the society. This is a necessary, if not sufficient, condition for the consolidation of the position of the emergent working-class.

As events have shown, nationalisation in Guyana has aided the expansion of the state in all three of the dimensions mentioned earlier (bureaucracy, ideology ad military). In so doing, it increased the capacity of the ruling PNC to assert its forms of authoritarian control over 'civil society'. This process, however, required other accompanying developments.

Production and reproduction in the capitalist world economy have always been accompanied by 'crises' and/or 'interruptions' in the process of accumulation. Since the mid-1970s, there has been such a continuing 'crisis/interruption' in the capitalist world economy. In the non-petroleum-producing countries on the capitalist periphery, this has been reflected in low or negative rates of growth of real output per head, increasing unemployment, inflation and acute foreign exchange and balance of payments crises. These, in turn, have exacerbated the widespread conditions of poverty which are perennial in these societies.

Guyana is no exception to this general process but two characteristics of the society have exacerbated the process. One was the lack of 'legitimacy' of the PNC regime, given the basis on which it came to and held power. The other was that in the process of its consolidation, the regime greatly expanded the state productive sector through nationalisations, with the state, as we noted, controlling over 80 per cent of the economy. Having acquired power in the way that it did, the Burnham Administration consistently used the state to promote a base in the system of production for the class that it represented. In pursuance of this goal, it contributed much to the destruction of the productive capability of the traditionally dominant industries which underlined the economic crisis which faced Guyana.

In Guyana, a production crisis of unprecedented dimensions has been raging since mid 1975. A decade and a half after Independence there had been no noticeable diversification of the economy, as the country remained as dependent as ever on the three traditional primary commodities — rice, bauxite-alumina and sugar. In the agricultural sector, domestic food production and the livestock industry averaged only about 7 per cent of gross domestic product. At the same time, manufacturing (other than the processing of rice and sugar) accounted for only 8 per cent of gross domestic product.

Despite the absence of any significant diversification of the economy, physical output in the sugar and bauxite-alumina industries declined seriously, producing at levels substantially below the capacity developed in them over the previous past 15 years. Thus, over the period 1980-81, sugar production averaged about 285,000 tons, while the annual rated output capacity of the industry was 450,000 tons. Indeed, as far back as 1971, the industry already produced 369,000 tons. Dried bauxite production in 1980 was 1.6 million tons compared with 2.3 million tons in 1970. Calcined bauxite produced in 1980 was 602,000 tons compared with 992,000 in 1970. Alumina production in 1980 was 211,000 tons as compared with 312,000 tons in 1970. Rice production in 1980 was 160,000 tons as compared with an annual output capacity of 200,000 tons. These output levels were about 20 per cent below the targets set by the Government over the period, even though, as can be inferred from the figures given here, targets were substantially below the rated capacity levels of the industries.

The collapse of the traditional producing sectors, with little or no diversification of output taking place, was accompanied by a deterioration of the services of the various public utilities, a decline in the quality of social services available, and a considerable flight of persons from the country. All the major public services - electricity, pure water supply, public transport, postal services, telephones, and sanitation - had deteriorated so much as to constitute major bottlenecks in the production process. Thus, electricity 'outages' occurred for several hours daily in the main production and residential areas. Public transport was so poor that workers' representatives claimed that as many as four hours per day on average had to be spent on commuting to and from work.

All the major social services — education, health, social welfare and housing — also deteriorated drastically. For example, in the state health services, foreign medical personnel (mainly from Cuba, India and the Phillipines) accounted for 75 per cent of the doctors. Less than 10 per cent of health personnel were engaged in preventive medicine. In housing, the targeted production for the development plan period 1972-76 was 65,000 housing units; of these 6,000 were built. Since then, because of the collapse of the main producing sectors and declining employment and incomes, housing construction was at a near standstill.

Finally, out of a natural population increase of about 180,000 persons during the inter-censal period 1970-80, approximately one-half, or 90,000, migrated from Guyana, principally to neighbouring countries in the Caribbean, especially Suriname, Europe and North America.

The result of the above was a serious decline in real per capita income. Official estimates placed this at 15 per cent between 1976 and 1980, but these estimates have been seriously challenged as being too low because of the price deflators used. Unemployment had also been increasing and was officially estimated at over 40 per cent of the labour force. Between 1976 and 1981, annual rates of inflation had been well into the double digit rate. Official estimates indicated a 70 per cent rise in consumer prices between 1976 and 1980, but this also has been challenged as a serious underestimate. Declining output of the main export commodities together with the inflationary rise in import prices created a serious balance of payments problem, with additional pressures being placed on the external account by the burden of foreign debt created through the nationalisations discussed above.

The Government's initial response to the crisis was to assume it was short-lived, that is, another 'normal' downswing in the post-World War II business cycle. An effort was made to buy time through printing money and borrowing. Between 1973 and 1975, the money supply doubled and, between 1975 and 1977, it grew by a further 38 per cent. But, by then, the problems were clearly not of the usual type. Yet, between the beginning of 1977 and the end of 1979 the money supply grew by 41 per cent and in 1980-81 it rose again by about 30 per cent. The public debt, which stood at G$267 million in 1970 had risen to G$673 million in 1974 and to $1.3 billion in 1976; at the end of 1981, it was over G$3.1 billion, of which G$1.9 billion was internal, and G$1.2 billion external, debt. It was no surprise that this easy money policy was associated with (although it was not necessarily the principal cause of) a progressive decline in external reserves. At the end of 1975, net international reserves were approximately G$200 million but, by the end of 1977, the figure was minus G$100 million and, at the end of 1980, minus G$396 million.

The easy money policy of the initial years only added fuel to the economic crisis which was worsening on the external front on account of a number of structural features, for example the world-wide inflation, the 'oil crisis', and the depression in the main capitalist centres. In the face of these developments, the Government turned to the IMF for balance of payments support in 1978. The result was that in August of that year a one-year IMF standby facility of 15 million special drawing rights (SDR) was negotiated but, as the expected balance of payments turnaround did not materialise, in August 1979 resort was made to a further three-year extended fund facility. However, the Government was unable to meet some of the economic and financial targets set under this arrangement, and the facility was interrupted. As production continued to fall and the turnaround in the balance of payments still did not materialise, a new three-year extended fund facility was agreed upon in July 1980. This involved a loan of 100 million SDRs as well as a World Bank structural adjustment loan of US$23.5 million. The former was subsequently increased to 150 million SDRs, or 400 per cent of the Guyana quota of 37.5 million SDRs with the IMF.

The treatment accorded to the PNC regime by these institutions contrasted strongly with the highly publicised destablising attitudes which they displayed in their dealings with the People's National Party Prime Minister Michael Manley regime in Jamaica in the same period. Two factors would seem to account for this difference in attitude. One was that, despite the socialist rhetoric, the Burnham regime, which was installed in the Anglo-US-CIA pre-Independence manoeuvre, continued to serve the fundamental interests of American capital better than Manley's 'democratic socialism'. We have noted earlier that in Guyana, opposition to the State comes from the left; in Jamaica by contrast, the main opposition to the Manley regime was the conservative Jamaica Labour Party led by Edward Seaga, the subsequent prime minister.

The second factor was that the main lines of Government policy genuinely conformed to the IMF recipes for this situation. The economic crisis was seen as first and foremost a crisis of sustained external disequilibrium and the key to the solution, in conditions where the obvious mismanagement of the state sector meant that export supply increases could not be produced in the short run, was seen as a lowering in the workers' living standards in order to reduce the levels of real consumption; given the high marginal propensity to import, this was expected to achieve a drop in foreign exchange expenditure.
Even before the highly publicised resort to the IMF in 1978, i.e.,

from the first signs of a prolongation of the drain in foreign resources, the Government had instituted massive deflationary policies. Thus, the 1977 Government budget cut public expenditure by 30 per cent. In addition, subsidies on a wide range of consumer items, many of which were introduced during the colonial period to ease the pressures on the poorest sections of the work force, were removed. Indirect taxes were also increased and the state sector proceeded to charge commercial prices for items it produced or handled; this meant, in effect, that they used their monopoly position to generate revenues so that cash surpluses could be achieved.

Large-scale retrenchment of the work force in the state sector was instituted. Later in 1979, this policy was to be extended into a wage freeze that denied to state employees any increase in wages, including normal increments. In 1980 and 1981, wage increases of 5 per cent and 7-12 per cent respectively were allowed, but these were substantially below the inflation rate indicated earlier. Finally, expenditure on the social services was also drastically cut. However, despite these deflationary measures and extensive resort to foreign exchange rationing (first introduced by the Government in 1976), the balance of payments showed no signs of reversal. The result was that in 1981 even more massive deflationary measures were introduced and the currency devalued by 18 per cent against the US dollar.

It was clear that whatever might have been its original objectives, the policy of deflation had intensified the production crisis outlined above, and continued to do so. To give a few examples, as the availability of public transport deteriorated and electricity supplies became grossly irregular and unreliable because of reduced spending and mismanagement of the public utilities, these hampered production and hindered worker productivity. Workers spent so much time queuing for food or transport, or without electricity and pure water, as to be unable to sustain the required levels of effort at work. The policy of state borrowing to finance expenditures created a serious fiscal constraint. Thus it was found that, in 1980, debt charges payments by the state accounted for 37 per cent of current expenditure as compared with 31 per cent for current spending on the social services and 32 per cent on personal emoluments for employees in the Government.

The production crisis and the mismanagement of this in terms of both its internal and international dimensions had been self-reinforcing. This self-reinforcement, which brought the economy to its then current stage of collapse, was also responsible for the emergence of a built-in repressive escalator in the state in Guyana which reflected the dialectical relation between oppression as a ruling-class solution to the crisis, and a crisis which was increasingly taking the form of popular resistance to the imposition of power as it was constellated in the state. This had been brought to issue because of both popular demands for change and the ruling regime's option to rule out all legal or constitutional means of changing the Government. In this section we shall briefly outline the working of this thesis as the main point to emerge from the study of the post-colonial state and politics in Guyana.

The first stage of repression developed in response to the situation in which the Government sought to enforce a reduction in the real wage in order to overcome the production crisis and its manifestations of declining output, sales and surpluses in the state sector, domestic inflation and foreign exchange and balance of payments crises. Nationalisations having resulted in the state being the major employer of labour, in order to fulfil its class function the state intervened to alter the historically determined system of industrial relations. This meant among other things: reducing the power of the trade unions; raising to the level of national policy the elimination of all wage payments which had as their aim the restoration of the purchasing power of the worker if the general price level increased; linking all wage increases exclusively to increases in productivity as defined by the state; and taking advantage of the state's position as common employer over a wide range of activities to insist on wage agreements across the board for all unions. This latter had also meant negotiating wages with the central trade union organisation and rejecting the historical role of individual unions in the wage determination process.

Justification for these measures had been couched in ideological terms, for example, 'the need to replace the colonial system of wage determination by a socialist one'; strikes in the state sector at a time of economic crisis were 'treasonable and political', and so on. Here, the propagandist aim had been to legitimise the use of the severest force in implementing the state policy of maximising, at all costs, the rate of surpluses in the state sector. This policy, as we have noted, had been since 1978 pursued in alliance with the IMF, to which the Government had turned for balance of payments support. The principal focus of repression in this stage was the containment of workers' rights inherited under the existing system of industrial relations. In pursuit of this the state employed three broad strategies. The first was to undermine the right to work. As the Guyana Human Rights Association (GHRA) in its 1980-81 report (1981: 39) has pointed out:

> the extensive control over employment exercised by the Government as a result of 80% of the economy falling within the state sector is being increasingly used as a form of political coercion. A large number of persons have been dismissed, or transferred for reasons which constitute a violation of the right to work. This trend goes back to 1978. Dismissals are not restricted to the State sector, they have occurred in the private sector also under direct pressure from Government officials.

The report then proceeded to list, under Article 23 of the *Universal Declaration of Human Rights* and Articles 6, 7 and 8 of the *Covenant on Social Economic and Cultural Rights*, evidence in support of this allegation for the period 1978-81.

The second strategy employed had been to undermine the right to strike by invocation of the doctrine of the 'political strike'. This doctrine claimed that any strike which the Government did not 'approve' as being industrial, is in effect, 'political'; in these circumstances, 'no holds are barred'. By this was meant that unapproved strikes were treated as subversive activity, that is, as attempts to undermine the state, and that the state was consequently justified in using its full repressive weight to break them. This doctrine was first invoked in 1977 during a strike in the sugar industry, in the course of which military and paramilitary personnel were brought in to cut the sugar cane, striking workers were physically attacked, and a general campaign of terror introduced into the sugar belt. The doctrine was again invoked in 1978 and 1979 to crush industrial actions by the workers.

The third strategy of the state had been to manipulate the composition of the executives of as many trade unions as it could, in order to determine the final composition of the national Trades Union Council (TUC). This had been made possible by resort to rigged union elections and by using the state's 'muscle' as the major employer in the country to determine which union was recognised as bargaining agent. This line of attack revealed that, in a country such as Guyana where there is a noticeable absence of an enforceable right to work, the weapon which the state controlled as the principal employer in the country could not be underestimated.

The second stage of this process of increased repression developed as repression of the work force inexorably spread to the repression of legality and human rights for all citizens. This progression followed because it was impossible to separate the rights of trade unions and trade unionists from the larger exercise of rights of citizens within a framework of justice. Worker repression therefore required the setting in place of mechanisms to ensure more generalised repression. This attack on human rights was in the first instance focused on the courts, where efforts were made to 'bend' the judiciary to support the executive arm of the state. Thus the GHRA report of 1980-81 observed:

> The courts have been used as an instrument of political harassment on a widespread scale. This has been made possible by the subordination of the Judiciary to the political executive in a number of ways. (GHRA 1981: 21).

It then proceeded to list the following: interference in the appointment of judges; political instructions on specific issues; political interference in specific cases; the *Administration of Justice Bill* (explained below); the *Criminal Law Bill* (explained below); blank warrants signed by magistrates; and trials with a political dimension. Specifically, the GHRA report indicated that the *Administration of Justice Bill* was denounced as 'obnoxious' by the Guyana Bar Association because, among other features, 'it removed in the majority of cases, the right of the accused to elect to be, and to be tried by, a judge and jury', and permitted the Court of Appeal to enter 'a guilty verdict even where the accused has been acquitted by jury'. The grave implications of this latter point were fully appreciated when account was taken of the interference of the appointment of judges noted above. The introduction of the *Criminal Law Bill* was met by a boycott of the courts staged by the Guyana Bar Association. The Organisation of Commonwealth Bar Associations also condemned the *Bill* because of 'its infringement of the citizens' right to trial by jury', and its deliberate aim of having 'retrospective effect on pending criminal proceedings to annul decisions of Courts of Justice and to abrogate the civil liberties of the citizens of Guyana'.

As the mechanisms for more generalised repression were set in train, an important transformation in the nature of resistance became manifest. The continuous attack on industrial rights and the merging of industrial rights issues into human rights issues were accompanied by the submerging of ethnic differences among the work force and an increasing class solidarity that cut across traditional racial boundaries. Thus, the 1977, 1978 and 1979 strikes saw the bauxite and sugar workers acting in greater unison than they had ever done since 1953.

In the third stage, the attacks on due process, legality and human rights generally became increasingly politicised and this led to a qualitative intensification of the process of fascistisation of the state. Opposition political formations organised in defence of democracy and, as claims to a popular base of the state disappeared in the face of growing repression, the regime extended its repression to opposition political groups in order to survive. To sanction this process under some form of legality, the state was 'legally' restructured, as the existing *Constitution* was found to be 'unworkable' for the newer forms of dictatorship.

In this stage, political assassination, direct repression of all popular manifestations, and a rapid growth of the security apparatuses of the state took place. These developments were propagandised with the familiar claims of 'law and order', 'the necessities of development of a poor country', and 'we cannot afford the luxuries of democracy'. The fascistisation of the state was now very much on the way and from here on, the Government, through state-manipulation, propaganda and force, made it unmistakably clear that it could not be changed by legal or constitutional means. Evidence in support of the workings of the repressive escalator as it led up to the constitutional restructuring of the state can be gleaned from the following:

- The rigging of national elections held in 1973.
- Local Government elections constitutionally due every two years since 1970 were never held.
- When national elections constitutionally fell due in 1978, they were postponed and, in their stead, a national referendum was held. Under the previous *Constitution*, only a referendum could change entrenched provisions, for example, the life of Parliament. The purpose of the referendum was to remove the referendum safeguard so that these entrenched provisions could be changed by a two-thirds majority in Parliament which the PNC had already rigged the 1973 election in order to acquire. A Committee of Concerned Citizens (1978) who surveyed the 1978 referendum claimed that the.maximum possible turnout of voters was 14.01 per cent, yet the Government claimed a turnout of 71.45 per cent of the voters, with itself winning 97.7 per cent of the votes cast!

- National elections were held under a new *Constitution* in 1980. A team of international observers sponsored by the Guyana Human Rights Association who came to Guyana during the election period to observe these denounced the elections as the 'most blatant fraud'. They went on to point out in their report (International Team of Observers 1980: 28) that:

  > We came to Guyana aware of the serious doubts expressed about the conduct of previous elections there, but determined to judge these elections on their own merit and hoping that we should be able to say that the result was fair. We deeply regret that, on the contrary, we were obliged to conclude, on the basis of abundant and clear evidence, that the election was rigged massively and flagrantly. Fortunately, however, the scale of the fraud made it impossible to conceal either from the Guyanese public or the outside world.

Because the new *Constitution* which came into operation in 1980 marked the formal stage of the restructuring of the state as the process of facistisation proceeded, the nature of this restructuring, as it was revealed in the provisions of the *Constitution*, requires brief mention. Under the 1980 *Constitution*, by 'law', Forbes Burnham became Executive President before elections were held, but nevertheless 'as if he had been elected thereto'. The dictatorial purposes of the *Constitution* were revealed in the array of powers that the Executive President commanded. Thus:

- Article 182 (1) says that the President 'shall not be personally answerable to any court for the performance of the functions of his office or for any act done in the performance of those functions, and no proceedings, whether criminal or civil, shall be instituted against him in his personal capacity in respect thereof either during his term of office or thereafter'.

- In the *Constitution*, the President was head of state, supreme executive authority and commander-in-chief. In addition he was supreme over the National Assembly, the local democratic organs, the National Congress of Local Democratic Organs and the Supreme Congress of the People, all created by the new *Constitution*. This supremacy was embodied in his powers 'to summon, suspend or dissolve all' these so-called 'democratic' and 'supreme' organs. He also had a veto over the elected National Assembly.

- The President's powers also required him to appoint the chairpersons of the Elections Commission, the Public Service Commission, the Police Service Commission, the Judicial Service Commission and the Teaching Service Commission. In addition, he had the power to appoint either a majority of the members or the whole of each commission. Furthermore, the President appointed the army Chief of Staff and all army commanders, the Director-General of the National Service and his deputies, the Attorney-General, the Chancellor of the Judiciary, the Chief Justice, the Director of Public Prosecutions and literally every other important official of the state. In those circumstances, the practice noted by the GHRA in its report (GHRA 1981: 7) for: 'Burnham... to adopt the dress of the Chief-of-Staff of the Army (he was the only general), the Commissioner of Police, and so on' took on a significance greater than that of a national joke.

The absolute powers conferred on Executive President Burnham under the *Constitution* mirrored the absolute powers conferred on him as 'leader' of the PNC. In that Party's *Constitution* it is stated that:

> ...the reserve powers of the Leader are (a) If the Leader in his deliberate judgement is of the opinion that a situation of emergency has arisen in the Party, he shall have power, notwithstanding any provision in these Rules, on giving written notice to the General Secretary of his opinion, to take all action that he may in his absolute discretion consider necessary to correct such a situation; and for this purpose, he may assume and exercise any or all of the powers of the Biennial Delegates' Congress, the General Council, the Central Executive Committee, any other Committee, Group, Arm, Organ or of any officer or official of the Party. (b) If General Council, the Central Executive Committee or the Administrative Committee has not been constituted or for any reason cannot function, the Leader may exercise all or any of its powers or may authorise such members as he may deem fit to exercise its powers for the time being.

The stages of repression highlighted here should not be interpreted mechanistically. They were the products of the dialectical interaction of the main forces of repression (the state) and liberation (the workers, independent trade unions, opposition parties, democratic social groups, and so on). Because of the dialectical nature of this process, other issues have to be borne in mind when studying the state and politics during this period.

In Guyana the use of state violence, political murder and open terroristic rule which characterised the third stage of the fascistisation of the state was associated with the increasing militarisation of the society. A number of new military and paramilitary agencies, all pledged to defend the ruling Party, had been created: the National Service, the People's Militia, the National Guard Service and an armed youth arm of the ruling Party, the Young Socialist Movement. Danns (1978) estimated that by 1977 Guyana had a ratio of 1:35 of the population in one or other military or para-military organisation. This total did not include what the GHRA in its 1980-81 report termed the 'private strong arm groups... the most notorious [being] a sect known as the House of Israel, whose members are freely used by the ruling Party to break up opposition meetings' (GHRA 1981: 7).

Over this period, the growth in the numbers of security personnel had also been associated with an orientation of the state towards 'security' matters, which was another way of saying towards the harassment and containment of the regime's political opposition. This constituted an 'economically non-productive' utilisation of the social surplus while it increased the orientation of the state to its self-preservation above all else, with the usual consequences for public sector efficiency and productivity.

Finally, it should be noted that the process of militarisation had been accompanied with the progressive politicisation of the security services. This began with efforts to make the security forces act and think partisanly, in favour of the ruling Party. It is for this reason that such rituals as the daily raising of the national flag were combined with the daily raising of the PNC flag in places such as National Service camps, and the attendance of security personnel (in mufti) at Party rallies was enforced. The deprofessionalisation of the security services which this entails, however, does not stop here. It led one stage further into the constitution of a definite PNC 'political element' within the security services. This was somewhat akin to the development of the 'political police' within developed fascist states, and constituted in Guyana an important stage in the transformation of state and political relations.

Historically, ruling classes have preferred the threat of the sanction of the force which they monopolise, rather than its routine use, as the basis of their rule. In other words, government with the consent of the governed is always sought after in class societies. That is why the development of open terroristic forms of rule always signifies a particular stage of degeneracy in the political culture. In this regard, Guyana offers no exception. The increased resort to terroristic rule by the regime is the dialectical opposition of increased popular resistance to the form of state domination. But because such methods were not compatible with the long-run survival of the regime, it sought to combine its increasing militarisation with increased control of the ideological and propaganda arms of the state. The hope was always that the more successful the propaganda, the less the need to resort to physical repression which, by its nature, is more obvious than other forms of repression and thus increases the chances of armed uprising by the oppressed classes and groups.

In Guyana, the PNC used all the ideological apparatuses of the state to project its legitimacy and paramountcy. The chief ideological line had been to identify the 'leader', Burnham, as embodying the PNC, the PNC as embodying the state, and the state as being identical with the country as a whole, or with society at large. All anti-PNC or anti-Burnham activity was therefore projected as being anti-state or anti-national and hence subversive. This ideological stance also was associated with calls for unity of all peoples and classes (though not of all parties) in the country in the face of the economic difficulties which were 'thrust' on the country by developments in the world economy. For obvious reasons, no local mismanagement of the economy was ever admitted as a major or contributory factor. This national consensus rhetoric was also linked with calls to produce more and to defend the country against territorial claims made by Venezuela. The means to put this propaganda into effect was the nationalisation of the private media allied with administrative or other obstacles to the publishing by independent or opposition groups and their exclusion from the use of state organs to propagandise their ideas. Thus, in Guyana, the so-called national radio stations and national press functioned as PNC organs in the most insulting of senses. The language used, and the style of reporting, perhaps, gave the quickest insights into the degeneracy of the political culture that accompanied the dictatorship. Meanwhile, the opposition was refused newsprint as in the case of the Party organ of the PPP, the *Mirror*, and a democratic church newspaper, the *Catholic Standard*, was denied the use of the state facilities to print; the organ of the Working People's Alliance, *Dayclean*, had to be published illegally, with two of its leading members going to prison for this reason; and the printing machinery and equipment of trade unions and other opposition groupings were frequently seized by the police.

Control of the media facilitated cover-ups of the evidence of terroristic methods of rule. Even the Parliament could not be heard or read through these media, thereby removing the last vestige of Parliament's usefulness to the opposition. Thus, it was possible to clamp the news lid on the 'crime of the century', the Jonestown murders, the murder of Vincent Teekah (a Minister of Education) and the assassinations of Walter Rodney, Ohene Koama, Edward Dublin and Fr. Bernard Darke. As the GHRA in its 1980-81 report has pointed out (GHRA 1981: 28):

> Strict political control is exerted over the content of the *Chronicle* and the state-owned radio. This is done by directive and personal intervention rather than by a formal censorship arrangement. The extent to which news is kept from the Guyanese people can be judged by the fact that an event as important as Jonestown was learnt by the Guyanese people from the BBC over 24 hours after it had happened. An instance of gross distortion is the manner in which the death of Walter Rodney was reported. For almost 12 hours the national radio carried a story to the effect that a man had been killed when a bomb which he was carrying exploded, but that the man was unrecognisable because his face had been blown off. In fact, Rodney's face was not in the slightest way disfigured and he was immediately recognisable. Distortions of events reached such proportions that in February 1980 a directive was circulated to all members of the *Chronicle* staff to the effect that 'contrived' photographs must no longer be used, and that the newspaper 'must never be seen to be lying on behalf of the Government'.

A further complement to this misuse of the media was the attempt to force the participation of the public in PNC events. State employees were routinely forced to attend PNC Party events at the risk of being fired. When these events were held, state facilities were commandeered and given over to the PNC free of charge to organise them. This development was, of course, common to many dictatorships, particularly in the context of a populist tradition in politics such as we had in Guyana. More threatening, however, was the stage in this phenomenon when the dictator came to believe that the crowds were evidence of real support, and that the unpopularity of the regime was due merely to the propagandising of a few dissidents and opposition elements who should be removed. This stage of self-deception was the most dangerous, as it merged into the use of state violence and political murder. In this process, the regime misjudged its own capacity for action (i.e. repression), and the extent to which this could be 'popularly' accepted. In the process of finding out its miscalculation, however, the historical evidence shows that many, many tragedies had occurred.

As the repressive escalator operated, the divorce of elementary forms of the democratic process from the state machinery rapidly proceeded and deprived the state of all its pretences to be building socialism. The growth of state property was more and more clearly seen as a path of development for those in control of the state. Even in the so-called co-operative sector this was rapidly observed, as consumer and producer co-operatives alike were organised along capitalist lines, with extensive use of wage labour and accumulation by a few proceeding apace.

Meanwhile, in the state sector, capitalist managerial prerogatives prevailed and worker control was absent. In the absence of any alteration of the capital-labour relation, those who controlled the state machinery used their prerogatives to help their stratum/class (mainly through family and friends) to accumulate wealth in enterprises which they privately owned. Given the colonial forms of domination that have historically prevailed, the location of the petty bourgeoisie in the system of economic reproduction in Guyana was initially somewhat tenuous. Consequently, as we have pointed out previously, the state was used as the principal instrument to secure the material basis for the extended social reproduction of this class. As this process developed, however, the class character of the state became more and more obvious, and the state capitalist form which 'co-operative socialism' took degenerated into openly authoritarian forms of rule. This development was generated both by the internal contradictions referred to here and the specific manner of Guyana's insertion into the capitalist world system. Indeed, it was the pattern of this insertion that principally explained the rapid generalisation within Guyana of the structural crisis of world capitalism.

The degeneration of the state capitalist model in the face of the structural crisis of world capitalism and the internal crisis in Guyana into authoritarian forms of state rule, raised one question which will be tackled briefly by way of conclusion, that was, the issue of the relation of political democracy to socialism. This question I have discussed in a number of other places (Thomas 1978, 1982) and the main burden of my position is that socialism cannot be built without a democratisation of all social relations, including the power relations of the state. It follows, therefore, that we must bear the following in mind when assessing co-operative socialism in Guyana:

- All democratic rights within the society have to be seen as the gains of mass struggles and not gifts bestowed by the former colonial masters to be taken away at the behest of their inheritors in the post-colonial situation.

- The task of socialist development, if it is being seriously pursued, has to rest on the progress of these rights in the society and on their progressive endowment with socio-economic content.

- Bread (i.e. development) cannot be traded for justice (i.e. social equality) as was commonly propagandised by the state in Guyana for, in the context of historically determined underdevelopment, there can be no development to socialism that is not based on justice.

- Political democracy and socialism are therefore not counterposed as far as working-class interests are concerned. They are counterposed by the propagandists of the ruling class only in order to bolster its claims to hegemony.

The authoritarian state form that accompanied the growth of state capitalism in Guyana was therefore the direct antithesis of socialism. This view is an old, sometimes forgotten, one, in socialist theory. As it is impossible to improve on Rosa Luxemburg's formulation of it (Looker 1974: 244-245), I shall quote an important, but frequently neglected observation of hers:

> Freedom only for the supporters of the Government, only for the members of Party - however numerous they may be - is no freedom at all. Freedom is always and exclusively freedom for the one who thinks differently. Not because of any fanatical concept of 'justice' but because all that is instructive, wholesome and purifying in political freedom depends on this essential characteristic, and its effectiveness vanishes when 'freedom' becomes a special privilege.

She then goes on to warn (Looker 1974: 246-247):

> The public life of countries with limited freedom is so poverty-stricken, so miserable, so rigid, so unfruitful, precisely because, through the exclusion of democracy, it cuts off the living sources of all spiritual riches and progress. Public control is indispensably necessary. Otherwise the exchange of experiences remains only with the closed circle of the officials of the new regime. Corruption becomes inevitable... with the repression of political life in the land as a whole, life in the soviets must also become more and more crippled. Without general elections, without unrestricted freedom of press and assembly, without a free struggle of opinion, life dies out in every public institution, becomes a mere semblance

> of life, in which only the bureaucracy remains as the active element. Public life gradually falls asleep, a few dozen party leaders of inexhaustible energy and boundless experience direct and rule. Among them, in reality only a dozen outstanding heads do the leading and an élite of the working-class is invited from time to time to meetings where they are to applaud the speeches of the leaders, and to approve proposed resolutions unanimously - at bottom, then, a clique affair - a dictatorship, to be sure, not the dictatorship of the proletariat, however, but only the dictatorship of a handful of politicians.

The relationship highlighted here between the democratisation of the state and political relations and the building of socialism reinforces the earlier observation that was made: that in Guyana the expansion of state property has nothing to do with socialism. State property of itself does not automatically ensure the use and management of those resources by the people, which constitutes a fundamental condition of the socialist path of development. Indeed state property can, as it has happened in Guyana, produce the worst of all possible worlds.

In the first instance, state property has not solved, or even seriously approached, the problems of lack of national control over the economy. Indeed, because of slow rates of growth of output, productivity and surpluses in the state sector, the society's ability to exercise control over the national economy has been further reduced and not enhanced.

The most crippling manifestation of this has been the operational constraints posed by the acute foreign exchange crisis that plagued the country. Because state property has been promoted principally to strengthen the positions of the ruling petty bourgeoisie, it also fostered the growth of corruption, elitism and clientelism in the society. At the same time, in the absence of any real socialist intent on the part of those who control the state machinery, the work force was not promoted into positions of effective control in these enterprises. Indeed, these state enterprises, sensitive to declining rates of profit, sought to reduce the effectiveness of existing worker organisations.

This occurred because of the need to contain wage demands in the face of declining living standards in the country and also because of the broader intent of containing the political power of working-class organisations in the society, thereby serving the real class interests of those who control the state.

Note

1. It was the burning of this building in July 1979 that led to charges of arson against three members of a political grouping known as the Working People's Alliance (WPA). This led to loud popular protest, mass demonstrations, and the transformation of the WPA into a political party in the same month. In 1980, one of the three accused, Walter Rodney, was assassinated by state agents. Later in 1981, the other two accused (Roopnarine and Omawale) were acquitted.

References

Burnham, L.F.S. 'A Vision of the Co-operative Republic', in L. Searwar (ed.), *Cooperative Republic: Guyana*, Georgetown, Guyana, 1970.

Burnham, L.F.S. *Declaration of Sophia: Address by the Prime Minister to the Special Congress, 10th Anniversary of the PNC Government, Georgetown*, 1975.

Committee of Concerned Citizens. *A Report on the Referendum held in Guyana, 16 Jul. 1978, Guyana*, 1978.

Danns, G.K. 'Militarisation and Development: An Experiment in Nation Building', *Transition*,. 1, (1978), 1, 23-44

Guyana Human Rights Association, *Human Rights Report: Jan. 1980-Jun. 1981*, Georgetown, Guyana, 1981.

International Team of Observers at the Elections in Guyana, *Report: Dec. 1980*, London, Parliamentary Human Rights Group, House of Commons 1980. Reprinted by the Guyana Human Rights Association, 1981.

Jagan, C. *The West on Trial. The Fight for Guyana's Freedom*. Berlin, Seven Seas Publication, 1966.

Kwayana, E. 'Pseudo-socialism', Paper presented to seminar, University of the West Indies, Trinidad, 1976.

Looker, R. (ed.), *Rosa Luxemburg: selected political writings*, New York: Grove Press, 1974.

Mandle, J. 'Continuity and Change in Guyanese Underdevelopment', *Monthly Review*, 28, 4, (1976), 37-50.

Mandle, J. 'The Post-Colonial Mode of Production in Guyana', University of Guyana and Temple University, mimeo, 1978.

Mars, P. 'Co-operative Socialism and Marxist Scientific Theory', *Caribbean Issues*, 4, 2, (1976), 71-106.

Thomas, C.Y., *Dependence and Transformation: the Economics of the Transition to Socialism*, New York and London: Monthly Review Press, 1974.

Thomas, C.Y. 'Bread and Justice: The Struggle for Socialism in Guyana', *Monthly Review*, 28, 4, (1976), 23-35.

Thomas C.Y. 'The Non-Capitalist Path as Theory and Practice of Decolonisation and Socialist Transformation', *Latin American Perspectives*, 5, 2, (1976), 10-28.

Thomas, C.Y. *Plantations, Peasants and State: A Study of the Modes of Sugar Production in Guyana*, Los Angeles: University of California Press, 1984.

Thomas, C.Y. 'From Colony to State Capitalism', *Transition*, V, 1981.

Thomas, C.Y. *The Rise of the Authoritarian State in Peripheral Societies. New York: Monthly Review Press*, 1984.

16: The Situation of African-Guyanese in the Economy

by
Clive Y. Thomas

This essay offers a portrait of the economic situation of African-Guyanese based entirely on available statistical information. Apart from the details presented below, there are five general preliminary observations to be made about the available statistical information.

First, as you will observe, it is in some ways far better than is usually assumed in public discourse on these matters.

Second, even though this is so, the available information is nevertheless deficient in two main ways. To begin with, most of it is based on the population censuses of 1960, 1970, 1980 and 1991, and the *Household Income and Expenditure Survey (HIES)* and the *Living Standards Measurement Survey (LSMS)* databases which were both compiled during the years 1992-93. While the survey data are extraordinarily detailed, they are somewhat dated now, 4-5 years later. Furthermore, much of the data, and in particular the population census data, have taken far too long to be processed. To date, the 1991 Census has still not been fully processed, and there is more than a hint that this delay is a carryover from the pre-1992 period, when economic and social data were hoarded by those who produced them.

Thirdly, the data sets, while surprising in their availability, are still limited. For example, we do not have basic data on things as fundamental to the economy as the ownership of productive assets (business, land, equipment, capital goods, access to credit) broken down by ethnic groups. Nor, for that matter, do we have an ethnic breakdown of corporate decision-making, that is, the ethnic composition of Boards of Directors, CEOs, Personnel Managers, etc. There is a mistaken view that the mere act of collecting such data is itself too politically sensitive and feeds racial insecurity.

Fourthly, it should be recognized that a statistical portrait such as I am presenting, while important in sorting out fact from fantasy, is by itself not enough. The reason for this is obvious. Such portraits emphasize the quantitative, as against the qualitative, dimensions of a matter when, in truth, neither a quantitative nor qualitative portrait by itself will ever be adequate. Both have to be brought together.

Finally, a portrait such as that which I am offering has its fullest meaning only when brought into comparison with the situation of other ethnic groups. From time to time, I will therefore make such references.

In concluding this introduction, I will try to highlight a few of the policy issues which need to be addressed with a sense of urgency.

The most important asset of any community is its people and I begin, therefore, with a portrait of the African-Guyanese population in the national context. After a century of continuous growth (1881-1980), in which the population trebled, data since 1980 indicate a sharp reversal. Most of the increase in the population between 1881 and 1980 was due to indentured immigration during the period 1835 - 1917 and its subsequent effects. After the 1946 Census, population growth peaked at 2.86 per cent per annum. But between 1970 and 1980, the annual growth of the population was reduced to only 0.4 per cent, and between 1980 and 1996 this rate became negative, showing an annual average decline of 0.1 per cent. By the end of 1996, the total population had only reached approximately 721,000 persons, with about 80 per cent of persons living in Regions 3, 4, 5 and 6. The rural/urban division of the population is estimated to be roughly 69:31.

Based on the 1991 Census, the ethnic distribution of the population shows that just over 49 per cent is made up of East Indians, about 36 per cent African-Guyanese, 7 per cent Mixed, just under 7 per cent Amerindians, with the remaining ethnic groups constituting less than one per cent of the population. A comparison of the census data between 1960 and 1991 reveals that the East Indian population first held an absolute majority in 1970 (52 per cent) and then again in 1980 (51 per cent), but in 1991 the data showed that this group was just under 50 per cent. The proportion of African-Guyanese in 1991 was 34 per cent, the highest since 1960 (Tables 14, 15, 16).

The regional distribution of the population by ethnic group shows that African-Guyanese are the largest group in Regions 4, 7 and 10, and that East Indians are the most numerous in Regions 2, 3, 5 and 6. However, while Amerindians only account for 6 per cent of the population, they are the most numerous group in Regions 1, 8 and 9 (Table 17).

Data on the national population by age group reveal that 35 per cent of the population was in the age group 0-14, and 22 per cent in the age group 15-24 years (Table 18). When examined by ethnic grouping, African-Guyanese have 37 per cent of their population in the age group 0-14, and 29 per cent in the age group 15-29. The combined total is 66 per cent or two-thirds of African-Guyanese, younger than 30 years of age. This should be compared with totals of 64, 72 and 68 per cent respectively for East Indians, Amerindians and Mixed groups (Table 19).

If the data on ethnicity by age group also include gender, we find that African-Guyanese males outnumber females in the age group 0-14 by a significant margin. The reverse, however, is true in the age group 15-29 and, indeed, 30+ as well (Table 20).

We are, of course, interested in ethnic characteristics of the population, other than location, age and gender. Two other such characteristics are family status and household size. The data show that, based on HIES definitions, less than 35 per cent of the African-Guyanese population, 15 years and over, enjoys a 'legal union.' This compares to more than 51 per cent for East Indians, just under 50 per cent for Amerindians, and 39 per cent for the Mixed groups. The national average is 45 per cent. For common law relations, there is less divergence among the ethnic groups. Thus, for the country as a whole, this averages just under 17 per cent while, for African-Guyanese, East Indians, Amerindians and the Mixed groups, the figures are 18, 16, 18 and 18 respectively. In addition to the above, the single population is 46 per cent for African-Guyanese, 33 per cent for East Indians, 33 per cent for Amerindians and 40 per cent for the Mixed group. The national average is 38 per cent (Table 21).

At the national level, the average household size is estimated at 4.28 persons. All the Regions, except 1 and 9, have below 5 persons per household. In Regions 1 and 9, the Amerindian population group is the largest and the average household size is 5.51 in Region 1 and 5.96 in Region 9. Indeed, the data show a larger variation of household size when compared to income, than to ethnicity; the range between the top and bottom fifth of households ranked by income is from 3.4 to 5.6 persons.

The most important role of an ethnic group within the population is to be found in its employment characteristics. What do we find? In the surveys, the population has been divided into the economically active (comprising those employed and unemployed, i.e. the labour force) and the economically inactive (comprising those at school, performing household duties, pensioners, disabled and others). The data collected show that 63 per cent of the total African-Guyanese population is economically active, with 9 per cent of this total unemployed. For East Indians the comparable figures are 55 per cent active with 6 per cent unemployed. Amerindians show 74 per cent economically active with 4 percent unemployed and the Mixed group 61 per cent active with 6 per cent unemployed. The national averages are 60 and 7 per cent respectively for the economically active and the unemployed (Table 22).

The employed population in the economically active category has been further sub-divided into categories of self-employed, regular salaried and casual labour. The data indicated that the average for all races is 40 per cent self-employment. This is the same for East Indians. However, for African-Guyanese this figure is only 31 per cent. The corollary of this is that 63 per cent of the African-Guyanese population could be found in waged or salaried employment as compared to 50 per cent for East Indians, and 52 per cent for all races. As we all know, much of this employment was in the public sector. Unfortunately, however, between 1980 and 1992, both in absolute and relative terms, the number of salaried jobs fell mainly because of a decline by nearly 40 per cent in public sector employment. There was a slow growth in private sector employment which was clearly insufficient to compensate for this decline. By 1992, the public sector contributed 7 per cent to total employment in the country, as compared with 15 per cent in 1980.

In terms of overall employment creation, between 1980 and 1992 the fastest growing sectors were commerce, finance, insurance and real estate (14 per cent each), while agriculture and construction grew by just over 4 per cent each, and services just under 4 per cent. The manufacturing, public and utilities sectors all showed decreases. Mining and quarrying were nearly static at 0.44 per cent. The special cultural situation of the Amerindian population is reflected in the fact that 75 per cent of this group is self-employed and only 19 per cent is in waged or salaried employment.

The figures for casual labour are low for all races, with only 6 per cent of the African-Guyanese population in this category, while for East Indians it was 10 per cent. The national average was 8 per cent (Table 23). The data on unemployment by ethnic group show that, while the national unemployment rate in 1992 was 11.7 per cent, for the African-Guyanese population this was higher, at 13.6 per cent. For East Indians the figure was 11.5 per cent. The data on unemployment by age group are startling. These show that over 44 per cent of African-Guyanese youths aged 15-19 years were unemployed, as compared to 36 per cent for East Indian youth and a national average of 37 per cent. For persons in the age-group 20-24 years, the figure was 24 per cent for African-Guyanese, also well above the national average of 19 per cent, and that for East Indians being 18 per cent. A similar picture is seen in the data for the group 25-29 years (Table 24).

The industrial structure of the work force by ethnic group is shown in Table 25 for 18 industrial groups. The African-Guyanese population is the leading ethnic group in 12 categories, but only by a significant extent in four of these, namely: mining, public administration and defence, education, health and social work. East Indians dominate in agriculture, hunting and forestry, and lead significantly in manufacturing, wholesale and retail trades. The percentage distribution of employed persons by occupational categories and ethnicity shows marked variations as well, with African-Guyanese in the majority in categories such as, technicians and assistant professionals, professionals, clerical and service workers/sales workers, and defence. East Indians are in the majority in the senior officials/managers, plant and machine operators and assemblers, and elementary occupations (Table 26). There are a number of analytical inferences which can be drawn from these employment data:

- The outcome for participants in the labour force is highly dependent on age, gender, ethnicity and location. Labour is not a homogeneous product in the market place. The market is biased against women and youth, women in rural areas, as well as African-Guyanese employment in the public sector. There is considerable inequality.

- While the contraction of state employment appears to have had a most calamitous impact on employment opportunities generally, its impact on African-Guyanese youth appears to have been particularly marked. This reinforces the importance of ethnic balance in the promotion of economic activities, and a focus on youth in the population.

- The contraction of state employment has not only impacted itself on overall employment and the African-Guyanese work force heavily concentrated there, but it seems also to have narrowed the range of occupational opportunities for the entire work force.

The skills of the work-force determine its effectiveness in the economy. We therefore look at the data on education to evaluate this. The education data suggest high levels of literacy in Guyana, averaging about 96 per cent for the population as a whole. For African-Guyanese the figure is 98 per cent, the highest for any ethnic group. East Indians average just over 94 per cent. As would be expected, Amerindians are lower than the average, 92 per cent. Except for African-Guyanese, all other ethnic groups have a higher proportion of females than males not literate (Table 27).

In terms of level of educational attainment, about one-fifth of the population lies within the 'below primary' educational level, just over half in the primary, under one-quarter in secondary, and above one per cent in the graduate and post-graduate category. For African-Guyanese, about one-sixth was below primary, just over one-half primary and one-fifth secondary. The African-Guyanese group has the lowest ratio below primary and the highest in the graduate and post graduate category. Indeed, about 30 per cent of all African-Guyanese have secondary and above levels of educational attainment, a figure significantly above the national average of 24 per cent (Table 28).

Data on functional literacy of out-of-school youth gathered in 1995, however, challenge these positive figures for African-Guyanese. These data show about 79 per cent of this ethnic group at moderate to low levels of functional literacy and 11 per cent at high levels. The data for Indian-Guyanese show 13 per cent at the high level and 77 per cent at moderate to low levels. Again, the disadvantagement of Amerindians is revealed as only 6 per cent is in the high category and 94 per cent in the middle to low categories (Table 29).

Poverty and related data inform us on the extent to which economic processes marginalize ethnic groups. In this regard, data collected in the LSMS survey reveal that 43.2 per cent of the population fell below the poverty line and 27.7 per cent fell below the critical poverty line, that is, below the ability to even provide food for survival. The data for the former reveal marked variations by ethnicity. For African-Guyanese the proportion below the poverty line is the same as the national average (43 per cent). However, for the Amerindians, this figure reaches a staggering 88 per cent of their total population. For East Indians, the figure is 34 per cent and for the Mixed group, 44 per cent (Table 30).

Related data on nutrition among school children are revealing in a different way. Using the much criticised and disputed height-for-age (HA) and weight-for-age (WA) anthropometric measures, GAHEF discovered in a survey of school children completed during 1993, that African-Guyanese children were above the national average for both HA and WA measures. Indian-Guyanese were below in both, showing the lowest mean weight in the sample for the WA measure, while African-Guyanese children showed the highest mean weight. Amerindians were the shortest and also below the mean weight in the sample (Table 31). A follow up survey one year later produced similar findings. While 14 per cent of the sample had low HA measures, for African-Guyanese the percentage was only 7, as compared to 62, 12, and 10 for the Amerindian, Mixed and East Indian groups respectively. About 8 per cent of the sample had low WH measures but, again for African-Guyanese, the figure was only 3 per cent. For East Indians the figure was as high as 14 per cent, while for the Amerindians there was a reversal in their fortunes, the figure was lowest at just over one per cent (Table 32).

There are two observations which I would like to make about recent economic performances. Firstly, the data above show the African-Guyanese work-force to be heavily centered in mining and quarrying, and the public sector, with the East Indian workforce heavily concentrated in agriculture, hunting and forestry and in various service trades (Table 24). Nearly one-third of the East Indian work-force is in agriculture, and half in the two other listed categories. The African-Guyanese have only 20 per cent of their work-force in the two categories listed. Data on the recent overall growth of the economy and its sectoral performance are quite revealing, when compared with these results. Between 1988 and 1996, overall GDP (in constant 1988 prices) increased by 40 per cent. Measured on the same basis we find that:

- sugar expanded by 65 per cent;
- rice expanded by 154 per cent;
- forestry expanded by 186 per cent;
- distribution and services expanded by 42 per cent;
- Government's growth was zero per cent;
- mining and quarrying expanded by 52 per cent.

Much of the growth, especially in rice, sugar and services, has occurred since 1991. There is a striking contrast, therefore, in the performance of the ethnic group predominantly in the Government and the economic gains obtained by that group, before and after the 1992 elections.

The second observation is that, prior to the foreign exchange liberalisation and other ERP measures introduced in 1991, a highly clandestine, and at the time illegal, economy flourished as a result of repressive Government economic measures directed at regulating the demand and supply of what were very scarce commodities. This clandestine economy was not dismantled as the economy became progressively liberalized. Instead it was transformed, and is now focused on six major areas:

- Narco-economy, i.e., the production and trafficking in narcotics;
- Money laundering;
- 'Back-tracking', or body smuggling;
- Commodity smuggling ;
- Gold smuggling (this is being reduced as Gold Board regulations are being liberalized); and,
- Makeshift construction firms and operators, designed to exploit public sector infrastructural project contracts.

By their nature, no firm data exist about the details of these operations. However, based on media reports and informal sources, three points seem to emerge:

- That the prosperity of some local firms is based on linkages between this new form of the clandestine economy and legitimate business. The appearance of prosperity, therefore, may have more to it than meets the eye.

- Based on reports in the media and public discussion, most of the top level operators in this transformed clandestine economy carry East Indian names.

- Based on similar reports, African-Guyanese names are prominent in street-running and the enforcement end of these activities, and also in supplying the 'official' lines and access, without which these activities would not flourish.

In conclusion, I draw attention to a few of the policy issues which arise from the above description and analysis. To begin with, it is clear that an essential requirement for intelligent action is the provision of appropriate databases from which one can act. This entails work in two principal directions, namely, keeping the already available data sets up-to-date and current, as well as expanding these into new areas of coverage. As mentioned earlier, there is a misguided belief that the mere collection of socio-economic data by ethnic group is divisive. This is wrong. Without hard empirical information, fact, fantasy and stereotype all become intertwined and intelligent or rational action stifled.

Secondly, without focussed and targeted action by the Government, the problems confronting the African-Guyanese community and indeed the impoverished sections of all communities will not be overcome. Community self-help, while essential to progress, cannot by itself overcome the many constraints which the data above indicate. Similarly, the market mechanism on its own cannot ensure enough trickle-down to secure an acceptable ethnic balance in the economy. To be effective, such Government action should have at least six major priorities:

- Youths, where the levels of unemployment are so high. How can young people be expected to develop stable family/household structures, if so many are neither at work nor at school?

- Education and skills, again focussed principally on youths.

- The promotion of small business both through training and the provision of specially designed credit programmes.

- Land reform. It is one of the paradoxes of Guyana that, despite the fact that every Government since 1953 has described itself as progressive, pro-poor and pro-worker and pro-farmer, no systematic programme for the radical restructuring of our land ownership system has been put in place. A positive land reform strategy would be an important foundation on which to launch a programme for enhancing the productive assets at the disposal of poor and marginalized communities, thereby benefiting the African-Guyanese community substantially.

- No programme to enhance ethnic balance and security would proceed far without well-established public policies in support of affirmative action in such areas as employment and housing. To be effective, such policies will have to draw heavily on accurate databases, thereby reinforcing the urgency of the first set of priorities mentioned above.
- In addition to the above, a whole range of 'multicultural policies' will have to be put in place, ranging from the use of language in the public media to cultural education in schools and universities.

Finally, the African-Guyanese community will have to contribute through its own action as a community to its upliftment. A number of priorities flow from this. One is the importance of the promotion of our culture in enhancing self-identity, group cohesiveness and non-conflictual modes of behaviour among African-Guyanese and between African-Guyanese and other ethnic groups. Another is the promotion of civic Organisations, from developmental NGOs to cooperatives within the African-Guyanese community. And yet another is for umbrella Organisations such as African Cultural and Development Association (ACDA) to make their own contributions in the area of the economy.

Why not, for example, promote the formation of an ACDA development bank?

Tables

Table 14: Population Census Data, 1946-1996

Year	1946	1960	1970	1980	1991	1996 (est.)
Amount ('000)	375.7	560.3	701.7	759.6	723.8	720.7

Source: Bureau of Statistics.

Table 15: Population: Regional Distribution of the Population 1991

Region	Region	Per cent of Total
1	Barima-Waini	2.6
2	Pomeroon-Supenaam	6.0
3	Essequibo Is.-W. Demerara	12.7
4	Demerara-Mahaica	41.4
5	Mahaica-Berbice	6.9
6	Cuyuni-Mazaruni	19.1
7	Berbice-Corentyne	2.1
8	Potaro-Siparuni	0.8
9	U. Takutu-U. Essequibo	2.1
10	U. Demerara-Berbice	5.5

Source: Bureau of Statistics.

Table 16: Population by Ethnicity: 1960, 1970,1980, and 1991

Ethnic Group	1960	1970	1980	1991
East Indian	47.8	51.8	51.4	49.5
African	32.8	31.2	30.5	35.6
Chinese	0.7	0.5	0.3	0.34
Amerindian	4.5	4.9	5.3	6.8
White	0.6	0.3	0.1	0.7
Mixed	12.2	10.3	11.0	7.0
Other	1.5	0.85	0.4	0.03
Not Stated	0.04	0.07	1.0	--
Total	100	100	100	100

Source: Bureau of Statistics, Statistical Yearbook, 1994.

Table 17 : Population by Ethnic Group of Head of Household (1992/93)

Region	Ethnic Group						
	Indian (1)	African (2)	Chinese (3)	Portuguese (4)	Amerindian (5)	Mixed (6)	Total
1. Barima-Waini	742	1,599	243	162	14,075	1,769	18,590
2. Pomeroon-Supenaam	23,234	10,399	-	443	5,728	2,965	42,769
3. Essequibo Is-West Demerara	64,699	19,001	532	156	289	6,651	91,328
4. Demerara-Mahaica	126,004	142,226	1,355	2,981	1,467	23,034	297,162
5. Mahaica-Berbice	29,643	15,417	52	84	2,383	1,919	49,498
6. East Berbice-Corentyne	106,192	28,022	125	511	2,380	5,609	142,839
7. Cuyuni-Mazaruni	2,425	5,383	24	80	4,614	2,731	15,342
8. Potaro-Siparuni	242	538	-	-	4,218	739	5,737
9. U. Takutu-U. Essequibo	354	1,226	48	-	12,194	1,265	15,087
10. U. Demerara - Berbice	1,557	31,806	54	234	1,511	3,872	39,106
Total	355,092	255,617	2,433	4,651	48,859	50,554	717,458
Per Cent	49.49	35.63	0.34	0.65	6.81	7.05	100.00

Source: Bureau of Statistics, HIES database.
Source: Calculated by Author from Bureau of Statistics, HIES database 1992-93.

Table 18: Population by Age Group, 1991

Age Group (Years)	Per cent of Total
0 - 14	34.8
15 - 24	22.0
25 - 34	17.2
35 - 44	11.1
45 - 54	6.6
55 - 64	4.2
65+	4.1

Source: Bureau of Statistics.

Table 19: Population by Ethnic Group and by Age Group, 1992-1993

Age Group	Indian	African	Amerindian	Mixed	Remainder*	Total
0 - 14	31.6	37.1	46.1	37.1	28.1	34.9
15 - 29	32.6	29.3	25.4	30.6	28.3	30.7
30 +	35.8	33.6	28.5	32.3	43.6	34.4
Total	100.0	100.0	100.0	100.0	100	100

*Notes: *Chinese, Portuguese and Other in HIES Classification*
Source: Calculated by the Author from the Bureau of Statistics, HIES Database, 1992/1993

Table 20 : Population Distribution by Ethnic Group, 1992/1993

Age Group	Indian		African		Amerindian		Mixed		Remainder*		Total	
	Male	Female	Male	Female	Male	Female	Male	Female	Male	Female	Male	Female
0-14	32.1	31.1	39.2	35.1	45.9	46.1	40.6	33.8	26.1	30.1	36.1	33.7
15-29	32.3	33.0	28.4	30.1	25.0	25.7	28.8	32.1	29.9	26.7	30.2	31.3
30+	35.6	35.9	32.3	34.8	29.1	28.1	30.6	33.9	44.0	43.2	33.8	34.9
Total	100	100	100	100	100	100	100	100	100	100	100	100

Notes: *Chinese, Portuguese and Other in HIES Classification

Source: *Calculated by the Author from the Bureau of Statistics, HIES Database, 1992/1993*

Table 21: Population Distribution of Persons 15+ by Ethnic Group and Marital Status, 1992/1993.

Martial Status	All Races	Indian	African	Amerindian	Mixed	Remainder **
Legal Union***	44.5	26.6	12.9	2.8	2.7	0.5
Common Law	16.7	8.1	6.2	1.0	1.3	0.1
Single	37.7	17.0	15.7	1.9	2.7	0.4
Other*	1.1	0.6	1.7	0.5	3.0	2.2
TOTAL	100	100	100	100	100	100

Notes: * *Visiting and Other*
** *Chinese, Portuguese and Other*
*** *Married, Widowed, Divorced and Separated*
} *According to HIES Classification*

Source: Calculated by the Author from the Bureau of Statistics HIES database, 1992-93.

Table 22 : Population Distribution of Persons Economically Active and Inactive by Ethnic Group and Age Group (15 years and over), 1992/1993.

Race	Economically Active			Economically Inactive	Total
	Employed	Unemployed	Total		
Indian	49.0	6.4	55.4	44.6	100
African	54.5	8.6	63.1	36.9	100
Amerindian	70.0	3.8	73.8	26.2	100
Mixed	55.2	6.4	61.5	38.4	100
Other*	50.2	3.6	53.8	46.2	100
All Races	52.5	7.0	59.5	40.5	100

Notes: * *Chinese, Portuguese, Other.*
Source: Calculated by the Author from the Bureau of Statistics HIES database 1992-93

Table 23 : Population Distribution of Employed Persons 15 Years and over by Ethnic Group and Employment Status, 1992/93.

Race	EMPLOYMENT STATUS			
	Self-Employed	Regular Salaried	Casual Labour	Total
All Races of which:	39.5	52.4	8.1	100
Indian	39.8	50.1	10.1	100
African	31.1	62.6	6.3	100
Amerindian	75.0	19.0	6.0	100
Mixed	42.3	52.4	5.3	100
Other*	43.6	53.2	3.2	100

Note: **Chinese, Portuguese and Other, in HIES classification.*
Source: *Calculated by Author from the Bureau of Statistics HIES database.*

Table 24 : Unemployment by Ethnic Group

		Age Group		
	Unemployment Rate	15-19	20-24	25-29
All Races	11.7	36.6	19.5	10.4
Indian	11.5	36.1	17.6	9.7
African	13.6	44.4	24.4	12.3

Note:
National female unemployment was 18.11 per cent compared to 8.4 for men. There was a similar disparity between urban and rural areas where the figures were 9.0 and 8.2 per cent respectively for men, and 16.2 and 19.3 per cent respectively for women.

Source: Calculated by Author from Bureau of Statistics, HIES database 1992-93.

Table 25 : Population Distribution of Employed Persons 15 years and over by Ethnic Group, Industry and Employment Status

Industry	All Races	Indian	African	Amer-Indian	Mixed	Other
1. Agricultural, Hunting & Forestry	27.1	32.1	13.1	69.1	22.2	10.7
2. Fishing	3.0	4.9	0.7	2.7	1.7	5.9
3. Mining & Quarrying	4.0	1.3	7.0	5.4	6.3	3.2
4. Manufacturing	11.2	12.8	10.6	3.4	10.1	18.5
5. Electricity, Gas & Water	1.1	0.6	1.8	-	1.5	1.4
6. Construction	4.1	4.2	4.6	1.9	3.5	1.4
7. Wholesale & Retail Trade	16.0	18.2	15.7	2.1	18.3	30.0
8. Hotels & Restaurants	1.3	1.1	1.7	0.5	1.7	-
9. Transport , Storage & Communications	5.1	5.7	5.3	0.9	5.1	6.1
10. Financial Intermediation	1.1	0.6	2.0	-	1.4	1.5
11. Real Estate, Rent & Business Activities	2.0	1.5	2.9	0.3	2.4	4.2
12. Pub. Admin. & Defence, etc.	7.4	3.5	13.4	2.0	8.8	8.5
13. Education	3.5	2.3	4.9	5.0	4.0	2.2
14. Health & Social Work	2.0	0.9	3.5	1.2	2.3	1.0
15. Other Com. Social & Personal Services	4.0	3.3	5.2	1.9	4.9	2.0
16. Private H.H. with Employed Persons	3.6	3.8	3.7	1.8	3.6	1.5
17. Extra-territorial Organisations & Bodies	0.05	0.04	0.1	-	-	-
18. No Industry	3.2	3.2	3.8	1.7	2.4	1.8
Total	100	100	100	100	100	100

*Note: *Chinese, Portuguese and Other in HIES Classification*
Source: Calculated by Author from IADB Labour Market Survey Report Statistical Annex, 1994

Table 26 : Population Distribution of Usually Employed Persons 15 Years and over, by Ethnic Group and Occupation, 1992/93.**

Occupation	Indian	African	Amer-indian	Mixed	Other	Total
1. Legislators, Senior Officials and Managers	50.1	33.9	0.9	11.2	4.0	100
2. Professionals	31.8	51.8	5.7	9.8	0.9	100
3. Technicians and Assistant Professionals	28.4	53.4	7.4	9.4	1.4	100
4. Clerks	36.1	51.4	1.4	9.5	1.6	100
5. Service Workers and Shop Sales Workers	35.1	52.9	1.3	9.1	1.6	100
6. Agricultural, Forestry and Fishery Workers	46.9	15.8	30.1	6.5	0.5	100
7. Craft and Retail Workers	44.6	42.7	3.6	7.5	1.5	100
8. Plant and Machine Operators and Assemblers	54.9	36.8	2.1	5.5	0.8	100
9. Elementary Occupations	60.2	29.0	4.0	6.0	0.8	100
10. Defence Force	--	97.0	3.0	--	--	100
11. Not stated	47.9	41.8	4.3	5.3	0.6	100

Note:
**Chinese, Portuguese, and other in HIES classification.*
***Usually employed in HIES definition comprises self-employed, regular salaried and casual labour.*
Source: Calculated by Author from the Bureau of Statistics, HIES Database.

Table 27: Population Distribution of Persons 15 years and over by Ethnic Group, Literacy and Gender.

Ethnic Group	Not-Literate		Literate				Not Stated	
			Without Schooling		With Schooling			
	Male	Female	Male	Female	Male	Female	Male	Female
All Races	1.85	2.2	1.52	1.7	95.5	95.1	1.1	1.0
Indian	2.4	3.1	2.0	2.3	94.8	93.8	0.8	0.8
African	1.0	0.8	0.5	0.5	96.9	97.5	1.6	1.2
Amerindian	3.3	4.4	4.3	5.3	91.5	89.1	0.8	1.2
Mixed	0.6	2.0	0.8	0.7	97.9	96.4	0.5	0.9
Other*	0.6	0.7	-	0.5	98.0	98.7	1.3	-

*Notes: *Chinese, Portuguese and Others*
Source: Calculated by the Author from Bureau of Statistics HIES Database, 1992/1993.

Table 28: Population Distribution of Persons 15 years and over with Formal Education by Gender and General Education Attainment.

Ethnic Group	Below Primary		Primary		Secondary		Graduate and Post Graduate		Total	
	Male	Female	Male	Female	Male	Female	Male	Female	Male	Female
All Races	20.8	20.4	53.4	54.2	22.5	24.1	1.3	1.3	49.1	50.9
Indian	21.3	21.0	57.3	58.2	20.4	20.0	1.0	0.8	50.0	49.5
African	17.9	7.0	53.6	50.1	26.6	30.8	1.9	2.0	47.1	52.9
Amerindian	36.0	37.3	58.9	57.6	5.1	5.1	0.06	0.06	51.8	48.2
Mixed	19.9	21.8	48.8	46.0	29.3	30.8	2.0	1.3	47.6	52.4
Other*	11.0	11.0	40.6	49.5	48.4	39.0	-	0.5	50.7	49.3

*Note: *Chinese, Portuguese and Other.*
Sources: Calculated by Author from Bureau of Statistics, HIES Database 1992/1993

Table 29: Functional Literacy Levels by Ethnic Group

Functional Literacy Level	African	Indian	Mixed	Amer-indian	Other	Not Stated	Total
High (above 29.92 or 77%)	125 10.9 %	155 13.2 %	55 10.6 %	7 6.3 %	7 12.5 %	5 6.4 %	354 11.5 %
Moderate (20.21-below 29.92 or 51.8%-below 77%)	696 60.7 %	762 65 %	343 65.8 %	70 63.1 %	29 51.8 %	27 34.6 %	1927 62.4 %
Low (Below 20.21 or 51.8%)	326 28.4 %	256 21.8 %	123 23.6 %	34 30.6 %	20 35.7 %	46 59.0 %	805 26.1 %
Total	1147	1173	521	111	56	78	3086 *

Note: Missing cases.
Source: Z. Jennings, et al., 1995.

Table 30: Poverty (Head Count) by Ethnic Group

Region	Percent of Population[1]	Head Count
All Guyana	100.0	43.2
Indian	45.9	33.7
African	36.7	43.0
Amerindian	10.7	87.5
Mixed	6.2	44.0
Other	0.9	-

Note: [1]Living in households headed by ethnic group.
Source: World Bank, 1994.

Table 31: Mean and Standard Deviation (SD) of Measurements of Primary School Entrants by Ethnic Groups, 1993.

	AGE (mth)	HEIGHT(cm)	WEIGHT (kg)	TOTAL
Entire Sample	72.25+ - 8.82	112.03+ - 5.96	18.19+ - 2.85	3213
Amerindian	72.91+ - 13.26	107.89+ - 6.28	17.93+ - 2.76	429
African	71.68+ - 7.86	113.34+ - 5.58	18.81+ - 2.81	1257
East Indian	72.57+ - 6.15	111.63+ - 5.02	17.25+ - 2.56	1008
Mixed	72.46+ - 9.97	113.11+ - 6.64	18.73+ - 3.07	489
Other*	72.69+ - 18.28	112.51+ - 5.43	18.45+ - 2.70	30

*Notes: *Chinese, Portuguese and Other.*
Source: GAHEF Nutrition Surveilliance ***Bulletin*** *No.6, Apr. 1994.*

Table 32: Anthropometry by Ethnicity (1994)

Ethnic Group	Anthropometry by Ethnicity	
	Low Height for Age %	Low Weight for Age %
Indian	10.4	14.3
African	7.5	3.1
Amerindian	61.7	1.5
Mixed	12.3	4.3

Note: National percentage of low Height for Age is 13.7 per cent and low Weight for Age is 8.1 per cent
Source: From data - GAHEF. Nutritional Surveilliance ***Bulletin*** *No.7, Jan. 1995.*

Bibliography

Primary Sources

British Colonial Office Records (C.O.) (Public Record Office: P.R.O.)

C.O. 111, British Guiana: Original Correspondence

C.O. 111/1, Kingston to Townshend, 13 Jan. 1783.
C.O. 111/3, Hopkinson to Huskisson, 29 Jul. 1795.
C.O. 111/3, Beaujon to Portland, 24 Jan. 1799 and enclosures.
C.O. 111/3, Beaujon to Portland, 9 Apr. 1799.
C.O. 111/4, Hislop to Turnbull, 12 Jan. 1801.
C.O. 111/4, Hislop to Turnbull, 12 Jan. 1801.
C.O. 111/4, Produce of Demerary and Essequibo for Six Years, as taken from the Customs House Books, n.d. (1803)?
C.O. 111/5, Sayers to Sullivan, 21 Oct. 1803.
C.O. 111/6, Courher to ?, 1 Mar. 1806.
C.O. 111/7, The Petition of Roger Leigh to Liverpool, 13 Jul. 1807.
C.O. 111/8, Bentinck to Castlereagh, 28 Jan. 1808.
Encl. in Kortright to Kimberley 140, 4 Aug. 1881.
C.O. 111/39, Amount of Clothing Received Annually for Slaves of the Civil Government of Essequibo and Demerara, 25 Dec. 1823.
C.O. 111/39, Murray to Bathurst, 24 Aug. 1823.
C.O. 111/39, Murray to Bathurst, 24 Aug. 1823.
C.O. 111/39, Murray to Bathurst, 24 Aug. 1823.
C.O. 111/39, Murray to Bathurst, 31 Aug. 1823.
C.O. 111/44, Murray to Bathurst, 14 Feb. 1824.
C.O. 111/44, "Regulations for the Treatment of Servants and Slaves," 1 Oct.1784.
C.O. 111/44, Convictions of Whites and Other Free Persons on Slave Evidence Between 1774 and 1824.
C.O. 111/44, Murray to Bathurst, 27 Aug. 1824.
C.O. 111/45, Durban to Bathurst, 9 Dec. 1824.
C.O. 111/45, Browne to Murray, 24 Jan. 1824.
C.O. 111/73, van Batenburg to Graham, 15 Sep. 1797.
C.O. 111/78, Gordon to Liverpool, 16 Dec. 1810.
C.O. 111/78, Statement Relative to the Colony of Berbice, 7 Oct. 1811.
C.O. 111/193, Light to Stanley, private, 1 Nov. 1842.
C.O. 111/200, Private and confidential, 13 Mar. 1843.
C O 111/227, Light to Stanley, 70, 7 Apr. 1845.

C.O. 111/252, Light to Grey, separate, 3 May 1848.
C.O. 111/277, Barkly to Grey, 173, 31 Dec. 1850.
C.O. 111/284. Governor Henry Barkly to Lord Grey, 164, 24 Nov. 1851,
C.O. 111/288, Barkly to Grey,. 26, 10 Feb. 1852.
C.O. 111/297, Walker to Newcastle, 102, 20 Oct. 1853.
C.O. 111/301, Wodehouse to Grey, 41, 21 Jul. 1854.,
C.O. 111/311, Wodehouse to Labouchere, 83, 23 Jun. 1856.
C.O 111/313, Attorney General's report in Wodehouse to Labouchere, 157, 24 Dec. 1856,
C.O. 111/316, Wodehouse to Labouchere, 29, 24 Feb. 1857.
C.O. 111/317, Wodehouse to Stanley, 68, 7 Jun. 1858.
C.O. 111/320, Wodehouse to Labouchere, 140, 6 Nov. 1856.
C.O. 111/336, Hincks to Newcastle, 140, 28 Jul. 1862.
C.O. 111/340, Governor Francis Hincks to Newcastle, 66, 20 Apr. 1863.
C.O. 111/345, Hincks to Newcastle, 84, 26 Apr. 1864.
C.O. 111/345, Hincks to Newcastle, No. 60, 18 Mar. 1864.
C.O.111/353, Hincks to Cardwell, 186, 23 Nov. 1865.
C.O 111/355, Hincks to Cardwell, 25, 22 Jan. 1866.
C.O. 111/364, Hincks to Buckingham & Chandos, 159, 20 Dec. 1867.
C.O. 111/383, Scott to Kimberley, 25, 23 Feb. 1871.
C.O. 111/398, Rushworth to Kimberley, 126, 7 Aug. 1873.
C.O. 111/398, Encl. in Kortright to Hicks Beach, 52, 24 Feb. 1879.
C.O. 111/412. Report of the inspector of villages, 29 March 1882.
C.O. 111/415, Young to Hicks Beach, 241, 4 Nov. 1879.
C.O. 111/419, Kortright to Kimberley, 229, 21 Jul. 1881,
C.O. 111/425, Governor Henry Irving to Kimberley, 285, 3 Oct. 1882.
C.O 111/428, Irving to Derby, 125, 5 May 1883.
C.O. 111/438, Irving to Holland, 76, 19 Feb. 1887.
C.O. 111/457, Governor Lord Gormanston to Knutsford, 248, 28 Jul. 1890.
C.O. 111/465, Sir Augustus Hemming, Gov. of B.G. to the Chairman W.I.Royal Commission.
C.O. 111/484, Hemming to Chamberlain, 153, 27 Apr. 1896.
C.O. 111/487, Gormanston to Ripon, 384, 25 Nov. 1892.

C.O. 114, British Guiana: Sessional Papers and Administrative Reports

C.O. 114/44, Report of the Inspector-General of Police for 1888.

C.O. 116, Blue Books of Statistics

Report on Blue Book, 1884.
Report on Blue Book 1885.
Report on Blue Book 1890.
Report on Blue Book 1891.
Report on Blue Book 1896.
Report on Blue Book 1897.
Report on Blue Book 1904.

C.O. 384, British Guiana: Emigration: Original Correspondence

C.O. 384/103, encl. in Longden to Carnarvon, 188, 7 Oct. 1874.

Minutes of the Court of Policy (Essequibo, Berbice and Demerara) (National Archives of Guyana: N.A.G.).

M.C.P., Berbice, 11 Feb. 1806.
M.C.P., Berbice, 13 Jan. 1807.
M.C.P., Berbice, 19 Apr. 1808.
M.C.P., Essequibo-Demerara, 1 Nov. 1808.
M.C.P., Berbice, 1 Oct. 1810
M.C.P., 21 Jul. 1823.
M.C.P., 21 Jul. 1823.
M.C.P., 19 Aug. 1823.
M.C.P., 5, 6 Sep. 1825.
M.C.P., 17 Apr. 1830.
M.C.P., 19 May. 1852
M.C.P., 16 Aug. 1855.
M.C.P., 18 Sep. 1855.
M.C.P., 25 Aug. 1857.
M.C P., 14 Dec. 1927.

British Guiana, Combined Court Sessional Papers, No. 779 of 1914.

Reports of the Proceedings of the British Guiana Legislative Council

Hansard, 18 Jun. 1953.
Hansard, 18 May - 8 Oct, 1953.

Hansard, 3 May. 1956.
Hansard, 1 Mar. 1957.

Legislative Council Papers

B.G., Fourth Legislative Council. Fourth Session, 1951-52.

Decennial Censuses

British Guiana: *Census Reports/Abstracts* 1831, 1841, 1851, 1861, 1871, 1881, 1891, 1911, 1921, 1931.
West Indian Population Census, Part C, British Guiana : 1946, 1960.
Commonwealth Population Census: Guyana : 1970, 1980,

Guyana National Archives Records (N.A.G.)

Governor Egerton to Secretary of State for the Colonies Harcourt, 13 Dec. 1912; 23 Jun. 1913.
Governor Hemming to Chairman of W.I. Royal Commission. 20 Apr. 1897.
A.A. Thorne and Philip N. Browne. "Memo to the Secretary of State with regard to the Administration of the Colony." Govt. Secretary's Office. 2425. 19 Apr. 1906. (Printed).
"Speech of His Excellency the Governor at the Opening of the Combined Court Annual Session, 1905", Court of Policy Hall, 10 Feb. 1905.
Irving to Holland, 407, 22 Oct. 1887. M.C.C., 29 Dec. 1927.
Attorney General Joseph Nunan to Egerton, 25 Jul. 1925. (Confidential).
Knutsford to Governor Gormanston, 30 Apr. 1890. (Confidential).
Governor H.T. Irving to Secretary of State Holland, 407, 22 Oct.
Governor Gormanston to Secretary of State Knutsford, 176, 20 May. 1888.
Hodgson to Lyttleton, 45, 14 Feb. 1906. Manuscript.
Knutsford to Governor Gormanston, . 300, 18 Nov. 1889.
Gormanston to Knutsford, 4, 3 Jan. 1890.
Governor Gormanston to Secretary of State Knutsford, No. 209, 20 Jun. 1890. Secretary of State Knutsford to Governor Gormanston, No. 261, 14 Oct. 1890.
Letter Patent, 5 Mar. 1891, in *Official Gazette*, 2 Jan. 1892.

Governor Gormanston to Knutsford,. 4, 3 Jan. 1980.
Letter from Agents for the Colonies to the Under Secretary of State for the Colonies, 1 Jan.1928.
Governor Gormanston to Knutsford, 3 Jan.1890.
Irving to Derby, 14 Oct. 1883.
Governor Wodehouse to Secretary of State for the Colonies Herbert, . 35, 23 Mar.1855.
Irving to Derby, 14 Oct. 1883. (Confidential).
Mr Cecil Clementi, O.A.G., to Bonar Law, Secretary of State for the Colonies, 31 Jun. 1916.
Governor Sir Walter Egerton, to Mc L. Harcourt, Secretary of State for the Colonies, 5 Jan. 1914.
Mc L. Harcourt to Governor Sir Walter Egerton, 21 Apr. 1914.
Governor Denham to Lord Passfield, 28 Jul. 1930. (Confidential).
Douglas Jones, Attorney General to Lord Passfield, 71, 30 Jan. 1930.
Governor Lethem to Lord Stanley, 8 Oct. 1943. Confidential.
Minute of W.A. Orrett to Colonel Secretary, 1 May 1951.
Reports of the activities of the British Guiana Labour Union, No. 173/ 32,
Ordinance No. XVII of 1921 entitled "An Ordinance to provide for the Regulation and Registration of Trade Unions."
Special Branch (British Guiana Police Force), "Report on a Mass Meeting held by the Trade Unions Council, GIWU, LCP, PPP and the FUGE at Bourda Greene (sic) on Sunday, 22 Mar. 1952." Wittenham to Col. Sect. 24 Mar. 1952. (Confidential).
Brentnol Blackman, Sect. BGTUC. to Col. Sect., 21 Mar. 1952.
John La Rose, Provisional Gen. Sect., West Indian Independence Party of Trinidad and Tobago to Governor of B.G., 5 Mar. 1953.
Proclamation by Governor Murray, 22 Apr. 1824.
Notes of the Shipping Arrivals in the Kyk-overal Diary.
Proclamation by His Excellency Major-General John Murray, Lieutenant Governor and Commander-in-Chief in and over the United Colony of Demerary and Essequibo, 16 Dec. 1823.
Proclamations of the Government of Berbice, 1796-1818.
Proclamation by Governor Sam Dalrymple, 1 Oct. 1810.
Publications and Ordinances, 1802 – 1810.
Publication by His Excellency Governor Beaujon and the Honourable Court of Policy, 25 May 1805.
Ordinance No. 15 of 1849.
Rules And Regulations For The Employment Of Labourers On Plantation... West Coast, Demerary, From And After 1st January, 1842.

(These records unfortunately are not catalogued and are without file or

reference numbers.)
Demerara and Essequibo Vade Mecum 1825.
1832 Local Guide of British Guiana.

British Guiana Boundary Arbitration and the United States of Venezuela. London, 1898.

Government Service Orders

G.S.O. No. 325. 14 January 1891. T.J. Wakefield and others to Governor – "Complaint of Present System of Registration of gold-labourers", Petition of 12 Jan. 1891.
G.S.O. 1536. 4 Mar. 1891. Petition of C.F. Hopkinson.

British Museum Documents

British Museum, London, E.G. (Egerton Papers) 1720. Douglas to Bentinck, 12 Jul. 1763.
British Museum, London, Additional *MSS, 42071*, Vol. 2, Sullivan to Grenville, 2 Apr. 1802, encl. Observations on Dutch Guiana by Lord Seaforth, 5 Feb. 1801.

London Missionary Society Papers

LMS, B.G. Demerara, Box 2/Folder 2/ Jacket A/, Smith to Burder, 7 May 1817.
LMS, B.G. Demerara, Box 2/Folder 2/Jacket A/, Smith to Burder, 17 May, 1817.
LMS, Papers, School of Oriental and African Studies, London, Smith's Journal.
LMS, Notebook entitled "Missions John Smith".
Report of the Trials of the Insurgent Africans (Georgetown, 1824).
London Missionary Society, *Report of the Proceedings against the late Rev. J. Smith of Demerara* (London, 1824).
LMS, "Missions John Smith"; *The Evangelical Magazine* (August, 1824).
LMS, 7/1 (Ber.), Roome to Tidman, 30 Jan. 1850.
LMS, 99/1, Scott to Tidman, 18 Feb. 1865.
LMS, 8b/4 (Dem.); Scott to Mullens, 8 Mar.1867, (Dem).
LMS, 10/1 Pettigrew to Mullens, 22 Feb. 1868, and Munro to Mullens, 21 Feb. 1870, (Ber.).

United Society for the Propagation of the Gospel Papers

SPG/E1O, Tanner to Hawkins, 18 Jan. 1862.

Hispanic Society of America Documents

Hispanic Society of America, New York, MS entitled "Gibraltar, Africa, West Indies from the Journal of Rev. W.R. Payne, Chaplain of H.M.S. Forte and Iphigenia, 1822, 1823, 1824, 1825."

Her Majesty's Government's Publications (Great Britain)

Report of the West India Royal Commission, 1897 (London: HMSO, 1897), Cmd. 8655.

Report by the Honourable E.F.L. Wood, M.P., Parliamentary Under Secretary for the Colonies, on his visit to the West Indies and British Guiana, Dec. 1921 – Feb. 1922 (London: HMSO, 1922), Cmd. 1679.

Report of the British Guiana Commission 1927 (London: HMSO, 1927), Cmd., 2841.

Memorandum Prepared by the Elected Members of the Combined Court of British Guiana in Reply to the Report of the British Guiana Commission (London : HMSO, 1928), Cmd. 3047.

Report of the West India Royal Commission, 1938 (London: HMSO, 1939), Cmd. 6607.

Parliamentary Papers

P.P. 1825, Vol. XXV, Copy of Major General Murray's Circular Instructions to the Magistrates of the Colony of Demerara, dated the 16 May 1823.

P.P., 1831-2, Vol. XX, Report from the Select Committee on the Commercial State of the West Indian Colonies.

P.P., 1831-2, Vol. XX, Report from the Select Committee on the Extinction of Slavery throughout the British Dominions.

P.P., 1833, Vol. XXVI, Return of the Numbers of the Slaves in each of the West Indian Colonies.

P.P., 1847 48, XXXIII, Pt. 11; Despatches Relative to the Present State and Prospects of the cultivation.

P.P., 1851., XXXIX, Despatches Relative to the Present State and Prospects of the cultivation.

Secondary Sources

Newspapers

Argosy, 1881-1900.
Berbice Gazette, 1838-1900.
Colonist, 1848-1884.
Creole, 1856-1882.
Daily Chronicle, 1895-1900.
Demerara Daily Chronicle, 1811-1884.
Guiana Graphic., 1944-1977.
Guiana Review, 1940-1942.
Guiana Times, 1840-1848; 1860-1866.
LCP Sentinel.
PAC Bulletin, 1946-1950.
Royal Gazette, 1838-1889.
The Daily Argosy, 1881-1960.
The Echo, 1887-1899.
The Mining Gazette,
The New Daily Chronicle.
The *Nugget*, 1858-1890.
Thunder, 1950-
Watchman, 1871-1879.

Journal Articles and Conference and Seminar Papers

ADAMSON, A.H. "Monoculture and Village Decay in British Guiana, 8541872", *Journal of Social History*, 3, (4), 1970.

ANSTEY, R. "The Volume and Profitability of the British Slave Trade, 1761-1807", in Engerman and Genovese, Race and Slavery in the Western Hemisphere. Quantitative (Princeton, 1975), pp. 33 48.

BENJAMIN, A.J. "Some Notes on the Origins of 1763," *Release*, *1*. 1979.

__________, "Background to the 1763 Berbice Uprising" (mimeo. Guyana, 1978).

BOLLAND, Nigel, O. "Systems of domination after slavery: the control of land and labor in the British West Indies after 1838", *Comparative Studies in Society and History* (hereafter *CSSH*), 23, (1981), pp. 591-619 .

_________, Reply to William A. Green's "The Perils of Comparative History", *CSSH*, 26, (1984), 120-25;

BRAITHWAITE. C.A. "The Growth of the African Population in Guyana 1871–1970". Unpublished Research Paper, Department of Geogra-

phy, University of Guyana, (1979).
BURNHAM, L.F.S. A vision of the Co-operative Republic', in L. Searwar (ed.), *Cooperative Republic: Guyana*, Georgetown, Guyana, (1970).
CARRINGTON, Winslow .The Trade Union Movement: Its History and its Growth (Georgetown: TUC, n.d.).
CLEMENTI, Sir Cecil. "Colonisation in British Guiana," *United Empire*, X111, 1922, 449 - 50.
CROPPER, J.B. "Our villages and countryparts", *Timehri*, 2 (2), (1912).
CRUICKSHANK, J.G. "The Beginnings of Our Villages," *Timehri*, 7, 3rd Series, 1921. 65-76.
DANNS, G.K. "Militarisation and Development: An Experiment in Nation Building", *Transition*, 1, (1978), 1, 23 – 44.
DAVIS, D. "The Records of British Guiana", *Timehri*, Vol. 11 (1888).
DAVSON, Edward R. "British Guiana and Its Development," A Paper read before the Colonial Institute, (24 Apr.1908).
DRAKES, Francis M. "The Middle Class in the Political Economy of British Guiana 1870 - 1928," Paper presented at Post-Graduate Seminar, Caribbean Societies, Institute of Commonwealth Studies, University of London, (3 Mar. 1987).
ELTIS, D. "The Traffic in Slaves between the British West Indian Colonies, 1807-1833", *Economic History Review*, 25 (1972).
FARLEY, Rawle. "The Rise of Village Settlement in British Guiana", *Caribbean Quarterly*, 10, 1. (Mar. 1964).
GREEN, William A "The perils of comparative history: Belize and the British sugar colonies after slavery', *CSSH*, 26, (1984), 112 119.
HALL, D. "Absentee Proprietorship in the British West Indies, to about 1850", *Jamaican Historical Review*, 4 (1964), 15-34.
HARPER-SMITH, J.W. "The Colonial Stock Acts and the 1891 British Guiana *Constitution*, *Social and Economic Studies*, Vol. XXV, 3 (Sep. 1965), 252 - 63.
INIKORI, J. "Measuring the Atlantic Slave Trade: An Assessment of Curtin and Anstey", *Journal of African History*, Vol. XVII, No. 2 (London, 1976) 197-223.
JAGAN, Cheddi. "Congress Speech Delivered at New Amsterdam, 1956" (University of Puerto Rico, College of the Social Sciences).
JAYAWARDENA, C. "Marital Stability in two Guianese Sugar Estate Communities", *Social and Economic Studies*, Vol. 9, No. 1 (1960).
KWAYANA, E. Pseudo-socialism', Paper presented to seminar, University of the West Indies, Trinidad, (1976).
KILKENNY, Roberta. "Women in Social and Political Struggle: British Guiana, 1946-1953", Paper presented at the Association of Caribbean Historians' Conference, (1984).
KIPLE K.F. and KIPLE, V.H. "Deficiency Diseases in the Caribbean,"

Journal of Interdisciplinary History, 11, (1980), 197 - 215.

KLEIN M. and LOVEJOY, P.E. "Slavery in Africa," in Henry Gemery and Jan Hogendorn, (eds.) *The Uncommon Market, Essays in the Economic History of the Atlantic Slave Trade* (New York, 1979), pp. 181 - 212.

KOPYTOFF, B. "The Development of Jamaican Maroon Ethnicity," *Caribbean Quarterly*, 22(2 - 3), (1976), 35 - 50.

LAMUR, C "Slave Mortality in Suriname in the 19th century: The Role of Internal Factors", (Paper presented at the Thirteenth Conference of Caribbean Historians,. Guadeloupe, 1981).

MANDLE, J. "Continuity and Change in Guyanese Underdevelopment", *Monthly Review*, 28, 4, (1976), 37 - 50.

________. "The Post-Colonial Mode of Production in Guyana", University of Guyana and Temple University, mimeo, (1978).

MARS, P. "Co-operative Socialism and Marxist Scientific Theory", *Caribbean Issues*, 4, 2, (1976), 71-106.

McGOWAN, W. "The French Revolutionary Period in Demerara Essequibo, 1793 - 1802", (Paper presented at the Thirteenth Conference of Caribbean Historians, Guadeloupe, 1981), 112.

____________, "Christianity and Slavery : Reactions to the Work of the London Missionary Society in Demerara, 1808 - 1813", in K. Laurence (ed.), *A Selection of Papers presented at the Twelfth Conference of the Association of Caribbean Historians* (1980) (Bridgetown, 1985), pp. 23-44.

MOORE, Brian L. "The Social Impact of Portuguese immigration into British Guiana after Emancipation," *Journal of Latin American and Caribbean Studies, No. 19, December 1975.*

____________, "The Social Impact of Portuguese immigration into British Guiana after Emancipation," *Boletin de Estudios Latinoamericanos y del Caribe*, Vol. X1X, (1975).

PAGET, Hugh "The Free Village System in Jamaica" *Caribbean Quarterly*, 10, (1 Mar. 1964).

PEARSON, J.G. "The Negro in the West Indies," *Timehri*, Vol. V111 (1889) .

____________, "The Negro's Grievance," *West Indian Quarterly* (1885-6).

POSTMA, J. "The Origin of African Slaves: The Dutch Activities on the Guinea Coast, 1675 1795", in S. Engerman and E. Genovese, *Race and Slavery in the Western Hemisphere. Quantitative Studies* (Princeton, 1975), pp. 33 48.

____________. "The Dimension of the Dutch Slave Trade from Western Africa", *Journal of African History*, Vol. XIII, No. 2 (London, 1972), pp. 237 348.

PREMDAS, R.R. *"The Rise of the First Mass-Based, Multi-Racial Party in Guyana", Caribbean Studies, XX, 314 (1974).*

ROBERTS G.W. and M.A. Johnson, "Factors Involved in Immigration and Movements in the Working Force of British Guiana in the 19th Century", *Social and Economic Studies*, 23(1), 1974).

_________, "Some Observations on the Population of British Guiana", *Population Studies*, Vol. 2 (1948), 185-218.

___________. "Immigration of Africans in the British Caribbean", *Population Studies*, Vol. 7(3), (1954) 235-62.

ROBINSON, P. D. "The Social Structure of Guyana" in, *Cooperative Republic of Guyana* (Georgetown, 1970).

RODNEY, W. "Slavery and Other Forms of Social Oppression on the Upper Guinea Coast in the Context of the Atlantic Slave Trade, *Journal of African History*, 7(4), (1966(, 431-43.

RODWAY, J. "Ruin", *Timehri*, 16, Vol. XI (Jun. 1887).

RODWELL, Sir Cecil."The Problems of British Guiana," *United Empire*, Vol. XV11, 3rd Series (1927),

SCHULER, M. "Akan Slave Revolts," *Savacou*, 1(1), (1970), 8-31. "Ethnic Slave Rebellions in the Caribbean and the Guianas," *Journal of Social History*, 3(4), (1970), 374-85.

SHERIDAN, R. "The Crisis of Slave Subsistence in the British West Indies During and After the American Revolution," *William and Mary Quarterly*, 33, 1976. 615-41.

SINGH, S. "Demographic Variables and the Recent Trend of Fertility in Guyana 1960-1971," *Population Studies*, 33(2) (1979), 295-334.

SPACKMAN, Ann. "Official Attitudes and Official Violence: The Ruimveldt Massacre, Guiana 1924", *Social and Economic Studies*, Vol. XXII, 3 (Sep. 1973).

TEIXEIRA, Gail. "Janet Jagan Honoured" (1989).

THOMAS, C.Y. Bread and Justice: The Struggle for Socialism in Guyana', *Monthly Review*, 28, 4, (1976), 23-35.

____________. "The Non-Capitalist Path as Theory and Practice of Decolonisation and Socialist Transformation", *Latin American Perspectives*, 5, 2, (1976), 10-28.

__________. "From Colony to State Capitalism", *Transition*, V, 1981.

THOMPSON, A. "Race and Colour Prejudices and the Origin of the Trans-Atlantic Slave Trade," *Caribbean Studies*, 16(3-4), 1976-77, 43-48.

VAN LIER, R.A.J. "African Slavery in Surinam," *Caribbean Historical Review*, 3-4, (1954).

VAN SERTIMA, J. "The Colony's Financial Position," *Timehri*, Vol. 111, 1 (1912).

VELZING, I. "The Berbice Slave Revolt of the 27th Feb. 1763," in W.

McGowan & I. Velzing, " Slave Resistance and Revolts" (mimeo. University of Guyana, 1980).
WATSON, K. "The TransAtlantic Slave Trade (with special reference to Barbados)" in A. Thompson (ed.), *Emancipation 1*, (Cave Hill, Barbados, 1986).
WILSON, Roy. and H. Snell, "The Future of British Guiana," West Indian Committee Circular, Vol. XL11, (14 Jul. 1927).
WILSON, Silvius "The Background to the Ruimveldt Incident of 1924", *History Gazette*, 67 (Apr. 1994).
__________, "The Causes of the Ruimveldt Incident of 1924," *History Gazette*, 68 (May, 1994).
WOOD, D. "Kru Migration to the West Indies" (Seminar Paper, University of London, 1978).
WOOLFORD, Hazel M. "Hubert Nathaniel Critchlow: The Crusader", *History Gazette*, 43 (Apr.1992).
__________, "History of the Guyana Labour Union 1919-1986" (Unpub. monograph).

Theses

CHANDERBALI, David. "Sir Henry Light: A Study of Protection and Paternalism," (M.A. Thesis, University of Guyana, 1977).
DRAKES, Francis. (Kimani Nehusi), "The 1905 Protest in British Guiana: Causes, Course and Consequences" (M.A. Thesis, University of Guyana, 1982).
FARLEY, R. "Aspects of the Economic History of British Guiana, 1781-1852", (Ph.D. Thesis, University of London, 1956).
LAURENCE, K.O. *Immigration into Trinidad and British Guiana 1834 - 1871*, (Ph.D. Dissertation, Cambridge University, 1958).
MANGAR, Tota "The Administration of Sir Henry Turner Irving as Governor of British Guiana 1882 - 1887: A Study in Astuteness and Resoluteness", (M.A. Thesis, University of Guyana, 1987).
POTTER, L.M. *Internal Migration and Resettlement of East Indians in British Guiana 1870-1920* (Ph.D. Thesis, McGill University, 1975).
THAKUR, Andra P. "Guyana: The Politics of Race and Class 1953-1964" (MA Thesis, Dept. of Anthropology, University of Alberta, Ed., Alberta, 1973).
WAGNER, Michael. "Structural Pluralism and the Portuguese in Nineteenth Century British Guiana: A Study in Historical Geography", (Ph D. Thesis, McGill University, 1975).

Bibliography

Books

ADAMSON, A.H. *Sugar Without Slaves: The Political Economy of British Guiana, 1838-1904*. New Haven: Yale University Press, 1972.

AJAYI, J. and CROWDER, M. (eds.). *History of West Africa* 1. London: Longman, 1971.

AYEARST, Morley. *The British West Indies: The Search for Self-Government*. Washington Square, New York University Press, 1960.

Beckles, H. *African Rebellion in Barbados: The Struggle against Slavery, 1627 - 1838*. Bridgetown, 1984.

BOAHEN, A. *Topics in West African History*. London: Longman, 1966.

BOLINGBROKE, H. *A Voyage to Demerary, 1799-1806* . orig. pub. 1807. Reprint Georgetown, 1941.

BOXILL, E.W. *The Golden Trade of the Moors*, Oxford, 1970.

DALTON, Henry. *The History of British Guiana*, 2 Vols. London, 1855.

DALY, V.T. *A Short History of the Guyanese People*. London: Macmillan, 1975.

DAVID, P.A. *et al., Reckoning with Slavery*. New York, 1976.

DAVIDSON, B. *The Growth of African Civilisation : A History of West Africa, 1000-1800,* 2nd edn. London: Longman, 1967.

DE AZURARA, Eannes. *Conquest and Discoveries of Henry the Navigator*. Ed. Virginia de Castro and Almeida. London, 1936.

DUFF, R. *British Guiana. Being Notes on a few of the Natural Productions, Industrial Occupations and Social Institutions*. Glasgow : Thomas Murray and Sons, 1866.

DUMONT, R. *The State of Urban Planning in Guyana*, Georgetown, 1974.

DUNN, R. *Sugar and Slaves. The Rise of the Planter Class in the English West Indies, 1624 - 1713*. New York, 1972.

ELKINS, Stanley. *Slavery. A Problem in American Institutional and Intellectual Life*. 3rd. ed., Chicago, 1976.

ENGERMAN, Stanley, and FOGEL, R. *Time on the Cross*. Boston, 1974.

________________, and GENOVESE, Eugene (eds.). *Race and Slavery in the Western Hemisphere. Quantitative Studies*. Princeton, 1975.

ENLOE, C. *Guyanese Political Response to Migration*. Clark University, 1972.

FONER, P. *A History of Cuba*. New York, 1962.

GOSLINGA, Cornelis. *The Dutch in the Caribbean and the Guianas, 1680-1791* Assen, 1985.

GREY, Earl. *The Colonial Policy of Lord John Russell's Administration.* 2 Vols. London: Richard Bent, 1853.

HARTSINCK, Jan J. *Beschrijving van Guiana of de Wildekust in Zuid America*. Amsterdam, 1770.

HIGMAN, B. *Slave Populations of the British Caribbean 1807 - 1834*. Baltimore, 1984.

HOPKINS, A. *An Economic History of West Africa*. New York: Columbia

University Press, 1973.

IRELAND, W. Alleyne. *Demerariana. Essays Historical, Critical and Descriptive*. Georgetown: Baldwin and Co., 1897.

JAGAN, Cheddi. *The West on Trial: The Fight for Guyana's Freedom*. Berlin: Seven Seas Publishers, 1966.

JAGAN, Janet. *Twelve Years of the PPP: An Account of the Party's Long Struggle against Privilege and for the Rights of the People*. Georgetown: New Guyana Co. Ltd., 1961.

JAKOBSON, S. *Am I Not a Man and a Brother? British Missions and the Abolition of the Slave Trade and Slavery in West Africa and the West Indies, 1786-1838*. Uppsala, 1972.

JOHNSTON, B.F. *The Staple Food Economies of Western Tropical Africa*. Stanford, 1958.

KIRKE, Henry. *Twenty-five Years in British Guiana*. London, Sampson Low & Co.,1898.

LEWIS, Gordon K. *The Growth of the Modern West Indies*. (London: MacGibbon and Kee Ltd., 1968.

LUTCHMAN, Harold. *The 1891 Constitutional Change and Representation in the Former British Guiana*. Georgetown: Critchlow Labour College, 1970.

_________________. *Planter Power in the Politics of Former British Guiana*. Turkeyen: University of Guyana, 1968.

_________________. *Some Aspects of the Crown Colony System of Government*. Turkeyen: University of Guyana, 1968.

MANDLE, J.R. *The Plantation Economy : Population and Economic Change in Guyana, 1838-1960*, Philadelphia : Temple University Press, 1973.

MARK, Francis X. *Organised Labour in British Guiana*. Puerto Rico, n.d.

MATTHEWS, L. and LEE, S.C. *Two Forms of Matricentrality : The Matrilineal Ashanti and the Matrifocal Guyanese*. American Sociological Association, 1975.

MEILLASSOUX, C. (ed.), *L'Esclavage en Afrique precoloniale*. Paris, 1975.

MIERS, S. and KOPYTOOF, I. (eds.) *Slavery in Africa*. Wisconsin, 1977.

MILLIROUX, M.F. *Demerara: The Transition from Slavery to Liberty*. Paris: 1843. Trans by J.R. Mac Farlane, London: 1877.

MOORE, Brian L. *Race, Power and Social Segmentation in Colonial Society: Guyana after Slavery*. New York : Gordon and Breach Science Publishers, 1987.

_______________. *Cultural Power, Resistance and Pluralism: Guyana 1838-1900*. Kingston, 1995.

NATH, Dwarka. *A History of Indians in British Guiana*. London, 1958.

NETSCHER, P.M. *History of the Colonies Essequibo, Demerara and Berbice. From the Dutch Establishment to the Present Day.* S' Gravenhage: Martinus Nijhoff, 1888. Trans. by W.E. Roth, Georgetown: 1929.

NEWMAN, P. *British Guiana : Problems of Cohesion in an Immigrant Society.* London : Oxford University Press, 1964.

NORTHCOTT, C. *Slavery's Martyr : John Smith of Demerara and the Emancipation Movement*. London, 1976.

PEOPLE'S PROGRESSIVE PARTY. *Constitution of the People's Progressive Party. Ratified and Adopted by First Congress of PPP on 1 April 1951*. Georgetown: Arcade Printery, 1951.

________________________. *Constitution of the People's Progressive Party. Revised and Adopted, 30 March 1958*. Georgetown: Labour Advocate Job Printing Dept. 1958.

________________________. *People's Progressive Party: 21 Years, 1950-1971*. Georgetown: New Guyana Co. Ltd., 1971.

PERKINS, H.J. *Notes on British Guiana and its Gold Industry with Maps*. 2nd. ed. London: Sampson Low, Marston and Company Ltd., N.D.C. 1896-97.

PITMAN, F. *The Development of the British West Indies 1700-1763*. London, 1967.

POPE-HENNESSY, James. *Sins of the Fathers. A Study of the Atlantic Slave Traders, 1441– 1807*. London : 1967.

PREMDAS, R.R. *The Rise of the First Mass-Based, Multi-Racial Party in Guyana*. Georgetown, 1972.

PREMIUM, B. *Eight Years in British Guiana, 1840 - 1848*. London, 1850.

PURCHAS, S. (ed.). *Purchas: His Pilgrims*. 1905 reprint. Glasgow, 1905

RANGER, T.O. *Revolt in Southern Rhodesia*. London, 1967.

RENO, Philip. *The Ordeal of British Guiana*. New York, Monthly Review Press, 1964.

RODNEY, W. *How Europe Underdevelopd Africa*. London: Bogle L'Ouverture, 1972.

__________. *A History of the Guyanese Working People, 1881-1905* . Baltimore: Johns Hopkins University Press, 1981.

RODWAY, J. *History of British Guiana from the Year 1668*. 3 Vols.

Georgetown, 1891-4.
ROSE, J.G. *The 1948 Enmore Incident*. Georgetown: Curriculum Development Centre - Ministry of Education Social Development & Culture, 1982.
ROWBOTHAN, Sheila. *Hidden from History: Rediscovering Women in History from the 17th Century to the Present.* New York: 1976.
SCHOMBURGK, Richard. *Travels in British Guiana*, Vol. 2. Georgetown, 1922.
SCOBLE, John. *Hill Coolies: A Brief Exposure of the Deplorable Conditions of the Hill Coolies in British Guiana and Mauritius*. London: Harvey & Darton, 1848.
SEARWAR, L. (ed.), *Cooperative Republic: Guyana*. Georgetown, 1970.
SHAHABUDDEEN, Mohammed. *Constitutional Development in Guyana, 1621-1978.* Georgetown: Guyana Printers Ltd., 1978.
_________________. *From Plantocracy to Nationalisation. A Profile of Sugar in Guyana*. Georgetown, 1983.
SHERIDAN, Richard, *Doctors and Slaves. A Medical and Demographic History of Slavery in the British West Indies, 1680-1834*. Cambridge, 1985.
SMITH, R.T. *The Negro Family in British Guiana*. London : Routledge and Kegan Paul, 1956.
STEDMAN, John G. *Narrative of Five Years' Expedition Against the Revolted Negroes of Surinam in Guiana on the Wild Coast of South America from the Years 1772 to 1777*. 2 vols. orig. pub. 1796. Reprint, Massachusetts, 1971.
SUKDEO, F. *The Impact of Emigration on Manpower Resources in Guyana*. Georgetown, 1972.
__________. *Malaria Eradication and Population Growth in Guyana*. Georgetown, 1973.
THOMAS, C.Y. *Plantations, Peasants and State: A Study of the Modes of Sugar Production in Guyana*. Los Angeles: University of California Press, 1984.
____________. *The Rise of the Authoritarian State in Peripheral Societies*. New York: Monthly Review Press, 1984.
____________. *Dependence and Transformation: The Economics of the Transition to Socialism*. New York, Monthly Review Press, 1974.
THOMPSON, A. *Bretheren of the Bush: A Study of Runaways and Bush – Negroes in Guyana c. 1750-1814*. Cave Hill, Barbados, 1975.
____________. *Colonialism and Underdevelopment in Guyana, 1580 - 1803*. Bridgetown, 1987.
TURNER, M. *Slaves and Missionaries : The Disintegration of Jamaican Slave Society, 1787-1834*. Urbana, 1982.
VAN HOOGENHEIM, Wolfert J. *Journal of van Hoogenheim, 1763 -*

1764. Trans. by Barbara L. Blair; mimeo. University of Guyana Library.

VAN LIER, R.A.J. *Frontier Society*, (orig. pub. as *Samenleving in een Grensgebied*). The Hague, 1971.

VAN'S GRAVESANDE, Storm L. *The Rise of British Guiana*, 2 Vols. - trans. and ed. by C. Harris and J. de Villiers. London, 1911.

VANSINA, J. *Kingdoms of the Savanna*. Madison: University of Wisconsin Press, 1966.

VOORHOEVE, J. *Suriname: Spiegel der Vaderlande Kooplieden*. Zwolle, 1958.

WALLBRIDGE, E. *The Demerara Martyr : Memoirs of the Rev. John Smith, Missionary to Demerara*. London, 1848.

____________. *The Demerara Martyr*. Orig. pub. 1848. Reprint, New York, 1969.

WEBBER, A.R.F. *Centenary History and Handbook of British Guiana*. Georgetown: Argosy Company Ltd., 1931.

WILL, W.A. *Constitutional Change in the B.W.I. 1880-1903 with special reference to Jamaica, British Guiana and Trinidad*. Oxford: Clarendon Press, 1970.

WILLIAMS, E. *From Columbus to Castro. The History of the Caribbean 1492-1968*. London, 1970.

YOUNG, Allan. *Approaches to Local Self-Government in British Guiana*. London, 1958.

Index

C

F

H

I

J

K

L

Q

R